Ethics In Applied Developmental Psychology:
Emerging Issues
In An Emerging Field

ANNUAL ADVANCES IN APPLIED DEVELOPMENTAL PSYCHOLOGY
VOLUME 4

VOLUME EDITORS:

Celia B. Fisher and Warren W. Tryon
Fordham University

SERIES EDITOR:
Irving E. Sigel
Educational Testing Service

ABLEX PUBLISHING CORPORATION
NORWOOD, NEW JERSEY

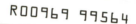

Copyright © 1990 by Ablex Publishing Corporation

Printed in the United States of America.

ISBN: 0–89391–598–X   ISSN: 0748–8572

Ablex Publishing Corporation
355 Chestnut Street
Norwood, New Jersey 07648

Contents

PART VI: COMMENTARY

List of Contributors

Diana Baumrind
Institute of Human Development
University of California
1203 Tolman Hall
Berkeley, CA 94720

Steven J. Danish
Virginia Commonwealth University
Department of Psychology
810 W. Franklin Street
Box 2018
Richmond, VA 23284–0001

David Elkind
Lincoln Filene Center
Tufts University
Medford, MA 02155

Celia B. Fisher (Editor)
Fordham University
Department of Psychology
Dealy Hall
Bronx, NY 10458

Lois Wladis Hoffman
University of Michigan
Psychology Department
529 Thompson Street
Ann Arbor, MI 48109

Gerald P. Koocher
Harvard Medical School
300 Longwood Avenue
Boston, MA 02115

Luis M. Laosa
Educational Testing Service
Princeton, NJ 08541–0001

Richard M. Lerner
The Pennsylvania State University
College of Health and Human
    Development
101 Beecher-Dock House
University Park, PA 16802

Michael Lewis
Institute for the Study of Child
    Development
University of Medicine and Dentistry of
    New Jersey
Robert Wood Johnson Medical School
Department of Pediatrics
One Robert Wood Johnson Place—CN19
New Brunswick, NJ 08903–0019

Harriette Pipes McAdoo
Howard University
School of Social Work
3034 Chestnut St. N.W.
Washington, DC 95064

Robert B. McCall
Office of Child Development
University of Pittsburgh
411 LRDC
3939 O'Hara Street
Pittsburgh, PA 15260

Gary B. Melton
University of Nebraska-Lincoln
Department of Psychology
209 Burnett Hall
Lincoln, NE 68588–0308

Susan A. Rosendahl
Department of Psychology
Fordham University
Dealy Hall
Bronx, NY 10458

Sandra Scarr
University of Virginia
Department of Psychology
Gilmer Hall
Charlottesville, VA 22903

Joan E. Sieber
California State University, Hayward
Department of Psychology
Hayward, CA 94542

Irving Sigel (Series Editor)
Educational Testing Service
Princeton, NJ 08450–0001

M. Brewster Smith
Board of Studies in Psychology
University of California at Santa Cruz
Stevenson College
Santa Cruz, CA 95064

Warren W. Tryon (Editor)
Fordham University
Department of Psychology
Dealy Hall
Bronx, NY 10458

Jonathan G. Tubman
The Pennsylvania State University
College of Health and Human
  Development
101 Beecher-Dock House
University Park, PA 16802

James Youniss
Youth Research Center
Catholic University
Washington, DC 20064

Preface

Irving E. Sigel, *Series Editor*

The subject matter addressed in this fourth volume in the *Advances in Applied Developmental Psychology* series is timely, since interest in ethical issues have been voiced recently in virtually every segment of our society. Research scientists and practitioners in the fields of medicine, psychology, and social work have become increasingly attentive to practical ethics (Sieber & Stanley, 1988). While the broad interest in ethics has existed since the days of the early Greek and Christian philosophers and theologians, the topic in academic circles has been subsumed under the rubric of moral philosophy. According to Singer, interest in applied ethics has emerged, due in part to the failure of moral philosophers to provide guidance for practical problems such as euthanasia, abortion, infant exposure, capital punishment, among others. Ethical issues also arose in the context of social action, so that in the 1960s and 1970s debates arose about the ethics of protest and civil disobedience. While on the social horizon decisions were being made about what was ethical, many of the practicing professions have concerned themselves with the ethics inherent in their practices. Lawyers, physicians, researchers in the life sciences, and many others have constructed ethical guidelines to insure that the practice of their profession would be within an ethical code. The dilemmas faced by each of these groups persist, and will probably continue to persist, because of the increasing complexity of social and individual rights and expectations. With an increase in sophistication of a public not tied to the authoritarian codes of religions, and with a continued development of individual responsibility, definition and resolution of ethical dilemmas and/or the establishment of a comprehensive code of ethical behavior will be increasingly problematical (Singer, 1986).

The emergence of this volume attests to the maturing process of applied developmental psychology. In order to discuss ethical issues in the field of *applied developmental psychology,* there has to be a definition of the field. Once that job is done or in progress, the need for definition of appropriate and inappropriate professional activities arises. And from such considerations, it then becomes necessary to deal with such questions as: Who is responsible for what? Who is accountable? Who will protect the public and thereby protect the profession and the professions? The questions that arise are manifold and it is for these reasons that this volume, edited by Celia Fisher and Warren Tryon, is timely. The authors of the chapters in this book do not solve all of the questions related to practical issues, but they do raise the issues. They do not provide a fixed set of guidelines, but they do express the types of guidance needed. They do not set up an institutional arrangement, but they do suggest the kinds of arrangements that are needed to insure maintenance of ethical standards for the field of applied developmental psychology.

As we read these chapters, it will become clear that the issues involved in ethics and the development of the field go hand in hand. As each new professional function arises or is defined in the purview of applied developmental psychology, so too do new ethical issues arise. Thus there can be no definitive set of guidelines carved in stone, but rather, they will evolve and in their evolution they will enhance the maturity and sensitivity of the field to the public. How each profession organizes itself, and what kinds of institutional safeguards become necessary, will have to wait. At least at this time Celia Fisher and Warren Tryon have created a valuable volume of thoughtful essays in which well-established science practitioners have addressed the ethical questions. This is an auspicious beginning because it comes at a time when society as a whole is faced with profound ethical dilemmas, from abortion rights to environmental protection. Applied developmental psychology is no exception to this upsurge in concern for the ethics of application of research to psychological practice. The strategies and subsequent standards set by the professionals who identify themselves as applied developmental psychologists may well contribute to the overall concern with applied ethics. This new field may augur well for an interdisciplinary approach to applied ethics, an approach that should lead to a consensual definition of a common and basic ethical stance, which in turn can become a living testament to applied ethics in the practical fields among which applied developmental psychology is but one among many.

REFERENCES

Sieber, J. E., & Stanley, B. (1988). Ethical and professional dimensions of socially sensitive research. *American Psychologist, 43,* 49–55.
Singer, P. (1986). *Applied ethics.* New York: Oxford University Press.

Acknowledgements

We are grateful to Irving Sigel for his encouragement and support. We thank Barbara Bernstein, Helen Burg, Carol Davidson, and Peg Tarnowsky for their invaluable assistance in preparing this volume. Finally, we would like to thank Gary, Brian, and Erica; Georgiana and Elizabeth, for keeping us mindful of the importance of caring and respect to individual and family development.

Acknowledgements

1 Emerging Ethical Issues in an Emerging Field*

Celia B. Fisher
Warren W. Tryon

We are at an exciting and challenging point in the history of developmental psychology. Developmental science, long a fundamentally academic and research discipline, has developed knowledge and expertise which can be applied to helping individuals. In response to the growing emphasis on the ecological contexts of human interaction, the recognition of social issues as points of departure for developmental theory, and the increasing emphasis on application within the marketplace and federal funding agencies, developmental psychologists have finally taken as their laboratory the society in which children grow (Bronfenbrenner, Kessel, Kessen, and White, 1986) and are playing a more direct role in the welfare of society and its members. In some ways we are experiencing a return to our roots: the mission-oriented goals of the early child welfare programs from which developmental psychologists sought a distinct identity (Sears, 1975; Siegel & White, 1982; see also Chapter 18). While the earliest attempts to use research to benefit children lacked methodological and scientific rigor (Morrison, Lord, & Keating, 1984), current applications do not.

As the activities of developmental scientists metamorphosize into direct application, the welfare of individuals evolves from an abstract ethical principle to a concrete, daily concern. The papers assembled for this volume were solicited to illustrate the applied activities in which developmental psychologists are currently engaged and to identify and provide guidelines for the ethical problems encountered in these activities. Applied developmental psychology is founded on the theories, procedures, and knowledge base of developmental science. For that reason we sought the contributions of senior scholars who are both noted for their contributions to empirical developmental and social science and engaged in applied activities. The authors have drawn from their experiences to identify issues that emerge as developmental psychology is applied beyond the laboratory.

This chapter is divided into three broad sections. First, we describe the current status of applied developmental psychology with respect to the spectrum of activities in which members of the field are currently engaged. Next, we highlight aspects of the applied developmental perspective influencing both the con-

---

* We would like to thank Diana Baumrind, Joan Sieber, and Irving Sigel for their thoughtful comments on a previous draft of this chapter.

1

duct of applied activities as well as the identification of ethical issues. Last, we identify three broad ethical values reflected in the chapters and relate them to the specific activities of applied developmental psychologists.

THE SCOPE OF APPLIED DEVELOPMENTAL PSYCHOLOGY

The extension of developmental science to social problems has been increasingly described as applied developmental psychology (Morrison, Lord, & Keating, 1984; Sigel & Cocking, 1980; Zigler & Finn, 1984). The extent to which activities subsumed under this appellation will be distinguished from generic development psychology on the one hand and child clinical and community on the other hand is still to be determined (see Chapters 13 and 14, respectively). There is, however, no doubt, that some individuals trained in the methodology and theory of developmental science are, and will be, engaged in applied activities. In this volume we have chosen to define applied developmental psychology as the activities and theoretical orientation guiding current applications of developmental principles and research methodology to real-world problems. We feel this de facto approach best represents the current status of this rapidly evolving field.

The Activities of Applied Developmental Psychologists

The activities of applied developmental psychologists span a continuum from knowledge-generation to knowledge-application (Fisher & Tryon, 1988; Morrison, Lord, & Keating, 1984; Scholnick, Fisher, Brown, & Sigel, 1988). On one end of this continuum are individuals engaged in knowledge generation who merge developmental theory with real-world problems by studying the applicability of scientific theory to growth and development in natural contexts or who study the correlates of social behaviors. In Chapters 2, 9, and 17, respectively, these activities are seen to generate knowledge about families and children germane to mental health professionals and which parents and educators need to bring up competent and moral children. The research activities described in this volume exemplify this level of application. These include adolescent health issues such as substance abuse and sexual behavior, correlates of maternal employment, parental teaching behaviors, child learning styles and causes of social class variation in achievement, self-esteem and racial identity within minority children, and physiological and social influences on aging. Ethical issues arising from mission-oriented developmental research conducted in natural contexts are most directly addressed in Part I of this volume.

A second set of applied developmental activities are aimed at change within social programs and within at-risk individuals. Developmental psychologists engaged in these activities may design and evaluate developmental intervention programs or developmental assessment instruments. As defined by Danish in Chapter 7, developmental interventions are planned programmatic efforts at altering the developmental process designed to optimize and enhance behavior. Developmental interventions described in this volume include infant stimulation and nutritional interventions, home- and school-based cognitive and behavioral management programs, adolescent substance abuse programs, and programs providing or adapting mainstream psychological services to members of culturally diverse populations. The chapters in Part II most directly address the ethical issues that emerge when developmental psychologists design and evaluate social programs.

A third set of activities of applied developmental psychologists concerns the dissemination of developmental knowledge to groups and individuals. Knowledge dissemination as described in the contributions to this volume include parent education workshops, literature written for parents, teachers, and mental health professionals, information imparted through the mass media, and expert testimony provided to participants in the legal system. The ethical concerns which go hand in hand with knowledge dissemination are raised by contributors to Part III of this volume.

A fourth set of activities associated with applied developmental psychology are directed at individual diagnosis and direct delivery of services for children and families in distress. At this point in time, few if any, graduate psychology programs exist that integrate developmental and clinical knowledge (Wertlieb, 1983). Developmental psychologists who wish to engage in direct delivery of services will need advanced specialization that places clinical acumen and exposure to behavioral problems within a developmental perspective (Scholnick, Fisher, Brown, & Sigel, 1988). The type of mental health services that such developmental psychologists may offer and the training they will require to perform these services raises ethical questions concerning the professionalization of applied developmental psychology. These issues are addressed in Part IV.

Diverse populations. The expansion of developmental psychology into the real-world arena is accompanied by an expansion in the types of populations encountered. While the research and theory of generic developmental psychology addresses itself to understanding the behavior of individuals at various points in the life cycle, applied developmental psychologists must seek to understand the behavior of individuals who vary with respect to cultural and ethnic background, economic and social opportunity, physical and cognitive abilities, and environment. Black and Hispanic families, poor families, single and working mothers, developmentally delayed infants, sexually active adolescents, and the institutionalized elderly are just some of the diverse populations considered within the chapters of this volume. Ethical issues concerned with cultural diversity and cultural bias are raised in Part V.

THE APPLIED DEVELOPMENTAL PERSPECTIVE

Applied developmental psychology approaches the activities and populations described above from a perspective which views individual functioning as a product of person-environment interactions that are continuously emerging and changing over time (Morrison, Lord, & Keating, 1984). Three substantive assumptions of the applied developmental perspective, chronicled in this volume, are identified below.

The Temporality of Individual Change

From the applied developmental perspective individual functioning is an ongoing process with a trajectory that extends and changes over time. Thus longitudinal data play a central role in deciding whether or not to embark upon a developmental intervention. For example, the decision to initiate the Athletes Coaching Teens Project to prevent substance abuse described by Danish in Chapter 7 was based in part on the findings of longitudinal studies indicating that adolescent drug use contributes to a wide variety of problems in adult life (Baumrind, 1987; Kandel, Davies, Karus, & Yamaguchi, 1986; Newcomb, Bentler, & Collins, 1986). Chapter 3, in which Scarr describes her 10-year collaboration to develop screening, assessment, and treatment programs for Bermuda illustrates how longitudinal research can be used to prevent the over- or underidentification of children needing treatment services.

As discussed by Lerner and Tubman in Chapter 8, the temporality of individual change implies that a natural stimulus or an intervention can have short- or long-term effects or compete with later experiences. Since change produced by intervention at one point in ontogeny may be only temporary, applied developmental psychologists recognize the limits of short-term focus in both research (Chapter 2) and intervention (Chapters 6 and 7). This leads to the development of long-term preventive strategies including lifelong dietary or exercise regimens for individuals at risk for certain physical diseases (Chapter 8), birth control information for sexually active adolescents whose infants would be at risk (Chapter 8; see also Chapter 2 for the potential pitfalls of sex education), or parent education programs designed to optimize the family environment of growing children (Chapter 12).

Individual Differences and Within-Person Change

From an applied developmental perspective a commitment to long-term goals in research and intervention must include recognition of individual variation and multiple influences that change people over time (Chapters 7 and 8). Throughout this volume an individual's response to the environment at any one period is seen as a function of prior experience and maturation level as well as historical, social, cognitive, and emotional factors. Humans are seen as neither interchangeable nor identical with themselves over time (Chapter 2). Since the effects on children of a particular intervention will vary as a function of the child's characteristics, applied developmental research and intervention strives to be multilevel. Lewis addresses this need (Chapter 6) by recommending a treatment by individual ability design for social programs which would provide a range of treatments designed to match the different characteristics of individuals, including their prior experience, attitudes, and aptitudes. The treatment by individual ability design calls for the simultaneous evaluation of multiple treatment approaches characteristic of Scarr's work in the Bermuda program.

Individuals not only differ in reaction to the environment, they also influence the environment. According to Lerner and Tubman, emphasis on the individual as producer of his or her own development (Lerner & Busch-Rossnagel, 1981) leads to a focus on processes of self-regulation, control, and self-efficacy in applied developmental research and intervention. Moreover, recognition of the role of the active, individually distinct person suggests that interindividual differences in the appropriateness of a given intervention for effecting change must be considered in the design and implementation of interventions.

The Centrality of Context in Shaping Developmental Phenomena

Knowledge of the historical, cultural, social, and physical context of the individual is critical to an understanding of real-world development. Chapters 3, 16, and 17, respectively, tie an understanding of poor families, dual-working families, and minority families to the role played by both mothers and fathers as well as the support of the extended family and community. Chapter 15 stresses the implications of a contextual perspective for the design and evaluation of instructional methods and curricular for students from diverse cultural backgrounds.

Cultural experience and values are seen to influence not only the developmental trajectories of individuals but the activities of psychologists as well. In Chapter 18, Youniss underscores this point in his description of the relationship between past and current concepts of childhood and the structural features of our society. Several authors (See Chapters 2, 5, 9, 15, 16, and 17) pursue this theme in discussing the importance of the social-political climate in shaping the decision-making processes of the applied developmental psychologist.

Ethical Implications of the Applied Developmental Perspective

The applied developmental perspective raises distinctive ethical issues. Emphasis on change over time (Chapter 8) raises questions about the point at which interventions take place and at which they should be evaluated. Some interventions may be more appropriate early in life when the system is being organized and there may be fewer constraints on its ability to change. Moreover, in evaluating these interventions the applied developmental psychologist must take into account the program's potential distal as well as proximal effects. A recognition of the temporality of individual change implies that behaviors which emerge in response to an intervention at one point in development will continue to be influenced by environmental factors at a later point in development. Along these lines, Lewis draws our attention to the unfair burden an expectation of permanent change places on social and educational interventions.

The focus on individual versus group developmental trajectories leads to the identification of ethical issues concerned with the relevance of developmental group data to decisions regarding the individual. As Danish points out (Chapter 7), the assumption of interindividual differences in intraindividual change with its complementary multilevel view of person-situation interactions means that if the level of intervention is inappropriate the solution can become the problem. Lewis extends this concern, warning us that an anti-individual difference perspective to social program evaluation and a univariate approach to problems will lead ultimately to negative assessments of social programs. Lewis calls for the assessment of multiple approaches and their effect on individuals.

A within-person change perspective also influences ethical decisions regarding how information about applied developmental research is communicated to research participants and consumers of developmental research findings. Fisher and Rosendahl (Chapter 4) discuss why applied developmental research with special populations requires informed consent procedures that reflect the developmental level, life-stage, cohort, and context of the individual and their guardians. Other contributors show why consumers of applied developmental research such as teachers (Chapter 9) and juries (Chapter 10) must be made aware of the limits of knowledge, including the leaps that are required to move from group data to a determination of facts about an individual.

The assumed centrality of context on development requires a similar responsibility of developmental scientists engaged in applied research to discuss caveats on how research is to be used (Chapters 2 and 3). Not only must we avoid advocating actions derived from research without clear evidence available to assess the integration of new data into a practical setting (Chapter 9) but we are also morally obligated to make appropriate disclaimers regarding the natural limitations on application created by context, developmental level, sex, and cohort (Chapter 2). The centrality of this issue to research with minority populations is emphasized by McAdoo in Chapter 17. She describes how participants in minority studies are often recruited from problem families or sampled as part of an intervention while majority families are randomly selected. McAdoo argues that the developmental contextual perspective must be equally applied to members of minority populations. For example when studying the correlates of single parenting among black families the researcher must make distinctions between female-headed households which start with an adolescent rather than an adult mother.

The contributors appreciate both the socio-economic political system's influence upon individual development, as well as how their own activities may be influenced by and in turn influence social attitudes and policy. In chapter 18, Youniss shows the reader how society's investment in children influences developmental theory, interpretation of data, and the consequent conceptualization of the child. This is underscored by an historical overview of the central role of religious and racial categories in the psychology of G. Stanley Hall, the founder of developmental psychology, and the equally value-laden, less overt, ideological influences on those who later sought to establish a "value-free" developmental science. Chapter 16, on the study of maternal employment, clearly illustrates how the biases of contemporary developmental psychologists affect the scientific process. This bias is reflected in the pursuit of differences among subgroups, in the choice of particular analyses and criteria, in the peer review process, and in the communication of information.

To help people deal with their values we have to deal with our own. McAdoo (Chapter 17) describes the special challenge to applied psychologists who are also members of ethnic groups. These professionals must work within a dual consciousness as they approach families of color to present a realistic and objective picture of minorities. The values of the psychologist also challenge those who seek to disseminate developmental knowledge to the public. McCall discusses how psychologists in the media must distinguish between research facts, theory, professional opinion, and speculation. Elkind (Chapter 12) asks us to recognize when the desire for self-promotion overrides commitment to provide the best possible information to parents. Melton (Chapter 10) points out that as an expert witness a developmental psychologist must discern which opinions are based on scientific fact as opposed to personal values. For example, while developmental data may be used to advocate for children, the psychologist must realize that the best interest of the child is a value-based, not an empirically-based, determination.

MORAL VALUES

The ethical concerns expressed by our contributors are based on the principles of beneficence, nonmaleficence, autonomy, and justice. The specific ethical dilemmas raised by the applied developmental perspective reflect recognition of the obligation to help others and to do no harm, to respect an individual's personhood and right to decision making, and to provide equally for all. Below we utilize these moral values to introduce the reader to additional ethical issues addressed in this volume and specific ethical principles which emerge from these concerns. We do so with the recognition that ethical dilemmas encountered in real world settings and in the situations described in the chapters of this book rarely reflect only one moral value. Although the following discussion is directed at applied developmental activities, ethical concerns arising from these moral values are relevant to related fields of applied psychology (e.g., child clinical, community, and school psychology).

Beneficence and Nonmaleficence

The principle of beneficence is embodied in the maximization of good outcomes and the avoidance of unnecessary suffering, injury, or other harm (Sieber, 1982). As developmental science extends outside the laboratory the potential to promote the welfare of individuals increases as does the potential to inflict harm. Both positive and negative results of applied research, program evaluation, and their dissemination can have long-lasting impact on social attitudes and social policy. This volume shows moral obligations derived from the principle of beneficence as emerging from a concern with the usefulness of one's work. For applied developmental psychology to be useful the psychologist must (a) conduct research, design interventions, and disseminate information that is as close as possible to the phenomena addressed; (b) ensure that the measures employed are reliable and that procedures are monitored and reliably applied; (c) carefully consider the criteria used to evaluate one's work; (d) translate information in a way that can be used by the knowledge consumer; and (e) provide services to groups and individuals which are compatible with one's graduate training and within one's area of competence. To ignore these principles is to risk ineffective social policies, the elimination of potentially helpful interventions, the misapplication of developmental principles to real world problems, and an erroneous public understanding of self and others.

   External validity. According to Sieber (Chapter 5) the conduct of useful applied developmental research requires that the research topic (a) be socially important; (b) be accurately formulated; and (c) correspond to the true character of the phenomenon as it arises in society. In drawing conclusions about scientific findings, the applied developmental psychologist must be aware that the last goal is not attainable in any one experiment. As Hoffman (Chapter 16) points out, any effect of a singular variable, for example, maternal employment, will be mediated through other variables and cannot and should not be reported with more certainty than is warranted. A problem for the applied investigator is that while research rarely yields cause-effect statements, that is what individuals and policy makers want to hear. Thus, developmental scientists conducting applied research must resist the pressures to make statements that go beyond the data.

   Lewis (Chapter 6) draws our attention to additional pitfalls related to a lack of external validity in intervention research. According to Lewis, the desire to implement the least-cost interventions leads to testing social programs in their weakest form (e.g., nutritional interventions for the poor are below middle-class levels) which, in turn, not only compromises the question of reaction to maximal enrichment but is biased towards the conclusion that interventions are ineffective.

Reliability. A criterion for whether information is useful for application rests on its reliability. Data intended to affect social policy should be highly reliable as well as ecologically valid. Scarr's description (Chapter 3) of ethical issues encountered in the Bermuda program illustrates how the reliability of assessment instruments in research or intervention can and should be an integral part of whether research is implemented and whether parents and children are recruited into a social program. According to Danish (Chapter 7), once a developmental intervention is implemented the monitoring of the process of intervention becomes a critical means of determining whether the program can be consistently implemented and whether the behavioral outcomes can indeed be attributed to the intervention process. Similarly, McCall (Chapter 11) raises the need for monitoring the quality and consistency of approaches in the mass media to assess whether call-in advice programs achieve their stated goals of providing beneficial psychological information to callers and listeners or fall short by giving the false impression that mental health services consist of context-free advice, absolute answers, and quick cures.

Evaluation criteria. The criteria chosen for program evaluation may present more direct and immediate threats to the usefulness of applied developmental activities. This is because a social program which has been negatively evaluated is often quickly terminated without assessing why the program failed. As discussed by Lewis (Chapter 6), an intervention which may be helpful to some individuals may be abandoned if the evaluation criteria focuses on permanent rather than limited "cure," universal rather than individual help, or general rather than specific change.

Translation. The ability to translate scientific information to the knowledge consumer often becomes the primary responsibility of those applied developmental psychologists who disseminate research findings. Melton (Chapter 10) discusses how in legal situations the developmental scientist as advocate of the data must present evidence in a comprehensible way to the court. For example, complex legal testimony can be inherently misleading when presented too briefly. Similarly, psychologists communicating knowledge of developmental research through the mass media (Chapter 11) need to educate themselves as to how to get points across to the audience while still communicating the limited applicability of these findings to individual problems.

A related danger is the misapplication of research due to the consumer's limited understanding. According to Sigel (Chapter 9) the applied developmental psychologist can take steps against consumer misapplication by approaching research design with an a priori concern for the context in which consumers of the research may attempt to apply the knowledge generated. For example, data on parental teaching styles and children's performance on intelligence tasks helps parents or educators only if the research report enables them to factor in the many conditions under which the study was conducted. How much experience a teacher needs to implement a particular intervention and exactly how to employ the method if it is new to him or her are examples of the type of information that enables a teacher to decide whether to apply the knowledge to his or her interactions with children.

Competence. Working outside one's area of competence is another example of applied activities which may harm the consumer. Ethical issues associated with the distinction between dispensing advice, educating the consumer, and providing psychotherapy are discussed in Chapters 11, 12, 13, and 14. In parent training workshops, hospital settings, or on radio talk shows applied developmental psychologists may be called upon to provide assessment or advice to particular individuals. Koocher (Chapter 14) argues that in the absence of training in individual assessment and direct intervention skills, applied developmental psychologists cannot adequately recognize psychopathology, measure individual developmental progressions, or assess individual behavioral change. In these situations the applied developmental psychologist must limit his or her activities to nontherapeutic interventions and must ensure the consumer understands these limitations as well (Fisher & Tryon, 1988). It is equally important that directors of training programs in applied developmental psychology assess the training and practice boundaries of the profession. Another training issue introduced by Melton (Chapter 10) concerns the ethical duty of the psychologist working with the courts not to exceed competence when giving expert testimony. This raises issues of the scientific foundation as well as training necessary to present opinions about social facts.

Autonomy and Respect for the Dignity of Individuals

The principle of respect reflects a moral concern for the autonomy of persons, their right to self-governance, and privacy of action and thought (Sieber, 1982). Developmental psychologists trained in traditional experimental child psychology programs are familiar with ethical guidelines designed to protect the dignity of individuals through informed consent procedures. Once outside the laboratory, however, the issue of respect becomes more complex. In this volume the moral obligations derived from the principle of respect emerge most clearly in concern for an individual's right to self-determination. For example, Baumrind (Chapter 2) discusses how deception, particularly with children, violates an individual's right to self-determination and the obligation of the applied developmental psychologist to be trustworthy. Fisher and Rosendahl (Chapter 4) extend this discussion to the increased risks to self-esteem posed by conducting deception studies in applied contexts. If applied developmental psychologists are to respect the dignity of those they study and serve they must (a) equip individuals with the information needed for informed and voluntary decisions about their participation in developmental research and intervention and/or the need to engage the services of other health care professionals, and (b) consider the right to confidentiality within the context of individual welfare.

Right to information. Applied developmental psychologists should strive to provide individuals with information enabling them to make autonomous decisions about (a) participation in developmental research or interventions and (b) the need for other psychological services. Laosa (Chapter 15), among other contributors to this volume, calls for the participant as partner in the decision-making processes leading to application, especially in the participant's right to learn of any known potential side effects of receiving treatment or control experiences. Self-determination may be indirectly threatened when participation in a study prevents a family from seeking the help for children they would otherwise have obtained. This issue, combined with the potential for developmental intervention studies to be coercive to families of at-risk or handicapped individuals are addressed in Chapters 3 and 4. Scarr (Chapter 3) raises the issue of parental rights to child assessment information, and the related problems of assessment quality and the competence of the developmental psychologist to communicate these results.

Another indirect threat to self-determination are activities directed at changing children's behaviors that usurp the parental role. Both Sigel and Elkind (Chapters 9 and 12) stress the fact that an intervention designed to change parental belief systems in ways that empirical research has shown is related to more positive academic attitudes or social development may in fact be a violation of privacy. They question whether parent education is, in fact, behavioral engineering.

Along somewhat different lines, Koocher (Chapter 14) raises concerns about the type of information provided graduate students seeking careers in applied developmental psychology. He argues that students need to be informed about employment opportunities currently available outside of academia as well as the complement (or lack thereof) of their training with credentialing in professional psychology and state licensure laws.

Confidentiality. Research designed to test a developmental theory in its natural context, to examine an immediate social problem, or to evaluate a social program will bring the applied developmental psychologist in contact not only with those participating in research and intervention but their caregivers, educators, and other helping professionals as well. These contacts may indirectly affect participants by changing the attitudes and behaviors of members of their social networks. Fisher and Rosendahl (Chapter 4) discuss steps that can be taken in order to reduce the risks posed to those individuals targeted as members of special populations in research, intervention, or dissemination.

A conflict between the moral values of beneficence and self-determination arises when a research participant, a participant in an intervention, or a radio caller indicate problems that place them or others in immediate danger. Scarr's position (Chapter 3) is that we cannot participate in screening programs without offering intervention alternatives. Several contributors to this volume discuss the responsibilities and limits of breaking confidentiality and providing referrals in these contexts. Fisher and Rosendahl (Chapter 4) describe procedures to follow when responses on a research instrument suggest a participant may be suicidal.

McCall and Elkind (Chapters 11 and 12) find similar problems emerge for developmental psychologists working through the media or conducting developmental education programs. They show how one can balance the obligation to preserve individual dignity, the right to choose treatment, and the right to a referral if needed.

Justice

The principle of justice refers to the moral value of equitable distribution of social benefit and costs. In this volume justice is expressed in concern with equal accessibility to valid services. For example, according to Sieber (Chapter 5), a science that focuses on the individual without critical analysis of the culture of the individual runs the risk of ethnocentric theories and cultural imperialism. To follow the principle of justice in research, intervention, and dissemination, applied developmental psychologists must strive to (a) recognize cultural differences without stereotyping members of a social category or depriving them of services, and (b) obtain an appropriate balance between good experimental design and the responsibility to provide equal distribution of psychological services when they are available.

Population validity. The heterogeneity of the American population poses the risk that research, intervention, and dissemination of research while appropriate for one segment of the population will be harmful to another segment. Laosa (Chapter 14) addresses this issue when discussing population validity, explaining that a measure of a psychological construct may or may not have the same or even similar psychometric properties or patterns of relationships with other variables in different populations. Thus an inference valid for one population may lead to incorrect judgments regarding another. An applied developmental psychologist designing interventions cannot assume that an outcome of a particular service can be generalized to different populations. While we must adapt and develop services to fit the target population, we must also recognize the risk of differential expectations and classification, plus different quality of services for minority groups. Both Chapters 15 and 17 address the tradeoff between mainstream and population-sensitive research and services as well as the consequences of failing to provide services to a population in need for whom there is still no guarantee of a positive outcome.

Provision of services. The problem of equal distribution also arises in intervention research where a control group must be considered. From an applied developmental perspective the decision not to intervene is itself an action (Chapters 7 and 8). In Chapter 4, Fisher and Rosendahl argue against the use of a control group when the deleterious effects of nonintervention are documented. Scarr (Chapter 3) discusses the costly tradeoff between ethics and research design when services are available to all participants.

CONCLUDING COMMENTS

While many of the issues raised and guidelines offered by our contributors can be related to the broad ethical principles currently provided by the American Psychological Association and the Society for Research in Child Development, the goal of this volume is to place these principles within the specific context of applied developmental psychology activities so that they can be of immediate practical use.

Ethics is not easy to write about. It requires self-reflection and the courage to analyze and reveal one's values. Elkind writes, "We must be reflective and that is perhaps the best we can do." And indeed that is what our contributors have done, generously sharing their experiences and concerns so that we might guide others in this emerging field.

REFERENCES

Baumrind, D. (1987). A developmental perspective on adolescent risk-taking in contemporary America. *New Directions for Child Development: Adolescent Health and Social Behaviors, 37,* 93–126.

Bronfenbrenner, U., Kessel, F., Kessen, W., & White, S. (1986). Towards a critical social history of developmental psychology: A propaedeutic discussion. *American Psychologist, 41,* 1218–1230.

Fisher, C.B., & Tryon, W.W. (1988). Ethical issues in the research and practice of applied developmental psychology. *Journal of Applied Developmental Psychology, 9,* 27–39.

Kandel, D., Davies, M., Karus, D., & Yamaguchi, K. (1986). The consequences in young adulthood of adolescent drug involvement. *Archives of General Psychiatry, 43,* 746–754.

Lerner, R.M., & Busch-Rossnagel, N.A. (1981). *Individuals as producers of their development: A life-span perspective.* New York: Academic Press.

Morrison, F.J., Lord, C., & Keating, D.P. (1984). Applied developmental psychology. In F.J. Morrison, C. Lord, & D.P. Keating (Eds.), *Applied developmental psychology* (Vol. 1, pp. 4–20). New York: Academic Press.

Newcomb, M., Bentler, P., & Collins, C. (1986). Alcohol use and dissatisfaction with self and life: A longitudinal analysis of young adults. *Journal of Drug Issues, 16,* 479–494.

Scholnick, E.K., Fisher, C.B., Brown, A., & Sigel, I. (1988). Report on applied developmental psychology. *APA Division 7 Newsletter, Spring,* 6–10.

Sears, R.R. (1975). Your ancients revisited: A history of child development. In E.M. Hetherington (Ed.), *Review of child development research* (Vol. 5, pp. 1–74). Chicago, IL: University of Chicago Press.

Sieber, J.E. (1982). Ethical dilemmas in social research. In J.E. Sieber (Ed.), *The ethics of social research: Surveys and experiments* (pp. 1–30). New York: Springer-Verlag.

Siegel, A.W., & White, S.H. (1982). The child study movement: Early growth and development of the symbolized child. In H.W. Reese (Ed.), *Advances in child development and behavior* (pp. 233–285). New York: Academic Press.

Sigel, I., & Cocking, R.R. (1980). Editors' message. *Journal of Applied Developmental Psychology, 1,* i–iii.

Wertlieb, D. (1983). Some foundations and directions for applied developmental psychology. *Journal of Applied Developmental Psychology, 4*, 349–358.

Zigler, E., & Finn, M. (1984). Applied developmental psychology. In M.H. Bornstein & M.E. Lamb (Eds.), *Developmental psychology: An advanced textbook* (pp. 451–492). Hillsdale, NJ: Lawrence Erlbaum Associates, Inc.

Part I
Ethics and Applied Developmental Research

2   Doing Good Well*

Diana Baumrind

I have entitled this chapter "Doing Good Well," in order to emphasize the crucial role of values in applied developmental research—in the choice of topics of study, in the way hypotheses are formulated, in the selection of research methods, in the manner in which results are probed with further analyses, in the generalizations that are drawn from these findings, and in the social policy recommendations that are based on these findings. In conducting scientific research, we are actors and not merely arbiters of social policy. Honest treatment of human subjects and humane treatment of animal subjects have become important social policy issues. My contribution to this volume will focus on the role of researchers in generating knowledge and telling the truth in a national climate of disinformation and self-delusion. The issues I consider are intended to be especially relevant to the generation of knowledge that parents and educators need to bring up competent and moral children. Applied developmental researchers have a special obligation to exemplify in their own professional conduct the values that define a fiduciary trust.

Scientific integrity is the crux of what I mean by doing good well. By *doing good* I mean to answer socially relevant questions using ecologically valid and ethically acceptable methods. To *do good* means that my work should be of sufficient social value to merit passionate personal commitment and that I treat my subject-participants as ethical agents in their own right with the power of informed consent. For me, the sine qua non of good research *done well* is the collection of high-quality data in natural settings, and careful articulation of conceptually meaningful theoretical constructs.

To the extent that our services as professionals and scholars are accorded public trust (as reflected in special privileges that enable us to perform our functions) and involve a *protective* obligation, a fiduciary relationship may be said to exist between the public and ourselves. As fiduciaries we are trustees of the values inherent in our activities—integrity, compassion, and trustworthiness. In the discharge of our fiduciary obligations, scientific integrity entails uncom-

* This chapter is revised from an invited contribution to the Symposium on Basic Research and Social Policy, at the Society for Research in Child Development, April 24, 1987. During its preparation, the author was supported by a Research Scientist Award (#1-K05-MH00485-01) from the National Institute of Mental Health. The William T. Grant Foundation has provided consistent and generous support of the author's work.

promising adherence to a code of values that avoids deception, expedience, and shallowness: The worthy end of doing good research well does not justify violation of any subject's right to informed consent; the need to obtain funding for doing good research well does not justify "pork barrel" research. Duties of nonmaleficence, to "do no harm," take precedence over duties of beneficence, to do good (e.g., Marshall, 1986; Beauchamp & Childress, 1983). Researchers do harm if we (a) violate the rights of subjects to informed consent, or (b) allow our scientific priorities to be determined by legislative mandate representing special interests or prejudices. I will discuss each of these two kinds of wrongdoing in turn.

INFORMED CONSENT AS THE CORNERSTONE OF ETHICAL RESEARCH

I have argued elsewhere (Baumrind, 1971, 1978, 1979, 1985) that the use of intentional deception in the research setting is unethical, imprudent, and unwarranted scientifically: The right of subjects to be informed *prior* to consent takes precedence over any considerations of scientific benefit that could accrue were we to violate that right. By "intentional deception" in the research setting, I mean withholding of information in order to obtain participation which the subject might otherwise decline, deceptive instructions and confederate manipulations in laboratory research, and concealment and staged manipulations in field settings. My judgment that intentional deception in the research setting is morally wrong is grounded in the rule-utilitarian view that truth telling and promise keeping serve the function in the social world that physical laws do in the natural world—to promote order and regularity. By acting in accord with agreed-upon rules, keeping promises, acting honorably, and following the rules of the game, human beings construct for themselves a coherent and consistent environment in which purposive behavior becomes possible. A violation of an individual's right of informed consent is a breach of the social contract and thus legitimates retaliative lawlessness because only in a rule-following environment may we be held fully accountable for the consequences of our actions. Therefore, social scientists must exercise their right to seek knowledge within the constraints imposed by the right to informed consent of those persons from whom they would obtain that knowledge.

Deceit in the research setting violates two principles intended to secure the common good: (a) the individual's right to self-determination, and (b) the obligation of a fiduciary to be trustworthy. Both warrant reflective comment.

First, the right of self-determination grants to each individual the freedom to do as one chooses (and to be left alone if one chooses), so long as one's behavior does not impinge on the rights of others or present a clear and imminent danger to oneself: In the research setting, the individual's right to be self-determining is abrogated whenever the researcher fails to obtain from subjects their informed consent or when consent is not freely given. When the researcher provides subjects with false or incomplete information, consent cannot be informed. If subjects are required to participate in an experiment, for example, in order to gain course credit, consent cannot be freely given. Subjects have the right to judge for themselves what constitutes psychological harm for them. For many, being lied to or learning something painful about themselves will constitute harm.

Second, the demands of a fiduciary relationship which obtain whenever one person (called the "fiduciary") is dealing with another (called the "beneficiary") in circumstances involving the placing of a special trust, are especially stringent. In such circumstances, the beneficiary (e.g., child, student, patient, or research subject) has a right to expect, and the fiduciary (parent, teacher, doctor, or social scientist) has the obligation to provide, a relationship characterized by trust and caring rather than one based on "caveat emptor." It is the fiduciary nature of the investigator-subject relationship that enables the investigator to recruit participants, and, by the same token, obliges the investigator to be trustworthy.

Violating one's fiduciary obligation to subjects who are children or students is especially blameworthy. The use of deception with children presents a particularly serious breach of our fiduciary obligation to them. Of the numerous examples of such research I will mention only one, the replication by Shanab and Yahya (1977) of the classic Milgram paradigm. Children as young as six were subject to the paradigm in which a confederate urged them to administer painful shock to an unfamiliar child of their own age. Graphic reports of the children's reactions document trembling, lip biting, and nervous laughter. College students are also at special risk when they serve as experimental subjects. Those who extend trust may, when they are later deceived, feel betrayed by the experimenter who in the academic context also serves as a teacher and professional model. As a model, the experimental psychologist is encouraging apprentice psychologists to dissimulate in the interests of science and career advancement when instead he or she ought to exemplify the rule of conduct that serves to justify scientific experimentation; that is, "You shall know the truth, and the truth shall set you free." Those young people still willing to consider a research career despite the decreasing grants available, and the negative image cast on scientific careers by evidence of fraud in scientific publications, deserve mentors who model high ethical standards and personal integrity.

The claim that deceptive manipulations are required to create an experimentally controlled psychological reality rests on two assumptions that have been challenged extensively by critics of Cartesian reductionism, the assumptions (a) that deceptive instructions create a uniform psychological reality without which valid inference is impossible, and (b) that causal inference in the social sciences can be achieved with a high level of certitude by using adequate experimental controls.

Among college students and adults, pervasive subject suspicion defeats the purpose of deceptive instructions, which is to control subject set. Subjects in social psychological experiments are as likely to role-play as to be truly naive and it is difficult to detect disingenuousness or skepticism without extensive questioning. Experimenters introduce deceptive strategies in order to increase experimental rigor; however, the potential effects of deceptive manipulations, and the influence of subject skepticism and incredulity, are not themselves rigorously evaluated. Page (1973) has shown that asking subjects fewer than four questions will classify only 5% of them as suspicious whereas extended questionnaires will yield about 40% suspicious subjects. But extended questionnaires are seldom, if ever, used to rule out suspiciousness. Thus, the methods which experimenters use to identify non-naive, suspicious subjects would not pass muster if evaluated by the same criteria as are applied to the experiments themselves. Since the behaviors of suspicious subjects in the experimental situation are generally found to differ systematically from those who are not, a covert source of ambiguity is introduced into experiments when investigators employ deception but fail to detect suspiciousness. Many subjects, particularly college students in heavily experimental departments, have come to expect rigged lotteries, deceptive instructions, and the use of confederates. Those who adopt a game-set will not feel betrayed because they do not assume that the experimenter is trustworthy. But to the extent that some students but not others are beguiled, experimental control has not been achieved by deceptive instructions, and there are no benefits to weigh against the costs.

Further, the claim that properly controlled observations can provide value-free, objective, and unassailable knowledge is certainly disputable. Over and above the ubiquitous issues of reliability and population generalizability, the level of certitude that can accompany any empirical generalization in the sociobehavioral sciences is limited by at least three factors: (a) human beings are not interchangeable or identical with themselves over time; (b) psychological laws operate within a dynamic and rapidly changing social context; and (c) given the complexity of social phenomena, the possibility of identifying, controlling, or ruling out all extrinsic factors is virtually nil. Ironically, to the extent that such controls *are* successfully instituted, the experimental paradigm becomes less ecologically valid. An ecologically valid context is one that is representative of those in which the participants normally conduct their affairs.

A hypothetical, counterfactual state of affairs constructed in the laboratory is of interest only if it constitutes a paradigm that could in fact be created in the real world. Generally, however, an experimental paradigm is not presented as a counterfactual but realizable ideal. Instead it is oriented towards testing mediational processes that are said to exist in the real world but in uncontrolled contexts (Berkowitz & Donnerstein, 1982). But if variables that are untied and independently manipulated in the laboratory setting in order to control them are necessarily or typically confounded in the natural setting, then conditions in the laboratory cannot or will not be replicable in the natural setting. Conversely, when such processes not only can, but do, typically operate in the real world, then they can be studied in natural or clinical contexts which do not require laboratory manipulation to produce. Thus, aggression researchers do not need to use deceptive sets to induce aggressive responses in the laboratory because they could instead study acts intended to harm others in the context of organized sports or the New York City subway system. These natural contexts vary along relevant parameters such as stress level, victim's vulnerability, and normative expectations, thus allowing natural experiments to be conducted.

Deceptive practices cannot be justified unless they result in findings that are controversial because the benefit to society of noncontroversial (that is, trivial) findings is minimal. If the phenomenon has already been shown to occur in real life it is not controversial. For example, Zimbardo and his colleagues (Zimbardo, Andersen, & Kabat, 1981) did not need to induce partial deafness through covert post-hypnotic suggestion because it is a generally acknowledged clinical observation that undiagnosed hearing loss in older people is often associated with increased suspiciousness (e.g., Corso, 1977; Knapp, 1948; Pfeiffer, 1977). Investigators interested in studying how people justify intentionally causing others to suffer in real life could examine the justifications offered by deception researchers themselves. Thus, in lieu of the familiar teacher-learner aggression paradigm (Berkowitz & Geen, 1966), in which a confederate makes a series of preplanned errors on a word-association task and subjects are urged to deliver "shocks" to the confederate, investigators and their confederates could examine their own motivation. It turns out, according to Kane and colleagues, that subjects in that familiar aggression paradigm believe that they are benefitting the learner and therefore are not behaving aggressively in the sense of intending to inflict harm (Kane, Joseph, & Tedeschi, 1976). Similarly, Milgram's (1964) ease in recruiting graduate student confederates to inflict suffering upon subjects demonstrated conclusively that normal, well-intentioned people such as his graduate-student confederates will willingly obey instructions to hurt others who are innocent. The confederates justified their actions in inflicting severe psychological pain on their subjects on the same bases that the subjects justified theirs, that they were inflicting no lasting harm and were contributing to science. Since these graduate student confederates were willing to cause others to whom they had a fiduciary obligation to suffer, Milgram's deceitful manipulation of subjects provided no new information.

I am *not* asserting that appropriate controls are unnecessary to reduce subjectivity and ambiguity. I *am* asserting that the reduction in ambiguity achievable by experimental controls is not sufficiently great or certain to justify, from a universalist or a utilitarian metaethical stance, violation of the informed consent provision of our code of ethics, especially when the subjects are children or students. Our attempts to justify deception research as necessary to do good science well ultimately undermines our credibility by equating our professional self-interest with the public interest. The rights or welfare of research subjects, especially of those to whom we are in a fiduciary role, should be defined so that these constitute obligatory conditions that *must* be met for a paradigm to be treated as ethically acceptable.

SCIENTIFIC INTEGRITY AND SPECIAL INTERESTS

A second kind of wrongdoing for researchers to avoid is to subordinate our quest for knowledge to our quest for funds or for social approval. Applied developmental psychologists now and in the future are addressing issues of the utmost importance to the public. Policy makers have a right to expect us to focus upon issues of social as well as scientific significance, and to share our knowledge with the public. However, we ought not to endorse false expectations that a short-term focus on each separate manifestation of a critical social malaise can produce socially or scientifically valid results. For example, adolescent drug use, sexual promiscuity, and delinquency are *symptoms* of a larger social malaise that has resulted in erosion of the ecology of family life. We have an obligation to reject the expectation that we can resolve any single symptom of the adolescent predicament—such as pregnancy or use of a specific drug such as cocaine—in the one to three years of funding typically allotted. We must resist the temptation to allow the government agencies that support our work to dictate our research agenda, although we should certainly engage in joint efforts to formulate national priorities and to lobby Congress for adequate funds to enable those priorities to be realized.

It is universally acknowledged that our adolescents are not thriving and that their problems lie largely in the domains of social and affective development and behavioral pediatrics. But despite the emphasis being placed now by all the National Institutes on adolescent health issues, adequate funds are not yet being appropriated. For example, the three institutes of the Alcohol, Drug Abuse, and Mental Health Administration (ADAMHA) jointly released a grant announcement in August, 1983, inviting methodologically rigorous applications using existing longitudinal data to improve our understanding of known risk factors and precursors of alcohol abuse, drug abuse, and mental illness in children and adolescents. Unfortunately, the total availability of funds for these new awards to be spread over the fiscal years of 1984 and 1985 was a mere $500,000! We should, through our professional organizations, protest such token support. When in fiscal 1987 a substantial sum of money was made available for treatment, research, and prevention of substance use, the National Institute on Drug Abuse flooded the field with Requests for Proposals (RFPs) that elicited an unprecedented number of applications (almost 900!) for review in the May-June Councils. Yet very few of those who applied could be funded. The monumental task of evaluating this number of proposals necessarily required the help of a large number of ad hoc reviewers, siphoned off a substantial portion of the available funds, and must have resulted in considerable disillusion on the part of new investigators who had responded with proposals to the special RFPs.

A one-to-three year focus on drug abuse, followed by a similar brief focus on pregnancy, displaced by a focus on AIDS will resolve none of these serious social problems. We must refuse to endorse by our complicity unrealistic expectations by policy makers of what our efforts can produce. Without secure, long-range funding, good investigative research, particularly longitudinal in design, cannot be sustained and ought not to be initiated. With funds increasingly scarce, and priority scores required to fund unusually stringent, it has become increasingly difficult for controversial or truly innovative work to be funded. Conversely, in the behavioral sciences it has always been difficult to obtain federal funding for replication studies that mitigate against fraud in the physical sciences. Applied developmental psychologists should urge funding agencies to set realistic priorities and to refrain from soliciting more proposals than there are funds available to support them; and to encourage review groups to seriously consider funding both highly innovative research by solid investigators, and replication studies where the conclusions have social policy applications.

LIMITATIONS OF SOCIAL SCIENCE RESEARCH

Program designers, the media, and policy makers may not want to hear disclaimers as to the limits of our certitude. However, *we* are morally obliged to make the appropriate disclaimers so that they *are* heard: Child development findings vary with the developmental level, sex, cohort, and social class of the child. They are limited by relevant extrinsic variables excluded from our model, by practical considerations, and by our own ignorance. At a minimum, the data upon which conclusions intended to affect social policy are based must be of high quality. We ought pay heed to the computer analyst's dictum, "garbage in, garbage out." We should be especially careful about the claims we make from so-called "causal analyses." Under the best of circumstances, and using the most sophisticated causal analyses, the truth value of a hypothesized causal connection cannot be established by inductive reasoning from associations which are not high (even if highly significant). Social scientists must still resort to the force of a better argument within some agreed-upon discourse system to resolve scientific disputes.

A particularly unfortunate example of the use of specious causal attribution to further an ideologically attractive hypothesis was the attempt by O'Donnell and Clayton (1982) to revive the hypothesis that marijuana use is a "stepping stone" to heroin use. The important social policy implications of this hypothesis were evidenced by the fact that then-director of the National Institute on Drug Abuse, William Pollin, brought the revised "stepping-stone hypothesis" to the attention of the Senate Subcommittee on Alcoholism and Drug Abuse (Scott, 1981) even prior to the paper's publication. O'Donnell and Clayton argued that the "recognition of the causal connection has implications for research and policy that are missed when the connection is denied" (p. 29). But their reformulated stepping-stone hypothesis was misleading because it was based on a parochial model of causality shared by neither laypersons nor philosophers of science (see Baumrind, 1983). O'Donnell and Clayton proposed a weak version of the regularity model of causality, which assumes that regularity of succession, contiguity, and covariation offer reasonable evidence of (or an approximation to) causation. In contrast, the model implicit in the common meaning of cause is generative. What the layperson and the social policy planner have in mind by "cause" is "a *necessary* connection or intrinsic bond embedded in the very nature of things;" that is, knowledge of the generative or productive mechanism. After a brief flurry, the "stepping-stone hypothesis" was again laid to rest, but not before an effort by social scientists to influence social policy had been discredited.

The planning of social interventions both presumes and requires a generative rather than a regularity causal model: That is, the presence of a nonspurious correlation which fails to vanish when the effects of other variables deemed to be prior to both of them are removed does not prove causation. The nature of statistical inferences, especially those based on probabilistic inductive models, provides only indirect support for an assertion, usually by casting doubt on an alternative assertion. Therefore language of proof such as "we have demonstrated" should be replaced by terms appropriate to the language of discovery (e.g., "we have good grounds for believing"), especially when speaking to the media or to policy makers. In view of the limits of our knowledge and wisdom, scientific integrity requires that when actively attempting to affect social policy decisions, we refrain from implying a level of certitude that our subject matter and research strategies do not justify.

RISKING THE FUTURE

Just as drug use was identified as the primary adolescent problem in 1986, adolescent pregnancy has been so identified in 1987. The National Research Council's panel report on adolescent pregnancy (1987), entitled "Risking the Future," is controversial, among other reasons because in its focus on a single symptom of the adolescent predicament it fails to deal with an even more devastating consequence of adolescent sexuality than pregnancy; that is, the risk of contracting a presently incurable, venereally transmitted disease. In strongly endorsing the use of birth control pills for sexually actively adolescent girls, the effect of the report may be to dissuade couples from using condoms which provide some protection against AIDS and herpes. Further, the Panel claims that there are no important health risks to the use of birth control pills, thus dismissing as unjustified the reservations of the Boston Women's Health Book Collective (1984) and many medical authorities, and the warning labels on the boxes themselves about the risks associated with the pill. In young women these risks include depression, greater susceptibility to yeast and urinary tract disorders, gum inflammation, increased nutritional needs (particularly for vitamins B6 and C), migraine, and acne. More serious risks are associated with a family history of diabetes or sickle cell anemia trait. In addition, there is some evidence from two studies (Olsen & Weed, 1986; Weed & Olsen, 1986) that school-based birth control clinics, which the Panel advocates, reduce live births by increasing abortion rather than by preventing pregnancy (in contradistinction to Zabin, Hirsch, Smith, Street, & Hardy, 1986). Their effect on the incidence of venereal disease is still not known.

Values, ours and our subjects, cannot be excluded from our work. I submit that at present social scientists are not perceived as credible because we render our values opaque by donning the veil of objectivity. The fact that we may feel strongly about such issues as sexual and ethnic stereotypes, exercise of arbitrary social control, or abortion on demand does not disallow us from gathering high-quality veridical data and reporting out results fairly. But in order for social scientists to appear credible in the eyes of those who do not share our values, we must (a) make our values explicit, and (b) then include persons with a wide range of explicit values among those who design and evaluate the results of experiments dealing with controversial subjects.

Value judgments generally presume the truth value of implicit premises and are therefore indirectly subject to disconfirmation. For example, presumptions underlying my personal values concerning adolescent sexuality which I have stated elsewhere (Baumrind, 1982) include the following testable hypotheses:

1. By virtue of adults' role as authorities, adolescents expect them to disapprove of teenage premarital sexual intercourse. For individuals whose morality is heteronomous, behavior which is mildly or inconsistently condemned is not seen as intrinsically wrong or even as violating consensual rules of conduct (Nisan, 1987). Nonreaction by adults under conditions of expected disapproval is likely to be interpreted by adolescents as approval. Thus Siegel and Kohn (1959) found that nonreaction by an adult present when a child was behaving aggressively results in greater incidence of such acts in the future. That is, when a young person whose morality is heteronomous misbehaves and an adult is present and does not express disapproval, the nonreaction is interpreted typically by the individual as approval and the future incidence of such behavior is increased.

2. Therefore, early adolescents who are still heteronomous in their judgments are likely to believe that teachers or Planned Parenthood counselors who provide them with information on birth control in a value-free context condone, or only mildly condemn, adolescent sexual intercourse, unless they are explicitly told otherwise when such information is im-

parted. The reality of moral norms proscribing sexual intercourse for individuals of their age is thus called into question.

3. Adolescents are likely to assume that the contraceptive methods suggested by trusted counselors are safe and morally acceptable to the counselors. Thus adolescents for whom oral contraceptives or the IUD are prescribed in a school-based family planning clinic, or with whom abortion as a feasible method of ending pregnancy is discussed in a value-free school context, are likely to discount the health hazards these contraceptive methods may present, unless explicitly warned against them. They are also more likely to attach no moral stigma to abortion than those who receive such information in an evaluative home-based or school-based context.

4. Adolescents who (a) discount the health hazards of the most effective methods of birth control, and (b) do not regard abortion as either dangerous to their health or as immoral, will express a more positive attitude toward engaging in sexual intercourse at their age.

5. Adolescents who express a more positive attitude toward engaging in sexual intercourse at their age will have a higher rate of sexual intercourse (which may result in a higher rate of venereal disease if not abortion) than those who do not, despite their greater access to effective methods of contraception. Thus, teenage involvement in value-neutral family planning programs may be followed not by a reduction in overall adolescent sexual activity and pregnancy rates but rather by an increase in abortion and/or sexually transmitted diseases.

6. Adolescents who either (a) attach no moral stigma to abortion or (b) rule out abortion for any person under any circumstances will be less prosocial (compassionate, altruistic) in their attitudes and behavior than those who say they would choose to have an abortion to terminate an unwanted pregnancy but also that they would feel sad or guilty for having destroyed an incipient life.

Despite or perhaps because of its controversial recommendations, the Panel report is a worthy example of an effort by child development specialists to apply scientific knowledge to a critical social problem, and to develop recommendations and guidelines for policy makers, service providers, and families. How it is received and used may tell us something about how the public evaluates our knowledge and our wisdom.

If we believe that human nature is shaped in important ways by environment than we have an obligation to determine what kind of environment is truly human. Whatever our specific area of knowledge, each of us must consider questions of obligation, duty, fairness, and compassion; give some thought to the nature of the good life and the good society; and make an intellectual commitment to a line of inquiry that we believe is meaningful and socially significant.

The scientific endeavor like any other human endeavor should be directed at valued goals. How we choose to conduct ourselves as scientists, as much as the knowledge we produce defines our professional contribution to the national interest. We cannot control, although we can influence, the use that is made of the knowledge we produce. We *can* control our own conduct, fulfill our fiduciary obligations faithfully, and behave with utmost integrity, aspiring to do no harm, in our efforts to *do good well*.

SUMMARY AND CONCLUSIONS

Scientific integrity is crucial to knowledge generation, especially when that knowledge is obtained in order to be applied to social problems. Intentional deception in the research setting, particularly with children as subjects, is unethical, imprudent, and unwarranted scientifically: It violates the individual's right to self-determination, and the obligation of a fiduciary to be trustworthy. Deceptive instructions do not assure a uniform psychological reality, or confer a high level of certitude and so cannot be justified on these bases. Our quest for knowledge ought never to be subordinated to our quest for funds or social approval. Rather than allow funding agencies to dictate our research priorities, we should take an active role in encouraging them to set realistic priorities, and to fund both more innovative designs and more replication studies. Data intended to affect social policy should be highly reliable and ecologically valid. Scientific integrity requires that we refrain from implying a level of certitude that our subject matter and research strategies do not justify. Values cannot and should not be excluded from scientific endeavors, but instead should be made explicit. Credibility requires that when evaluating a body of data about controversial issues, for example school-based contraceptive clinics, persons with a wide range of explicit values be included as judges. As applied developmental psychologists, we are judged by our professional conduct as well as by the quality of the knowledge we generate, as we strive to do good well.

REFERENCES

Baumrind, D. (1971). Reactions to the May 1972 draft report of the Ad Hoc Committee on Ethical Standards in Psychological Research. *American Psychologist, 26,* 887–896.

Baumrind, D. (1978). Nature and definition of informed consent in research involving deception. In *The Belmont Report: Ethical principles and guidelines for the protection of human subjects of research* (DHEW Publication No. (OS) 78-0014, 23-1-23-71). Washington, DC: The National Commission for the Protection of Human Subjects of Biochemical and Behavioral Research.

Baumrind, D. (1979). IRBs and social science research: The costs of deception. *IRB: A Review of Human Subjects Research, 1*(6), 1–4.

Baumrind, D. (1982). Adolescent sexuality: Comment on Williams' and Silka's comments on Baumrind. *American Psychologist, 37*(12), 1402–1403.

Baumrind, D. (1983). Specious causal attributions in the social sciences: The reformulated stepping-stone theory of heroin use as exemplar. *Journal of Personality and Social Psychology, 45*(6), 1289–1298.

Baumrind, D. (1985). Research using intentional deception: Ethical issues revisited. *American Psychologist, 40,* 165–174.

Beauchamp, T., & Childress, J. (1983). *Principles of biomedical ethics.* London: Oxford University Press.

Berkowitz, L., & Donnerstein, E. (1982). External validity is more than skin deep: Some answers to criticisms of laboratory experiments. *American Psychologist, 37,* 245–357.

Berkowitz, L., & Geen, R.G. (1966). Film violence and the cue properties of available targets. *Journal of Personality and Social Psychology, 3,* 525–530.

Boston Women's Health Book Collective. (1984). *The new our bodies, ourselves.* New York: Simon & Schuster.

Corso, J.F. (1977). Auditory perception and communication. In J.E. Birren & Schaie (Eds.), *Handbook of the psychology of aging* (pp. 535–561). New York: Van Nostrand Reinhold.

Kane, T.R., Joseph, J.M., & Tedeschi, J.T. (1976). Person perception and the Berkowitz paradigm for the study of aggression. *Journal of Personality and Social Psychology, 33*(6), 663–673.

Knapp, P.H. (1948). Emotional aspects of hearing loss. *Psychosomatic Medicine, 10,* 203–222.

Marshall, E. (1986). Does the moral philosophy of The Belmont Report rest on a mistake? *IRB, 8*(6), 5–6.

Milgram, S. (1964). Issues in the study of obedience: A reply to Baumrind. *American Psychologist, 19,* 848–852.

National Research Council. (1987). *Risking the future: Adolescent sexuality, pregnancy, and childbearing.* Washington, DC: National Academic Press.

Nisan, M. (1987). Moral norms and social conventions: A cross-cultural comparison. *Developmental Psychology, 23*(5), 719–725.

O'Donnell, J.A., & Clayton, R.R. (1982). The stepping-stone hypothesis—marijuana, heroin, and causality. *Chemical Dependencies: Behavioral and Biomedical Issues, 4,* 229–241.

Olsen, J.A., & Weed, S.W. (1986). Effects of family planning programs for teenagers on adolescent birth and pregnancy rates. *Family Perspective, 20*(3), 153–170.

Page, M.M. (1973). On detecting demand awareness by post-experimental questionnaire. *Journal of Social Psychology, 91,* 305–323.

Pfeiffer, E. (1977). Psychopathology and social pathology. In J.E. Birren & K.W. Schaie (Eds.), *Handbook of the psychology of aging* (pp. 650–671). New York: Van Nostrand Reinhold.

Scott, C. (1981, November 13). Teen marijuana use declines, Pollin tells Congress. *ADAMHA News,* p. 3.

Siegel, A.E., & Kohn, L.G. (1959). Permissiveness, permission, and aggression: The effects of adult presence or absence on aggression in children's play. *Child Development, 30,* 131–141.

Shanab, M.E., & Yahya, K.A. (1977). A behavioral study of obedience in children. *Journal of Personality and Social Psychology, 35,* 530–536.

Weed, S.E., & Olsen, J.A. (1986). Effects of family-planning programs on teenage pregnancy—replication and extension. *Family Perspective, 20*(3), 173–195.

Zabin, L.S., Hirsch, M.B., Smith, E.A., Street, R., & Hardy, J.B. (1986). Evaluation of a pregnancy prevention program for urban teenagers. *Family Planning Perspectives, 18*(3), 119–126.

Zimbardo, P.G., Andersen, S.M., & Kabat, L.G. (1981, June). Induced hearing deficit generates experimental paranoia. *Science, 212*(26), 1529–1531.

3 Ethical Dilemmas in Recent Research: A Personal Saga

Sandra Scarr

Writing this chapter is a welcome opportunity to share some ethical concerns that have arisen in my research in the past 10 years. My research abounds with ethical dilemmas of several sorts. Studies of racial differences in intelligence and school achievement, of adoptive and biologically related families, and of the causes of social class variation in achievement raise many ethical issues for investigators, as one conducts the study and as one presents the results to participants, to the scientific community, and to lay audiences. In my experience, there are few guiding principles for dealing with the ethical problems in such situations.

In this chapter, I will not deal with ethical problems in research on race, social class, and IQ. Having recently published "Race and gender as psychological variables: Social and ethical concerns" (Scarr, 1988), I will focus here on ethical considerations in other aspects of my research: (a) screening, assessment, and intervention programs, (b) research with "at-risk" groups, (c) government interference, (d) ineffectual programs, (e) cross-cultural collaborations, and (f) interpreting the results of day care research on infants and toddlers. Although the list may seem heterogeneous, it is probably not unusual for applied developmental psychologists to encounter such a range of ethical problems in their work. In any case, these are my recent ethical problems in applied development research.

GENERAL PRINCIPLES

Nearly all of the *Ethical Principles in the Conduct of Research with Human Participants* (APA, 1982) deal with the rights of research participants and the obligations of investigators to protect those rights. Ethical principles in research rest on but one of the APA's ethical principles, number 9; the others apply more generally to all psychologists or to the practice of psychology. Protection from harm, informed consent to participate, the competence of the participant to give informed consent without coercion, and the protection of participants' anonymity and the confidentiality of the data are major issues set forth in Principle 9. Let us assume that applied developmental psychologists subscribe to the general principles of ethical research, or else they should not be psychologists at all.

But there are no examples that illustrate the ethical problems of applied research or of developmental psychology in the *Ethical Principles,* in the recently published *Casebook on Ethical Principles of Psychologists* (APA, 1987), or in the ethical guidelines of the Society for Research in Child Development, currently under revision. One can imagine many examples of ethical problems in applied developmental research; for example:

- A newborn is assessed; do parents have a right to the investigator's report? What if the infant is abnormal but the researcher is not a licensed clinician and not entitled under state licensing law to offer clinical evaluations to parents of abnormal infants?
- What advice, if any, should be given to parents who participated in a research project about family life or their children's development? What if parents request information about sibling rivalry or parental conflict, as they affect family relations? Is the applied developmental researcher obliged to inform parents of his/her best judgment or is the investigator forbidden from giving "clinical" advice?
- What if an intervention program is found to be ineffective; do the research investigators have a right or even a responsibility to report their results to the families who participated in the study? Do the sponsors of the evaluation of an intervention program have the right to restrict access to information about the negative evaluation of their program?
- If an applied developmental investigator discovers in the course of a research project cases of incest or child abuse, when the families have been guaranteed confidentiality, is that investigator obliged to report the parents to appropriate authorities, as are medical personnel, or is this a breach of confidentiality, which is covered by our ethical principles?
- Are intervention programs that offer participants considerable benefits (e.g., free day care, toys and books, medical and social service programs) unduly coercive, such that the "right to withdraw" from the program is meaningless? Applied developmental psychologists face such dilemmas in asking for the cooperation of research participants in programs the participants cannot afford to refuse.
- Are screening programs that identify children's problems, but do not offer help, ethical? Should we participate in screening programs without intervention alternatives?

Applied developmentalists encounter ethical dilemmas in screening programs that do not offer treatment, evaluations of intervention programs that are *intended* to help participants but may not, assessment devices with less than perfect reliability that will be used to make life decisions, organizational sponsors that may not respect participants' rights to anonymity and confidentiality of their data, and seemingly undesirable social policy implications of the research results. There are doubtless other ethical problems for applied developmentalists, but these will be the focus of this chapter.

SCREENING, ASSESSMENT, AND TREATMENT PROGRAMS

In this section I tell the story of a 10-year collaboration to develop screening, assessment, and treatment programs for Bermuda and the ethical dilemmas encountered. In 1978, I was asked to develop a research design and evaluation of an early childhood intervention program (Scarr & McCartney, 1988) that had already been piloted on the island. Personnel had been trained, and it was clear that the HOME program was to be tested against a no-treatment control group. Because the Bermuda government was concerned that all of their children could possibly benefit from early intervention, the program was to be tested with a representative sample of families with young children.

I had no ethical problems with the random assignment of families to the intervention or control groups, as all were members of the general population with no identified developmental problems. Indeed, one of the goals of this research was to estimate the extent of developmental problems in the Bermudian population, where few data were available on the developmental status of young children.

In addition, parents were fully informed at the time of their participation in the pre-program assessment that some would receive additional services and some would not—the luck of the draw. As Wortman and her colleagues (Wortman, Hendricks & Hillis, 1976) have shown, participants in randomized trials who are informed of the design *before* participation are not as reactive as those who become aware of the design during the course of their participation. Thus, fully informed participants provide a better test of treatment results than participants who are told later of the randomized trial. Not only is random selection of participants a fair means of selection, it is also to the benefit of the research.

The assessments, both at intake and at outcome, were an extensive combination of standard measures and observations of children, their mothers (fathers were for the most part absent or unavailable), and the interactions of mothers and their children in an experimental setting. The reliability of the measures and of the battery as a whole was excellent, so that we felt fairly confident that our program evaluation was on firm measurement footing.

From this extensive evaluation of the HOME program in a representative sample of Bermudian families, Kathleen McCartney and I (Scarr & McCartney, 1988) found the HOME program to be of little benefit to these families, most of whose children were functioning quite well without planned intervention. (One of the most valuable aspects of this study was the normative data on the functioning of Bermudian preschoolers.) Most Bermudian children are in preschool programs and day care from infancy; thus, the additional stimulation from the HOME program is largely redundant.

We did find that about 15% of children (as in any population) had developmental delays or behavior problems that could possibly be ameliorated by early intervention. Thus, we designed a second study—Islandwide Screening, Assessment, and Intervention—that posed more acute ethical and research problems.

RESEARCH WITH AT-RISK GROUPS

Developing a screening battery for 2-year-olds could have been the first step in a research plan. A rational stepwise plan would have begun with validating a reliable screening battery, continued with a second step of validating an assessment battery, and finally moved to evaluating alternative treatment programs. But I have never approved of identifying problems without providing treatment that may ameliorate them. Separation of the identification of problems from attempts to treat them seems to me unethical. Similarly, separation of assessment from treatment seems untenable for the same ethical considerations. At the least, separation of screening and assessment from treatment poses an ethical problem that I cannot resolve.

Reliability of Assessments

Therefore, we launched simultaneously into the evaluation of screening, assessment, and treatment programs. Based on prior research we assembled a battery of reliable screening devices to identify mental delay, language delay, and behavior management problems. The intermediate step was finer-grained assessment to assure ourselves and the program staff that those children assigned to treatment programs had "real" problems and that other children not assigned to treatment did not need services. Happily, the screening and assessment programs turned out to be very effective in identifying children with "real" problems and in not overidentifying others who do not need treatment services (Scarr, McCartney, Miller, Havenstein, Goldfarb, Ricciuti, & Ming, 1988).

We found that of 40 children who passed the cognitive assessment at 2 years, only 1 failed the 4-year assessment for cognitive skills. Of the 29 children who failed the cognitive assessment at 2 years and who were assigned to cognitive treatment, 10 failed the 4-year assessment, despite 2 years of cognitive intervention. In the language delay group, results were similar: Of 58 children assigned to language treatment at age 2, 44% failed language assessment at age 4, whereas only 6% of children who passed language assessment at age 2 failed the assessment at age 4.

Assessment of behavior management difficulties was far less successful. Although we hoped that we had identified contrariness in 24-month-olds that was beyond parental tolerance and parents who were relatively intolerant of normal 2-year-old oppositional behavior, it turned out that we were not good at predicting behavior problems in 4-year-olds. Of families that passed the 24-month assessment, 9 of 40 mothers reported behavior problems at 4 years; of 29 mothers in the cognitive delay group, 9 reported behavior problems at 4; of 58 in the language delay group, 9 reported later behavior problems; and of 35 in the behavior management treatment group, 10 reported problems at 4 years, despite treatment. Although there are statistically significant differences among the groups, with the cognitive and behavior management treatment groups reporting the largest percent of behavior problems at age 4, the 24-month assessments were not good at identifying those individual children who would have later behavior problems.

Unreliable assessments that result in individual treatment decisions, whether yes or no, pose ethical dilemmas. I feel confident in telling parents that our assessments of cognitive and language delays result in highly probable treatment decisions for their children. But I do not think that parents ought to be recruited into the behavior management programs unless they feel they could personally benefit from some training, because our assessments are not reliable.

Dilemma of No-Treatment Controls

The final step in the research project was to institute several treatment programs whose effectiveness could be compared. Ideally, we would have had a no-treatment control group to compare with the various treatment groups. But how could we ethically identify children with problems and not provide any treatment? Even if we did not know which kind of treatment was most effective, could we legitimately provide *no* intervention for children with identified problems?

Despite the advantages to the research design, I could not in conscience arrange for a no-treatment control group. Given the commitment of the government to provide the necessary resources for treatment of all eligible children, the decision to deny some participation in the service of the evaluation seemed to me ethically questionable. On the other hand, if the government had decided to conduct a limited trial, where allocated resources would cover treatment for only some of the eligible participants, a randomly selected control group would have been not only ethically acceptable but preferable to the research design we used.

Random selection from a pool of eligible participants seems to me the fairest way to select potential beneficiaries for intervention programs—far more equitable than "first come-first served" or other voluntary selection criteria. Furthermore, it is my experience that participants, even low-income families, see random selection as the fairest means to allocate benefits (Justice is blind?). In the first intervention study in Bermuda (Scarr & McCartney, 1988), only 7% of eligible families refused participation in the randomized experimental versus control group design. Given the restrictions on what one can infer from results of nonrandomized evaluations, it seems almost unethical to use any other design, if there are limited resources. In one case in the United States, which shall remain anonymous, I have literally knocked on doors in a catchment area to create more eligible and willing participants than the resources could accommodate in order to institute random assignment to treatment and control groups. The importance of this research issue cannot be underestimated.

The decision about randomized groups when there are unrestricted resources and identified developmental problems, however, results in an ethical dilemma

of research design versus potential benefits to all participants. The ethical decision against a no-treatment control group in the islandwide screening, assessment, and treatment program cost the research project important kinds of inferences that could be made with no-treatment control group. For example, we
cannot evaluate the effects of *any* treatment, given that all participants who failed
screening and assessment received some kind of services. We cannot infer that
treatment per se is better than no intervention at all. This is an unestimable loss to
the research design, and it was based entirely on ethical concerns for the participants. Many of my colleagues think that decision was a grave mistake, because
we will never be able to demonstrate that it is better to provide early services for
children with problems than not to provide services at all. I still worry about it.
But what can you do if a government is willing to provide services to all who
need them (regardless of whether or not *any* service would be effective)?

The research results show that our approaches to treatment services—specialized professional services versus paraprofessional home visiting—have
equivalent outcomes (Scarr et al., 1988). But we will not know whether any of
these approaches was worth the money invested in early intervention. The tradeoff of ethics with research design can be a costly one.

Who Intervenes?

In this study, the local staff of masters-level educators, counselors, and psychologists conducted and supervised the interventions. As in many other countries,
the pool of more highly-trained people is extremely limited. And it is not clear to
me that more highly trained *research* personnel are needed to provide family
services.[1] The government personnel delivered their own services, which we
evaluated. This arrangement provokes conflicts between service and research
personnel, about which I will speak later.

In the case of evaluation of screening, assessment, and intervention programs,
psychologists cannot avoid interactions with families that offer the families advice, services, and evaluations of the family's circumstances. If psychologists in
the United States were to conduct such a study, they would be well advised to be
licensed in most states, because they do consult with families about the diagnosis
and treatment of their children's problems. I am licensed in Virginia, and I would
advise other applied developmental psychologists to seek licensure in their states.
Licensure in most states does not require that you be a professional (clinical,
counseling, or school) psychologist. Rather, licensure is generic, as in medicine,

---

[1] I know that this statement will get me into hot water with many practitioners who believe that
the PhD. or PsyD. is the entry level degree for such services, but I think we see masters-level social
workers and marriage and family counselors providing the same services more cheaply and effi-
ciently, even in the United States.

and it is up to the candidate to specify his or her competencies to practice. Applied developmental psychologists are well positioned to apply for competencies in developmental assessment, intervention, and program evaluation that do not include individual psychotherapy. This advice may not apply in all states, as each differs in requirements for licensure.

ORGANIZATIONAL CENSORSHIP

Changes in government personnel can threaten research. Sometimes, funds are suddenly terminated. At other times, personnel are withdrawn, fired, or intimidated. In my experience the most threatening crisis of government interference in the Bermuda research occurred with censorship. One of the new and highly placed bureaucrats decided that her permission was required for us to publish any results of the studies, even though my prior oral agreement with other Bermuda government officials included free publication of research results in all studies. For me the ethical dilemma was clear: I would never undertake a classified or proprietary study, whose results could not be added to the scientific literature. Her position was also clear: She did not want any research results reported that might in any way damage Bermuda's image in the world.

I explained that my university did not permit classified research or research that required sponsor approval for publication. Furthermore, I was personally unwilling to enter into an agreement where anyone had censor's rights over my scientific publications. She explained that she had to protect Bermuda's image (not from me, but for tourism). We reached a nervous compromise: I would submit all papers (articles, chapters, presentations) to her for review and comments. Her review was not binding but advisory, as I did not intend deliberately or inadvertently to offend the people of Bermuda. Indeed, the comments of several of our Bermudian colleagues have helped to improve papers, but this was not her intent. If I did not hear from her within two weeks of her receipt of the paper, I could assume approval and submit the paper for publication. To date, approximately 15 papers have been submitted to this bureaucrat, and I have never received a comment. Such is the power of government officials. And such are the ethical dilemmas of dealing with some of them.

INEFFECTUAL PROGRAMS VERSUS COMMITMENT TO THE PROBLEM

Some years ago, Donald Campbell (1969) wrote a wise paper about action research, in which futile attempts are often made to ameliorate an identified problem. He warned that all interventions are sampled from a universe of possible interventions. Other interventions that have not been tried have unknown effects that may not generalize from those that have been tried. The one or few interventions that are evaluated may prove ineffectual, but that unfortunate result should not diminish our commitment to solve the problem. Rather than give up our interest in the problem, we must try another—more effective, one hopes—approach to solution.

And so it is in applied developmental psychology. In the Islandwide Screening, Assessment, and Treatment Program, we found that none of the treatment approaches prevented many children from continuing to function in impaired ways. As noted earlier, the cognitive and language assessments at 24 months directed children to treatment programs that did not always ameliorate their problems, at least to a level of normal functioning. Nor was one program more effective than another. Such a result undermines sponsor's confidence, parents' beliefs about the services, and the attitudes of program personnel, who must believe in their program in order to implement it effectively.

To try an intervention and to find it wanting is a painful experience. Government sponsors often fail to understand Campbell's call for commitment to the problem, not to a particular solution. And they may turn their attention, and resources, to other problems that are perceived to be more amenable to solution. Even though a selected program may not be of great benefit to the participants, it is very tempting to continue it, for fear that all will be lost if it is revealed to be useless. To be so tempted is human; to give in to the temptation, unethical.

Parent participants in intervention programs also want to believe that their efforts are worthwhile. To tell them that the program in which they worked with their child has proved of little value and that another approach might be better is a difficult public relations job, to say the least. And yet, do we not owe participants the truth, as we know it?

Evaluators are loath to tell committed program personnel that their efforts have been useless. Rather, researchers tend to gloss over the bad news, if possible. But that means that resources will continue to be spent on ineffectual programs, rather than used to continue the search for better programs.

Commitment to the problem requires that one look for more effective means to ameliorate it, not to perpetuate a particular program. In this intervention program, it was a constantly recurring effort to remind the program staff that the program was being evaluated so that they could deliver effective services. If the services they were currently delivering were found to be ineffective, they would be expected to try other approaches.

It is very difficult, however, to keep an enthusiastic staff in intervention programs if one is genuinely serious about one's evaluation having the possible outcome of no effects. The necessary tension in program evaluation between those who implement the intervention and those who evaluate it has been the source of a great deal of discussion in applied research. And there are ethical aspects to the tension.

The program staff are themselves participants in the research; it is not clear that investigators always understand the ethical problems of informed consent and voluntary participation for program staff, whose life work is the subject of the evaluation. It is ethically imperative that those who implement the programs being evaluated be informed participants in the research, even if this causes uncomfortable moments in staff meetings. At present, the staff have taken seriously our finding of no differences between professionally-delivered services and those delivered by paraprofessionals and have combined programs and tried to tailor their services to individual family's needs. The usefulness of this approach needs to be evaluated. It is possible that they need an entirely new approach, or no approach.

And so we have continued to try out various combinations of services to Bermuda's young children with identified problems, in collaboration with a staff whose commitment to the problems of young children and their families has carried them through rough times in the evaluation and troublesome changes in the direction of their programs. Realistic goals do not include making all developmentally delayed children function like unimpaired children, but do include having the greatest impact possible for the resources invested.

CROSS-CULTURAL COLLABORATION

Participation in research is voluntary, for the most part, in the United States. The degree of informed consent may vary somewhat from one situation to another, but federal Department of Health and Human Services regulations control coercion, deception, and exposure to physical and mental harm for research participants in most situations. Few other countries have such stringent regulations about the behavior of research investigators.

When another government's program is designed to benefit participants, voluntary participation in the program may be assumed, rather than sought. Leaving aside totalitarian governments that care little for individual freedoms, most other societies have less stringent rules about the conduct of research than the United States. This is especially true for applied developmental research, where the participants are often the intended beneficiaries of the program being evaluated.

In other societies, the welfare of citizens is of greater government concern than in the United States. The welfare of children, especially, is not left entirely to the good or bad circumstances of their biological parents. Rather, the community and the government assume some responsibility to make sure that children benefit from available resources. Thus, parental consent may not have the same force in other countries as it does in the United States.

Different values about parental informed consent can place applied developmentalists in ethical conflicts. If one subscribes to our own code of ethics, research on programs in other countries that do not adhere closely to principles of voluntary participation and informed consent can be problematic. In fact, this was not a great problem in Bermuda, although, like Britain, their Department of

Health and Social Services has legal obligations to provide services to young children that we in the United States might consider intrusive. For example, health visitors, who are similar to our public health nurses, have the legal authority to enter the homes of all new parents to examine conditions and to advise the parents on the care and welfare of the new baby. If health nurses suspect any neglect or abuse of children or other family members, they can go into the home as frequently as they feel is necessary. In the United States, such provisions are regulated by court orders in each individual case.

Other countries, such as France, have permitted research on families that we could not (in conscience or otherwise) do. For example, Michel Schiff and his colleagues (Schiff, Duyme, Dumaret, Stewart, Tomkiewicz, & Feingold, 1978) discovered from birth and adoption records a sample of low-income families who had relinquished infants for adoption to higher status families and later had additional children whom they retained. The adoptive families and the biological families of the adopted children were recruited for the study of genetic and environmental variation in intelligence and school achievement under patently false pretenses. The investigators presented the study to the parents as though their children had been chosen randomly from classrooms in which they were enrolled. U.S. investigators would be unlikely to receive permission from an Institutional Review Board (IRB) to conduct such a study under these recruitment conditions.

The tradeoffs are not simple. The French study is an important one, widely cited in support of environmental enrichment. But the circumstances of the data collection raise ethical issues in many of our minds, I suspect. But, given the cultural acceptance of this research in France, is the study justified? Should an American investigator have participated in it, had anyone been asked? Should a U.S. IRB give approval to the research to be conducted abroad by U.S. investigators, where there were no ethical objections to it? Cross-cultural research is fraught with ethical problems that arise from different ideas about participants' rights to voluntary participation, informed consent, and the value of the research to the society.

Many cross-cultural psychologists have worried a great deal about differences between the research ethics of their country and those of other countries, and I have only my own standards on these matters. When children are benefited by governmental interventions that we might consider intrusive and where social programs may not require the same kind of voluntary participation that we expect, it seems to me benign to accept another society's definition of who is responsible for children and young families, as long as the participants also accept that definition of the situation. British and Bermudian parents do not object when the health visitor arrives to see their newborn; indeed, they would object if the service were not given. Much of this is an endless debate about individualism versus community responsibility for citizens.

Much more objectionable, of course, are situations where the government intrudes in ways that are harmful and that the participants do not agree to. Fortunately, I have not encountered those.

CHILD CARE RESEARCH ON INFANTS: IMPLICATIONS OF THE RESULTS

Currently, a controversy about the alleged effects of extensive infant day care, especially on boys, rages in the journals and in the popular press. Belsky (1986) claims that more than 20 hours per week of day care in the first year of life makes infants more likely to be insecurely attached to their mothers and more aggressive as children. (He also finds that infants at home full-time with mothers are more likely to be insecurely attached to their *fathers* than infants in day care (Belsky & Rovine, 1988), but that finding is little cited. Other investigators have either disputed Belsky's conclusions (e.g., Phillips, McCartney, Scarr, & Howes, 1987) or trivialized them (e.g., Clarke-Stewart, 1989). The worst-case scenario from Belsky's own claims is that 7% more infants are insecurely attached to their mothers (not fathers or caregivers) if they have been in full-time child care in the first year of life (not a big difference). The consensus among developmentalists is that the quality of care is what matters (see Scarr, Phillips, & McCartney, in press). This is not the forum for recapitulation of the controversy. Rather, I want to draw out the ethical implications of presenting unpopular or unsavory research results.

First, I believe that investigators have an ethical responsibility to draw social policy implications from their research, especially those that can be easily anticipated (Scarr, 1981, 1988). If one knows that studies of racial differences in IQ scores can be interpreted in unfavorable ways, one has a responsibility to interpret one's own data, acknowledging that others are free to disagree. In the case of infant day care, it is not much of an inferential leap from reputed findings about infant insecurity and later aggression among day care children to advice to mothers to leave their jobs and tend their babies. I think one could anticipate that implication being drawn by guilt-ridden parents, the media, and conservative politicians. To my knowledge, Belsky has not written about the policy implications he draws from his findings.

Second, I do *not* think that one can hold research investigators ethically responsible for distal or unlikely implications drawn by others from their research findings. Behaviorists who developed aversive conditioning techniques are not ethically responsible for their use in political torture, nor are sleep researchers responsible for knowledge about sleep deprivation being used in brainwashing and cult indoctrination. If Belsky's conclusions about infant day care were to be used to justify *purdah* (the complete isolation of women in the home) in Saudi Arabia, I would not hold Belsky responsible.

To make clear what I see as ethical considerations in reporting potentially damaging research results, let us consider a hypothetical case. Suppose that infants of employed mothers grew up to be nonfunctional adults, emotionally isolated and insecurely attached to any other human beings. Suppose, also, that more than 50% of the mothers of infants are currently in the labor force (not a hypothetical scenario). What is the ethical way to handle such devastating research results, in the face of the compelling economic necessity for maternal employment in most families?

I suppose that if most of us who study child care had discovered such devastating effects of day care per se, we would feel ethically impelled to reveal our findings to the world.[2] In my view, an ethical stance requires that we present both the developmental implications of maternal employment for the child and the economic requirements of maternal employment for the family. One implication is not sufficient; both are necessary.

The ethics of the situation also depend on the actions the investigators derive from their findings. On the one hand, one could merely imply that mothers ought to stay home. That would not be a very constructive approach to the research results, given the number of women and children in poverty (Let them eat cake?), but it is an ethically plausible conclusion. On the other hand, one could campaign for parental (maternal) leaves, for family allowances, and for other measures that would permit mothers to stay home with their infants without the family starving. One could also stress the need to know more about infants' relationships with their fathers, other family members, and their caregivers before one reached drastic conclusions about the importance of *maternal* care (Scarr, Phillips, & McCartney, in press).

Social science research is always conducted in a social and political context, where one can be (a) understood; (b) misunderstood; or (c) an easy tool for whatever political forces can use the research for their own ends. The goal is to have one's interpretation of one's research understood, which means that one has to explain it. I do not apply any political test; one does not have to adhere to any political implications that happen to be popular. Burton White (1988) has been outspoken about what he considers the value of maternal care in the first three years of life. This is the implication he draws from his research. Although I do not agree with his logic (Scarr, 1984), he is ethically sound to make his inferences clear.

SUMMARY AND CONCLUSIONS

Applied developmental research propels investigators into ethically problematic situations, both in the protection of human participants and in personal value

---

[2] Of course, if infant day care had such devastating effects, we would not need research to discover them; they would be obvious to everyone in the population.

conflicts about ethics and research design and the implications of research findings. It is in the nature of applied research on important issues in people's lives that such ethical problems arise.

In this chapter, I have discussed ethical problems associated with screening, assessment, and treatment programs for young children and their families, research designs with children identified at risk for developmental delays and behavior problems, intervention programs that prove ineffective, cross-cultural collaborations, government interference in reporting of research results, and the social policy implications of potentially dangerous research results.

The major themes are investigators' responsibility to adhere to the APA's ethical standards and to develop sensitivity to the additional ethical issues that are not well detailed in those standards. Perhaps, the best summary statement is that research investigators in any field, but particularly in applied psychology, must have consummate *integrity* and *truthfulness* to themselves. From these flow ethical behavior toward others.

REFERENCES

American Psychological Association. (1982). *Ethical principles in the conduct of research with human participants*. Washington, DC: American Psychological Association.

American Psychological Association. (1987). *Casebook on ethical principles of psychologists*. Washington, DC: American Psychological Association.

Belsky, J. (1986). Infant day care: A cause for concern? *Zero to Three, IV*(5), 1–9.

Belsky, J., & Rovine, M.J. (1988). Nonmaternal care in the first year of life and the security of infant-parent attachment. *Child Development, 59*, 157–167.

Campbell, D.T. (1969). Reforms as experiments. *American Psychologist, 24*, 409–429.

Clarke-Stewart, A. (1989). Infant day care: Malignant or maligned? *American Psychologist, 44*(2), 266–273.

Levenstein, P. (1977). *The Mother-Child Home Program*. In M.C. Day & R.K. Parker (Eds.), *The Preschool in action* (pp. 159–183). Boston: Allyn & Bacon.

Phillips, D., McCartney, K., Scarr, S., & Howes, C. (1987). Selective review of infant day care research: A cause for concern! *Zero to Three* (pp. 18–21).

Scarr, S. (1981). *Race, social class, and individual differences in IQ*. Hillsdale, NJ: Lawrence Erlbaum Associates, Inc.

Scarr, S. (1988). Race and gender as psychological variables: Social and ethical issues. *American Psychologist, 43*, 56–59.

Scarr, S., & McCartney, K. (1988). Far from home and experimental evaluation of the Mother-Child HOME Program in Bermuda. *Child Development, 59*, 531–543.

Scarr, S., McCartney, K., Miller, S., Hauenstein, E., Goldfarb, A., Ricciuti, A., & Ming, C. Evaluation of an islandwide screening, assessment, and treatment program. Submitted for publication.

Scarr, S., Phillips, D., & McCartney, K. (in press). Dilemmas of child care in the United States: Working mothers and children at risk. *Canadian Psychology*.

Schiff, M., Duyme, M., Dumaret, A., Stewart, J., Tomkiewicz, S., & Feingold, J. (1978). Intellectual status of working-class children adopted early into upper-middle-class families. *Science, 200*, 1503–1504.

White, B. (1988). *Educating the infant and toddler*. Lexington, MA: Lexington.

Wortman, C.B., Hendricks, M., & Hillis, J.W. (1976). Factors affecting participant reactions to random assignment in ameliorative social programs. *Journal of Personality and Social Psychology, 33,* 256–266.

4   Psychological Risks and Remedies of Research Participation*

Celia B. Fisher
Susan A. Rosendahl

In recent years developmental psychology has entered what Pion and Lipsy (1984) have coined the "decade of applied research." Developmental psychologists are increasingly acting as problem solvers outside the laboratory, taking the developmental perspective into the broader arena of real-world problems. Concern with the practical implications of our research has expanded the diversity of individuals and problems studied. This has widened the spectrum of problems addressed to include research on developmental patterns in socially disfavored and developmentally vulnerable populations and examination of the efficacy of developmental interventions.

As developmental science extends beyond the laboratory we are working with new populations, in new places, in new ways. Researchers engaged in these pioneering activities are grappling with questions for which traditional laboratory-based ethical guidelines offer incomplete answers. In this chapter we address one area of growing concern: the impact of applied research on the welfare of research participants. Our purpose is to identify potential risks of applied research participation and offer nine principles for remedying these risks. There are no easy answers to ethical dilemmas facing applied researchers, and new dilemmas await developmental psychologists as they continue to enter social agencies and community organizations. We hope these prescriptions will contribute to an ongoing dialogue on ethical practice in applied developmental psychology.

ETHICAL RESPONSIBILITIES AND APPLIED DEVELOPMENTAL RESEARCH DESIGN

The goals and attitudes of social groups, as well as research literature and public practice, should be used as background information for the design of socially sensitive research. This provides a check on the implicitly value-laden nature of any research and enhances external validity.

Experimental activities subsumed under the Applied Developmental Psychology (ADP) umbrella extend across a spectrum of empirical goals ranging from stud-

* The authors thank Judy Hall, Claire Kopp, Joan Sieber, and Irving Sigel for their thoughtful comments on a previous draft of this chapter.

ies designed to test the validity of a developmental theory within a natural context to studies designed to test the effectiveness of a developmental intervention. When research is conducted in applied settings or designed to address issues of immediate social relevance it is more likely that information gained may influence public practices. This information can result in public policies harmful to participants. This places the applied developmental psychologist in what Veatch (1987) has coined the "scientist-citizen" dilemma: the need to reconcile our commitment to the pursuit of knowledge with our commitment to the promotion of human welfare.

Consideration of Social Issues in Research Design

Whether investigators should consider potential applications of their research before generating results that may influence public practices has been heatedly debated with respect to participant autonomy versus academic freedom (e.g., Sarason, 1984; Scarr, 1988). We believe that when research is designed to address an immediate social problem, concern for the consequences of experimental findings reflects appropriate scientific procedure rather than censorship. In applied research, consideration of public practices and social issues facing members of a social group under investigation are essential for the selection of appropriate experimental variables. For example, following the 1954 and 1955 Supreme Court decisions on school desegregation, social science research focused on the relationship of classroom racial composition to school achievement. While findings from these studies were used to justify desegregation methods such as court-ordered busing, investigators failed to incorporate examination of the effects of these procedures (e.g., competition for a limited number of benefits, frequency of cross-racial contacts, equivalence of positions among racial groups in the desegregated setting) into their research design (Hennigan, Flay, & Cook, 1980). By not considering the practical consequences of research linking school integration to academic performance, social science produced a body of knowledge which left public policy makers unprepared for the complexity of individual responses to desegregation policies.

Ethical dilemmas also arise from the well constructed developmental study which strives for an acceptable balance between internal and external validity, but whose findings risk yielding unfavorable results for a politically vulnerable group. One approach to the scientist-citizen dilemma when designing these studies is to survey the concerns of social groups and formulate these concerns into researchable questions. For example, concerns of older constituents that studies of intellectual decline may negatively impact employment opportunities could lead the applied researcher to include measures of compensatory skills into the study. Research designed for direct action is often based on institutional evaluations of social problems rather than input from those groups themselves, and it is these institutional values which are often implicitly a part of our research designs. An added scientific benefit of community surveys is to provide a check on institutional bias and enhance external validity through a broader perspective of the problem under investigation.

Participant Education

A final means of fulfilling our scientist-citizen obligation to members of disfavored groups who we study is to incorporate into our research procedures participant education on the workings of social research. This will enable participants and gatekeepers (e.g., parents, teachers, principles) to better evaluate information disseminated to the public and public policies influenced by the results of experimentation. As yet, we know little about how to convey scientific information to populations of different cultural backgrounds and developmental levels. Confronting these ethical dilemmas opens up new areas of researchable topics for applied developmental psychologists.

PARTICIPANT RECRUITMENT

Recruitment of high-risk or disfavored populations must be designed to include positive information in describing the target population. Every precaution should be taken to guarantee that neither participants nor their social group will be perceived negatively because of exposure to the hypotheses under investigation.

Indirect Effects of Recruitment Procedures

Once we have designed a research project, we face the problem of participant recruitment. When conducting applied research the recruitment process is often conducted within the everyday social environment of the research participant. This may mean contacting personnel at schools, hospitals, or community settings to explain the purpose and procedures of the investigation. When describing a study to institutional staff we rarely consider whether they take the explanation of a hypothesis as a statement of fact rather than a possible (and at best partial) explanation for a given pattern of behaviors. Nor do we consider how this knowledge may indirectly influence subsequent relationships between personnel and research participants or nonparticipants of their social category. For example, involvement in a study on the relationship of maternal employment to school behaviors (e.g., asking teachers to rate disruptive classroom behaviors) risks oversensitizing teachers to the behavior of children of employed mothers or further stigmatizing these mothers within the school setting.

To address this risk, the applied developmental psychologist must set up recruitment procedures which not only describe the nature of the study, but also educate participants, their guardians, and institutional staff to the multideter-mined nature of behavior and caution them about the limitations of generalities based on hypotheses and the results of singular studies. Additionally, the descrip-tion of studies which focus on the negative behaviors of a particular population should be balanced with information concerning previous work stressing the positive characteristics of these groups.

Direct Effects of Recruitment Procedures

A related issue concerns the direct effect of being targeted as a "subject" popula-tion. For example, adopted children may not perceive themselves as members of a "special" group prior to exposure to recruitment. This may raise psychological concerns not previously present. Consequently, identifying individuals as mem-bers of a vulnerable population may precipitate potentially distressing self-eval-uations. Individual differences in reactions to normative or nonnormative life events (Danish, Smyer, & Nowak, 1980) can also play a role in a participant's response to subject recruitment. For example, individuals over 65 who view retirement as a loss of a valued part of the self (Hornstein & Wapner, 1985) would be most vulnerable to recruitment procedures which focus on threats to self-esteem in prospective retirees.

Because subject recruitment itself is potentially harmful to the participant, psychologists should draw upon knowledge about self-concept and self-esteem in the target population to identify its vulnerabilities to the intended recruitment procedures. Moreover, recruitment procedures for vulnerable populations should emphasize individual and general strengths of the target population. We recently utilized this approach when we recruited individuals over 60 years of age for a study on visual information processing. Visual decline is a fact of old age and was of particular interest for this study. We specifically designed our recruitment procedures to both acknowledge the visual deficits that accompany aging as well as to stress the fact that adults live longer, have more active lives than ever before and, in so doing, utilize compensatory activities that allow them to function effectively on everyday visual tasks.

A related problem illustrated by this study concerns selection procedures which screen out certain individuals. In our study we could not use individuals who had an artificial lens (after cataract surgery) or individuals with glaucoma. In communicating the constraints on subject participation we spent time explain-ing why these individuals would not be appropriate for our study. Specifically, we indicated that these conditions introduced an element into the experiment which would prevent us from drawing conclusions about more typical visual development. We also provided information on visual diseases in the elderly which framed these problems in an optimistic light.

INFORMED CONSENT

When planning informed consent procedures investigators need to take into account the participant's developmental level, cultural background, cohort membership, social expectations, and the current context under which participation is being sought. Efforts should be made to ensure that guardian consent is received in conjunction with the assent of the child, although this does not release the experimenter from obtaining child assent at the time of experiment.

Informed consent is seen by many as the major means of protecting the rights of research participants. The three basic guidelines for consent are that participant involvement in research be informed, voluntary, and rational (Freedman, 1975). When conducting laboratory research we typically provide participants with a form describing the general purpose of the study, the procedures to be followed, statements about the confidentiality of the data, and the right to withdraw. With the signing of this form we proceed on the assumption that relevant information has been conveyed in a noncoercive manner within a context conducive to rational decision making.

Participant Misconceptions of Informed Consent

The fallacy of the above assumption when research is conducted in applied settings is illustrated in the following case example concerning the grandmother of one of the authors (CF), Mrs. B., an amputee, residing in a hospital geriatric center where there was an impending threat of a staff strike. Mrs. B. was fearful that she would have to be moved out of the hospital if she was viewed as incompetent. During this stressful period a graduate student in gerontology asked her to participate in a dissertation study on geriatric care. Upon signing the informed consent form she began to answer his questions:

"Do you know where you are?"

"Yes in LIJ Geriatric Center"

"Can you recite the alphabet?"

"Backwards or forwards?" she asked to demonstrate her intellectual competence.

"How do you like the service here?"

"Oh it's great!" answered Mrs. B., who constantly complained to her family about the poor hospital service and bad food.

"How do you like the food here?"

"It's delicious," she replied.

Mrs. B.'s anxiety was rising, and midway through the questioning she asked the student, "Did I pass the test?"

"What test?" he asked.

"The one for whether I can stay in the hospital."

"I'm not working for the hospital," he replied, and with that Mrs. B. spun her chair around and wheeled herself away.

While in principle, this budding psychologist was following ethical procedures of informed consent, he had not considered that a member of Mrs. B's generation might be unfamiliar with the concept of research aimed at getting a Ph.D. and thus, without more information, could not understand the purpose of the study; that her consent was, in fact, coerced due to her view that anybody in a position of authority was a member of the hospital staff; and that the stress experienced by her current situation worked against approaching consent in a rational manner. While poor judgment is not synonymous with unethical behavior, the implementation of standard ethical procedures without regard for the context in which the participant receives them is poor ethics.

Had the student approached the informed consent procedures in the same way good developmental research is designed, he would have taken into account Mrs. B's cohort membership, social expectations, and the current context under which testing was being conducted (see Chapter 8 for a detailed discussion of the importance of developmental contextualism for ethical practice). In addition he would have developed a method of assessing the participant's understanding of the procedures to design a consent form in a format conducive to her developmental level. These considerations would have allowed Mrs. B. to make a voluntary, informed, and rational decision to participate and would have guarded against the collection of invalid data based on participant misconceptions.

Applied developmental researchers, especially those working with parents of at-risk infants, must be particularly sensitive to the fact that hopes and wishes for betterment of their condition may interfere with a participant's ability to rationally understand the limitations of experiments (Carroll, Schneider, & Wesley, 1985; Fisher & Tryon, 1988). Attention to reasons for subject attrition can be used as a means of understanding stress-related misconceptions of informed consent procedures. For example, in a recent study on social interaction of preterm and full-term infants five mothers of preterms who wished to discontinue "reported that they no longer felt their infants were in jeopardy or felt that they were being adequately followed by private, primary-care physicians (Crnic, Ragozin, Greenberg, Robinson, & Basham, 1983, p. 1201)." This response is striking in light of the fact that the research was not an intervention study. Reports such as these contribute to the ongoing development of procedures which can effectively communicate to high-risk individuals and their guardians the absence of benefits resulting from their participation.

Guardian Consent and Child Assent

Developmental psychologists have been relatively more sensitive to the inadequacies of informed consent procedures for children and other vulnerable populations such as the mentally retarded. Unfortunately, we have attempted to remedy this concern by relying predominantly on parental or guardian consent. Not only does this procedure when taken alone underestimate children's competence (Melton, Koocher, & Saks, 1983) but it is based on the erroneous assumption that reliance on guardian consent safeguards the participant from exposure to personally upsetting material. There is a wealth of literature on cognitive development to suggest that adult guardians and their children perceive social situations in very different ways (Sigel, 1985). This problem is even more complicated when children from abusive families are the focus of inquiry (Kinard, 1985).

One way to increase the likelihood that guardian consent represents the wishes of the minor is to have parental consent procedures include discussion of participation with the child. This can be accomplished by having an age-appropriate child assent form accompany the parental form, which in turn includes instructions to the parent to discuss the procedure with the child prior to signing. This joint-decision making approach (Weithorn, 1983) provides a noncoercive environment for the child to ask questions about the research and decide whether to participate as well as the opportunity to communicate his or her decision to the parent.

Guardian consent should never preclude child assent procedures at the time of the experiment. While the age of the child will determine the assent format (e.g., it is inappropriate to ask young children to sign assent forms), we would agree with attorney Bersoff (1983) that "rather than assume that children are too young emotionally, experimentally, and cognitively to make appropriate decisions, we can alternatively presume that children are capable of making those decisions no more disastrously than adults" (Bersoff, 1983, p. 170). Assent procedures should incorporate an explanation of the confidentiality of the information at a level the child can understand as well as an explanation of scientific methods which explains the contribution the child can make to the general welfare of others or to science. Finally, children, individuals with learning disabilities, or elderly with poor vision may have difficulty reading informed consent sheets. However, embarrassment over this difficulty may cause them to inefficiently scan a written consent form rather than ask for clarification. When these populations are tested, forms should be read to the participant.

POWER RELATIONSHIPS

Specific mechanisms to facilitate withdrawal from the study or requests for additional information by distressed or fatigued subjects should be incorporated into standard experimental procedures.

Once an individual assents to research participation we must be sensitive to power relationships and attitudes toward authority which may interfere with the ability to exercise the right to withdraw or ask for more information. As a graduate student one of us (CF) became sensitive to how compliance to the researcher's authority can influence performance under the most arbitrary and seemingly unstressful conditions. I was testing preschoolers on a left-right visual discrimination problem in which they had to make same-different judgments to stimuli presented in a light-tight box which I illuminated with a switch during test trials (Fisher, 1979). One little boy was dutifully responding "same" or "different" to successive presentations of the stimuli, when after 10 trials he paused and asked me, "When are you going to turn on the light?" Unbeknownst to me the light bulb had burned out and this child was responding "same" and "different" to my requests for a response even though he was seeing nothing but total darkness.

In both this example and the situation the Ph.D. student found himself in with Mrs. B, if the participants had not spontaneously told the investigators of their concerns, we would not have realized the invalidity of their data. Thus, seeking to insure that consent procedures are designed to meet the individual needs of participants to make informed and voluntary decisions is not just good ethics, it is good science!

How do we guarantee that participants will feel free to communicate their concerns during experiments, especially in exercising their right to withdraw? Keith-Spiegel (1983) has suggested that we be more sensitive to behavioral indicators that children do not want to participate. While crying and requests to go back to the classroom are obvious indicators that the session should be ended, what about other more subtle signs such as multiple yawns, foot tapping, or "I want to go to the bathroom?" One solution to this dilemma is to provide explicit pre-experiment instructions on how to withdraw from participation. Children or mentally retarded individuals can simply be instructed to say "I'd like to stop now," or to signal their reluctance to continue by picking up an arrow provided by the experimenter and pointing it toward the door. Procedures for requesting breaks should be part of the experimental instructions for participants, like the elderly, who may experience fatigue or minor discomforts from sitting in one position for a particular length of time. If too many participants take the option to withdraw, the procedures and assumptions about the cost/benefit ratio of the study should be reassessed.

DEBRIEFING

When working with vulnerable populations or on problems related to psychological or physical disabilities, researchers should routinely provide referral sources and information related to the topic of the experiment and the particular population studied.

Participant Reactions to Planned Procedures

Studies exploring development of vulnerable individuals can pose ethical problems since they have the potential for tapping sources of psychopathology or psychological distress. For example, in a doctoral project conducted at Fordham University, James Reid (1988) investigated the relationship of family environment to psychological stress reported by chronically ill elderly men and women. One of Jim's measures, the Brief Symptom Inventory (Derogotis, 1975) included two questions concerned with suicidal ideation and thoughts of dying. When designing the study the question arose as to what Jim should do if a participant responded that he or she had thoughts of ending his or her life. The APA Ethical Principles of Psychologists (APA, 1981) clearly indicate the overriding importance of the individual's welfare and provides guidelines for breaking confidentiality in life-threatening situations (APA, 1977). As an applied developmental psychologist, however, Jim is neither trained to make a clinical judgment as to the psychological status of the respondent nor to counsel the participant. Moreover, even a psychologist trained in these procedures would clearly not use two responses on a questionnaire as the basis of a diagnosis (Stanton & New, 1988).

In the obligation we had to the welfare of Jim's participants, we arrived at the following two procedures: First, an on-site physician and members of our clinical faculty agreed to be available as consultants if a respondent appeared extremely distressed. Second, during debriefing all participants were given a list of community psychological resources, a brief explanation of the services, and a discussion of the nonstigmatizing nature of contacting these agencies (for additional discussion see Loo, 1982).

Referrals as Standard Practice

The incorporation of referral sources into debriefing procedures need not be tied to imminent risk. When working with vulnerable populations or on problems of social relevance, investigators should routinely provide referral sources and information related to the topic of the experiment and the particular population studied. In our investigation of visual information processing in the elderly, we give all participants brochures explaining aspects of visual aging such as low vision, glaucoma, and cataracts as well as the telephone number of an agency that provides free opthamalogical services for those who cannot afford them. We also provide participants with measures of their visual acuity and discuss the benefits of yearly eye examinations. By using the debriefing period as a means of sharing our knowledge of specific developmental processes and problems we have an opportunity to promote human welfare by "giving psychology away" (Miller, 1969).

DECEPTION, DEBRIEFING, AND THREATS TO SELF-WORTH

Consideration of the psychological effects of deception and the efficacy of debriefing should be included in the design stage of applied research. Evaluation of risk should be based on information concerning the cognitive level, sociocultural context, and life stage of the participants.

The employment of deception has been heatedly debated by social scientists concerned with the psychological costs of research participation (e.g., Baumrind, 1985; Sieber, 1982; see also Chapter 2). Decisions regarding the adequacy of debriefing procedures have too often relied on studies of participant reactions to dehoaxing procedures which are themselves confounded by social pressures and power relationships inherent within the experimenter/participant relationship. This problem is compounded when special populations (e.g., minorities, developmentally disabled, elderly) are the target of investigation, since assessments of debriefing procedures have typically involved college students as subjects. A direct implication of these limitations for developmental psychologists is that dehoaxing procedures which appear to alleviate negative self-attributions in college freshman should be viewed with caution, especially when the target of investigation are learning disabled children or frail elderly whose histories lead them to view failure as additional evidence of their disability.

At minimum, the decision to deceive participants should be based on information concerning the cognitive level, sociocultural context, and life stage of each individual. This information, considered within the context of knowledge on how members of the target population respond to threats to self-esteem and moral dilemmas, should provide the framework for decisions regarding threats posed by exposure to deceptive research. For example, studies indicating that children as old as eight or nine do not incorporate intentionality as a defining feature of the concept of deceit (Piaget, 1965; Wimmer, Gruber, & Perner, 1985) suggest that younger participants may merely conclude from dehoaxing that psychologists are adults who lie. Similarly, evidence that high school students who experience unsuccessful performance in a deception study persist in erroneous self-assessment following debriefing (Lepper, Ross, & Lau, 1980) suggests that this population may be vulnerable to experimentally produced threats to self-worth.

To Debrief or Not Debrief

In response to this problem some have suggested that it may be wiser not to debrief younger subjects (Achenbach, 1978). One problem with this solution is that it leaves participants uninformed with respect to attributions for their behavior. Consider, for example, the psychological consequences for children who have been tempted by the experimental condition to perform moral breaches such as playing with a forbidden toy (Walters & Parke, 1964) or pressing a button they believe will hurt another child (Liebert & Baron, 1972). In the absence of debriefing, these individuals are at risk for attributing their actions to negative self-worth. In these cases it would be immoral not to debrief the child.

The above indicates that consideration of the potentially damaging effects of deception as well as the efficacy of debriefing must contribute to the design of applied developmental research. If deceptive practices have the potential to elicit anxiety, antisocial behavior or lowered self-esteem, and if there is developmental evidence to suggest that debriefing may be inadequately understood by the participant, steps should be taken to remedy this situation within the research design itself. If the researcher cannot be confident that debriefing procedures will eliminate all residues of experimentally produced distress, he or she should refrain from employing deception by investigating threats to self-esteem or antisocial behavior within natural contexts when they emerge (Geller, 1982).

APPLIED DEVELOPMENTAL RESEARCH AS INTERVENTION

In research in which participants or their families may experience the experimental condition as intervention, control groups should not be used merely to replicate an already substantiated finding, especially in light of evidence that the control condition is deficient and one of the treatments is effective. Consideration of participant preferences for the treatment versus control conditions should be part of the research design. Opportunities for developmental stimulation should be provided to controls once the efficacy of an experimental condition has been determined.

As developmental scientists continue to devote attention to problems associated with at-risk populations, the boundary between research designs utilizing experimental and control groups will become increasingly indistinguishable from intervention designs utilizing treatment and nontreatment groups. Applied developmental psychologists must familiarize themselves with ethical issues associated with intervention research. In this section we will review several of these issues as they relate to the assignment of individuals to control groups.

Control Groups and Participants Known to be At Risk

The boundary between experimentation and intervention is particularly salient in studies of the influence of added-stimulation on developmental delays associated with high-risk infants. As the field advances, investigators are focusing on the relative efficacy of treatment approaches. In designing these studies one must ask whether it is ethically responsible to assign infants to a control condition which has been shown to produce poor developmental outcomes when the effectiveness of one of the experimental conditions is also well documented? The issue here is not whether control groups should be used when the effect of a treatment is unknown (see Chapter 3), but whether control groups should be used merely to replicate an already substantiated finding, especially if the control condition has been associated with developmental delays.

Participant Misconceptions

The above example underscores the importance of taking time to determine whether an experiment will have the impact of an intervention. When the nature of an investigation is not clear, families and researchers may hold very different views of the goals of the study. As noted previously, families under stress may see any experience with professionals as a means of promoting their child's development. Under these conditions, parents who have volunteered to partici-pate in what the experimenter considers a "nonintervention" study may er-roneously believe that the measure used to assess their infant's development over the course of the experiment are in fact techniques that will help the baby. A second consequence of failing to view certain types of applied research as inter-vention is that, unlike informed consent procedures designed for intervention studies, families may be kept in ignorance concerning the (known) consequences of participating in the control condition. This ignorance combined with the erroneous assumption of beneficial consequences of participating in the study may deter parents from seeking other forms of treatment for their infants.

Random Assignment of Participants to Treatment and Control Groups

If the applied developmental psychologist takes an intervention approach to the research design, then he or she will inform the participants of random assignment and the risks associated with participation in the treatment and control condi-tions. What happens when subjects or their families have a preference for one arm of the research, that is, the treatment group? A traditional response has been to eliminate these individuals from the subject pool. The problem with this procedure is twofold: First, a study which offers a 50% chance of effective intervention versus no participation compromises the voluntary nature of in-formed consent for individuals who are desperate to help themselves or their family members. Second, eliminating subjects who do not agree to these condi-tions limits the generalizability of findings to individuals and their families who are willing to be randomly assigned.

Veatch (1987) has developed a unique approach to this situation called the semirandomized clinical trial. This research design includes four experimental conditions: two randomized groups consisting of participants who have agreed to be randomly assigned to the control and experimental group and two nonran-domized groups who have chosen to be in either the control or experimental groups. The semirandomized clinical trial respects participant autonomy and at the same time allows the investigator to compare the performance of participants who have agreed to randomization and those who have not.

Treatment Opportunities for Control Group Members

A third consideration when research is viewed as intervention is how to provide treatment for participants assigned to the control group once the effect of the experimental condition has been evaluated. In research designed to evaluate the effectiveness of different psychotherapeutic techniques, it is standard ethical procedure to provide participants in the least effective conditions with the treatment found to be most effective following completion of the study (Imber et al., 1986). This task is more difficult for applied developmental psychologists since they are dealing with longitudinal studies which are typically designed to evaluate the effectiveness of an early intervention on behaviors characteristic of a later developmental period.

Several steps can be taken in longitudinal designs to fulfill our responsibility to provide effective interventions to members of the control group. First, applied developmental researchers can incorporate midexperimental checks into the research design. If the experimental group is at midpoint, already showing significant improvement over the control group, than a decision must be made to provide the latter with the experimental stimulation. Long-term effects can be evaluated at a later developmental point by comparing those participants who received stimulation in the beginning of the experiment with those who received stimulation at midpoint. When only long-term rather than midpoint evaluations of the research groups yield significant effects, the investigator should, at the completion of the study, provide a stimulation experience appropriate for the child's post-experimental developmental level.

PUBLISHING APPLIED DEVELOPMENTAL RESEARCH

Citations of published research conducted under questionable ethical conditions must be accompanied by an ethical critique.

Reporting the results of applied research brings with it a host of ethical issues. For example, when publishing research directed at immediate social problems or special populations the investigator must consider the limitations of the findings such as generalizability (to populations and contexts not tested) and inappropriate assumptions likely to be drawn from the data (e.g., that correlational findings indicate causal relationships). In disseminating this information to the public the researcher must consider the sophistication of his or her audience and the extent to which conclusions drawn are based on replicated experiments. These and other ethical considerations concerned with publishing applied developmental research have been discussed elsewhere (see, for example, Fisher & Tryon, 1988; Maccoby, Kahn, & Everett, 1983) and in this volume (see Chapters 5, 9, and 16).

Citing Research Conducted Under Questionable Ethical Conditions

Another issue related to publication is the citation of scientific works which have used questionable ethical procedures. We take the position that when investigators cite research conducted under unacceptable ethical conditions without comment, they are implicitly condoning the unethical practice. A case in point involves the frequent citation in articles and developmental textbooks of a study on sensory-motor development conducted by the Dennises in the late 1930s (Dennis, 1941). The couple secured 36-day-old female twins from the social service department of their university to launch a "natural" experiment to determine whether very severe restriction of opportunities for practice of motor skills (such as those found in orphanages) retard motor development. For twelve months the twins were confined to a nursery in the Dennis home which contained a minimal amount of furniture, no toys, and a barrier between the cribs. In order to restrict experience, the infants were taken from the cribs only for feeding, bathing, or experimental demands. The Dennises worked hard to achieve "indifferent behavior" (Dennis, 1941, p. 150) towards the twins' activities. This included efforts not to smile, fondle, or speak to the infants. During the course of the study it was observed that both subjects were retarded with respect to activities (e.g., sitting without support, reaching for a dangling object, supporting body weight with one's feet) the "practice of which were totally ruled out by the conditions of the experiment (Dennis, 1941, p. 147)."

It is not our purpose to cast judgment on the decisions made by the Dennises within a historical context different from our own. For example, this experiment was conducted during a period when the debilitating conditions of 1940s orphanages, to which the twins might have been assigned, had recently been documented and data on the impact of physical and social deprivation on infant development had yet to be obtained. Nonetheless, it is disturbing that those who cite the experiment fail to comment on its ethics. By implication authors who unquestionably refer to this study may be communicating to their colleagues, and perhaps more importantly their students, that research procedures inappropriate under today's ethical standards will be judged acceptable if they yield important scientific results.

It is often difficult to evaluate, and thus improve upon, ethical procedures employed in current developmental research. For example, in some of the recent work on vicariously induced emotional reactions, children are exposed to films or situations designed to induce emotions of anxiety/apprehension and empathic sadness. Measures of heart rate, self report, and facial indices are taken to demonstrate that indeed the children experience the emotions presented. In none of the most recent studies or reviews are debriefing procedures or ethical implications of the work mentioned. One way to remedy this problem is for journal editors to require ethical review by consulting editors and description of ethical issues involved in the research design and implementation by authors (Fisher & Tryon, 1988).

SUMMARY AND CONCLUSIONS

Promotion of human welfare whether it be of a social group or individuals should play an integral role in applied developmental research.

In this chapter we identified ethical issues emerging as developmental science is applied to investigations of social problems, behaviors of vulnerable populations, and developmental interventions. Recommendations for ethical practice in applied developmental research across a broad range of populations and activities were provided. These include consideration of social implications of applied research, direct and indirect effects of subject recruitment procedures, the psychological context in which informed consent is sought, power relationships which may interfere with the participant's right to withdraw, the availability of referral sources for at-risk subjects, participant reactions to deception and debriefing procedures, the consequences of control group assignment, and the inclusion of ethical issues in published works.

As developmental science is directed at social problems and behaviors of vulnerable populations, applied developmental psychologists can utilize current knowledge of developmental processes and social-cultural contexts to anticipate and prevent undesirable psychological costs of research participation. The actions we must take to design research which will benefit both the individual participant and society (Smith, 1976) will most certainly make the task of applied developmental psychology more challenging, but it will also provide more externally valid and useful knowledge, and promote the welfare of children and adults who place their faith in us.

REFERENCES

Achenbach, T.M. (1978). *Research in developmental psychology: Concepts, strategies, methods.* New York: The Free Press.

American Psychological Association. (1977). *Standards for providers of psychological services.* Washington, DC.

American Psychological Association. (1981). Ethical principles of psychologists. *American Psychologist, 36,* 633–638.

Baumrind, D. (1985). Research using intentional deception: Ethical issues revisited. *American Psychologist, 40,* 165–174.

Bersoff, D.N. (1983). Children as participants in psychoeducational assessment. In G.B. Melton,

G.P. Koocher, & M.J. Saks (Eds.), *Children's competence to consent* (pp. 149–178). New York: Plenum Press.

Carroll, M.A., Schneider, H.G., & Wesley, G.R. (1985). *Ethics in the practice of psychology*. Englewood Cliffs, NJ: Prentice-Hall.

Crnic, K.A., Ragozin, A.S., Greenberg, M.T., Robinson, N.M., & Basham, R.B. (1983). Social interaction and developmental competence of preterm and full-term infants during the first year of life. *Child Development, 54*, 1199–1210.

Danish, S.J., Smyer, M.A., & Nowak, C.A. (1980). Developmental intervention: Enhancing life-event processes. In P.B. Baltes & O.B. Brin, Jr. (Eds.), *Life-span development and behavior* (Vol. 3, pp. 341–366). New York: Academic Press.

Dennis, W. (1941). Infant development under conditions of restricted practice and of minimum social stimulation. *Genetic Psychology Monographs, 23*, 143–189.

Derogotis, L.R. (1975). *Brief symptoms inventory*. Baltimore, MD: Johns Hopkins University School of Medicine, Clinical Psychometrics Unit.

Fisher, C.B. (1979). Memory for orientation in the absence of external cues. *Child Development, 50*, 1088–1092.

Fisher, C.B., & Tryon, W.W. (1988). Ethical issues in the research and practice of applied developmental psychology. *Journal of Applied Developmental Psychology, 9*, 27–39.

Freedman, B. (1975, August). A moral theory of informed consent. *Hastings Center Report, 5*(4), 32–39.

Geller, D.M. (1982). Alternatives to deception: Why, what, and how? In J.E. Sieber (Ed.), *The ethics of social research: Surveys and experiments* (pp. 39–56). New York: Springer-Verlag.

Hennigan, K.M., Flay, B.F., & Cook, T.D. (1980). "Give me the facts": Some suggestions for using social science knowledge in national policy-making. In R.F. Kidd & M.J. Saks (Eds.), *Advances in applied social psychology* (Vol. 1, pp. 113–148). Hillsdale, NJ: Lawrence Erlbaum Associates, Inc.

Hornstein, G.A., & Wapner, S. (1985). Modes of experiencing and adapting to retirement. *International Journal of Aging and Human Development, 21*, 291–315.

Imber, S.D., Glanz, L.M., Elkin, I., Sotsky, S.M., Boyer, J.L., & Leber, W.R. (1986). Ethical issues in psychotherapy research: Problems in a collaborative clinical trials study. *American Psychology, 41*, 137–146.

Kinard, E.M. (1985). Ethical issues in research with abused children. *Child Abuse, 9*(3), 301–311.

Keith-Spiegel, P. (1983). Children and consent to participate in research. In G.P. Melton, G.P. Koocher, & M.J. Saks (Eds.), *Children's competence to consent*. New York: Plenum.

Lepper, M.R., Ross, L., & Lau, R.R. (1986). Persistence of inaccurate beliefs about the self: Perseverance effects in the classroom. *Journal of Personality and Social Psychology, 50*, 482–491.

Liebert, R.M., & Baron, R.A. (1972). Some immediate effects of televised violence on children's behavior. *Developmental Psychology, 6*, 467–475.

Loo, C.M. (1982). Vulnerable populations: Case studies in crowding research. In J.E. Sieber (Ed.), *The ethics of social research: Surveys and Experiments* (pp. 105–129). New York: Springer-Verlag.

Melton, G.B., Koocher, G.P., & Saks, M.J. (1983). *Children's competence to consent*. New York: Plenum Press.

Maccoby, E.E., Kahn, A.J., & Everett, B.A. (1983). Role of psychological research in formation of policies affecting children. *American Psychologist, 38*, 80–84.

McCall, R.B., Gregory, T.G., & Murray, J.P. (1984). Communicating developmental research results to the general public through television. *Developmental Psychology, 10*, 45–54.

Miller, G.A. (1969). Psychology as a means of promoting human welfare. *American Psychologist, 24*, 1063–1075.

Piaget, J. (1965). *The moral judgment of the child*. (M. Gabian, trans.). New York: Free Press. (Original work published 1932.)

Pion, G.M., & Lipsy, M.W. (1984). Psychology and society: The challenge of change. *American Psychologist, 39*, 739–754.

Reid, J. (1988). *Family environments mediating psychological distress in physically ill elderly*. Unpublished doctoral dissertation, Fordham University, Bronx, NY.

Sarason, S.B. (1984). If it can be studied or developed, should it? *American Psychologist, 39*, 477–485.

Scarr, S. (1988). Race and gender as psychological variables: Social and ethical issues. *American Psychologist, 43*, 56–59.

Sieber, J.E. (1982). Deception in social research I: Kinds of deception and the wrongs they may involve. *IRB: A review of human subjects research, 4*, 1–6.

Sigel, I.E. (1985). *Parental belief systems: The psychological consequences for children*. Hillsdale, NJ: Lawrence Erlbaum Associates, Inc.

Smith, M.B. (1967). Conflicting values affecting behavioral research with children. *Children, 14*, 53–58.

Stanton, A.L., & New, M.J. (1988). Ethical responsibilities to depressed research participants. *Professional Psychology: Research & Practice, 19*, 279–285.

Veatch, R.M. (1987). *The patient as partner*. Bloomington, IN: Indiana University Press.

Walters, R.H., & Parke, R.D. (1964). Influence of response consequences to a social model on resistance to deviation. *Journal of Experimental Child Psychology, 1*, 260–280.

Weithorn, L.A. (1983). Involving children in decisions affecting their own welfare: Guidelines for professionals. In G.B. Melton, G.P. Koocher, & M.J. Saks (Eds.), *Children's competence to consent* (pp. 235–260). New York: Plenum Press.

Wimmer, H., Gruber, S., & Perner, J. (1985). Young children's conception of lying: Moral intuition and denotation and connotation of "to lie." *Developmental Psychology, 21*, 993–995.

5 How to be Ethical in Applied Developmental Psychology: Examples from Research on Adolescent Drinking Behavior

Joan E. Sieber

Applied developmental psychology takes the psychologist to settings that lie far outside the conceptual reach of standard tenets of scientific ethics. Even in the more traditional scientific settings, intuition and good intentions are rarely sufficient to keep scientists out of ethical dilemmas. Those problems are compounded in applied developmental psychology where there are two overarching ethical issues, or principles: (a) The research must be *useful,* and (b) the scientific knowledge gleaned must be *validly translated* (generalized) to applied settings. Attention to these two ethical issues is a distinguishing aspect of the applied, in contrast to the traditional, approach to developmental psychology.

The first issue, usefulness, pertains primarily to discussions regarding the design of research. The second issue, translation, pertains primarily to decisions regarding the application of knowledge gained from this research. However, the two issues are intertwined with each other and with the issue of validity, so that they cannot truly be separated. In this chapter we examine why these are different, but intertwined issues, and just what kinds of ethical principles pertain to both matters. Finally we examine some of these problems in the context of the study of adolescent drinking behavior.

DESIGNING AND CONDUCTING USEFUL RESEARCH

Useful Research

Ironically, it is easy to formulate trivial research that does not raise issues of risk, consent, confidentiality, or community sensitivity—we shall call these the *little ethical problems.* However, while doing trivial research in which it is easy to solve the little ethical problems, we create the big ethical problem, that of ignoring important problems. Most research in applied developmental psychology that is useful is also difficult to do ethically because it raises many of the "little" ethical problems.

For example, knowledge of the actual socialization processes that underlie alcohol abuse in adolescents would be of interest to mental health practitioners, educators, and parents. However, as we will see later on in this chapter, one cannot make simple generalizations about these processes. Socializing agents include the family, peers, the church, the culture, and the special qualities of being adolescent (Chambers, Inciardi, & Siegal, 1982; Holck, Warren, Smith, & Rochat, 1984; Schuckit, 1985; Streit & Nicolich, 1977). As Jessor (1984) points out, adolescence is a time when the individual actively seeks to transform his or her social identity by seeking new self-definition, patterns of interpersonal relationships, skill, and so on. Alcohol use and abuse (apart from family norms and expectations about drinking) can serve various purposes in this time of self-redefinition. It may be (a) an expression of opposition to adult authority and conventional society, (b) a way to cope with anxiety, frustration, inadequacy, and failure in relation to school performance, peer expectation, or parental high standards, (c) a way to gain admission to peer groups and to express solidarity with peers or demonstrate identification with the youth subculture, (d) confirmation of personal identity characteristics, for example, machismo, "experience," or "coolness," or (e) a transition marker, that is, a symbol of having gone form less mature to more mature status.

Thus, the applied developmental psychologist who wished to observe the processes underlying the observed demography of adolescent drinking would face the following monumental tasks, and many more:

1. Drawing upon all that is known about the demography of adolescent drinking, socialization in and outside of the family, and extant models of socialization, the researcher must judiciously select a problem that is researchable and will yield information that is useful to parents, psychologists, educators, and policy makers.
2. The research design task would involve selecting appropriate sampling frames, identifying the factors that seem to warrant study, and developing data-gathering instruments appropriate to the study of these factors.
3. The actual conduct of the research may involve complex problems of consent and confidentiality.

While it would be useful to include in the sample those families where problems of abuse and violence occur, the legal implications for the researcher of observing reportable criminal behavior are enough to deter all but the most dedicated. Moreover, the demographic data leave one with the distinct impression that some of the most censorious and repressive of religious and socioeconomic settings produce the most serious adolescent drinking problems. How is it possible to observe the way families cope with the very problem they are most eager to deny?

4. Finally, the dissemination of findings poses some interesting problems. Many popular myths will be shattered by competent research on family

processes that influence adolescent drinking. It would be convenient for the researcher to bury the findings in obscure journals that are unlikely to be read by those whose lifestyle is exposed. But usefulness means that the research find its way into literature that is read by policy makers, parents, and members of the various helping professions. Responsible disclosure of findings to the press is warranted. As a consequence of this publicity and resultant exposure of hypocrisy of some powerful social institutions, the life of the researcher may become rather uncomfortable.

In short, there may be little personal or professional incentive for conducting important research that promises to usefully enlighten crucial social interventions. Indeed, research that is likely to generate knowledge that is useful to applied developmental psychologists is also likely to raise tough ethical problems of consent, confidentiality, how to frame the problem so as not to blame the victim, and so on.

The following sections discuss several aspects of designing useful applied developmental research.

Values and Epistemology

How psychologists define reality and their relationship to that reality affects theory, method, and practice. For example, although the moderate drinkers and those least likely to become alcoholic tend to come from homes in which wine is often served with meals, and in which children drink wine responsibly with their parents, (e.g., Lolli, Serianni, Golder & Luzzatto-Fergiz, 1958) there are psychologists who believe that any adolescent drinking leads to problem drinking and drug abuse (e.g., Hawkins, Fine, & Sweany, 1986). The holding of this belief demonstrably has a strong influence on the way one researches the relationship between adolescent drinking and subsequent behavior, and on what one finds. Unfortunately, the scientific method is not entirely objective, especially when used by psychologists who are quite convinced of what they will find; indeed, scientists often arrange to find what they are looking for. The nature of one's beliefs about reality, coupled with "scientific proof" of that belief, can turn an otherwise intelligent psychologist into a dogmatic advocate of a bad idea. A skeptical mind is all the more important in applied developmental psychology, and this skepticism should be applied to the basic assumptions or guiding theory, as well as to other aspects, of the research and development enterprise.

Validity

For science and technology to be ethical it must be valid. In applied developmental research, there are many temptations to compromise research designs for humanitarian and practical reasons, or to study easy problems that raise fewer ethical problems, including fewer problems of internal validity, but which raise serious problems of external validity. In the development and use of applications, practical considerations (e.g., lack of training of personnel) may result in the administration of a technique that resembles the original concept in name only. For example, when many of the Head Start programs were evaluated, it was found that they involved little use of the curriculum that the community volunteers presumably were following. Unfortunately, most applied developmental intervention programs have not been as well-funded as Head Start, nor had the luxury of process evaluation that would indicate whether the presumed program was in fact being administered (see Chapter 7).

Equitable Treatment of Participants

Procedural and distributive justice arise as issues in many parts of the research and application process. Who sponsors and pays for the research and development? Who benefits? How are participants for research or treatment selected? How is the power of the psychologist balanced against the powerlessness of the participants? Applied developmental research and development programs often are mandated in response to some public perception of the problem that is to be solved. That perception may not be appropriate. Moreover, the pressure groups that define the problem and demand action may be a part of the actual problem, but would resist any effort that would implicate them. For example, the current public perception of teenage drinking is that it is invariably excessive and inappropriate, getting worse during the last decade, characteristic of teens from the wrong side of the tracks, worse in America than elsewhere, exacerbated by advertising, and caused by unavoidable peer pressure. All of these perceptions are wrong, as we shall see in the latter section of this chapter. Parents and other adults who scapegoat adolescents in this way probably exacerbate problems of adolescent drinking. Research and interventions based on such misperceptions of the problem are likely to be useless or harmful.

Risk and Benefit

Scientific knowledge may bring risk of harm or wrong to individuals, as well as economic cost to some sector of society. When is this cost ethically justified? Typically, Institutional Review Boards (IRBs)[1] and other decision-making bodies

---

[1] Federal Law (National Research Act, Public Law 93-348, July 12, 1974) specifies that any institution that expects to obtain Federal funding of research must establish an Institutional Review Board (IRB) to review research involving human subjects in order to assure that the rights of human subjects are protected. The investigator must submit a research protocol to the IRB and have the protocol approved prior to performing the research. In the protocol, there must be a description of the

consider risk as occurring in the research process, and benefit as a promised event that might (or more likely might not) occur later. In applied developmental psychology, it is the responsibility of psychologists to integrate risk/benefit considerations across the research and application spectrum: One should not fail to do risky research that has a serious promise of leading to great benefit in application, and should not fail to consider the risks or lack of benefit that may arise from misapplication of knowledge or lack of external validity. The psychologist must then persuade the IRB of this reasoning.

The identification of risks and estimation of degree of risk is a process still in its prescientific stages. Risks to research subjects, research populations, and community members stemming from products of the research or development need to be considered. However, here is another catch-22 for applied developmental psychology: We tend to be risk averse, regardless of the possible payoff of the project. Hence, some important and high payoff projects are unlikely to be done if the risk is also high.

The ethical justification for research and development is that it is beneficial. What the benefits of specific work may be, how these may be estimated or maximized ahead of time, and how they may be measured after the research or development has occurred needs to be considered carefully if planning is to be ethical.

Communication Processes and Agreements

Informed consent. Here I refer to informed consent not as a legal process or as a written form, but as a communication process that extends beyond the legally mandated actions. There are many contexts in which the psychologist and participant communicate with one another and reach agreements. The adequacy of these communication processes deserves serious scrutiny. The ramifications of this process for the success of the project are many, as the anecdote about Celia Fisher's grandmother would suggest (see Chapter 4).

Deception. This includes any concealment, intended deception, mental reservations, perceived deception, or the use of devices intended to take the subject's attention off of the main purpose of any activity in order to evoke spontaneous behavior. Deception in social science ranges along a continuum from everyday management of the perceptions of others by the use of tact and body language—forms of deception that we encounter regularly in interpersonal relations—to lies which may undermine the confidence of persons in themselves and others, may leave persons seriously deluded, and damage the reputation of psychology.

---

research project and the subjects to be used, a comprehensive discussion of possible risks and benefits and the procedures employed to minimize risk and maximize benefit, and discussion of the informed consent procedure.

In applied development psychology, when research and treatment moves into sensitive contexts such as the family, there is pressure on psychologists to engage in various forms of deception in order to maintain rapport with socially deviant participants. How, for example, does one explain to prospective participants that the purpose of one's project is to learn more about the dynamics of abusive families. Typically, a more euphemistic explanation is used: for example, "We want to observe the different ways parents interact with their children." There is a fine line between tact and deception, and the applied developmental psychologist often must balance the pros and cons of total honesty versus euphemistic explanations. Just as one should not tell one's 16-year-old daughter that her purple prom dress matches her pimples, there are some observations about one's research participants that may better be left unsaid.

Relationships as sources of data. Qualitative social research, such as participant-observation in family settings, involves getting to know persons and then reporting on some aspect of their life. Much more research of this kind is needed in order to understand the dynamics of social development. However, the kind of critical analysis of findings that is published is likely to be inconsistent with the way the informant expected or wanted to be represented to the world; that is, the "friendship" that the investigator established to obtain data may turn into a betrayal, as far as the subjects are concerned. Apart from the possibility of perceived betrayal, the establishment of a rather intimate relationship with, say, a family in their home, may produce knowledge, attitudes, and commitment in the investigator that, in turn, may subtly affect many other aspects of the research, the definition of the research problem, the collection and organization of the data, the framing of research reports, and the dissemination and utilization of the findings. The ethically aware scientist must recognize that friendship may affect objectivity and professional judgment in these ways.

Restriction of Research

Government regulations and IRBs. Government regulations and institutional review boards contribute much to the ethical socialization of scientists, but also impose a bureaucracy with rules that are sometimes in conflict with tenets of valid and useful research. In applied developmental psychology, there is a clear need to undertake research and experimental interventions with vulnerable populations in sensitive settings. Unfortunately, IRBs are not necessarily as concerned about fostering useful research as they are about protecting the research institution from controversy and lawsuits; hence, they are risk-averse. Solving the myriad of "little ethical problems" that accompany useful applied developmental projects is the task of the investigator, who must then persuade the IRB that the project is safe. Hence, IRBs are yet another source of pressure to do trivial but safe projects.

Controversial topics. While science and society value freedom of inquiry, there is some question as to whether certain topics should be studied, especially those supported by public funds. There are various kinds of concerns about controversial topics: Will the truth cause serious or irreparable social harm? Will scientists produce misleading results that will then be misapplied? Will the truth be highly offensive to some, or be used in ways that are politically or personally harmful to some groups or individuals or to society at large? The study of racial, ethnic, or gender differences in ability is a case in point.

Scientific freedom. Both scientists and subjects have rights and responsibilities. The right of the investigator to conduct research must be balanced against the rights of those studied, but there must also be consideration of the obligations of all citizens to contribute to the development of scientific knowledge. When sensitive research on vulnerable populations is at issue, the balancing of these rights and responsibilities may become quite a complex undertaking.

Ethics and politics. Values and distinctions between moral and immoral behavior are frequently based on subjective or political criteria. Critics who approve of a particular cause regard projects that support its aims as moral. Charges of immorality or scientific irresponsibility may mask profound ideological disagreements. For example, persons who believe that any and all drinking by adolescents is wrong and leads to substance abuse would formulate a different research agenda from that of persons who stress the socialization of responsible drinking.

TRANSLATION OF KNOWLEDGE TO APPLIED SETTINGS

Translation or generalizability of knowledge to applied settings is the problem of external validity and much more. Many of the "general principles" of developmental psychology that one may find in the scientific literature are, in fact, principles whose generality across populations is not known (see Chapter 15). The problem of external validity (generalizability across major populations, for example, across sex, age, ethnicity, race, social class) is endemic in psychology. Many researchers seek to study general or nomothetic processes and eschew the study of differences. In fact, such investigators may be studying a phenomenon that is highly idiosyncratic to the population employed, but remain ignorant of that fact until other populations are studied.

In addition to establishing the limits of generalizability across populations, the applied developmental psychologist should be concerned to show the reader how a given piece of new knowledge or a new technique is useful to specific populations; that is, the applied developmental psychologist is engaged in technology transfer and should act accordingly. A sailing proverb says "it does no good to push a rope." It seems that many technology transfer efforts seek to "push" a new technique by emphasizing its novelty and power, rather than by creating a pull. One could create a "pull" by making the new technique truly more attractive—that is, more relevant to the needs of the target population. The ethical issues we discuss in this section are all pertinent to the transfer of new behavioral technology.

There are at least seven major problems that the applied developmental psychologist must take into account, in order to translate or generalize knowledge validity; they are discussed next.

Studying a Range of Populations

Even the most dedicated applied developmental psychologists may be deterred from studying populations that don't fit standard theory or paradigms—that is, populations that differ in many respects from the populations typically studied. Why, for example, are there so few controlled comparisons of socialization across radically different ethnic groups? Why, for example, is so little known about the socialization of drinking in black adolescents, apart from the fact that they tend not to abuse alcohol? An investigator who sets out to do such a comparative study will quickly learn that (a) there is no overarching theory to describe socialization of drinking in all homes, (b) there is little commonality of family settings across black and white homes, (c) there are enormous problems of gaining entree to homes in cultures not one's own, and (d) there are complex methodological problems of establishing comparability of procedures and data. The difficulties of doing a valid, and hence ethical, comparison are overwhelming.

Cultural Imperialism

Given that vital knowledge about diverse populations is often unavailable and is difficult and costly to obtain, how do applied developmental psychologists serve those diverse populations? Most of the world looks to American psychology (read: middle-class white, and perhaps even student, psychology) as the last word. We find that Third World psychologists import American psychological theory unquestioningly to settings that differ critically from the setting in which the theory was developed. So do we. In the absence of comprehensive comparisons across cultures or other relevant groups, how does one ethically seek to generalize findings to new settings? In a word—cautiously. It is important that the applied developmental psychologist employ a healthy skepticism, be a good field worker, consult with many others who are more experienced with the subject population, find good native informants to interpret what is happening, do a thorough evaluation, and try numerous promising alternative interventions before settling on a solution to the problem at hand.

Prevention

Prevention is the laudable notion that knowledge can enable psychologists and members of other helping professions to identify populations that are vulnerable, and to provide an intervention that will reduce their vulnerability. The main ethical problems with prevention have to do with inaccuracy of identifying the target population, stigmatizing those identified, and possibly giving them an intervention that does more harm than good. A case in point was the proposal, made during the Nixon administration, that boys carrying XYY chromosomes be identified and given special counseling and guidance to deter the criminal tendencies they were believed to have!

Individual Versus Cultural Psychology

In *Psychology Misdirected*, Seymour Sarason (1981) eloquently argues that psychologists miss half their target by focusing on the individual without critical analysis of the culture of the individual. The psychologist tends to apply an implicit personal theory about the nature of the society in which the individual functions, how that society works, and how to get things done in it. Even when the initial scientist is aware of the cultural factors involved and mentions them clearly, as Binet did concerning the cultural determinants of IQ scores, others will apply the idea to individuals blindly with regard to cultural factors.

To be powerful, interventions must take cultural context into account. It is hardly surprising that the most powerful interventions to prevent teenage drunk driving have been those of Friday Night Live, a high-energy extracurricular teen organization that, among its other activities, develops contracts for teens and their parents to sign, in which the teen agrees never to enter a car when he or others have been drinking, and the parent agrees to respond to any phone call from their teenager to come and pick them up with no blame laid. A back-up program consists of trained teen chauffeurs who are available on a hot line every Friday and Saturday, at all hours, to respond, on a strictly confidential basis, to calls from teens whose parents wouldn't sign such a contract. Sacramento County, California has cut its teen DUI and auto injury rate in half since instituting Friday Night Live (1987).

Engineering

Dewey (1978) pointed out that social scientists err in assuming that once scientific research has generated basic knowledge, it can simply be applied without any kind of "engineering" activity. In fact, he points out, theory and practice must inform one another; and any theory-practice dichotomy will involve poor theory and poor practice. Applications need to be researched as carefully as the original research that informed the application, and the findings must be fed back to the initial theory.

Superficial Evaluation

Most programs produce disappointing results. Unfortunately, however, the evaluations of the programs typically are not designed to indicate why they failed;

they typically focus on the product, which is easy to measure, and not the process involved in producing the product. Process-oriented evaluation is far more complex and costly, but would provide the information needed for effective "engineering" as discussed above, and would provide needed insight into cultural differences as discussed above.

Poor Market Research

When one seeks to disseminate a new social technology or social intervention, one faces problems similar to those who seek to market any other kind of technology: Who will use it? What can be done to interest potential customers in using it? What are the characteristics of the target population to which the product needs to be tailored? How does one work with the target population to perfect the product for their purposes? Who bears these developmental costs? We are again revisiting issues discussed above but now from the perspective of technology transfer, and sales engineering.

ADOLESCENT USE AND ABUSE OF ALCOHOL

The purpose of this chapter is to offer, as an heuristic, a taxonomy of ethical issues that arise in applied developmental psychology. However, in actual applied developmental psychology projects, these issues do not arise simply, one by one, or in a social or political vacuum. Rather they tend to arise due to the enormous difficulties of defining an applied project in logical yet workable terms, separating truth from the fictions that abound in society about social problems, and dealing with public opinion surrounding the research. In the preceeding discussion, we have seen numerous ways in which the study of adolescent use and abuse of alcohol may raise ethical issues. However, without a fuller examination of this area of research and development, it is not possible to understand how embedded these ethical issues are in the very nature of the problem as it exists in society today. Indeed, there is not much agreement on the nature of the problem; hence there is limited social support for valid and useful research on this socially sensitive issue. Myriads of problems await the applied developmental psychologist who seeks to do useful and valid projects in this area. We turn now to an examination of some of these problems.

Adolescents fascinate and worry adults because they mirror qualities of their elders and are the inheritors of their culture. Since adults have a major practical and emotional investment in adolescents, the topic of how adolescents learn to use and abuse alcohol is hardly a neutral one. Like other salient behaviors of adults, their drinking is emulated by youngsters. But, perhaps more than any of the other habits that young persons emulate and learn from their elders, adolescent drinking is denied, exaggerated, and scapegoated by adults. About every thirty years, a new generation of sincere, civic-minded adults rediscovers that adolescents are drinking alcoholic beverages, and typically equates use with abuse. While the turn-of-the-century literature on adolescent drinking is much more naive and unscientific than that of the last decade or two, then, as now, the conclusion typically is that adolescents simply should not drink at all.

The student of human development and social learning readily senses that something is wrong with popular conceptions of adolescent drinking. The learning of appropriate, problem-free patterns of adult drinking is the result of complex learning over the years of childhood and adolescence. Likewise, the learning of comfortable and satisfying patterns of abstinent behavior is based on a complex set of beliefs and behaviors requiring extensive prior learning. Driver-education movies showing wrecked cars and dead teenagers, and adults who say "Do as I say, not as I do" obviously do not fulfill scientific requirements for an effective alcohol use or abstinence learning program for adolescents.

Since American society is once again putting considerable political energy and federal funding into programs to combat an allegedly new epidemic of teenage alcohol abuse, this is an appropriate time for applied developmental psychologists to examine the nature of adolescent drinking and prospects for promoting more responsible approaches to the socialization of alcohol use or abstinence in the young. However, as we shall see, the problems of defining and approaching these problems in a useful and valid way are considerable.

Defining Adolescent Use and Abuse of Alcohol

Adolescent drinking is a complex as well as socially sensitive topic. Each of the words—adolescent, use, abuse, and alcohol— refers not to a single entity but to a complex concept. It is not surprising that the psychological literature and the media abound with oversimplifications and inconsistent use of these terms. Adolescence refers to an age span of 13 through 19 or 12 through 20. Because adolescence is a time of rapid development, it is not meaningful to consider a 12-year-old's drinking equivalent to a 20-year-old's drinking; or a 12-year-old's abstinence equivalent to a 20-year-old's abstinence. Young adults (age 20 to 25) are the segment of the population containing the heaviest and most problem drinkers (apart from alcoholics). This category of drinkers obviously contains "spill over" of rebellious youngsters who are taking a long time to grow up, hence is not unrelated to adolescent drinking. However, statistics on this young adult category are often cited, mistakenly, in connection with concern about adolescent drinking.

Alcohol refers to quite different beverages which may be categorized as beer, wine, and spirits. Although most research on adolescent drinking does not take beverage specificity into consideration, the research that does so indicates that adolescent drinking behavior is highly beverage-specific. Beer is the beverage of choice of adolescents and young adults. The ratio of beer drinking to wine or liquor is typically at least two to one, for both boys and girls. Beer is the preferred drink of men and young adults, with older drinkers and women showing a preference for wine and spirits. The behavioral implications of these differences in beverage preference are quite dramatic. Those who prefer beer typically drink to higher levels of intoxication, are more likely to drive after drinking, and tend to consider driving while intoxicated to be less serious. These findings generalize across age, sex, education, income, and marital status. Thus, although beer has the lowest concentration of alcohol, it is not actually the drink of moderation (Berger & Snortum, 1985).

Use of alcohol may refer to any of an incredibly diverse set of uses. It may refer to the Jewish youngster who drinks wine with his family regularly; Jews have a low rate of per capita consumption and a low rate of alcohol-related problems, although most are drinkers and have been wine drinkers since childhood (Adler & Kandel, 1982). It could refer to the girl whose parents insist that she drink whiskey with them when they are on an alcoholic binge, and who is likely to be haunted by alcohol-related problems all her life. It could refer to the young women whose parents invite and permit her to join adult guests in having a cocktail at parties given in their home, and who learns responsible drinking behavior. It could refer to the teenager who drinks beer in cars because he is not allowed to drink at home, and who outgrows this form of rebellion in a few years, but not before getting into a scrape with the law.

Each of these cases depicts a very different meaning of alcohol use. To put this point more technically, the meaning of alcohol use depends on (a) quantity, (b) frequency, (c) weight of the drinker, (d) duration of drinking episode, (e) user's experience, (f) context of use, (g) psychological and physiological status of the user, (h) the way the role of the drinker is defined, (i) the way the act of drinking is defined, and (j) the patterns of alcohol use over time (Bacon, 1976). Because of the difficulty of employing an adequate operational definition of drinking (abusive or otherwise), the literature abounds with the oversimplified and inconsistent definitions. As an example, Bacon (1976) notes that two major studies of adolescents (each having over 10,000 subjects) defined drinking as having more than one sip a year, and drinking at least five days out of every week, respectively.

Quite apart from such oversimplification and inconsistency, no research could feasibly employ all 10 of the above factors in its definition of alcohol use, despite the importance of making those distinctions. The typical operational definition of alcohol use takes quantity and frequency into account. For example, national surveys of adolescent drinking completed in 1974 (Rachal et al., 1975), 1978 (Rachal, Maisto, Guess, & Hubbard), and 1980 (Zucker & Harford, 1983) followed Cahalan, Cisin, and Crossley's (1969) system, classifying respondents into six drinking categories:

1. Nondrinkers or abstainers—don't drink or drink less than once a year.
2. Infrequent drinkers—drink once a month at most, and have one drink or less per typical drinking occasion.

3. Light drinkers—drink once a month and have small amounts typically.
4. Moderate drinkers—drink at least once a week and have small amounts, or drink less than once a week and have medium amounts, or drink no more than once a month and drink large amounts (five or more drinks).
5. Moderate to heavy drinkers—drink at least once a week and drink medium amounts, or drink three or four times a month and drink large amounts.
6. Heavy drinkers—drink large amounts weekly.

Alcohol abuse is almost impossible to define in adolescents. In adults, abuse or problem drinking is defined as repeated use of alcoholic beverages in ways that lead to problems of health or interpersonal relationships, destruction of sense of self-worth, and interference with ability to carry out responsibilities to family, job, and community in accordance with prevailing social expectations. However, problem drinking in adolescence is more difficult to define. Even those adolescents who drink excessively have not yet developed chronic psychological or medical problems, and they do not yet have work and family responsibilities that are vulnerable to their alcohol abuse.

Consequently, adolescent problem drinking tends to be defined as drunkenness, especially when this involves drunk driving, or trouble with family, teachers, police, or friends. Defined in this way, "adolescent problem drinking" is often a transitory testing of limits set by the adult world, which soon gives way to moderate and responsible drinking. This concept of problem drinking does not imply an entity such as "alcoholism" or any kind of pathology or illness (Donovan & Jessor, 1978; Jessor & Jessor, 1977; Cahalan, 1970), but only that other problems arise in association with the drinking. This conceptualization leads to arbitrariness in the operational definition of problem drinking in adolescents. For one investigator, a problem drinker might be anyone between the age of 12 and 20 who reports having gotten drunk, while for another it may be any adolescent who was found to have been drinking at the time he or she got into a scrape with the law (Berger & Snortum, 1985). Obviously, the percentage of adolescents found to be problem drinkers varies greatly with the operational definition employed.

Unfortunately, these problems of defining and measuring adolescent drinking are not understood by naive investigators and by nonscientists who crusade against "the epidemic of alcohol." Social scientists and allied crusaders have made this error before. For example, in the research done on mental retardation at the turn of the century, investigators found that among persons arrested for prostitution, delinquency, alcoholism, and vagrancy, some were retarded. They went on to warn policy makers that unless the retarded are prevented from reproducing, these problems would be multiplied, threatening the extinction of Western civilization (Doris, 1982). Unfortunately, the current lay literature on adolescent drinking abounds with warnings that drinking leads to undesirable social behavior such as teenage pregnancy, dropping out of school, getting poor grades, using drugs, engaging in burglaries, and so on. This scare propaganda misleads society to focus on alcohol as the root cause of antisocial behavior and to ignore the complex psychosocial factors that appear to underlie both drinking and the problems associated with it.

Prevalent Misconceptions about Adolescent Drinking

Prevalent misconceptions about adolescent drinking make it difficult to approach this topic objectively. The actual problems that appear to warrant research differ from what the mass media depict. Some misconceptions are summarized here.

Adolescents are not typically depicted as drinking responsibly or moderately, but as guzzling and carousing. When an adult drinks, we say, for example, that she is having a beer, a glass of wine, or a cocktail—implying something appropriate and moderate. However, when a teenager drinks, we say she is drinking (often with about the same tone of voice used when mentioning that someone has cancer), implying pathology, excess, or inappropriateness. Newspaper and magazine coverage of teenage drinking is likely to depict a boy in a parked car with a whiskey bottled raised to his lips. However, empirical research indicates that most teenage drinking occurs at home with parents, or at chaparoned parties in the homes of friends (Bacon & Jones, 1968; Milgram, 1982).

The media imply that teenage drinking is on the increase. In fact, there was a dramatic increase throughout the Western world in adolescent drinking between 1940 and 1965, but since about 1965, it has leveled off (Blane & Hewitt, 1976; Zucker & Harford, 1983). It is also suggested that problem teenage drinking is found especially among youngsters from the "wrong side of the tracks," minorities, and those who are socially maladjusted. In fact, drinking is more prevalent among whites than blacks or other minorities, highly prevalent among white middle- and upper-middle class teens (Higgins, Albrecht, & Albrecht, 1977; Zucker & Harford, 1983; Forney, 1984) and bears no relationship to whether the youngster is a member of student organizations, participates in scholastic activities, holds office in organizations, or comes from a broken home (Forney, 1984).

Teenage drinking and the onset of drinking in the early teens is depicted as an American problem. In fact, statistics comparing the onset and patterns of drinking of American youth are virtually identical to those from Canada and many Western European countries. Studies of drinking conducted throughout the Western world (Moser, 1983) indicate that most youngsters have tasted alcoholic beverages by the time they enter their teens and the percentage who drink occasionally increases throughout the adolescent years; a considerable number of teens abstain or rarely drink. Moser (1980) notes that the greatest threat of alcohol problems in adolescence is probably to be found in areas of the world undergoing rapid sociocultural and economic change, for example, Africa and Latin America. These problems are especially acute among primitive peoples in settings where formerly effective sociocultural controls on overindulgence have broken down and alcohol has become more available.

Advertising and the peer culture are often depicted as luring teenagers to drink against their parents' wishes. However, research indicates that advertising does not have a noticeable effect on adolescent drinking (Smart, 1979). Moreover, research indicates that there is an overall tendency for teenagers to respect their parents' wishes, and that many parents permit their teenagers to drink under certain circumstances. The children of abstaining parents typically are abstainers. Keller (1964) points out that while peer group participation may expose youngsters to models of behavior other than those of their parents, adolescent cliques tend to form around similarity of lifestyle of the members' families. Thus, peer group drinking behavior reflects that of the parental models, though "perhaps in caricature and to an extent that parents would consider premature and excessive for the adolescent" (Keller, 1964, p. 8). Moreover, peer pressure is reciprocal. The teen who has responsible attitudes is very likely to impose these attitudes on others who have lower standards.

Young people do not invent ideas about drinking or abstinence, but learn them in the process of learning how adults act. Teenagers do differ from adults in their attitudes toward alcoholism, but they differ in the direction of being more moralistic and blaming. While about two-thirds of the adult population accepts the medical model of alcoholism as illness, about two-thirds of the teen population rejects this model and regards alcoholism as symptomatic of immorality or lack of will power (Lorch & Hughes, 1986).

There are indeed problems connected with teenage drinking—enough to occupy the attention of a large number of social scientists, teachers, and policy makers. But there is a related set of interesting psychological questions that need to be answered about the motivation of adults to create and maintain misconceptions about adolescent drinking that probably harm rather than benefit teenagers. Negative and repressive approaches to socializing adolescents with regard to alcohol are unlikely to produce responsible alcohol use or a healthy basis for abstinence. Yet, such issues are not the ones that some advocacy organizations want to fund or to address.

What models of socialization will prevail in the next decade? What can social science do to understand and change the motivation of adults who misattribute teenage drinking and to foster the use of positive and effective models? A new-style temperance movement is gaining momentum in American society. Fifteen years ago, many states lowered the drinking age on grounds that 18-year-olds can vote, fight wars, marry, and hold jobs—and should also be allowed to drink. But now the Federal government is threatening to cut off federal highway funds to states that do not again raise the drinking age to 21. Perhaps a more effective way to prevent drunk driving is through education and stiffer penalties aimed at adult, as well as teenage, drivers. These and related other policy issues remain to be enlightened by ethical and committed applied developmental psychologists.

The concern, of course, is not just with drunk driving, but also with substance abuse generally. Popular concerns about health are spawning a wide range of social and political movements, including movements to abolish tobacco, alcohol, drugs, and "impure" foods. Grass-roots groups of sincere nonprofessionals, such as Mothers Against Drunk Driving (MADD), Students Against Drunk Driving (SADD), and the National Federation of Parents for Drug Free Youth are organizing, with guidance from central offices which distribute materials and handle political strategy, to inform the public that action must be taken against irresponsible drinking. These groups resemble the Anti-Saloon League of the 1890s in structure, but their current approaches are largely positive. As illustrated by the results of the Prohibition Act, and of the "new prohibition" against marijuana (Kaplan, 1970), the potential of such well-meaning movements to do social harm, as well as good, is enormous. Whether the current wave of programs continues to develop psychologically and sociologically sound approaches to the socialization of adolescent use of alcohol will probably depend on the quality and amount of input received from applied developmental psychologists and other social scientists. That input must be guided by ethical considerations of the kinds discussed earlier.

SUMMARY AND CONCLUSIONS

Manifold ethical issues arise in connection with the design and conduct of useful developmental research and the transfer of new knowledge to applied settings. The design and conduct of useful developmental research require that the investigator be sensitive to the values and epistemology underlying the research. The research participants must be selected and treated in an equitable manner. Respectful communication between researchers and subjects and careful consideration of the rights and interests of subjects are essential to the ethical and scientific integrity of the research. Potential risks and benefits must be assessed as accurately as possible and steps taken to minimize risk and maximize benefit. Institutional Review Boards tend to be risk averse; hence, it falls to the researcher to persuade the IRB that risk has been minimized and that the importance of the research problem and the validity of the research design justify any residual risk.

The effective translation of knowledge into useful application requires both external validity of the research and effective technology transfer. The applied developmental psychologist needs to create a "pull" from the population that is to use the results, rather than attempt to "push" the results on them. To create a "pull," the researcher must also be a field worker and clinician who learns much about the culture and needs of the population to which the results are to be applied. The setting and the early attempts at application should be researched as carefully as the original research that informed the application, and the findings fed back to the initial theory. In this way, application enriches research, and vice versa.

REFERENCES

Adler, I., & Kandel, D.B. (1982). A cross-cultural comparison of sociopsychological factors in alcohol use among adolescents in Israel, France and the United States. *Journal of Youth and Adolescence, 2,* 89–113.

Bacon, M., & Jones, M.B. (1968). *Teenage drinking.* New York: Crowell.

Bacon, S. (1976). Defining adolescent alcohol use: Implications for a definition of adolescent alcoholism. *Journal of Studies on Alcohol, 37,* 1014–1019.

Berger, D.E., & Snortum, J.R. (1985). Alcoholic beverage preferences of drinking driving violators. *Journal of Studies on Alcohol, 46*(3), 232–239.

Blane, H.T., & Hewitt, L.E. (1976). *Alcohol and youth: An analysis of the literature.* Document prepared for the U.S. National Institute on Alcohol Abuse and Alcoholism, Washington, DC.

Cahalan, D. (1970). *Problem drinkers: A national survey.* San Francisco: Jossey-Bass.

Cahalan, D., Cisin, I.H., & Crossley, H.M. (1969). *American drinking practices: A national study of drinking behavior and attitudes* (Monograph No. 6). New Brunswick, NJ: Rutgers Center Of Alcohol Studies.

Chambers, C.D., Inciardi, J.A., & Siegal, H.A. (1982). The use and abuse of licit drugs in rural families. *Chemical Dependencies: Behavioral & Biomedical Issues, 4*(3), 153–165.

Dewey, J. (1978). Psychology and social practice. In E.H. Hilgard (Ed.), *American Psychology in Historical Perspective.* Washington, DC: American Psychological Association.

Donovan, J.E., & Jessor, R. (1978). Adolescent problem drinking: Psychosocial correlates in a national sample study. *Journal of Studies on Alcohol, 39*(9), 1506–24.

Doris, J. (1982). Social science and advocacy. *American Behavioral Scientist, 26,* 199–234.

Forney, M. (1984). A discriminant analysis of adolescent problem drinking. *Journal of Drug Education, 14*(4), 347–355.

Friday Night Live. (1987). *Friday Night Live DUI Statistical Handout.* Sacramento, CA.

Hawkins, J.D., Fine, D.N., & Sweaney, S.L. (1986). *The effects of parental attitudes on teenagers' use of gateway drugs.* Unpublished paper. Center for Social Welfare Research, University of Washington, Seattle, WA.

Higgins, P.C., Albrecht, G.L., & Albrecht, M.H. (1977). Black-white adolescent drinking: The myth and the reality. *Social Problems, 25*(2), 215–224.

Holck, S.E., Warren, C.W., Smith, J.C., & Rochat, R.W. (1984). Alcohol consumption among Mexican American and Anglo women: Results of a survey along the U.S.-Mexico border. *Journal of Studies on Alcohol, 45*(2), 149–154.

Jessor, R. (1984). Adolescent development and behavioral health. In J.D. Matarazzo, S.M. Weiss, J.A. Herd, & N.E. Miller (Eds.), *Behavioral health: A handbook of health enhancement and disease prevention* (pp. 69–90). New York: Wiley.

Jessor, R., & Jessor, S.L. (1977). *Problem behavior and psychosocial development: A longitudinal study of youth.* New York: Academic Press.

Kaplan, J. (1970). *Marijuana-The new prohibition.* New York: World.

Keller, M. (1964). In introduction to G.L. Maddox and B.C. McCall (Ed.), *Drinking among teenagers* (pp. 1–17). New Haven, CT: College & University Press.

Lolli, G., Serianni, E., Golder, G., & Luzzatto-Fergiz. (1958). *Alcohol in Italian culture: Food and wine in relation to sobriety among Italians and Italian-Americans.* Glencoe, IL: The Free Press.

Lorch, B.D., & Hughes, R.H. (1986). Youths' perceptions of alcoholism. *Journal of Alcohol and Drug Education, 31,* 54–63.

Milgram, G.G. (1982). Youthful drinking: Past and present. *Journal of Drug Education, 12*(4), 289–308.

Moser, J. (1980). *Prevention of alcohol problems. An international review of preventive measures, policies and programmes; compiled with the help of contributors from more than 80 countries in the six WHO Regions.* Toronto: Addiction Research Foundation.

Moser, J. (1983). Alcohol problems in children and adolescents: A growing threat? *Child Health, 2,* 147–159.

Rachal, J.V., Maisto, S.A., Guess, L.L., & Hubbard, R.L. (1980). *A national study of adolescent drinking—1978.* Prepared for the U.S. National Institute on Alcohol Abuse and Alcoholism. Research Triangle Park, NC: Research Triangle Institute.

Rachal, J.V., Williams, J.R., Brehm, M.L., Cavanaugh, B., Moore, R.P., & Eckerman, W.C. (1975). *A national study of adolescent drinking behavior, attitudes and correlates.* (Report No. PB-246-002; NIAAA/NCALI-75/27). Springfield, VA: U.S. National Technological Information Service.

Sarason, S. (1981). *Psychology misdirected.* New York: Free Press.

Schuckit, M.A. (1985). Genetics and the risk for alcoholism. *JAMA, 254,* 2614–2617.

Smart, R.G. (1979). Priorities in minimizing alcohol problems among young people. In H.T. Blane & M.E. Chafetz (Eds.), *Youth, alcohol, and social policy* (pp. 229–261). New York: Plenum Press.

Streit, F., & Nicolich, M.J. (1977). Myths versus data on American Indian drug abuse. *Journal of Drug Education, 7*(2), 117–122.

Zucker, R.A., & Harford, T.C. (1983). National study of the demography of adolescent drinking practices in 1980. *Journal of Studies on Alcohol, 44*(6), 974–985.

Part II
Ethics and Developmental Intervention

6   Assessing Social Intervention: Scientific and Social Implications*

Michael Lewis

Within the search for methods to improve the lives of children and families, our society has undertaken massive efforts at intervention. Perhaps no social system in history has been so willing and capable of altering instances of perceived injustice through educational and social reform. As part of this effort, we attempt to evaluate the success or failure of these reforms. It appears reasonable to ask whether what we have proposed makes a difference. Social scientists have assumed responsibility for evaluating the effectiveness of many reforms that have been undertaken. While no one doubts that answers to the effectiveness of reform and their cost are important, we hope to raise some question as to the usefulness of evaluation in light of the problems with conducting such studies. More specifically, we hope to show that evaluation as most often performed, or even by necessity, cannot help but lead to the conclusion that intervention does not work. Thus, our methods may unwittingly lead us toward a conservative conclusion, one which generates the belief that individuals are fixed rather than flexible and that national resources could be better spent elsewhere.

We do not argue for the proposition that it is unnecessary to evaluate societal reform and the expenditure of resources. Rather, some forms of social reform may not be amenable to evaluation as currently conceived. The criteria for the "success" of a particular program may be simply to observe its face validity; that is, does it appear to work. Much of our investment in programs related to the society's interest cannot be readily evaluated using objective methods. For example, we spend tens of billions of dollars in the design, construction, and deployment of atomic weapons under the proposition that this will safeguard us from atomic war. The expenditure of resources are justified by the belief that the building of these weapons will prevent the need to use them. This hypothesis is not subject to test since there is no way we would decide whether building these weapons will be a true deterrent. History may provide clues, but the hypothesis is accepted largely based on its face validity, its emotional appeal, and belief that it will work. Moreover, our society is willing to expend enormous sums of time, energy, and resource on projects without formal evaluation. For example, we

* This chapter was supported by a grant from the Robert Wood Johnson Foundation.

invest a large percentage of our resources on the production and employment of weapon systems without knowledge of their effectiveness as deterrents to war. Likewise, we increase our police force in an attempt to limit crime. Neither program is evaluated, either from a historical or concurrent perspective. It is not clear what rule may be governing which expenditures are put to the test. Evaluation may be used by our society as a political weapon, it being required only of those programs which are politically vulnerable. Moreover, if evaluation is likely to lead to a conservative conclusion, it may provide the means of eliminating certain types of expenditures. What is certain is that formal evaluation is employed selectively. If, in addition, it turns out to be the case that evaluation cannot help but lead to a conservative outcome, then social scientists may be participants in a political as well as scientific venture.

The problem of evaluation focuses on five features which most likely lead to a conservative conclusion. Others may be found; however, these five are central to evaluation and present problems inherent in designing and conducting evaluation about intervention.

EFFECTIVENESS AND COST: ASKING TWO QUESTIONS AT THE SAME TIME

The attempt to initiate change in any culture always is associated with the question of cost. For example, if we wish to provide increased medical care for all our citizens, we know that this increased care will cost more money. That both questions exist does not mean that both need to be addressed at the same time. When they are, incomplete answers for both questions result. For example, this is apparent in some of the earlier studies of nutrition and how increasing the available food affects children's behavior (Irwin et al., 1979; Klein, 1979; Mora, Christiansen, Ortiz, Vuori, & Herrera, 1979). The effectiveness question that is asked in such studies is whether increased nutrition will result in increased well-being of the child. More specifically, will children be brighter and more able to learn if they (and their families) have proper nutrition? Such a question is reasonable and would be of interest to study if for no other reason than to demonstrate the relationship between nutrition and intellectual ability, especially to demonstrate the importance of increasing the nutritional diet of poor people, be they South American Indians or inner-city poor. How would we go about testing the proposition that increased diet results in increased ability? One approach would be to provide the equivalent of a middle-class diet to the children at risk for inadequate nourishment. The outcome measures of growth, intellectual ability, or school performance could be related to middle-class standards in these areas.

Unfortunately, many studies of nutritional intervention do not pose the question in this form (Ricciuti, 1981). If we look at the nutritional supplements often given to the study population, we would find them far below the level received by the middle class. Why should a study of the potential effect of nutrition be tested in its weakest form? If the question had focused solely on whether certain nutritional supplements improve children's development, then a maximally enriched diet should be provided. However, a second question is being asked at the same time. This question, how to implement such programs in a most-cost-effective fashion, may seriously compromise the ability to answer the first question.

When both questions are asked at the same time, the most likely answer is the one that states that the intervention has no effect. The danger in trying to answer two questions at once is that a failure to demonstrate positive effects cannot be interpreted properly. In times of political and fiscal conservatism, the lack of a clearly demonstrated benefit is likely to be used as a basis for stopping all such intervention. Proper evaluation requires that, first, we need to evaluate the full range of intervention effects *when provided under optimal conditions*. Only then can we proceed to study alternative means of implementing the intervention on a cost-effective basis.

It may not be possible to address the question of whether intervening in the lives of families will increase outcomes without committing considerable resource to the effort. Consider the case of educational opportunity. While programs such as Head Start provide additional hours of instruction a day, few would argue that this is a sufficient test of an ideal instructional environment as it affects young children's subsequent intellectual development. To test such an effect correctly, we need to supply both child and family with an array of tutors, special educators, and a set of instructors who spend all their time working with them. George Bernard Shaw understood the need for such intense instruction in *Pygmalion* (Shaw, 1916). Liza was not given several hours of instruction but lived a different life. The cost for such intervention would be tens or even hundreds of thousands of dollars per family. Using such resources, we should be able to demonstrate that children subjected to high quality education show increased intellectual capacity. Only after such a demonstration should we ask, "For how much less could this be achieved?" By not testing the proposition using maximum resources, we bias the results. Under minimum to moderate levels of educational resource, we fail to demonstrate much effect on children's capacity (Westinghouse, 1969). This failure allows us wrongly to conclude the general proposition that remedial educational opportunity does not work. Such a conclusion allows us to avoid the expenditure of money for such programs. It would appear as if the testing of the proposition "does it work" at the same time we test the cost issue must provide a less-than-adequate test of the intervention and thus increases the likelihood that we will find no effect. The combining of questions provides for a politically conservative conclusion.

CARING FOR CHILDREN

Intervention usually means the selection of one new procedure which is administered to everyone. While the choice of a single procedure is not necessary, the costs involved usually made complex intervention procedures too expensive to undertake. This limitation requires us to assume that a single procedure is likely to help large numbers of people, for without that assumption our methodological design of comparing an experimental and control group would make little sense. If large numbers of people are not helped by a single procedure, then no differences between groups will be found and the conservative conclusion will be confirmed. Let us explore this problem in more detail.

At times, we may pick several variations of an intervention but, in general, we usually propose that a particular intervention is likely to work for everyone. This neglects the likelihood that different interventions may be necessary to achieve the same goals for different types of people. When we present only a single variation, we act contrary to what we know about variation in human development and individual differences, and increase the likelihood of finding little effect. For example, consider how to test the general proposition that increased exposure to educational materials would result in better general intellectual ability. If a particular curriculum is selected to test the general proposition, the effects will be limited. If we presented a single curriculum to 100 different children, we might find that particular curriculum was effective in altering general intellectual ability of 10 of those 100 children. Since only 10% of the group was affected, there would be little difference between the experimental and control groups. We would conclude that this particular curriculum is not effective in altering children's intellectual ability. If we employ nine other different curricula, which would affect a different 10% of the 100 children, we would be forced to conclude that not one of these 10 curricula had a significant effect. Although all 100 children, using 10 different curricula, in fact were helped, one would conclude that all intervention curriculum procedures were ineffective since not one of them was able to result in a significant difference between experimental and control groups. Here we see that a serious problem in intervention resides in the assumption that a single variation is capable of proving the general proposition. This limitation is particularly important when we consider the likely ramifications of such a fallacious assumption. If environmental stimulation did not lead to gains in intellectual ability, then it might be assumed that general intellectual ability is due to genetic differences in children. This conclusion is most likely to occur if we are unwilling, or, because of costs, unable to understand that no single intervention procedure is likely to result in sweeping changes. We need to provide multiple experiences in order to match the characteristics of individuals, including their prior experiences, attitudes, and aptitudes (Berliner & Cahen, 1978).

This proposition is rarely explored fully, in part because the concept of *univer-*

sal help or a *best way* dominates our social reform mentality, and, in part, because of the expense of such an intervention effort (see Louis Laosa's discussion of population validity in Chapter 15.) Return to our example; what would happen if we could specify who among the 10 subjects were likely to be helped by each curriculum? Having identified which of the 10 children are likely to be affected by a particular intervention, it would be possible to select a new sample of 100 children with those particular characteristics and demonstrate significant change. This treatment by individual ability design would permit a far more powerful test of our general proposition. Even more exciting is the opportunity to evaluate the processes different types of children use to learn, which is possible only when varied interventions are implemented for a heterogeneous group of children (Berliner & Cahen, 1978).

Given the intervention methodology currently being used, one which focuses on a single procedure, we are likely to conclude that intervention does not work. We are forced to such a conclusion by our emphasis on a single cure for all; itself a rather anti-individualistic perspective. Exactly why we have chosen such a methodology is unclear; perhaps because of limited theory and statistical ability, more likely the lack of resource to invest in multiple programs, or even the limited concept of universal help. Whatever the reason, the selection of a single procedure inherently is likely to lead to a politically conservative conclusion.

THE NATURE OF CURE

When we intervene in people's lives we can expect many different levels of effect varying from limited change—both in level and duration—to permanent change. While for many areas of intervention, we do not require permanent change to conclude success, within social reform we most often expect and require it. Using permanent change as the only criteria of success biases the conclusions that can be reached by settling on the most conservative outcome.

When considering most intervention efforts, we tend to select success criteria which are most stringent. To understand this situation, we will use the term "cure" to better focus our discussion; the use of the medical examples allows for a clear articulation of the issues providing the backdrop to our analysis of social reform. Cures come in many forms. The first type of cure is temporary, altering behavior or a disease state only for a brief period. Administering nitroglycerin to patients with angina temporarily relieves the pain, but does not remedy the cause of pain or provide long-term relief. The second type of cure is prosthetic, involving use of special devices or supports. Poor vision is prosthetically cured by corrective lenses. This cure is effective as long as the patient uses the prosthesis, such as eyeglasses. At any point that the patient ceases to wear the glasses the poor vision returns. This cure is absolute but not permanent. The cure for poor vision is achieved through the intervention of eyeglasses; however, the eyes never are corrected. Most forms of disease are cured using this model; hypertension is cured through the use of particular medication or/and diet which, when stopped, returns. We could find more examples; however, they are not necessary since these few suggest that absolute but not permanent cure is most common in our daily experience.

Another model of cure, by far the most longed for, is one that is both *absolute and permanent*. A permanent cure relies on the discoveries of ways to correct or eliminate the disorder so that the negative features can never be reactivated. We might operate upon an aneurysm, for example, removing a portion of artery and cure the particular problem.

Of these three types of cure, the third is undoubtedly the most preferred. For most social reforms, the criteria for success are high, requiring demonstration of permanent changes that continue even after the intervention itself has stopped. If such stringent criteria had been used to evaluate the effectiveness of correctional lenses for poor vision, we would have rejected them as a cure because poor vision remains when treatment ends. In testing early intervention on subsequent school achievement, we adapt a standard of judging effectiveness of success that requires lifelong, major, and permanent change. For example, programs such as Head Start and early childhood stimulation have been criticized because the effects of these interventions have been shown to disappear several years after the intervention has stopped (Bronfenbrenner, 1974). This critique is remarkable because intervention did lead to increased learning and improved cognitive ability in the short run. Such expectation of permanence places an unfair burden upon social and educational interventions that is rarely, if ever, used in other areas of our life such as health or technology. Why is there this demand that socioeducational procedures provide an absolute and permanent cure? Is there a unique and defensible rationale requiring that psychosocial and humanitarian intervention be both absolute and permanent? There appears to be no logical or a priori justification. The demands for effectiveness of human services and interventions are unrealistic and probably self-defeating. We need to further explore the political, emotional, and economic forces that have contributed to the maintenance of unrealistic and unfair criteria for evaluating the benefits of social reform. Even when biomedical treatments impact on relatively minor aspects of a larger disease process or when they are applicable only to a subgroup of patients with disease, they are used and accepted as valid if they result in some measurable degree of "cure." In a broader sense, social scientists need to consider how their conclusions subserve various political agendas and policy decisions, especially since the definition of cure tends to limit what is considered effective change.

WHAT TO MEASURE

Issues of measurement are at the heart of the scientific enterprise. Even so, there are no explicit theories of what to measure. What to measure is determined by implicit theories of human nature or behavior as well as the beliefs of the scientist. Given the evidence for a conservative view of change, there is some concern that the selection of measures of change may be affected by a similar view.

The selection of measures potentially affects the conclusions that are reached. An analogy to such measurement problems can be seen if we look at the public school system. Imagine that after each course in geography or history children are given overall IQ tests to evaluate whether these specific courses altered their ability. Clearly such activity would be foolish. We evaluate children's learning of history by seeing how much more history they know. We evaluate classes in English composition by seeing how much better they can write. We do not evaluate specific programs by asking how children's overall ability changes. This seems obvious, yet any number of intervention programs, especially those in early childhood, rely on measuring very broad and nested outcomes as a way of validating the usefulness of the intervention.

Most intervention programs specify their goals, relating their program/treatment choices to particular hypotheses or assumptions. If intervention simply relies on an obvious hypothesis, such as, providing food will reduce hunger, it is unlikely to receive much scientific attention. More typically, the hypotheses are broad, reflecting a global view that correcting almost any negative aspect of a child's life will lead to improvement in many areas. For example, instead of saying that better nutrition will result in less illness, we state that improved nutrition will result in better school performance. This hypothesis is based on the following rationale: First, increased nutrition should result in better health and school-age children spending less time thinking about food. Children thus will be more attentive and alert, prerequisites for doing well in school. If the evaluation of nutritional programs was school performance, we run the risk of concluding that the program is not effective. School performance itself represents a complex outcome of many influences, not only the child's nutritional status. While there may be little scientific doubt that amount and quality of nutrients impact the developing central nervous system and ultimately behavioral competence in school performance, this effect is not likely to be detected immediately. Even more importantly, the effectiveness of a nutritional program should not be centered primarily around general outcomes such as school performance.

Intervention projects are thought unsuccessful because the nested hypotheses lead to claims that cannot be met. Consider an example. A group of economically impoverished parents and children are the subjects of an intervention study. The intervention is designed to improve the children's nutrient intake by educating the parents about proper diet (Johnson, 1982). The investigators claim that this would result in smarter children who would do better in preschool. The intervention itself consists of adult education courses. Parents are taught about nutrition and urged to buy certain foods. The outcome measures are changes in children's performance on standard psychometric tests. The intervention would be judged a failure if the children's abilities did not change even though information including type and amount of food in the refrigerator before and after the mothers' education program indicated that the families had less soda and more milk, fewer fast food snacks, and more nutritional food. Yet, even with these significant and positive changes, the final conclusion would be that intervention failed since there was no improvement in school performance. Had evaluation been based on the more relevant outcome of whether families altered their food buying habits when taught to do so, then the program would have been considered successful. Even if the long-range goal was that such dietary changes could foster better child outcomes in areas such as school performance, we must determine what outcome measures constitute success for any given intervention.

This same type of difficulty arises often: Specific intervention programs are believed to result in *general changes* in ability. Ideally, a program which leads to large pervasive changes will be better received than one which affects only limited or modest aspects of the recipients' lives. Until we can articulate a theory which unites a specific intervention to more general hypothesis of skill development and competence, we are at high risk for ignoring small real changes that result from interventions, simply because we fail to consider these changes important enough. We must focus first on the most direct and measurable outcomes likely to result from a particular intervention; only when these are demonstrated and we have additional reasons for estimating the breadth or duration of effect should we generalize to broad outcome possibilities. To continue to focus exclusively on broad outcomes for relatively focused (slender) intervention procedures must result in rejection of intervention as a means for altering human well-being and behavior.

TEMPORAL PARAMETERS IN MEASURING CHANGE

We are a young and relatively vigorous society. We believe in change and we believe that change can take place quickly. Given this belief, we should not be surprised that we hope to see immediate and impressive effects of our efforts. We readily view failure to document such change as adequate evidence that our intervention has failed. Such a belief is tenable only if we have a cohesive theory of human development on which to base our choices about when change should take place (Lewis & Schaeffer, 1981). Without a temporal theory of change, we are forced to conclude that there is no change if not immediately evident. Such a strategy is conservative since it limits the likelihood of demonstrating a significant effect. The assumption of immediacy of effect, while deemed desirable, is not required for all our endeavors; why then this assumption for social reform?

Again let us use a medical model of cure and consider some temporal dimension related to cure. As we all know, there are certain medications which can be taken and which offer close to immediate relief. If one has a headache, an analgesic can provide comfort within a short time. Alternatively, other medications take a long time to initiate change. Both beta blockers and diuretics assist in relieving hypertension but may take days, weeks, or months before the patient shows improvement. These temporal effects in intervention should alert us to analyze when we expect change to be demonstrated. Interventions, unfortunately in both medical and socioeducational areas, have temporal parameters which are not yet well understood; some interventions with no immediate effects may have delayed impact.

Let us consider examples of delayed effects. Lazar and Darlington (1982) found that while the early positive effects of the infant stimulation program wore off several years after the intervention, there were effects 15 years later. Children who received these infant programs were much more likely to be enrolled in school (that is, they did not drop out) and to have stayed out of trouble with the law compared to children from similar backgrounds who did not receive the infant programs. Negative sleeper effects also exist, and within medicine are all too familiar. We know that many drug therapies initially effective lead to unanticipated side effects. DES daughters who survived in utero because their mothers received DES are at high risk for cervical vaginal cancer (Westerholm, 1984).

What is missing in our studies of intervention effectiveness is a good temporal sense. We know that good parenting affects children's adjustment and the type of parent they become. Harlow and Harlow's (1965) demonstration that monkeys reared without mothers become themselves terrible parents is an example of an intergenerational temporal outcome. From such studies we should anticipate that good early daycare programs will have an influence on children when they become parents, when they make choices about the kinds of environments to create or make available to their own children, not two or three years after the program is over.

The restless nature of our culture makes long-term study of effects unlikely; the biases about social reform and fiscal conservatism make the situation even worse. The possibility to conclude intervention works has become restricted to the consideration of immediacy in spite of the evidence of long-term effects. Such bias must result in the conclusion that social change as a function of intervention is unlikely.

SUMMARY AND CONCLUSIONS

Our society, at least ideologically, is committed to change. Planned intervention in the lives of our citizenry, be it for the very young, old, or even the majority of healthy adults, is predicated on the belief that change can be evaluated in terms of our stated goals. As we have tried to point out, the evaluation of intervention is at best a difficult task. The difficulty lies not only in our incomplete scientific understanding, but also in our requiring evaluative research to do more than it is capable. If we rely upon the commonly held procedures and standards for evaluating intervention, we are likely to continue to arrive at the conservative conclusion; that is, commit a type two error; ignoring a valid result (cf. McCall, 1986). While science favors such errors, when applied to humans and the ability to change behavior patterns it becomes an argument favoring the status quo.

The problems with the evaluation of social reform may involve more than incomplete understanding; they may involve implicit assumption about the nature of human behavior and human beings. It is to this regard that social science also must attend; namely, that we may not be neutral to the proposition that human beings can change given the opportunity and resource. If our reforms are too little and the measure of their effectiveness too conservative, then unwittingly (or not) we favor the proposition of the fixity of human nature. This is not an anti-intellectual argument against evaluation. Face validity needs to be considered more in social reform as a means to evaluate the effectiveness of intervention and its cost. The same validity reasoning which allows us to conclude that it is better for us to have weapons to protect ourselves from our enemies also should allow us to conclude that it is better for children to be fed and to have schooling than to be hungry and ignorant.

As presented here, we have attempted to delineate some of the critical issues which limit our ability to conduct entirely comprehensive or timely evaluations. If, as an informed citizenry, we understand these limitations, we can better use what knowledge we have to evaluate outcomes in a proper perspective. In this regard, it is necessary that we utilize our moral sense, our commitment to common good, our reliance upon common sense, and above else, the utilization of all evaluation methods deemed possible and responsible. To simply ask, in the absence of good evaluative procedure, whether or not reform is good is to place too great a burden on the scientific community and not enough burden on our sense of justice and the needs of human beings as we see them.

REFERENCES

Berliner, D., & Cahen, L.S. (1978). Trait-treatment interactions and learning. In F.N. Kerlinger (Ed.), *Review research in education* (Vol. 1). Ithaca: Peacock.

Bronfenbrenner, U. (1974). *A report on longitudinal evaluations of preschool programs: Is early intervention effective?* (DHEW Publication No. OHD 74–24). Washington, DC: Office of Child Development.

Harlow, H.F., & Harlow, M.K. (1965). The affectional systems. In A.M. Schrier, H.F. Harlow, & F. Stollnitz (Eds.), *Behavior of non-human primates, Vol. II* (pp. 287–334). New York: Academic Press.

Irwin, M.H., Klein, R.E., Townshend, J.W., Owens, W., Engle, P.L., Lechtig, A., Martorell, R., Yarbrough, C., Lasky, R.E., & Delgado, H.L. (1979). Effects of food supplementation on cognitive development and behavior among rural Guatemalan children. In J. Brozek (Ed.), *Behavioral effects of energy and protein deficits* (pp. 239–254). Bethesda: Department of Health, Education and Welfare (NIH).

Johnson, D.L., (1982). In J. Andrews (Ed.), *The skills of mothering: A study of parent child development centers: Houston.* Monographs of the Society for Research in Child Development, Serial No. 198, *47* (6), pp. 33–42.

Klein, R.E. (1979). Malnutrition and human behavior: A backward glance at an ongoing longitudinal study. In D.A. Levitsky (Ed.), *Malnutrition, environment and behavior: New perspectives* (pp. 219–237). Ithaca, NY: Cornell University Press.

Lazar, I., & Darlington, R.B. (1982). Lasting effects of early education with commentary by Craig T. Ramey. Monographs of the Society for Research in Child Development, *47* (2–3), Serial No. 195.

Lewis, M., & Schaeffer, S. (1981). Peer behavior and mother-infant interaction in maltreated children. In M. Lewis & L.A. Rosenblum (Eds.), *The uncommon child: The genesis of behavior, 3,* 193–224. New York: Plenum Press.

McCall, R.B. (1986). *Fundamental statistics for behavioral sciences.* New York: Harcourt, Brace, Jovanovich.

Mora, J.O., Christiansen, N., Ortiz, N., Vuori, L., & Herrera, M.G. (1979). Nutritional supplementation, early environment, and child development during the first 18 months of life. In J. Brozek (Ed.), *Behavioral effects of energy and protein deficits* (pp. 255–269). Bethesda, MD: Department of Health, Education and Welfare (NIH).

Ricciuti, H. (1981). Developmental consequences of malnutrition in early childhood. In M. Lewis & L. Rosenblum (Eds.), *The uncommon child* (pp. 151–172). New York: Plenum Press.

Shaw, G.B. (1916). *Pygmalion.* New York: Brentano.

Westerholm, B. (1984). Sex hormones. In M.G. Dukes (Ed.), *Meyler's side effects of drugs.* New York: Elsevier.

Westinghouse Learning Corporation for Federal Scientific and Technical Information, U.S. Institute for Applied Technology. (1969). *The impact of Head Start: An evaluation of Head Start on children's cognitive and affective development.* (Report No. P.B. 184.238). Washington, DC: Clearinghouse for Federal Scientific & Technological Information. Report presented to the Office of Economic Opportunity, pursuant to Contract B 89-4536.

7 Ethical Considerations in the Design, Implementation, and Evaluation of Developmental Interventions*

Steven J. Danish

The movement of another segment of psychology toward an applied focus seems like a natural progression for our discipline (Howard et al., 1986; Pion & Lipsey, 1984). Since World War II psychology has become a more applied discipline. Training programs in clinical, counseling, and school psychology place a greater emphasis on practitioner skills sometimes to the exclusion of scientific training. Furthermore, an increasing number of these new practitioners are trained to deliver one-to-one remedial counseling and therapy such that the practice of psychology more closely mirrors the other health care professions than any other time in our history (see Chapter 13). The practice of psychology as conceived by many of these new practitioners can be best characterized as having a disease conception and a waiting-mode style of delivery (Rappaport, 1977). In other words, individuals with problems "develop" pathology, become clients, and are treated in offices or clinics by experts. As a result decreasing attention is being paid by applied psychologists to understanding, enhancing, and intervening in the process of individual development.

Given these changes, other psychologists, including developmental psychologists, have become involved in the conduct of interventions, especially those oriented toward preventing dysfunctional behaviors or enhancing empowering behaviors (Rappaport, 1981). As one might expect the traditional clinical and counseling psychologists have been opposed to the involvement in such activities by developmental psychologists and have invoked both legal and ethical arguments (see Chapter 14).

It is beyond the scope of this chapter to discuss the legal issues involved and their appropriateness. My colleagues and I have discussed them elsewhere (Danish, 1980; Danish & Smyer, 1981). However, it is reasonable to consider the

* Preparation of this chapter was supported in part by Office of Substance Abuse Prevention Grant 1-H84-AD00489-01. Its contents are solely the responsibility of the author and do not necessarily represent the official views of OSAP.

The author wishes to thank Drs. Cathy Howard, Albert Farrell, Rick Birkel, and Mr. Mark Mash for their comments and suggestions.

effectiveness and inherent value of the "preventive" interventions being developed, implemented, and evaluated by applied developmental psychologists. To do so implies consideration of the extent to which the conduct of developmental interventions meets the ethical obligation of psychologists to competently promote and protect the welfare of individuals. By intervention, I am referring to planned, programmatic efforts usually conducted in groups directed at altering the developmental process. My focus in this chapter will be on considering selected issues involved in the design, implementation, and evaluation of interventions and describing some of the prerequisite knowledge and skills necessary to meet ethical standards. I will consider these three components of an intervention separately; however, to some degree treating them as distinct components obscures the actual process. In reality, the three must be considered simultaneously. In the second section of the chapter an example of a comprehensive intervention being conducted by the author and several colleagues will be described. In the final section I will consider what training is necessary to conduct such interventions.

DESIGNING THE INTERVENTION

Identifying the Goals of an Intervention

In the 1960s a number of disparate groups within mental health began to write about different types of interventions. The Division of Counseling Psychology of the American Psychological Association published a definition of counseling psychology identifying three roles for counseling psychologists.

> Counseling psychologists play three different but complementary roles when engaging in practice, as contrasted with related research teaching or administration. One is to help persons who are presently experiencing difficulty. This is the remedial or rehabilitative role. Another is to anticipate, circumvent, and if possible, forestall difficulties that may arise in the future. This is the preventive role. A third role is to help individuals plan, obtain and derive maximum benefit from educational, social, avocational, vocational, and other kinds of experiences that will enable them to discover and develop their potentials. This is the educative and developmental role. The counseling psychologist is therefore as concerned with facilitating optimum development as he is with remedying faulty development, as interested in cultivating assets and potentials as he is in correcting and overcoming deficits and shortcomings. (Whiteley, 1980, p. 181)

At about the same time, Caplan (1964), a psychiatrist, adapted public health concepts and applied them to mental health. He identified three levels of preventive interventions: primary, secondary, and tertiary which parallel the roles identified by counseling psychology but are applied to working with communities rather than with an individual. Primary prevention involves steps taken to prevent the occurrence of a disease or other form of dysfunction. The key strategy is to counteract circumstances before they have a chance to produce the illness. Secondary prevention is the detection and early treatment of an existing problem for "at risk" populations. Tertiary prevention is designed to increase the likelihood that a normal level of functioning can be approximated and that recurrence of the problem can be minimized.

The decision as to what kind of intervention is developed, be it for rehabilitation or tertiary prevention, secondary prevention or primary prevention is related to two factors. The first is an understanding of theories of individual development *and* societal functioning. The second is to be able to recognize one's values and norms about what is desirable (Baltes & Danish, 1980).

To have an understanding of theories of development and societal functioning enables one to delineate the differences and similarities between the normative, dysfunctional, and optimal development of the target population. Without this understanding discriminating between normal and abnormal behavior is difficult, if not impossible.

Emphasizing the need to understand development to applied developmental psychologists would seem to be an example of "preaching to the converted," yet simply to know what are usually considered the criteria for understanding development is insufficient. One must know more than the theories of development and the criteria by which changes in development are measured. The designer of a developmental intervention must understand societal functioning as well since development does not occur in a vacuum. For this reason a knowledge of the assumptions inherent in a life-span human development perspective is helpful. Several of these assumptions are: (a) developmental change is a continual process, not limited to any one stage in life; (b) change occurs in various interrelated social, psychological, and biological domains of human development and therefore one must develop a multidisciplinary, multidetermined focus; (c) change is sequential and therefore it is necessary to place any "stage" of life within the context of the preceding and following developmental changes; and (d) changes in individuals must be considered within the context of the prevailing norms of the day as well as the historical time within which one lives (Baltes, Reese, & Lipsitt, 1980; Danish, Smyer, & Nowak, 1980).

As to the issue of values, it is argued that any decision to intervene presupposes a dimension of quality of functioning of what is and what should be. However, what constitutes effective behavior may not be altogether clear, consequently the goal(s) of an intervention may not be well thought out. Therefore, it becomes necessary for interveners to recognize both the intended and unintended consequences of an intervention. Without such an analysis the impact of the unintended consequences of an intervention may overwhelm the impact of the intended consequences.

One value stance that may be adopted is that to prevent a problem from occurring if it is or will be detrimental to an individual or group is more "ethical" than treating the individual or group once the problem has occurred. Further, to enhance an individual or group's development is probably even of greater value than to wait until the individual or group is "at risk" and prevention is necessary.

The decisions, then, about the goals for intervention come from multiple sources and it is necessary for the applied developmental psychologist designing the intervention to answer the question, "Intervention—why, how and for what purpose?"

Determining the Target of an Intervention

When one examines the different potential goals of an intervention, it becomes evident that the decision whether to intervene is a complex one. One of the first questions one must address is *why*. As noted earlier the answer to this question is clearly rooted in one's understanding of life span development. If the intervener concludes that an intervention is appropriate, determining *where* to intervene becomes the next question. Rappaport (1977) has described six levels of organization which may make up the "social order." Each level serves as a potential point of intervention. These levels include: the individual, group, organizational, institutional, community, and society level (Rappaport, 1977, p. 129). A decision to intervene at one level as opposed to another has implications for the values and goals, conceptual frameworks and strategies of the intervener. For example, Ryan (1971) has passionately decried our tendency to design interventions which are "victim blaming." He states:

> The formula for action becomes extraordinarily simple: Change the victim. All of this happens so smoothly that it seems downright rational. First, identify a social problem. Second, study those affected by the problem and discover in what ways they are different from the rest of us as a consequence of deprivation and injustice. Third, define the differences as the cause of the social problem itself. Finally, of course, assign a government bureaucrat to invent a humanitarian action program to correct the differences. (Ryan, 1971, p. 8)

His commentary has been very instrumental in the decision of community psychologists to design social interventions at the more complex levels of organization.

While the question of where to focus the intervention is, in part, a "values" question, it also has significant implications for the effectiveness of the intervention. Regardless of how well an intervention is designed, if change at the level at which the intervention is not appropriate for the solution of the problem, the solution itself will become a problem (Rappaport, 1977).

Such a perspective has been proposed by Watzlawick, Weakland, and Fisch (1974). They refer to three solution errors in intervention: (a) action is necessary but not taken; (b) action is taken but not necessary; and (c) an error of "logical typing" occurs. Logical typing errors are most relevant to the present situation. One form of logical typing errors takes place when a *system* level problem is taken care of by an *individual* level solution. It establishes a "Game Without Ends" where the intervention leads to no change because it is the wrong kind of intervention and more and more of the same intervention is called for without success.

The response of interveners to what is perceived as a crisis often leads to errors in logical typing. For example, the impact of the farm crisis on rural communities has led mental health and human service workers to focus their response on the farmers and their families (Meyer, 1988; Jane Paulsen, 1988; Julie Paulsen, 1988). The situation described by these authors and the interventions developed seemed to represent effective *short-term* help. However, it was proposed that such responses may not be directed at the right level for a long-term impact (Danish, 1988). It was suggested that an intervention directed at the community might be necessary for growth and change to take place.

The closer one is to a person in need, the more we tend to direct our energies at the individual. While such a decision may make us feel more useful and the recipient feel better temporarily, if our goal is to help alleviate the circumstances, we must intervene in the larger system.

The inability to solve a problem because the intervention is directed at the wrong level is frustrating. However, the situation described by Watzlawick et al. (1974) when action is taken which is not necessary is equally disconcerting. The plight of latchkey children may be such an example. The concern expressed by parents, the press, and the writings of researchers like Long and Long (1983) have led to calls to develop extensive after-school care (Vandell & Corasaniti, 1988). However, research by Rodman, Pratto, and Nelson (1985); Sternberg (1986); and Vandell and Corasaniti (1988) suggest that concerns about the problems faced by latchkey children may be overstated. While interventions designed to increase after-school care opportunities may be extremely valuable, what are the unintended consequences of frightening parents of latchkey children about the detrimental effects of leaving their children alone after school?

IMPLEMENTING THE RESEARCH

In this section two separate activities will be described: the development of the intervention technology, and the actual carrying out of the intervention. Although they will be described separately, in actuality the process requires that both activities be integrated. Places where such integration is necessary will be pointed out. Also, even though an intervention can be implemented at any level, for example, individual, group, organizational, institutional, society, or community, the focus of this section will be on the individual and group levels since these levels are the likely targets for applied developmental psychologists.

Developing the Technology

In constructing an intervention, the applied developmental psychologist must become an educational technologist. Decisions have to be made as to *what* is being taught and *how* it will be taught. Determining what is taught is directly related to the goals of the intervention. The content of the intervention must be consistent with the goals. For example, if the goal were to prevent burnout of employees in the workplace, it would be necessary to determine at what level the intervention should be directed and carefully define what constitutes burnout. Too often the construct is not well specified, leaving the content of the intervention unfocused and the projected goals unattained.

While the question of "how" to teach the intervention is related to the content, it is still a distinct decision. Teaching or disseminating knowledge or skills or attitudes requires different strategies. Moreover, teaching problem solving skills in a school setting is very different than disseminating information about healthy lifestyles through the media. Finally, the intervener must be sensitive to the population which serves as the target of the intervention. The mores, values, and cultural differences, let alone the educational levels, of different groups must be considered.

It is unfortunate that journal articles do not generally consider in detail the intervention methodology (see Chapter 9). Consequently, while *what* is taught may be specified, *how* it is taught is usually not. For example, if a skill were being taught, a format consistent with "skill learning" should be developed (Gage, 1963; Gagne, 1970). Such a format includes: (a) specifying an explicit goal or objective as behaviorally as possible; (b) clarifying the rationale (understanding the importance) for learning the skill; (c) presenting sequentially aspects of the skill so the dimensions of the skill are known; (d) modeling effective and ineffective examples of the skill; (e) encouraging active participation and practice both during the training session and in the environment where the skill is to be employed; and (f) providing immediate feedback about the appropriateness of the practice.

The result of a carefully constructed technology is an intervention that can be replicated. Very often interventions are developed, evaluated, and found to be effective. However, when the intervention is replicated elsewhere it is not found to be equally as effective and questions are raised about the program. What often has occurred is that the intervention itself is not actually replicated. When interventions are adapted for other settings, it must be predetermined whether the actual intervention is being conducted as designed and whether the purposes of the intervention are the same. For this reason the most effective interventions are ones that have been documented so that others can see how to apply them. When the intervention is dependent on the charisma of the intervener it cannot be adequately replicated.

Ensuring that the intervention is important for the participants is critical. Most interventions take place in a very brief time period. If it is to have impact on the participants it must be meaningful and become an integral part of their lives. One key question to be addressed in developing the intervention is whether the intervention is to be conducted *on, for* or *with* participants. Obviously, the more an intervention is done "with" participants, rather than "on" or "for" them, the greater the participants' motivation to learn will be. Kelman (1958) has identified three levels of motivation: compliance, identification, and internalization.

Compliance occurs when participation in an intervention is done to gain rewards or avoid punishment. Participants perform the required behaviors to achieve favorable reactions rather than due to a belief in the effectiveness of the intervention. When participation is the result of compliance, learning is not retained.

A higher level of motivation is identification. Learning occurs because participants like the intervener and wish to establish or maintain a good relationship. Problems occur with retention when the intervener's influence is no longer present; that is, when participants move out into the natural environment.

The highest level of the motivational processes is internalization. This occurs when the rationale for learning agrees with the participants' value system. Because performance is intrinsically rewarding, learning is more likely to be maintained in diverse environments. Internalization can be facilitated if the relevance of what is learned is perceived. This requires that significant others in the natural environment model effective use of the behaviors and reinforce participants for responding appropriately.

The actual conduct of an intervention is somewhat similar to the processes involved in both counseling and teaching. It cannot be done effectively by individuals who have no training or experience. Conducting interventions is a skill and the process of learning requires skill learning similar to the format described earlier. We do not learn how to teach, conduct research, or play tennis by reading about it; nor can we learn to conduct interventions by reading.

Carrying Out the Intervention

Interventions do not get carried out in a vacuum. For example, if they are conducted in schools the intervener must contend with school-related groups such as administrators, school boards, teachers, parents, the school's environment, and the students. Logistical considerations are as important as the design of the intervention. Carrying out an intervention in the schools or in any complex organization requires "getting your hands dirty." It is not an "ivory tower" exercise which can be controlled in the same manner as a laboratory experiment.

Before the intervention begins, the intervener must lay the groundwork for conducting the actual intervention. For example in a school, approval may be necessary by the administrator, the school board or both. Writing up a description which emphasizes how the intervention will meet their needs is necessary. Equally as important is convincing them that the intervention will be valuable while not impinging significantly on their schedule. Many a good idea has gone awry because the demands created by the intervention require too great a commitment on the part of the school and its students. The intervener is a guest in someone's "home" and must be sensitive to this role. Above all, carrying out an intervention requires patience and flexibility. Things will go wrong regardless of planning.

Obtaining permission to conduct an intervention is just the first step. In a system, if authority is decentralized, it will be necessary to "sell the project" all over again at each level. For example, if the administration of a school district has approved a program, it will be necessary to gain the support of each school's principal and teachers. It will also be critical to understand the calendar of the school, when statewide testing takes place, when examinations are given, and what the school norms are. Securing liaisons at different levels of the system will be of tremendous value.

Once the intervention starts, continual feedback to system representatives and participants is necessary. Informing and thanking those who have helped will be appreciated. Recognizing that neither the intervener nor representatives of the setting will totally understand the other's environment increases the need for continual feedback. For example, individuals in the intervention setting will not understand requirements such as passing the intervention project through an institution's Human Subjects Review Committee. There are rituals in every setting which require that continuous communication take place.

In this section I have tried to identify a number of the details involved in carrying out the intervention. To understand all the details one must participate in such a project. In sum, two aspects stand out. First, carrying out an intervention requires more than just making an appearance during the intervention itself. It is an excursion into an ongoing system; a system that the intervention project will disturb and one which must be prepared for the disturbance. Second, systems will be more willing to be part of a program when they see the benefit of the intervention *for them* and when there is some indication that the intervener is willing to make an ongoing commitment beyond the intervention. When the intervener disappears as soon as the intervention ends to analyze and publish the results, the commitment of the system to future proposals will be minimal.

EVALUATING THE INTERVENTION

Intervention action is not necessarily effective nor is it always effective as it was planned. Therefore, evaluation becomes an essential component of any developmental intervention. The purpose of this section is to describe what constitutes evaluation and its role in the intervention process.

Purposes of Evaluation

There are three basic purposes for evaluating a program. One is *to prove* that an intervention was effective or successful, that it was valuable, that it did what it was intended to do. Evaluations designed to prove effectiveness are often used to convince decision makers and funding sources that the intervention has "redeeming social value."

Interventions which are successful when evaluated receive a much greater emphasis in an age of accountability. Decision makers and funding sources want evidence which will help them determine which programs should be continued and which should be dropped. For that reason in an age of accountability, the other reasons for evaluating programs are often overlooked.

The second reason for evaluating interventions is *to improve* them. The emphasis here is on gathering the information and making the judgments needed to help the intervener make changes in a given aspect of the intervention. These changes should lead to a honing or refining process which ultimately improves the design and impact of future efforts.

Ideally, these first two purposes of evaluation are interactive. We do need to prove that our interventions are effective. We also need to improve their effectiveness. Thus, we need to learn from our successes as well as our mistakes.

The third purpose to evaluating interventions is to advance scientific knowledge. Traditionally distinctions have been made between empirical and evaluation research with the former aimed at advancing scientific knowledge and the latter aimed at establishing the worth, effectiveness, and efficiency of an intervention (Scriven, 1972). However, interventions serve not only a knowledge application function but a knowledge generation function (Baltes & Willis, 1977). Therefore, the distinction between experimental and evaluation research is one of emphasis rather than qualitative difference. This is particularly true when theory-based interventions are conducted (Baltes & Danish, 1980).

The Process and Types of Evaluation

While the difference between experimental and evaluation research may be simply one of emphasis, the procedures are very different. The process of evaluation involves describing each step of the intervention and assessing both the impact of each step as well as the total intervention program.

The value of a step-by-step assessment is that any step within the intervention process that is not fulfilling its prescribed goal can be changed. The final result of an intervention is the summed impact of each step of the intervention and the relationship between these steps and the goals of the intervention. Evaluation, then, is a dynamic process. *For evaluation to be effective it must become a part of the intervention program development, not a process applied after its development* (Danish & Conter, 1978).

Two types of evaluation exist: process or formative evaluation; and outcome or summative evaluation. While the two are interrelated and generally going on at the same time, the goals are different. A process evaluation is conducted to monitor what is going on in the intervention; to determine how it is being received by the participants and whether it is reaching the target audience; to examine the unintended consequences, both good and bad, associated with the intervention; to assess the cost-effectiveness of the activity; to assist in making replication possible; and finally to pinpoint when the intervention program is sufficiently stable so an outcome evaluation can be conducted (Price & Smith, 1985). As part of these goals, monitoring the intervention will provide information on how well the intervention was planned, the quality of the materials developed, and of the presentations. A second series of questions will pertain to the participants. The evaluation will provide information on how appropriate the intervention was for the target population given their demographic characteristics and whether participants have gained the knowledge, skills, attitudes, and behaviors which were taught. The overall question being asked in process evaluations is whether the target population learned what was taught: if so, why; if not, why not?

The failure of the target population to learn what was taught may have nothing to do with the goals of the intervention but more with the process of its implementation. For example, if the content is not relevant to the objectives or goals of the intervention it should be redesigned. If the training was not delivered as planned, whether because of lack of "instructor" expertise, the inadequacy of the materials, or because of a poor fit between the learners and the intervention to be delivered, revisions must be made. Finally, the failure may be a result of difficulties such as scheduling problems or system-level resistance related to implementing the intervention. In sum, four program elements must be examined carefully: participants, instructors, topic areas, and the setting. A process evaluation will clarify the sources of any difficulty in these areas and direct possible solutions.

When we conduct an outcome evaluation we are asking whether our intervention goal was attained. In developmental interventions this goal will most likely relate to the reduction, delay, alteration, or enhancement of certain behaviors and whether this result can be attributed to the intervention. It is rare that a clear-cut relationship exists between Intervention X and Behavior Y which can be measured accurately and in a timely manner. What often occurs is the approximations of Behavior Y are assessed. These approximations are often called mediating variables. It is then up to the intervener to make the connection between the mediating variables and the developmental goal.

McCaul and Glasgow (1985) describe the process of determining construct validity of prevention programs, specifically preventing adolescent smoking. Past researchers have assumed, perhaps simplistically, that knowledge of the risks of smoking will lead to a decrease in smoking behaviors. Although this knowledge is relatively easy to teach it has not been found to change behavior. Thus, the mediating variable, knowledge of smoking, is insufficient, though perhaps necessary, for changes in behavior. The authors present a more complex and realistic representation of the possible relationships among treatment components, mediating variables and outcomes. They identify eight treatment components: health consequences information, pressures to smoke, social consequences information, use of peer leaders, assertion training/behavioral rehearsal, anxiety management training, public commitment, and decision-making training; and five mediating variables: knowledge, attitudes, subjective norms, social competence, and smoking intentions.

Generally, more successful interventions require a complex representation. In determining whether the results can be attributed to the intervention comparing different interventions and "control treatments" is necessary. While true experimental designs are preferable, the community generally differs dramatically from the laboratory in the kind of control which is possible. For example, random assignment is much more difficult. While difficult, experimental designs are not impossible and other quasi designs have been developed which are effective (Price & Smith, 1985).

"ATHLETES COACHING TEENS"—AN EXAMPLE OF A DEVELOPMENTAL INTERVENTION FOR PREVENTING SUBSTANCE ABUSE

Status of the Problem

Alcohol abuse and other drug-related problems (excluding tobacco) annually cost American society around $205 billion. This figure equals approximately $850 per person in the United States and includes costs for lost productivity, crimes, accidents, fires, treatment, and various indirect expenses (Office for Substance Abuse Prevention, 1987).

Recent epidemiological research indicates that substance use is statistically normative among American youth. Before graduating from high school, 92% of the young people in the United States have tried alcohol, 70% have smoked cigarettes, 51% have tried marijuana, and 38% have used an illicit drug other than marijuana (Johnston, O'Malley, & Bachman, 1987). Perhaps more importantly, cigarettes are used daily by 19% of high school seniors and alcohol and marijuana are used on a daily basis by 4.8% and 5% of high school seniors, respectively (Johnston et al., 1987).

Considerable evidence suggests that adolescent drug use may have adverse consequences in young adulthood. Longitudinal studies indicate that, even when initial individual differences in adolescence are controlled for, adolescent drug use contributes to a wide variety of problems in adult life including: greater drug use; impaired performance in adult roles of work and family; more delinquency, particularly theft (Kandel, Davies, Karus, & Yamaguchi, 1986); greater dissatisfaction with peer and parental relationships; and greater dissatisfaction with free time, and with life in general (Newcomb, Bentler, & Collins, 1986). Such findings suggest that adolescent drug and alcohol use may adversely affect developmental processes necessary for optimal adult functioning (Baumrind, 1987).

Recent national attention on the prevalence and consequences of alcohol and drug abuse has created great concern. In a survey of 1,000 Richmond, Virginia residents, both parents and children rated drugs and alcohol as the most serious problem they face (Youth Services Commission, 1982).

Such concern has led to increased efforts to reduce alcohol- and drug-related problems. The 1982 Federal Strategy for Prevention of Drug Abuse and Drug Trafficking called for a national "war" against drug abuse. The war on drugs has led to a proliferation of prevention programs, primarily targeted at adolescents. Adolescents have been targeted because research shows that almost no use of cigarettes, alcohol, or illicit drugs (with the exception of cocaine and abused prescription drugs) is initiated after age 25 (Office for Substance Abuse Prevention, 1987). In fact, most initiation of cigarette, alcohol, and marijuana use occurs prior to high school (Johnston et al., 1987; McLaughlin, Baer, Pokorny, Burnside, & Fairlie, 1984). Prevention efforts have primarily targeted cigarette and alcohol use because these are viewed as "gateway behaviors" which precede and significantly increase the likelihood of involvement with illicit drugs (Donovan & Jessor, 1983; Hamburg, Braemer, & Jahnke, 1975).

Two major prevention approaches have evolved in the last decade. One approach focuses on teaching youth specific skills for resisting peer and media influences to use substances. The battle cry for such programs is the much popularized slogan "Just Say No." The second approach targets a broader range of skills. In these programs youth are taught how to deal more effectively with general life problems and with specific temptations to use substances (Botvin, 1986). They emphasize one or more of the following life skills: decision making, social skills, problem solving, stress management, and assertiveness.

Development of the Intervention

To assess the effectiveness of different developmental intervention programs a three-year grant was received from the Office of Substance Abuse Prevention (OSAP). Three intervention strategies are being tested.

INFORM. This intervention consists of a presentation by a professional athlete and the distribution of drug awareness information. The presentation by the professional athlete takes place at a school assembly.

Athletes have been chosen because they are good role models for children, although for some the idea of athletes being role models is confusing. The use of drugs by athletes is well known. However, their commitment to excellence and their desire and dedication to succeed is also well known. Too often this dedication is obscured from the public because we see only the physical skills of the athlete. Scientists, writers, businessmen, and musicians, among others, have similar dedication. However, because both male and female adolescents look up to athletes, the athlete's commitment and goal-setting ability provide an optimal model for the behaviors we seek to teach.

The athletes' presentations are designed to disseminate information about the problems of substance abuse, to provide a perspective about the incompatibility between excellence in life and sports and substance abuse, and to communicate the need for making decisions based on one's own goals rather than peer influence.

SMART moves—a "just say no" program. SMART Moves (Boys Clubs of America, 1988), developed by the Boys Club of America is a drug, alcohol, and teenage pregnancy prevention program that has a refusal skills orientation. There are three parts of the program; *Start SMART, Stay SMART,* and *Keep SMART.* In this project we are using *Start SMART,* which is a refusal skill training program for preteens. This part of the program is based on Project SMART developed by the Health Behavior Research Institute (1986) at the University of Southern California. The focus of the program is to teach information about the dangers of drugs and alcohol, ways of saying "no," consequence analysis, dealing with peer pressure and media manipulation.

The ACT "what to say yes to" program. The ACT program is a seven-session skill-based program which involves student participation in small groups. These sessions are 45 minutes each and are conducted during health education classes. The program is delivered by selected high school student-athletes who have undergone special training to be a student trainer.

The program is based on several premises. First, drug use is one of a number of "health-compromising" behaviors (Jessor, 1982), such as drinking and driving, engaging in unsafe sex, smoking, eating incorrectly, experiencing too much life stress, not being able to manage anger, and even dropping out of school. Jessor (1982) suggests that individuals who have a problem in one of these areas are likely to experience problems in several of the areas. There is what might be called a "lifestyle syndrome" that develops, which must be attacked if we are to prevent these behaviors from occurring. Trying to focus on these behaviors one at a time is likely to be ineffective and time consuming.

Second, if we are to change lifestyle behaviors, we must emphasize teaching students new skills for living. Such an approach is not easy. Behaviors which have been learned over a number of years are not changed overnight. The specific skills taught were determined following an assessment of some of the underlying causes of health-compromising behaviors. Researchers (Johnston & O'Malley, 1986) who have studied drug use among adolescents for over a decade have identified several reasons why adolescents use drugs: a social-recreational factor ("to be part of the group" and "getting high with friends"); a factor related to coping with negative affect ("getting away from problems and frustrations" or "to relax and relieve tensions"); and a factor related to lack of optimism about the future. These three factors are seen as major reasons why adolescents engage in drug use and other health-compromising behaviors. Efforts must start as early as possible to address these factors and to prevent these health-comprising behaviors from becoming too entrenched. Two possible approaches exist to prevent such behaviors—weaken, reduce, or eliminate health-compromising behaviors or strengthen health-enhancing behaviors (Perry & Jessor, 1985). It is this latter strategy we have adopted. Eventually, if we are to be successful, a prevention program must include parents, the community, and the total school environment.

The ACT program is directed at preventing and changing health-compromising behaviors by teaching students ways to increase self-esteem, cope more effectively with the stress and confusion in their lives, and learn how to make better decisions.

Based on these premises, the focus of ACT is on goal setting. Students are taught the importance of dreaming and setting goals which are attainable. Attainable goals must be phrased positively, be more important to the goal setter than to others, be specific, and require the goal setter to change his/her behavior and not the behavior of others (Danish, D'Augelli, & Ginsberg, 1984). Students are also taught how to develop plans to reach the goals using a goal ladder. The potential roadblocks to reaching one's goals are discussed. Additionally, students are taught skills which will help them reach their goals, such as problem solving, evaluating consequences, seeking social support, and practicing positive self-talk. However, all skills revolve around the students knowing what they want and knowing how to reach for it.

Procedure

All seventh graders, approximately 1750 students, in the Richmond City Schools are involved in the intervention study. The student population of seventh graders is predominantly poor, black, and living in single-parent households. Of the 1750, 88% of them are black, 60% live with their mother only, 20% live in low-rent housing, and 63% receive free or reduced-cost lunches.

The intervention involves all the middle schools in Richmond. In four middle schools, all seventh grade students will be in one of three intervention programs: INFORM, SMART, or ACT. Within each of these schools one third of the seventh-grade health classes will be selected to participate in INFORM, another third in SMART, and the other third in ACT. The other middle schools serve as comparison schools. In these schools seventh-grade students are involved in the assessment and evaluation aspects but not with any of the intervention programs.

As was noted above, the ACT program is taught by high school male and female student-athletes. These students undergo extensive training (between 10–20 hours) conducted by college student-athletes and project staff. They are given teaching manuals to use as well. The SMART program also uses peer leaders but only to assist the adult trainer.

In a recent review, Botvin and Willis (1985) made a number of specific recommendations for improving current knowledge about substance abuse prevention programs. These recommendations included: (a) evaluating the impact of prevention programs on alcohol and drug abuse, in addition to tobacco use, (b) conducting an analysis of variables hypothesized to play a role in substance abuse prevention; (c) determining the extent to which prevention programs have utility for populations other than white middle-class students, for example, low socioeconomic status minority populations; (d) identifying the "active ingredients" or components of successful prevention programs; (e) identifying factors associated with positive and negative program outcome; (f) testing different substance abuse prevention models and programs against each other to determine their relative efficacy and cost-effectiveness; (g) developing procedures to insure the successful implementation of these programs in nonresearch settings; and (h) conducting large scale "clinical trials" with a broad range of students. The project design incorporates all of the above recommendations.

To assess the effects of the program a special survey was developed by project staff. The survey entitled "Lifestyles, Interest, Values and Expectations (LIVE)" is being administered pre- and post throughout the three years. It is about 45 minutes in length. The purpose of the survey is twofold. First, it is being used to survey the attitudes, values, interests, and expectations of the students. Second, it is both a process and outcome evaluation of the interventions. Five types of variables are measured. The first set of variables are *descriptive*. The purpose of this part of the instrument is to describe the population and to serve as predictor variables in examining differential outcomes. The second set of variables are *process evaluation* variables. The purpose of these measures is to assess whether the different interventions have achieved their instructional objectives. In other words, did the students learn what they were taught? The third set of variables are the *intervening* variables. The purpose of these measures is to show whether the intervention has impact on variables causally related to substance use and to determine whether these interventions have other desirable outcomes. Most of the constructs here are related to Jessor's (1982) problem behavior theory. Other constructs are derived from the literature on adolescent development. The fourth set of variables relate to *outcome evaluations* variables. The purpose of this part of the instrument is to demonstrate whether and how well the interventions met their ultimate objective—the prevention of substance abuse and other problem behaviors. Finally, the fifth set of variables are to determine whether *differential treatment* outcomes occur as a result of the intervention. For example, participation in the ACT program should result in more goal-oriented students who are setting and attaining short-term goals and behaving in ways consistent with the long-term goals.

What has been described is a comprehensive intervention and evaluation program. Two faculty, a full-time PhD project coordinator, and four graduate students work on the project. Such an extensive project is probably only possible with grant monies, since the logistics are enormous. Obtaining the support and cooperation of the schools is nearly a full-time job. Staff have met with the superintendent, the school cabinet, the high school and middle school principals, and selected high school and middle school teachers. The logistics of scheduling the training of the high school student-athletes, the transportation of these athletes to middle schools, the health classes, the testing, and the assemblies can be overwhelming. The time involved in these logistics is above and beyond developing the interventions and survey and scoring the student surveys.

NEEDED COURSES AND PRACTICAL EXPERIENCES

When psychology graduate students are being prepared in scientist-practitioner clinical and/or counseling graduate programs, they enroll in content-based courses in psychology, courses designed to disseminate information about the practice of psychology, and practica. A major focus of these programs is to integrate practice with theory and research as early in the student's career as possible. Such an approach is relevant to applied developmental psychologists as well. The only distinction is that the definition of practice differs for clinical and counseling psychologists as opposed to applied developmental psychologists.

In this section some of the necessary training experiences will be briefly described. Interested readers might also examine the Accreditation Handbook (American Psychological Association, 1986) and the proceedings of some of the many conferences held on graduate professional education by the American Psychological Association and its Divisions. It is not my suggestion that programs in applied developmental psychology delineate a required series of courses. On the contrary, I am opposed to identifying a sequence of required courses or experiences. I do, however, believe that an examination of the issues raised in these documents about professional education will be illuminating.

There are three general knowledge domains that students must understand: development and the contexts in which development occurs; measurement and evaluation methodology; and intervention methodology. If one is working to enhance optimal development or prevent dysfunctional development, it is essential to understand development. By development I am referring to a life-span human developmental framework. Such an understanding would include a knowledge of developmental processes, the procedures necessary to assess both the level of development and changes in development, and how different societal levels of influence (contexts) impact on development. These contexts would include groups such as families, organizations and institutions, and communities. Thus, some of the unique knowledge components applied developmental psychologists must have are courses/experiences in life-span developmental psychology and community psychology.

A second knowledge component relates to measurement and evaluation methodology. Courses and/or experiences in measurement concepts including such techniques as needs assessment are critical. Furthermore, the strategies and methods needed to evaluate community interventions are significantly different than those used for more "typical" developmental studies and must be taught. Some of these differences have been described earlier in this chapter; others are considered by Price and Smith (1985) and other evaluation methodologists.

The third knowledge component is intervention methodology. Methods related to developing educational technology, consultation, supervision, training, and program development will be necessary. As such the applied developmental psychologist could be considered a provider of indirect rather than direct service as is the clinician.

While these three knowledge domains are necessary they are insufficient. Knowing the procedures involved in intervening is different than having the skills to intervene effectively. When learning skills is required, practicum courses must be developed to ensure that students learn *how to* develop the skills of designing, implementing, and evaluating an intervention. An integral part of a practica is the supervision and feedback by an experienced mentor. Just as faculty serve as research supervisors in theses and dissertations they must provide supervision on practicum performance.

The development of such courses and experiences will likely add to the time necessary to complete a graduate degree. It will also add to the courses which an institution training applied developmental psychologists will need to offer. Consequently, an expense is involved. However, without such courses and experiences, students are violating one of the most basic ethical principles: The maintenance of high standards of competence which enable the psychologist to promote and protect the welfare of individuals.

SUMMARY

Throughout the process of developing, implementing, and evaluating an intervention there are many value-laden decisions that the intervener must make. Some of these have significant ethical implications. While I have touched on some of these, my focus in this chapter has been different. I have sought to identify what is involved in an intervention activity. Whether it is as comprehensive as the *Athletes Coaching Teens* project or is more circumscribed, the knowledge and skills necessary to undertake such a task are extensive. A thorough knowledge of developmental psychology is necessary but clearly not sufficient. Training and practice in program development and design, in evaluation and methods, and in community intervention is required. Without such training, one must question whether it is ethical to conduct interventions. From my perspective it is not.

One of the pressing problems faced by programs in applied developmental psychology is to ensure that faculty exist who have experience in the conduct of interventions and who can serve as mentors for students interested in such experiences. Coursework and practica experiences must be available as well.

REFERENCES

American Psychological Association. (Revised, 1986). *Accreditation Handbook*. Washington, DC.
Baltes, P.B., & Danish, S.J. (1980). Intervention in life-span development and aging: Issues and concepts. In R.R. Turner & H.W. Reese (Eds.), *Life-span developmental psychology: Intervention*. New York: Academic Press.
Baltes, P.B., Reese, H.W., & Lipsitt, L.P. (1980). Life-span developmental psychology. *Annual Review of Psychology, 31*, 65–110.
Baltes, P.B., & Willis, S.L. (1977). Toward psychological theories of aging and development. In J.E. Birren & K.W. Schaie (Eds.), *Handbook of the psychology of aging*. New York: Reinhold-Van Nostrand.
Baumrind, D. (1987). A developmental perspective on adolescent risk-taking behavior in contemporary America. *New Directions for Child Development: Adolescent Health and Social Behavior, 37*, 93–126.
Botvin, G.J. (1986). Substance abuse prevention research: Recent developments and future directions. *Journal of School Health, 56*, 369–374.
Botvin, G.J. & Willis, T. (1985). *Deterring drug abuse among children and adolescents*. National Institute on Drug Abuse Prevention Monograph Series, Prevention Research, U.S. Govt. Printing Office.
Boys Clubs of America. (1988). *SMART Moves*. New York.
Caplan, G. (1964). *Principles of preventive psychiatry*. New York: Basic Books.
Danish, S.J. (1980). Considering professional licensing from a social and historical context. *The Counseling Psychologist, 9*, 35–38.
Danish, S.J. (1988). A crisis is a turning point. *Journal of Rural Community Psychology, 9*, 23–26.
Danish, S.J., & Conter, K.R. (1978). Intervention and evaluation: Two sides of the same community coin. In L. Goldman (Ed.), *Research methods for counselors*. New York: Wiley.
Danish, S.J., D'Augelli, A.R. & Ginsberg, M.R. (1984). Life development intervention: Promotion of mental health through the development of competence. In S.D. Brown & R.W. Lent (Eds.), *Handbook of counseling psychology* (pp. 520–544). New York: Wiley.
Danish, S.J., & Smyer, M.A. (1981). The unintended consequences of requiring a license to help. *American Psychologist, 36*, 13–21.
Danish, S.J., Smyer, M., & Nowak, C. (1980). Developmental intervention: Enhancing life-event processes. In P.B. Baltes & O.G. Brim, Jr. (Eds.), *Life-span development and behavior* (Vol. 3). New York: Academic Press.
Donovan, J.E., & Jessor, R. (1983). Problem drinking and the dimension of involvement with drugs: A Guttman scalogram analysis of adolescent drug use. *American Journal of Public Health, 73*, 543–552.
Gage, N.L. (Ed.). (1963). *Handbook of research on teaching*. Chicago: Rand McNally.
Gagne, R. (1970). *The conditions of learning*. New York: Hold, Rinehart and Winston.
Hamburg, B., Braemer, H., & Jahnke, W. (1975). Hierarchy of drug use in adolescence: Behavioral and attitudinal correlates of substantial drug use. *American Journal of Psychiatry, 132*, 1155–1167.
Health Behavior Research Institute. (1986). *Project SMART: A social approach to drug abuse prevention*. University of Southern California.

Howard, A., Pion, G., Gottfredson, G., Flattau, P.E., Oskamp, S., Pfafflin, S., Bray, D., & Burstein, A. (1986). The changing face of American Psychology. *American Psychologist, 41*, 1311–1327.

Jessor, R. (1982). Critical issues in research on adolescent health promotion. In T.J. Coates, A.C. Petersen, & C. Perry (Eds.), *Promoting adolescent health: A dialog on research and practice* (pp. 447–465). Academic Press: New York.

Johnston, L. & O'Malley, P. (1986). Why do the nation's students use drugs and alcohol: Self-reported reasons from nine national surveys. *Journal of Drug Issues, 16*, 29–66.

Johnston, L., O'Malley, P., & Bachman, J. (1987). *National trends in drug use and related factors among American high school students and young adults, 1975–1986*. Rockville, MD: National Institute on Drug Abuse.

Kandel, D., Davies, M., Karus, D., & Yamaguchi, K. (1986). The consequences in young adulthood of adolescent drug involvement. *Archives of General Psychiatry, 43*, 746–754.

Kelman, H.C. (1958). Compliance, identification, and internalization: Three processes of opinion change. *Journal of Conflict Resolution, 2*, 51–60.

Long, T.J., & Long, L. (1983). *The handbook for latchkey children and their parents*. New York: Arbor House.

McCaul, K.D., & Glasgow, R.E. (1985). Preventing adolescent smoking: Have we learned about treatment construct validity? *Health Psychology, 4*, 361–387.

Meyer, M. (1988). Implications for assessment: Characteristics of rural families in crisis. *Journal of Rural Community Psychology, 9*, 12–15.

Newcomb, M., Bentler, P., & Collins, C. (1986). Alcohol use and dissatisfaction with self and life: A longitudinal analysis of young adults. *Journal of Drug Issues, 16*, 479–494.

Office for Substance Abuse Prevention, Alcohol, Drug Abuse, and Mental Health Administration. (1987). *Prevention: From knowledge to action*. Washington, DC: U.S. Government Printing Office.

Paulsen, Jane. (1988). Crisis, culture, and response. *Journal of Rural Community Psychology, 9*, 5–11.

Paulsen, Julie. (1988). A service response to a culture in crisis. *Journal of Rural Community Psychology, 9*, 16–22.

Perry, C.L., & Jessor, R. (1985). The concept of health promotion and the prevention of adolescent drug abuse. *Health Education Quarterly, 12*, 169–184.

Pion, G.M., & Lipsey, M.W. (1984). Psychology and society: the challenge of change. *American Psychologist, 39*, 739–754.

Price, R., & Smith, S.S. (1985). A guide to evaluating prevention programs in mental health. *Monograph of the National Institute of Mental Health, 6* (DHHS Publication No. ADM 85-1365). Washington, DC: U.S. Government Printing Office.

Rappaport, J. (1981). In praise of paradox: A social policy empowerment over prevention. *American Journal of Community Psychology, 9*, 1–26.

Rappaport, J. (1977). *Community psychology: Values, research, and action*. Chicago: Holt, Rinehart and Winston.

Rodman, H., Pratto, D., & Nelson, R. (1985). Child care arrangements and children's functioning: A comparison of self-care and adult-care children. *Developmental Psychology, 21*, 413–418.

Ryan, W. (1971). *Blaming the victim*. New York: Random House.

Scriven, M. (1972). The methodology of evaluation. In C.H. Weiss (Ed.), *Evaluating action programs: Readings in social action and education*. Boston: Allyn and Bacon.

Sternberg, L. (1986). Latchkey children and susceptibility to peer pressure: An ecological analysis. *Developmental Psychology, 22*, 433–439.

Vandell, D. & Corasaniti, M.A. (1988). The relation between third graders' after-school care and social, academic, and emotional functioning. *Child Development, 59*, 868–875.

Watzlawick, P., Weakland, J.H., & Fisch, R. (1974). *Change: Principles of problem formation and problem resolution*. New York: Norton.

Whiteley, J. (1980). *The history of counseling psychology*. Beverly Hills, CA: Sage.

Youth Services Commission. (1982). Unpublished report.

8 Plasticity in Development: Ethical Implications for Developmental Interventions*

Richard M. Lerner
Jonathan G. Tubman

All social and behavioral scientists are socialized to conduct their research and practice within the frame of the set of ethical standards extant at a given moment in history. This is certainly the case in the fields of human development and developmental psychology, wherein the key professional organizations (e.g., SRCD and Division 7 of APA, respectively) provide a codified set of ethical principles. The presence of these ethical rules seems to function as an appropriate constraint on the potential variability of research procedures applied to the people studied in social and behavioral science research. Exceptions, of course, occur, but usually only under perverse and (fortunately) rare historical conditions (e.g., as in the case of Konrad Lorenz, 1940, writing in support of genocide in the context of National Socialist German rule).

Typically, the ethical standards of a discipline function as templates applied to a set of procedures in order to evaluate whether their use entails greater human and/or societal benefits than human and/or societal risks and costs. Although these ethical evaluations may be, in many ways, integral components of the actual practice of a given discipline, they are not necessarily seen as a core component of the discipline's research agenda. However, in one instance of human development/developmental psychology, ethical evaluations do play such a substantive role in the research enterprise: In research associated with a developmental contextual model of development (Lerner, 1986; Lerner & Kauffman, 1985), for example, in the research associated with the life-span view of human development (Baltes, 1987; Lerner, 1984), ethics are a central part of the substantive issues a scientist considers in designing the procedures for his/her research. Because of the assumptions of developmental contextualism, research with humans is seen, in effect, to constitute an intervention into their lives. The act of studying people changes them in ways which would not have occurred had

* The preparation of this chapter was supported in part by a grant to Richard M. Lerner and Jacqueline V. Lerner from the W.T. Grant Foundation and by NIMH Grant MH3995. The authors thank Linda Burton, Laura E. Hess, Jacqueline V. Lerner, and Patty Mulkeen for their comments on a previous draft of this chapter.

they not been assessed (Riegel, 1975, 1976). Rather than being "alienated" from the targets of his or her research, the scientist and his or her procedures are part of a system of person-context relations involved in the production of human developmental change. Thus, issues pertinent to the ethics of intervention are always a substantive part of the research agenda of the developmental contextualist, and this is the case whether the investigator is conducting either "basic" research or intervention research, or whether he or she is implementing or evaluating an actual intervention program.

The purpose of this chapter is to explain the nature and the implications of the assumptions of developmental contextualism which lead to this view linking ethics and intervention to substantive issues of human development. Here, however, it may be useful to provide an overview of the essential features of the points to be developed in this chapter. The linkages among ethics, intervention, and the nature of human development derive from two assumptions within developmental contextualism. First, human development is reciprocally related to (i.e., "embedded within") changes in the biological and social contexts of life. Second, as a consequence of this embeddedness, there is a potential for *plasticity* across the entire course of the human life span, that is, for systematic alteration in the processes and products of human functioning (Lerner, 1984).

This focus on the potential for plasticity means that, beyond the description and the explanation of developmental change, developmental contextualism is concerned necessarily with the optimization of behavior (Baltes & Willis, 1977). This connection is central to understanding the substantive focus on ethics and intervention in developmental contextualism. To explain this connection we may note that reciprocal, or "dynamic" (Lerner, 1978), interactions among variables from multiple levels of analysis are believed within developmental contextualism to be the basis of human plasticity. These interactions provide conditions which may alter—at any point in ontogeny—the developmental trajectory. There is a virtual infinity of variables, from the multiple levels of analysis affecting human life, which may impact on the person. At the same time, however, the person is actively influencing this complex context. In other words, the person is a dynamically interacting level of analysis (i.e., the individual-psychological level, in Riegel's, 1975, 1976, terms). Thus, given these person-context interactions there is a rich and varied set of conditions which may be appraised in order to explain: (a) why a given person develops along a given developmental trajectory; (b) why interindividual differences in developmental trajectories appear to be the "rule" in ontogeny; and (c) why the ability to modify human functioning—either through altering actions of the context on the person and/or actions of the person on the context—seems virtually ubiquitous across the life span. The virtual ubiquity of this modification ability is the point wherein ethical and intervention issues enter into the substantive concerns of the developmentally contextually oriented researcher.

As we shall argue in more detail below, the ability to modify the course of life leads one to be optimistic about the potential for interventions to be effective at any point in ontogeny. On the other hand, since developmental contextualism stresses that people remain open to influence across their lives, that is, there exists a potential for plasticity across life, one must be cautious about one's interventions into the life course. Changes produced by interventions at one point in ontogeny may be expected to be only temporary, since the person continues to dynamically interact with his/her context. In addition, changes can be for the worse, either in the immediate period within which they are introduced and/or at a later developmental period. Thus, developmental contextualists must couple their study of modification with a concern for values—for example, "What constitutes a desirable change?"—and therefore with explicit statements about what makes a given intervention, both concurrently and in the future, an optimization of the person's possible developmental course.

In essence, then, a developmental contextual perspective raises issues of ethical practice that other developmental approaches may not as readily bring to the fore. First, this perspective raises the issue of person-context dynamic interactions, and hence of the reciprocal embeddedness of people in a complex, multilevel context. Second, this perspective stresses the importance of the individual as a producer of his or her own development. Third, the potential for plasticity across life is emphasized. Last, the temporality (and therefore the immediate and the long-term efficacy) of any intervention endeavor is an issue of central concern.

As we have noted, the potential for plasticity is central in depicting the ethical implications of developmental contextualism for interventions into the human life course. As such, it is useful to discuss this concept in detail.

PLASTICITY: BASES AND IMPLICATIONS

A developmental contextual perspective emphasizes that the potential for change exists across life as a consequence of active people reciprocally interacting in a changing world. As a consequence, the life course is always characterized by the potential for *plasticity,* that is, by the potential for systematic changes within the person in his or her structure and/or function (Lerner, 1984). While not denying that constancies and continuities can, and do, characterize much of many peoples' life courses, and that plasticity is therefore not limitless, proponents of developmental contextualism (Lerner, 1986; Lerner & Kauffman, 1985) hold that any particular features of life are not the only ones which may occur. Rather, interindividual differences, and not normative developmental functions (Wohlwill, 1973), are emphasized. In short, proponents of developmental contextualism contend that change and the potential for change characterize life because of the plasticity of the processes involved in people's lives. From the level of biology to that of culture, these processes are presumed to be changeable—on the basis of both their inherent character (e.g., could a life process be adaptive if it were not capable of change?) and their reciprocal relations (their embeddedness) with other processes.

The existence of such plasticity is not a point of minor practical significance. If all levels of analysis are available to be changed, then, as we have said, there is great reason to be optimistic about the ability of intervention programs to enhance human development. On the other hand, we have noted that there is great reason to be cautious and wary: A system open to change for the better is also open to change for the worse. Indeed, it is the double-edged nature of this plasticity—of this openness to change—in person-context relations which makes ethical considerations an inherent component of research and intervention associated with developmental contextualism. The character of this inherent link between ethical concerns and research/intervention is highlighted by a consideration of the nature and implications of the two key ideas upon which developmental contextualism is based: embeddedness and dynamic interactionism (Lerner, 1978).

Embeddedness and Dynamic Interactionism

The idea of embeddedness is that key phenomena of human life exist at multiple levels of being (e.g., the inner-biological, individual-psychological, social network, community, sociocultural, physical-ecological, and historical). At any one point in time variables and processes from any and all of these multiple levels may contribute to human functioning. Moreover, these levels do not function in parallel, as independent domains; rather, variables and processes at all levels are *reciprocally* influential: That is, there is a *dynamic interaction* among levels. An illustration of the integrated levels of analysis (Schneirla, 1957; Tobach & Greenberg, 1984) which comprise the person-context relation within a developmental contextual perspective is presented in Figure 8.1. Depicted here are intraindividual interrelations for a child and his/her parent, and bidirectional interindividual relations between them. Moreover, this dyad is enmeshed reciprocally in interlevel relationships with various networks (in which there exists as well intralevel interactions) and components of the broader, community and sociocultural contexts. Finally, all entities within this embedded, dynamically interactive system are changing across time (i.e., historically). Therefore, a change (e.g., as induced by an intervention) associated with one level of analysis will influence and be influenced by variables at other levels of analysis. Accordingly, and in particular regard to interventions, this dynamic interaction among the levels of analysis involved in change requires a broad (multilevel) contextualization of developmental assessment and evaluation.

An illustration of the view of developmental processes promoted by developmental contextualism may be seen in Gollin's (1981) statement that:

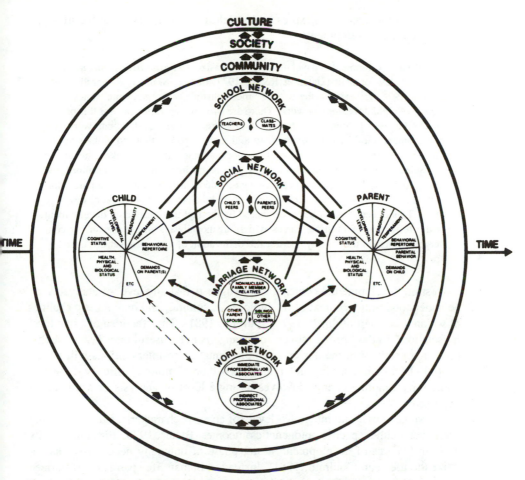

Figure 8.1. **A developmental contextual model of development (from Lerner, 1984, 1986).**

the relationships between organisms and environments are not interactionist, as interaction implies that organism and environment are separate entities that come together at an interface. Organism and environment constitute a single life process. . . For analytic convenience, we may treat various aspects of a living system and various external environmental and biological features as independently definable properties. Analytical excursions are an essential aspect of scientific inquiry, but they are hazardous if they are primarily reductive. An account of the *collective behavior* of the parts as an organized entity is a necessary complement to a reductive analytic program, and serves to restore the information content lost in the course of the reductive excursion. . . In any event, the relationships that contain the sources of change are those between organized systems and environments, not between heredity and environment. (Gollin, 1981, pp. 231–232)

A similar view has been expressed by Baltes (1979) in regard to the life-span view of human development:

> Life-span developmental psychologists emphasize *contextualistic-dialectic* paradigms of development (Datan & Reese, 1977; Lerner, Skinner, & Sorell, 1980; Riegel, 1976) rather than the use of "mechanistic" or "organismic" ones more typical of child development work. There are two primary rationales for this preference. One is, of course, evident also in current child development work. As development unfolds, it becomes more and more apparent that individuals act on the environment and produce novel behavior outcomes, thereby making the active and selective nature of human beings of paramount importance. Furthermore, the recognition of the interplay between age-graded, history-graded, and non-normative life events suggests a contextualistic and dialectical conception of development. This dialectic is further accentuated by the fact that individual development is the reflection of multiple forces which are not always in synergism, or convergence, nor do they always permit the delineation of a specific set of endstates. (p. 2)

In sum, developmental contextualism suggests that any level of analysis may be understood in the context of the biological, cultural, and ontogenetic changes of which it is a part (Tobach, 1978; Toulmin, 1981). Thus the idea of "one level in isolation" as the "prime mover" of change is not a useful one. Use of such a limited conception in the design or implementation of interventions will not be fruitful. That is, in our view, interventions will be of minimal efficacy if the sole focus for promoting change involves a single level of analysis or a univariate approach.

If change at multiple integrated levels of analysis characterizes the human life span, then neither specific ontogenetic outcomes (Baltes, 1979, 1987) nor totally uniform features of development at any phase of ontogeny necessarily characterize the life span (Toulmin, 1981). Instead, a human life span is characterized by the potential for individual flexibility as a consequence of multilevel, embedded plastic processes (Maier & Schneirla, 1935; Schneirla, 1957; Tobach & Schneirla, 1968), and human lives may differ in the incidence of flexibility because of interindividual differences in the functioning of plastic processes.

In short, then, dynamic interactions among multiple, embedded levels of analysis provide a basis for human plasticity. It is useful to note explicitly some of the key implications of the ideas of embeddedness and dynamic interaction.

Implications of Embeddedness and Dynamic Interaction

To briefly recapitulate the import of the two key ideas within developmental contextualism, let us note that the ideas of embeddedness and dynamic interactionism together mean that, first, individual developmental phenomena occur in the context of the developmental and nondevelopmental change phenomena of other levels of analysis; and second, that developments or changes on one level influence, and are influenced by, developments or changes at these other levels. There are at least three major implications of the ideas of embeddedness and dynamic interactionism. Although these implications have been suggested above, it is useful—for purposes of expansion—to discuss them in more detail here.

The potential for plasticity across life. The idea that changes at one level are reciprocally dependent on changes at other levels suggests that there is always some *possibility* for altering across life the status of a variable or process at any given level of analysis. The key concept here is *"potential for change."* Simply put, the character of the interaction among levels of analysis means that there is a potential to change the functioning, or at least the functional significance, of any target level (or target variable)—and indeed of the system of interlevel relations itself.

For example, medical research may some day uncover means to alter the motor functioning of a child with cerebral palsy (CP). Even if these means should not be found in the near future, however, a developmental contextual perspective would suggest that one may still alter the functional significance of CP for the child; for example, the child's self esteem and/or motivation may be altered and/or the perceptions or attitudes of the child's caregivers towards the disability may be changed (and, in fact, this latter change may be a basis for altering the child's self-esteem, etc.).

However, the potential for plasticity should not be construed to mean that there are no limits on change. By virtue of its structural organization a system delimits the range of changes it may undergo (Brent, 1984). Such a structural constraint holds for any level of analysis. For example, the prior developmental organization of a system constrains the potential of a later influence to effect a change in the system as easily as would have been the case if that same influence acted earlier in development (Lerner, 1978, 1979; Schneirla, 1957).

In this view, then, attempts to change behavior considered functionally deleterious to the individual may be bounded by previous patterns of behavior. Moreover, interventions aimed at changing behavior through attempting only to alter a single variable/level of analysis (e.g., and individual's motivation) will, in our view, have less of a chance of success than will a multivariate/multilevel approach. For instance, approaches to stopping substance abuse, decreasing the chances of exposure to sexually transmitted diseases, or curbing the incidence of eating disorders via interventions aimed only at the individual (e.g., in programs appealing to sexual abstinence or in attempts to have youth "just say no" to drugs) may have less probability of being effective than would be the case if they were coupled with interventions aimed at altering educational curricula, child rearing techniques, social policy, governmental funding priorities, and public attitudes.

That phenomena at one point in life may influence later functioning is summarized by life-span developmentalists in the concept of *developmental embedded-ness* (Parke, R.D., personal communication, December, 1982). Life-span devel-opmentalists emphasize that one must consider not only the changes across life but the constancies as well. Indeed, a key issue within the life-span perspective is to understand the relation between processes that serve to promote constancy and those that serve to promote change (Baltes, 1979; Brim & Kagan, 1980; Lerner, 1984). That is, life-span developmental psychology and the developmental con-textual perspective with which it is associated are concerned with understanding the developmental syntheses between continuous and discontinuous processes (Lerner, 1978, 1988; Lerner & Tubman, 1989).

However, despite the acknowledgment of limits and constraints on change and the emphasis on the concept of developmental embeddedness, life-span develop-mental psychology—as a key instance of a developmental contextual point of view—holds to the position that a potential for plasticity means, in effect, that human development systems are never necessarily completely limited or con-strained (Brim & Kagan, 1980). Instead, and as a consequence of the dynamic interaction among multiple integrated levels, means may be found to reorganize or restructure the system (Lerner, 1984)—given, of course, that there exists an adequate theoretical understanding of the processes that are involved in the functioning of the system.

The person as a producer of his/her own development. Within the devel-opmental contextual perspective it is possible to view variables from any level of analysis as an influence on variables from other levels (see Figure 8.1). For the individual-psychological level of analysis, this means that a person may affect any other level of the context that affects him or her, in essence providing feedback to himself or herself. In other words, the individual helps produce his or her own development (Lerner, 1982; Lerner & Busch-Rossnagel, 1981; Scarr & McCartney, 1983). This influence may occur by the individual constituting a distinct stimulus to others (e.g., through characteristics of physical and/or behav-ioral individuality), through his/her capabilities as a processor of the world (e.g., in regard to cognitive structure and mode of emotional reactivity), through active behavioral agency (Bakan, 1966; Block, 1973), and through—the most flexible means—by behaviorally shaping or selecting his or her contexts (Kendall, Lerner, & Craighead, 1984; Mischel, 1977; Snyder, 1981). The emphasis on the individual as a producer of his or her own development leads to a focus on processes of self-regulation, control, and self-efficacy (Baltes & Baltes, 1986). Therefore, the role of the active, individually distinct person, and of interin-dividual differences in the appropriateness of a given intervention for effecting change, must be included in the deliberations involved in the design and imple-mentation of interventions.

The potential for intervention. The potential for plasticity implies that means may be found to prevent, ameliorate, or enhance undesired or nonvalued developments or behaviors. Given the multiple integrated levels involved in plasticity, however, a search for such means should be multidisciplinary in scope

(Baltes & Danish, 1980; Lerner, 1984). Interventions which include only one source of influence (i.e., univariate/unilevel interventions) are more likely to provide only short-lived benefits and to produce relatively little change due to a lack of attention to altering concurrently relevant variables from other levels of analysis. In addition, the idea of developmental embeddedness suggests that one may take a historical approach to intervention, and for instance devise long-term preventative strategies (Lerner & Ryff, 1978). However, individual ontogeny is not the only aspect of history that may be considered here. One should appreciate also features of intergenerational transmission (e.g., see Bengtson & Troll, 1978).

For instance, one may envision the possibility of intervention with future parents to prevent undesired outcomes in yet-to-be-conceived offspring. An example is the possibility of changing the type of birth control precautions of sexually active young adolescents in order to prevent the conception and birth of a child consequently at risk for several health problems as a consequence of being born to a young adolescent mother. (See Chapter 2 for discussion of potential hazards of current approaches to sex education.) Alternatively, in some cases it may be more effective to direct interventions at targets other than the source of the "problem" behavior per se. For instance, rather than trying to alter the behavior of an Alzheimer's disease patient it may be more efficacious to attempt to alter a caregiver's skills in aiding the patient and/or the caregiver's social support system. Moreover, and seen in the context of a broad historical approach to intervention, it may be useful to try to alter social policies in the direction of enabling adult children to obtain the educational background and the financial resources needed to provide this skilled care to their aged parents.

Finally, the view that there is a potential for plasticity across life does not mean that one should ignore or not invest in treating problems in early life. Rather, we should keep in mind there are always constraints on change and that plasticity is not equipotential across life. That is, while plasticity may be considered ubiquitous, its potential for actualization operates within an increasingly narrower range of structures and functions with time (Baltes, 1987; Baltes & Baltes, 1980; Clarke & Clarke, 1976; Greenough & Green, 1981). Thus, interventions may be more appropriate early in life, when the system is being organized and there may be fewer constraints on its ability to change (Brent, 1984). Nevertheless, even if early intervention is not possible, according to the developmental contextual perspective there may still be means, albeit more difficult ones, to effect desired change.

For example, although means may be found across life to decrease or even eliminate the habit of cigarette smoking, interventions later in life—after a longer history of smoking—may require a greater expenditure of time and a more intricate involvement of the person's social context. For instance, greater coordination with family and peer support groups may be needed, and consultation with medical personnel may be necessary if the habit has resulted in physical diseases.

In addition, we should *not* expect that a single intervention, even early in life, will have an enduring influence on the person. Since the person retains some degree of plasticity across life, events subsequent to an initial intervention can alter the trajectory of development (Sigman, 1982). In turn, however, repeatedly applied preventive measures may produce enduring, desired outcomes; examples are lifelong dietary or exercise regimens.

Thus, interventions, and assessments of them, ideally should be longitudinal in character. We cannot be certain, therefore, from a single interaction with a person or appraisal of an intervention that we have permanently altered the life course for the good. As noted earlier, the relative plasticity of the person across life means that he or she may change for the worse. Thus, in projecting and/or evaluating the risk-benefit ratios of particular research treatments or intervention procedures, it is ethically incumbent upon the applied developmental psychologist to (a) take a long-term, change-oriented perspective, one which is sensitive both to person and context variables, and (b) to be familiar with the multiple processes believed to be involved in the behavior targeted for intervention.

Components of a Change-Oriented Perspective

What are the dimensions of change which need to be considered as a consequence of the embeddedness of person-context relations? In our view, there are at least four:

The intraindividual—interindividual. Within this dimension changes involve, on the one hand, within-person biological, psychological, and behavioral alterations *versus,* on the other hand, changes involving between-person social (dyadic) exchanges as, for instance, occur in child–parent relations. Although this dimension typically is studied through use of individual-psychological units of analysis, in a sense—given that the continuum includes both individual and dyadic changes—it is not discontinuous with the next dimension.

The intralevel—multilevel dimension. Changes involve variations over time which occur only within a level of analysis (e.g., between one social network and another) *versus* changes involving variables from two or more levels of analysis (e.g., between a social network and an individual). When multilevel changes occur, or in other words when interactions take place among variables from different levels of analysis, an important conceptual issue is raised pertinent to the measurement of change. Lerner, Skinner, and Sorell (1980) have discussed this issue under the phrase "non-equivalent temporal metric:" The appropriate temporal unit of analysis (i.e., the divisions one makes along one's "X" axis, one's time axis in developmental research) to detect change is not the same at different levels of analysis. Changes at the individual-psychological level of analysis may be detected by temporal divisions as small as a day or week (e.g., for some neonatal or infant neuromuscular, bioemotional, or bioregulatory variables) or as large as a year. However, divisions by decades usually are considered too gross to detect change: Too many important changes would fall "between the cracks," that is, between the X-axis divisions. However, to detect change at the sociocultural level, decade divisions may be the smallest ones appropriate for use. For instance, we could not expect a sociocultural change in social policies— for example, regarding nutritional programs for mothers and infants (see Chapter 6)—to have a detectable effect on the health and development of individuals or groups within a week, a month, or perhaps even a year.

Consideration of the nonequivalent temporal metric has implications for ethical practice regarding the evaluation of social programs are concerned. One must not evaluate the utility of a program introduced at one level of analysis in the context of the temporal metric appropriate at another level.

Jensen's (1969) review of compensatory education programs (e.g., Head Start) is perhaps the classic example of the failure to appreciate the issue of the nonequivalent temporal metric. Head Start, introduced in 1965, could not realistically have been expected to change intellectual and educational achievement outcomes by the time of Jensen's (1969) review. Such outcomes are embedded reciprocally in a system of multilevel relationships—involving intraindividual variables (e.g., motivation, self-esteem), social network variables (e.g., familial, and especially parental, attitudes toward educational achievement), community variables (e.g., regarding the physical characteristics of, and economic support, for schools), and sociocultural variables (e.g., regarding previous social policies, laws and statutes, and pejorative social stereotypes)—*all of which had been occurring for hundreds of years* (cf. Sarason, 1973). To have expected that change in such embedded outcome variables could have been detected after only a few years was either naive, or simply silly, at best, and was unfair, prejudicial, and socially mischievous, at worst. In short, a key concern for the applied developmental psychologist is deciding on the levels of analysis most appropriate for a given intervention. In some cases involvement of quite temporally extensive—historical—levels may be virtually mandatory.

The proximal—distal dimension. From a developmental contextual perspective any target variable is embedded in a system of changes akin to that depicted in Figure 8.1. Nevertheless, it is useful to organize one's analysis of this system of changes on the basis of those which occur in closer proximity to, versus more distally from, the target change. Such organization facilitates understanding of the extant and possible sources of influence on the target change *and* the possible routes of influence these sources may take.

Proximal influences have more direct or immediate effects on a target, but there are fewer routes (paths) through which these influences may travel. For instance, within an intact family with one child, a father may influence a child either directly or through his spouse. More distal influences are more indirect and less immediate, but they may affect the target through a large, and indeed in some cases perhaps an infinite, array of pathways.

These differences between proximal and distal influences have import both for planning interventions or research treatments *and* for evaluating the risks and benefits of such procedures. One must have theoretical and empirical understanding of a process, as well as of course practical experience with it, in order to be in the best position to design and implement effective interventions. One's plans and assessments must survey, or better model, both direct and indirect pathways of influence and, as well, influences which range in time from those which occur almost simultaneously with a target change versus those for which there must be some temporal delay in influence (e.g., "sleeper effects" in longitudinal studies are in this class of influences; Kagan & Moss, 1962). The inclusion of a temporal perspective in the proximal-distal dimension gives this continuum commonality with the last change dimension we shall note.

The temporally concurrent—historical dimension. Developmental contextualism is a perspective for understanding person-context developmental changes (Lerner, 1986; Lerner & Kauffman, 1985). As such, change is a dimension which is ubiquitous, which pervades all others. Analogous to the proximal-distal dimension, the temporally concurrent-historical dimension allows one to organize what are ubiquitous changes into: (a) more versus less immediate ones, and (b) short- versus long-term ones. Interventions or research treatments may be introduced to effect target changes either in the immediate developmental period of an individual and/or at a subsequent time in life. Indeed, as we have noted, one may intervene with people of one generation in order to influence the development of a subsequent generation. Recall, for instance, our example of the possibility of giving sexually active early adolescent females birth control information in order to prevent births of infants who might be at risk because of variables related to maternal age.

Similarly, the changes to be realized as a consequence of interventions or research treatments may be either immediate or long-term. For instance, one may intervene to influence contemporaneous performance in a particular high school course, or one may intervene to affect enduring values and attitudes regarding the importance of education in one's life. In turn, assessments of the outcomes or risk-benefit ratios of one's interventions or research treatments need to include appraisals of both immediate and/or short-term *and* delayed and/or long-term changes.

In sum, consideration of the above four dimensions indicates the complexity of the change perspective associated with a developmental contextual perspective. Together, these dimensions indicate that the assessment tasks required of an intervenor or researcher attempting to appraise the outcomes and/or risks and benefits of his/her work are similarly complex. Finally, the combination of the changes involved along these four dimensions underscores the basis of the developmental contextual view that *change is inevitable*.

Of course, not all changes may actually matter for the functional quality of a given target variable. That is, some changes may be beneath a "just noticeable difference" (j.n.d.). However, this point begs the question of whether change occurs. In fact, the ubiquity of change alters the scientific issue from one of deciding whether change is or is not present to one of determining whether change is or is not functionally significant for a given outcome variable.

The inevitability of change has ethical implications. The inevitability means that any intervention or research procedure—any interaction with the people whom one is studying—*may* constitute a sufficient condition altering the direction of development. However, not interacting may also alter development. As we have indicated previously, this situation arises because the researcher and his/her procedures are embedded *inextricably* in the same system of person-context relations as are the people he/she studies. In other words, developmentalists are part of the object of their own study (and therefore, from a developmental contextual perspective, there is a subject-object synthesis; Riegel, 1975, 1976). It is inevitable, then, that dynamic interactions will occur between developmentalists and those they study. Therefore, it is ethically incumbent on interventionists to be at least conversant with contemporary advances in research methodology and with the current theoretical and research literatures as well. Current issues of design, measurement, statistical analysis, and interpretation must be part of the interventionist's assessment and evaluation tools.

For instance, in regard to intervention per se, the ethical issue is *not* whether one should or should not intervene. Since both choices inevitably affect the behavior and development of others, failure to intervene is itself an intervention. It will keep the developmental trajectory on a course it otherwise may have been diverted from had one acted. The ethical issue is, then, "What are the relative costs and benefits of acting in one way (e.g., intervening) or another (e.g., not intervening)?"

But, how does one decide whether or not to act (since either course is, in fact, an intervention)? Since no one would argue that intervention should proceed without being ethical, one must decide therefore if one's action or inaction—or in the case of research, one's application of one or another particular research treatment (or experimental manipulation)—is more ethical.

ISSUES IN DECIDING ON THE ETHICS OF ONE'S RESEARCH PROCEDURES AND INTERVENTION STRATEGIES

The number and complexity of changes involved in the system of intra- and interlevel relations illustrated in Figure 8.1 means that while change is ubiquitous it is not fixed or certain in respect to norms. Instead, change is probabilistic (Gottlieb, 1970, 1983). Therefore, determination of the risks and benefits associated with a given intervention or research treatment also must be probabilistic. In short, probabilistic change means that there are *confidence intervals* surrounding any given developmental trajectory or any statement about the risks and benefits of an intervention or research treatment.

Here the concept of j.n.d. is again relevant. An example will help indicate why this is so. Any one genotype can give rise to an infinite array of phenotypes, depending on the similarly infinite array of environmental conditions with which that genotype may interact (Hirsch, 1970; McClearn, 1981). However, not all of these resulting phenotypes can be construed to be functionally different from each other. For instance, a final adult male body weight of 165 pounds may (in its functional significance for cardiovascular fitness, body image, or longevity) be less than a j.n.d. from a final adult male body weight of 166. However, an adult male body weight of 175 may be for some variables (e.g., body image) more than a j.n.d. different.

Thus, the determination of the confidence intervals surrounding a given target change is complicated by the necessity of considering how much of a difference matters—how much of the interval involves changes above or below a j.n.d. Moreover, there is a need to cast one's appraisal of "how much of a difference matters" in the context of specific target variables: "How much of a difference matters for a specific variable in which I am interested?" For some target variables the degree of change that is significant may be quite debatable. For instance, while a 10 pound difference in body weight (from 165 to 175 pounds) might affect the body image of a 40-year-old man bent on maintaining a youthful and healthy appearance, such a difference might be below a j.n.d. for the man's cardiovascular fitness or longevity.

Thus, risk-benefit ratios are not only probabilistic assessments. They are also assessments which, first, need to be partitioned into j.n.d. segments and, second, formulated in regard to specific outcome variables. How may such determinations be made?

First, one needs to consider and assess along the four dimensions of embeddedness noted above, a broad array of contextual and historical conditions in formulating one's risk-benefit ratio. Second, one needs to determine the conditions under which a given research treatment or intervention will or will not result in desired outcomes.

One needs to remember that more than one variable or target may be influenced by a treatment or an intervention. That is, any intervention or research treatment may radiate beyond a target variable or level of analysis (Lerner, 1984). In other words, there may be both indirect and unintended consequences of one's interventions or research treatments. Therefore, one must consider whether the amount of intervention resources required to affect a change in a target variable justifies the costs in terms of likely length of the change, unintended consequences, and time and money.

For instance, the 1982 review of 1,500 Head Start research and evaluation studies indicated that the program—as intended—*was* responsible for improvement in children's performance in school achievement tests, including gains in cognitive development (Lazar, Darlington, Murray, Royce, & Snipper, 1982). However, in illustration of the indirect and unintended (but, in this case, desirable) consequences which interventions may have, the program produced also a positive impact on child socialization, on the development of socially mature behaviors, and on the positive attitudes of parents toward their children. Furthermore, the program was associated with better nutritional practices and generally better health among participating children.

Of course, not all indirect or unintended consequences of an intervention or research treatment need be desirable. Certainly, what is or is not desirable depends on one's values, and therefore is ultimately a subjective appraisal. Nevertheless, our point is that within a developmental contextual perspective one needs to theoretically survey the potentially multilevel ramifications of one's interventions or research treatments, and formulate one's probabilistic risk—benefit assessments as a multilevel (and hence, multivariate) projection.

It is important to emphasize here a point noted earlier, in the context of our discussion of the concept of developmental embeddedness: In developmental contextualism, plasticity is not considered limitless. Any developmental phenomenon is a product of processes which both promote and constrain its change. Both contextual and/or biological conditions may delimit or constrain as well as promote change.

To illustrate, there is a growing technology in molecular biology which underscores the point that biological processes (e.g., genetic mechanisms) do not only constrain development; such processes also "liberate" development (e.g., see the literature on recombinant DNA technology and genetic engineering; Lerner, 1984). Thus, biological processes both enable and limit change.

In turn, social institutions similarly promote and constrain change. For instance, schools promote changes in academic skills, but do so within the context (and constraints) of particular curricular objectives and educational policies. Moreover, social policies and institutions which have an enduring historical character may act to support the "status quo" (Meyer, 1988; Sarason, 1973). Institutions have philosophical agendas which may constrain the targets of intervention, the levels of analysis involved in, and the methods appropriate for, a given intervention, as well as the funding levels probable for a given intervention target.

The presence, then, of *both* plasticity and constraints in development means that both sets of processes must be evaluated in: (a) planning one's research treatment or intervention; and (b) making risk-benefit assessments along the four dimensions of embeddedness noted above. Moreover, since social scientists are more familiar with, and skilled at, dealing with the individual and sociocultural levels of analysis, social institutions, programs, and policies should become *key* targets of evaluation in determining the processes which promote and constrain human development (see Brim & Phillips, 1988).

In this regard, we should note that policy is part of the "exosystem" of human ecology (Bronfenbrenner, 1979), part of the sociocultural level of analysis, depicted in Figure 8.1, which influences person-context relations through the creation and/or deployment of social programs and policies. The embeddedness of programs and policies within politics introduces an additional source of plasticity and constraints in development.

For instance, Steiner (1981) documents the inability of a federal administration to implement a coherent agenda of family-oriented policies due to the political pluralism of constituents. In a pluralistic democracy, where value systems among subgroups are not always congruent, attempts to intervene in human development through policy initiation may be thwarted by overarching considerations of a political nature.

This "policy-program-politics" interrelation is simply one more source of variation in evaluating the confidence intervals and risk—benefit ratios surrounding an intervention or research treatment. The presence of this interrelation underscores again the idea that developmentalists cannot separate themselves from the social (including political) realities of the world they study. If they do attempt such separation, then to paraphrase Eldridge Cleaver, they will not be part of the process but part of the problem.

SUMMARY AND CONCLUSIONS

Developmental contextualism emphasizes the dynamic interaction over time of individuals and the multiple contexts of life. The plasticity of the human developmental trajectory derives from this interaction. The existence of plasticity means that a potential exists across life for intervention. Several points must be attended to in order to insure that interventions are ethical.

The design and implementation of ethical interventions require a theoretical conception of the multiple processes involved in the multiple dimensions of developmental change. Such theoretical knowledge should guide the selection of research treatment conditions and intervention strategies. In addition, such knowledge should guide the assessments of the dimensions of embeddedness we have noted in this chapter, and thus guide as well the formulation of decisions about risk-benefit ratios. The investigator should also be able to determine the confidence intervals surrounding a given target change. Clearly, such knowledge needs to be sensitive to the multiple, integrated levels of human existence (Schneirla, 1957; Tobach & Greenberg, 1984) which comprise the domain of concern within developmental contextualism.

All these plans and evaluations must necessarily be multidisciplinary and probabilistic. The people and the world we study are similarly complex and probabilistic. The challenge before us is to design nonreductive approaches to our research and intervention efforts, and to accept that we are scientific, social, and political partners in the processes of human development we hope to understand and enhance.

REFERENCES

Bakan, D. (1966). *The duality of human existence*. Chicago: Rand McNally.

Baltes, M.M., & Baltes, P.B. (Eds.). (1986). *The psychology of control and aging*. Hillsdale, NJ: Erlbaum.

Baltes, P.B. (1979). Life-span developmental psychology: Some converging observations on history and theory. In P.B. Baltes & O.G. Brim, Jr. (Eds.), *Life-span development and behavior* (Vol. 2, pp. 256–281). New York: Academic Press.

Baltes, P.B. (1987). Theoretical propositions of life-span developmental psychology: On the dynamics between growth and decline. *Developmental Psychology, 23*, 611–626.

Baltes, P.B., & Baltes, M.M. (1980). Plasticity and variability in psychological aging: Methodological and theoretical issues. In G.E. Gurski (Ed.), *Determining the effects of aging on the central nervous system* (pp. 41–60). Berlin: Schering AG. (Oraniendruck).

Baltes, P.B., & Danish, S.J. (1980). Intervention in life-span development and aging: Issues and concepts. In R.R. Turner & H.W. Reese (Eds.), *Life-span developmental psychology: Interventions* (pp. 49–78). New York: Academic Press.

Baltes, P.B., & Willis, S.L. (1977). Toward psychological theories of aging and development. In J.E. Birren & K.W. Schaie (Eds.), *Handbook of the psychology of aging* (pp. 128–154). Belmont, CA: Wadsworth.

Bengtson, V.L., & Troll, L. (1978). Youths and their parents: Feedback and intergenerational influence in socialization. In R.M. Lerner & G.B. Spanier (Eds.), *Child influences on marital and family interaction: A life-span perspective* (pp. 215–240). New York: Academic Press.

Block, J.H. (1973). Conceptions of sex roles: Some cross-cultural and longitudinal perspectives. *American Psychologist, 28*, 512–526.

Brent, S.B. (1984). *Psychological and social structure: Their organization, activity, and development*. Hillsdale, NJ: Erlbaum.

Brim, O.G., Jr., & Kagan, J. (1980). Constancy and change: A view of the issues. In O.G. Brim, Jr. & J. Kagan (Eds.), *Constancy and change in human development* (pp. 1–25). Cambridge, MA: Harvard University Press.

Brim, O.G., Jr., & Phillips, D. (1988). The life-span intervention cube. In E.M. Hetherington, R.M. Lerner, & M. Perlmutter (Eds.), *Child development in life-span perspective* (pp. 277–299). Hillsdale, NJ: Erlbaum.

Bronfenbrenner, U. (1979). *The ecology of human development*. Cambridge, MA: Harvard University press.

Clarke, A.M., & Clarke, A.D.B. (Eds.). (1976). *Early experience: Myth and evidence*. New York: Free Press.

Datan, N., & Reese, H.W. (1977). *Life-span developmental psychology: Dialectical perspectives on experimental psychology*. New York: Academic Press.

Gollin, E.S. (1981). Development and plasticity. In E.S. Gollin (Ed.), *Developmental plasticity: Behavioral and biological aspects of variations in development* (pp. 231–251). New York: Academic Press.

Gottlieb, G. (1970). Conceptions of prenatal behavior. In L.R. Aronson, E. Tobach, D.S. Lehrman, & J.S. Rosenblatt (Eds.), *Development and evolution of behavior: Essays in memory of T.C. Schneirla* (pp. 111–137). San Francisco: Freeman.

Gottlieb, G. (1983). The psychobiological approach to developmental issues. In M.M. Haith & J.J. Campos (Eds.), *Handbook of child psychology: Infancy and biological bases* (4th ed., Vol. 2, pp. 1–26). New York: Wiley.

Greenough, W.T., & Green, E.J. (1981). Experience and the changing brain. In J.L. McGaugh, J.G. March, & S.B. Kiesler (Eds.), *Aging: Biology and behavior* (pp. 159–200). New York: Academic Press.

Hirsch, J. (1970). Behavior-genetic analysis and its biosocial consequences. *Seminars in Psychiatry, 2,* 89–105.

Jensen, A.R. (1969). How much can we boost IQ and scholastic achievement? *Harvard Educational Review, 39,* 1–123.

Kagan, J., & Moss, H. (1962). *Birth to maturity.* New York: Wiley.

Kendall, P.C., Lerner, R.M., & Craighead, W.E. (1984). Human development intervention in childhood psychopathology. *Child Development, 55,* 71–82.

Lazar, I., Darlington, R., Murray, H., Royce, J., & Snipper, A. (1982). Lasting effects of early education: A report from the consortium for longitudinal studies. *Monographs of the Society for Research in Child Development, 47* (Serial No. 195, Nos. 2–3).

Lerner, R.M. (1978). Nature, nurture and dynamic interactionism. *Human Development, 21,* 1–20.

Lerner, R.M. (1979). A dynamic interactional concept of individual and social relationship development. In R. Burgess & T. Huston (Eds.), *Social exchange in developing relationships* (pp. 271–305). New York: Academic Press.

Lerner, R.M. (1982). Children and adolescents as producers of their own development. *Developmental Review, 2,* 342–370.

Lerner, R.M. (1984). *On the nature of human plasticity.* New York: Cambridge University Press.

Lerner, R.M. (1986). *Concepts and theories of human development* (2nd ed.). New York: Random House.

Lerner, R.M. (1988). Personality development: A life-span perspective. In E.M. Hetherington, R.M. Lerner, & M. Perlmutter (Eds.), *Child development in life-span perspective* (pp. 21–46). Hillsdale, NJ: Erlbaum.

Lerner, R.M., & Busch-Rossnagel, N.A. (1981). *Individuals as producers of their development: A life-span perspective.* New York: Academic Press.

Lerner, R.M., & Kauffman, M.B. (1985). The concept of development in contextualism. *Developmental Review, 5,* 309–333.

Lerner, R.M., & Ryff, C.D. (1978). Implementation of the life-span view of human development: The sample case of attachment. In P.B. Baltes (Ed.), *Life-span development and behavior* (Vol. 1, pp. 1–44). New York: Academic Press.

Lerner, R.M., Skinner, E.A., & Sorell, G.T. (1980). Methodological implications of contextual/dialectic theories of development. *Human Development, 23,* 225–235.

Lerner, R.M., & Tubman, J. (1989). Conceptual issues in studying continuity and discontinuity in personality development across life. *Journal of Personality, 57,* 343–373.

Lorenz, K. (1940). Durch Domestikation verursachte Storungen arteigenen Verhaltens. *Zeitschrift fur angewandte Psychologie und Charakterkunde, 59,* 2–81.

Maier, N.R.F., & Schneirla, T.C. (1935). *Principles of animal behavior.* New York: McGraw-Hill.

McClearn, G.E. (1981). Evolution and genetic variability. In E.S. Gollin (Ed.), *Developmental plasticity: Behavioral and biological aspects of variations in development* (pp. 3–31). New York: Academic Press.

Meyer, J.W. (1988). The social construction of the psychology of childhood. In E.M. Hetherington, R.M. Lerner, & M. Perlmutter (Eds.), *Child development in life-span perspective* (pp. 47–65). Hillsdale, NJ: Erlbaum.

Mischel, W. (1977). On the future of personality measurement. *American Psychologist, 32,* 246–254.

Riegel, K.F. (1975). Toward a dialectical theory of development. *Human Development, 18,* 50–64.

Riegel, K.F. (1976a). The dialectics of human development. *American Psychologist, 31,* 689–700.

Sarason, S.B. (1973). Jewishness, Blackishness, and the nature-nurture controversy. *American Psychologist, 28,* 962–971.

Scarr, S., & McCartney, K. (1983). How people make their own environments: A theory of genotype-environment effects. *Child Development, 54,* 424–435.

Schneirla, T.C. (1957). The concept of development in comparative psychology. In D.B. Harris

(Ed.), *The concept of development* (pp. 78–108). Minneapolis: University of Minnesota Press.

Sigman, M. (1982). Plasticity in development: Implications for intervention. In L.A. Bond & J.M. Jaffe (Eds.), *Facilitating infant and early childhood development* (pp. 98–116). Hanover, NH: University Press of New England.

Snyder, M. (1981). On the influence of individuals on situations. In N. Cantor & J.F. Kihlstrom (Eds.), *Personality, cognition, and social interaction* (pp. 309–329). Hillsdale, NJ: Erlbaum.

Steiner, G.Y. (1981). *The futility of family policy.* Washington, D.C.: The Brookings Institute.

Tobach, E. (1978). The methodology of sociobiology from the viewpoint of a comparative psychologist. In A.L. Caplan (Ed.), *The sociobiology debate* (pp. 411–423). New York: Harper & Row.

Tobach, E., & Greenberg, G. (1984). The significance of T.C. Schneirla's contribution to the concept of levels of integration. In G. Greenberg & E. Tobach (Eds.), *Behavioral evolution and integrative levels* (pp. 1–7). Hillsdale, NJ: Erlbaum.

Tobach, E., & Schneirla, T.C. (1968). The biopsychology of social behavior of animals. In R.E. Cooke & S. Levin (Eds.), *Biologic basis of pediatric practice* (pp. 68–82). New York: McGraw-Hill.

Toulmin, S. (1981). Epistemology and developmental psychology. In E.S. Gollin (Ed.), *Developmental plasticity: Behavioral and biological aspects of variations in development* (pp. 253–267). New York: Academic Press.

Wohlwill, J.F. (1973). *The study of behavioral development.* New York: Academic Press.

9   Ethical Concerns for the Use of Research Findings in Applied Settings

Irving Sigel

Issues pertaining to ethics in social and behavioral science have been of long-standing concern. Works such as Diener and Crandall's volume *Ethics in Social and Behavioral Research* (1978) discuss ethics in relation to the psychologist's responsibility to participants and colleagues across selected research methodologies. Works such as Glenn's (1980) article "Ethical Issues in the Practice of Child Psychotherapy," focus on issues tied to treatment. All of these discussions distinguish between ethical issues associated with research and practice and thus do not refer specifically to questions that arise when one attempts to apply research knowledge in practical settings. The aim of this chapter is to raise issues which have ethical implications for the use of research findings in the field.

APPLYING DEVELOPMENTAL PSYCHOLOGY TO PRACTICAL PROBLEMS

Two questions have to be addressed at the outset: First, how and in which contexts is developmental research applied? Second, how are ethical questions relevant to these applications?

To identify the relevance of ethics for professionals engaged in applying developmental knowledge to practical problems requires a clear definition of these activities:

> Application of empirical knowledge to social problem-solving occurs in at least three ways. It happens when the practitioner develops a new perspective regarding a set of events as a result of some research. For example, reading a review of research on affect development, a teacher might gain new insight into children's affect. The effect may range from the teacher's attitudes toward children in general to curriculum innovations. A second type of application is a direct use of an idea in the service of a program. A dramatic example of this is Skinner's discovery of the effect of operant conditioning with pigeons which subsequently led to employment of operant procedures for treating a variety of human problems. A third type of application is the modification of a situation (or a practice or policy) based on discoveries from controlled experimental research. Application of this type has

appeared in the mental health movement, where it was found, for example, that bringing patients from "back" wards into dayroom social contacts with others tended to improve their mental status. While these three types of application are not exhaustive, they do represent ways that research knowledge is utilized for application. (Sigel & Cocking, 1980, p. ii)

Working with this concept of application, the potential for doing harm involves the implementation of an inappropriate application as a consequence of misinterpretation of developmental research or failure to evaluate the effects of the application (Sigel, 1983). The relevance of this exhortation for caution is tied to the fact that consumers of research are free agents to do as they wish with the results of research.[1] The only constraints utilizers of research findings have are their own professional standards. There are no monitoring agencies serving as watchdogs. A professional interested in applying research findings to a field situation will do so solely in terms of her own judgment. This is in contrast to the original investigator whose work is monitored in a number of ways: IRBs, journal reviewers (usually peers), and government agencies. In effect, *there are more guidelines relative to carrying out developmental research than there are for using the products of this research.*

Knowledge Generators and Knowledge Users

As indicated above, activities associated with applied developmental psychology are conducted by three categories of professionals: the knowledge generator (usually referred to as the basic scientist); the knowledge user (usually referred to as the practical or applied professional); and the professional who combines both roles (usually referred to as the scientist-practitioner). In this essay I would like to address ethical issues which arise when the application of developmental knowledge to real-world problems is the product of the independent activities of two different professional groups: the developmental scientist generating information and the practitioner (e.g., clinician[2] or educator) applying that information in a practical setting. If the goal of applied developmental research is to generate useful knowledge, then to succeed at his or her investigatory function the applied developmental psychologist must take into account the potential applications and misapplications of that knowledge by practitioners.[3] In the

---

[1] I use the term *consumer* to refer to everyone other than the original investigator, for example: service practitioners, journalists, and science writers. To be sure, scientists are consumers of research, but this is part of the ongoing process of scholarship and research. A discussion of how this is done is another issue and refers less to ethics than to quality of scholarship.

[2] Clinical is used in the broad sense of service settings, for example, psychotherapy, social case work, and the like. I distinguish it from educational settings in schools and universities.

[3] There are some journals which are particularly oriented to application, for example, *Journal of Developmental Psychology, Journal of Applied Developmental Psychology.*

remaining sections of this chapter I wish to focus on ethical concerns involving the types and bases of misuse of research by knowledge consumers.

MISUSE OF RESEARCH REPORTS

Research findings are available to practitioners in many forms, for example, professional journals, conferences, news media. Irrespective of the means of communication, the extent to which a practitioner can appropriately apply these findings to his or her particular area of responsibility will be limited by the quality of information provided. This raises ethical issues concerning the reporting of research results.

Responsibilities of the Knowledge Generator

Knowledge generators are expected to report their results in full, describe the limitations of their findings in terms of research issues, and report their research procedures in detail thereby providing the consumer with an adequate basis for interpretation, application, and replication of the study. Finally, researchers must not intentionally furnish misleading research information for personal gain.

The current controversy regarding the role of scientists in the tobacco industry provides an example of an ethical issue tied to the intentional misuse of research. It has been asserted that the relationship between smoking and illness was suspected as early as the 1950s and that tobacco company advertising continued to deliberately misinform the public (Radio broadcast, National Public Broadcasting, Morning Edition, May 4, 1988). If in the initial report the company withheld information, then the company behaved unethically (Koffler, 1988). If scientists employed by the tobacco industry interpreted the data consistently with company policy, regardless of the true pattern of results, they were also behaving unethically. Under these circumstances the smoker is the injured party because he did not have adequate information about the consequences of his behavior.

If, on the other hand, the company acted responsibly in reporting and the consumer still persisted in smoking, there is no ethical issue involved. The smoker makes her own decision as a free agent.

To summarize, scientists are responsible for reporting their research in sufficient detail, to describe the limitations of the findings in terms of research issues, and to report their results fully and without bias. What are not currently reported and do not have to be reported are caveats relative to application of the findings. Should this be part and parcel of the reporting process?[4] Many basic researchers

---

[4] The issue of social responsibility has been articulated since 1945 by the atomic scientists when they came to realize the consequence of their discovery on how to harness atomic energy. I shall not

would contend they are not qualified to address the practical issues and that application of their research results is not their responsibility (see for discussion, Scarr, 1988; Sieber & Stanley, 1988). In the last analysis, the consumer of the research is the responsible agent for use. After all, it is the practitioner who bears the primary responsibility for forging a link between the practical and basic research. The applied person has a choice as to how to use the material. He or she can, of course, make personal contact with the knowledge generator and seek help in considering the "hows" and the "whys" of application. Chances are, however, the practitioner will work from the document using whatever information is available.

Responsibilities of the Knowledge User

First, the practitioner has to ascertain in detail the implications of applying any research to his situation. For example, when using research data as a basis for intervention, the user has to pay particular attention to the potential consequences of the application, such as employing appropriate educational intervention techniques which will not be harmful to clients. One ethical issue that immediately arises in this context is the truthfulness of the claim that individuals participating in such interventions have a high probability of profiting from the intervention. For example, claims emanating from advocates that reducing sugar or red dye will help children learn border on the potentially unethical in the absence of data directly testing these claims. It does not matter whether the research shows advantages of a procedure; the practitioner has to weigh these claims in terms of the clientele to whom it will be applied as well as the solidity of the research.

It is also unethical when the person applying the information does not assure herself that the research findings to be applied are based on complete information. For example, one should not use ideas obtained from reviews of the literature or from some lay publications, since these summaries will not provide the type of detail (found in the original research report) necessary for decisions concerning applicability.

In the field of psychological testing, it would be unethical for an inexperienced examiner to test an individual and claim that the results are valid. This is the case also for the application of research findings to practical situations. From my bias, such application has to proceed tentatively until there is some assurance that the mode of application, and the setting in which it is done, are appropriate. For example, in some of our work we discovered that when parents use didactic, authoritarian, and parent-oriented teaching strategies with their preschool children, the children do not do well on intellectual tasks (Sigel &

reinvent this discussion except to say that I do not think behavior scientists have faced this issue as sharply as the atomic scientists have.

McGillicuddy-DeLisi, 1984). How are practitioners to use this information? The information is useful, provided the consumer takes into account the many factors and the conditions under which this research was done. Thus, there will have to be qualifications relative to the age of the children, the social status of the families, the fact that these results were obtained in an experimental situation, and so on. These are but some of the questions that must be considered before these findings are applied to a particular parent or group.

To further illustrate the boundaries between responsibilities of the knowledge generator and the knowledge consumer let me give a hypothetical example using my own work. I did a study some years ago designed to investigate the development of representational competence, that is, the understanding of signs and symbols among low-income children (Sigel, 1978). I found that low-income Black children had difficulty understanding the representational nature of pictures, which in turn I interpreted as one possible source of their difficulty in learning to read. Let us suppose that an educator read this paper and decided it had some relevance to his work on reading programs for children from low-income, Black families. Since I did not present any practical implications, nor provide guidelines as to the limitations of this study for application, the educator becomes the primary interpreter of the findings for potential use in a practical setting.

What are the ethical issues for the practitioner in this situation? First, the level of sophistication of the educator will define how that person interprets the applicability of the findings. It is thus the knowledge user's responsibility to assess his or her competence to interpret research results for practical use. Additionally, when deciding to incorporate these findings into their professional activities the knowledge user must not profess more expertise in the application of the material than is the case or make claims concerning the potential outcomes of application for which there is no evidential base.

The above suggests the consumer of research, rather than the knowledge generator, is responsible for how research is used. It is also the case, however, that the developmental scientist has not fulfilled his or her ethical responsibilities if the research report leads the public consumer to erroneously believe that the data had more direct relevance for practice than was actually the case.

PROFESSIONAL RESPONSIBILITY, COMPETENCE, AND THE APPLICATION OF FINDINGS TO PRACTICAL SETTINGS: EXAMPLES FROM EDUCATION

In this section, I will expand upon our discussion of the problems faced by knowledge consumers when they attempt to apply developmental research findings to practical situations. I will focus on two broad types of research applications in educational settings: (a) the incorporation of research findings into ongoing practice, and (b) the initiation of new research-based educational interventions. In the former case a teacher who reads of some new ideas in a research journal might incorporate them by making minor changes in her ongoing teaching program. In the latter case, the educator might embark on a new programmatic effort to enhance children's reading ability. Each of these types of applications raises ethical issues for the practitioner regarding the professional responsibility to incorporate new ideas into practice and the competencies required to use new knowledge successfully.

The incorporation of new knowledge into ongoing practice is a generic expectation for professional growth and development. However, no specific guidelines exist for helping teachers decide on the type of information and training required to incorporate information into their teaching practices. For example, a preschool teacher reads a journal article which reports that for young children an inquiry teaching strategy is more effective than a didactic one (Sigel & Kelly, 1988). The teacher may reject this finding out of hand because it does not square with his teaching ideology. However, if he accepts the idea, what does he need to know before attempting to apply it? The research he reads about merely says there were two classes—a didactic class and an inquiry class. The article does not state how much experience the teacher needs to have in either method before attempting it, nor does the researcher describe how the teacher is to employ (or come to be able to employ) the inquiry method if it is new to him. Even if the methods were not new, the article may not provide enough information for the teacher to assess whether or not he is doing the same thing as was done by the teachers in the experiment?

The responsible teacher in this case would determine whether the new procedure is within her professional competence. She would also have to decide whether or not the application is appropriate for her students. Her ability to make these decisions will rest on skills derived from her own professional training *and* the quality of information provided in the research report. A skilled teacher, reading a report with insufficient detail for application, must ethically decide not to apply this knowledge in her work. Therefore, the extent to which knowledge generators address the practical implications of their work sets limits on the extent to which developmental knowledge can be utilized by practitioners.

Now let us take the teacher who is assigned to implement a reading program which is new to the school. If the teacher has never conducted this type of program before, should he obtain the consent of the parent prior to introducing the program? How much information should the parent have before accepting or rejecting participation? If the teacher is to employ a program new to this population, should there not be some previous training for the teacher to work with the new group?

The responsible teacher in this case would have to evaluate the degree of technical competence required to include the new approach in the classroom as well as the consequences of this innovation to her particular students. If, in the teacher's judgment, the innovation has the potential for harm, or in some way may have a deleterious effect on the children—an effect unknown but possible at the outset—then it would behoove the teacher to openly discuss this with the administrator and parents. If, on the other hand, in the teacher's judgment the innovation is consistent with what has been done with similar groups, requires skills that she already possesses, and does not include a potential for harm, then the program can be implemented. Once again, the degree to which the teacher can evaluate the appropriateness of the intervention to her particular setting will depend upon the amount of information provided in the research report.

INTERVENING IN PARENTING PRACTICES

Intervention refers to the active process intended to change the ongoing behaviors of others. Developmental intervention programs operate on the assumption that the trajectory of behavioral development without intervention will lead to undesirable outcomes unless corrective measures are applied to alter the direction of the trajectory from the predicted socially undesirable to the socially desirable. In most recent years intervention, with the deliberate intention to change, has been an interest of educators, particularly as evidenced in programs for "disadvantaged" children and their parents.

In this section I will address ethical issues tied to programs geared to enhance children's intellectual development and their ability to take advantage of available educational opportunities. Most of these programs are established by professional educators. This fact, as well as others to be discussed below, underscores a presumption common to current approaches to intervention: The established education community knows what is best for children and also knows how best to achieve the societal goals of the program. This simple statement is crucial for our discussion because it sets the stage for the ethical argument of the right of parents to determine social goals for their children.

COMMUNICATING PROGRAM OBJECTIVES AND MUTUAL RESPONSIBILITIES IN PROGRAM PARTICIPATION

Let me start with a discussion of the ethical issues involved when a practitioner enrolls a family in a preschool program. The professional, typically an educator, describes the program to the parents, tells them the requirements of the program, and may or may not hold out some positive outcomes for participation. Assuming that the educator has determined the appropriateness of the intervention for this population and the staff's competence to implement the program (as discussed above), the professional must now guarantee that the parents (a) understand the goals of the program, the potential risks (if any), and the requirements as far as their participation is concerned; (b) do not feel coerced into participating; and (c) do not feel that participation in the program has the potential to create conflict between parent and child.

The obligation to assess whether the program has the potential to create family conflict implies that the goals of an intervention program may be at odds with the family values of participants. Specifically, imagine a program where the children are encouraged to explore, to be curious, to ask questions, and to develop a sense of entitlement in asking parents to justify certain decisions. It may well be that these educational objectives run counter to how a parent believes children should act. The only way the professional would get to know this is to learn the cultural meaning that the parent attributes to situations which may arise from the intervention program.

Professionals applying developmental knowledge to change individuals must understand that the appropriateness of an intervention can be evaluated from two different views: a view from outside the culture and one from within. The first so-called "objective" or *etic* view would evaluate an intervention on the basis of its potential to facilitate children's learning in a way that is consistent with research knowledge on how children develop intellectually. The second, "subjective" or *emic* view would evaluate an intervention on the basis of its compatibility with the cultural values of the participants. Fry and Keith (1980) put this into context:

> Data are not just plain data and facts are not simple facts. Culture filters out what is important and has meaning. But, whose culture are we using? "Etic" refers to the culture of science . . . "Emic" is the inside view of another culture. (p. 17)[5]

If the knowledge user becomes sensitive to the significance of the "emic" perspective, he may be more willing to seek ways to accommodate to the cultural factors of the intervention population. This has significance not only for obtaining parental permission for participation at the outset of an intervention, but for interpreting the results of the program to parents. The evaluation procedure usually fits into the etic mode, that is, objective tests are given and the child is usually asked a series of questions about quantity, colors, or memory for sentences, and so on. Interpretation of test results that do not take the child's cultural heritage into account may well mislead everyone—teacher, child, and parent (Laosa, 1979, chapter 15, this volume).

---

[5] Quoted in Reese, H.W., & Adams-Price, C.E. (1987). *An "emic" study of children's memory in nursery school.* Unpublished manuscript, West Virginia University.

THE USE OF INTERVENTION AND POLICY SITUATIONS
AS EXPERIMENTS

One of the current methods of application is to establish groups of individuals to test the efficacy of an intervention program where the program is an outgrowth of research findings in a more experimental situation. Let me present another hypothetical situation derived from my own research. In our studies we have found that there is a relationship between parents' beliefs and children's school performance (Sigel & McGillicuddy-DeLisi, 1984). Some beliefs predict to negative academic achievements, while others do just the reverse. On the basis of these findings a hypothetical practitioner might design an experimental intervention to change the beliefs of parents holding negative beliefs in the hopes of enhancing their children's academic outcomes. An experiment is designed which includes both a control group and experimental group. The control parents are not provided any intervention, but their children are tested prior to and following the experimental program (for a discussion on ethical issues associated with assignment to control groups see Chapters 3 and 4). Parents in the experimental group are informed that they are participating in a parent education program aimed at fostering parental attitudes which are considered predictive of "good" outcomes for children's academic achievement. While parents are chosen to participate on the basis of their "negative" beliefs, they are not told that the purpose of the program is to "change" their way of thinking about their children.

In evaluating issues associated with implementing this type of an intervention the intervener must ask what function these "negative" beliefs play in the lives of the families involved? To what extent are these beliefs reflections of other perspectives such as one's religious orientation, one's life goals, or a host of other beliefs which the parent has held for some time and is perfectly comfortable with? To investigate such questions may be an invasion of the individual's privacy—but to attempt to change an individual's beliefs in the absence of such knowledge is a violation of their right to self-determination.

SUMMARY AND CONCLUSIONS

In this chapter I have attempted to highlight ethical issues that arise when knowledge generation and knowledge application are seen as independent rather than interdependent aspects of applied developmental psychology. While in the last analysis, responsibility for knowledge use rests with the practitioner, in order to succeed at his or her investigatory function an applied developmental psychologist must have an understanding of how developmental knowledge is applied and misapplied in practical settings. Sensitivity to the contexts in which developmental knowledge is applied should lead to research reports which assist the knowledge consumer in evaluating the applicability of the research to their professional activities.

Embedded in all decisions regarding the application of developmental principles to induce change in individuals is the fundamental problem of value orientation and value commitment of the investigation and intervention professionals. For me, the guidelines for ethical actions on the part of all professionals involve concern for the welfare and dignity of others which can best be achieved by treating them as *participants and not subjects* (Lincoln & Guba, 1987). We must continue to reflect on the ways we can do applied developmental psychology in an ethical and forthright manner without compromising the science, the application, and above all, our professional relationship with our constituents.

REFERENCES

Diener, E., & Crandall, R. (1978). *Ethics in social and behavioral research.* Chicago: The University of Chicago Press.

Fry, C.L., & Keith, J. (1980). Introduction. In C.L. Fry & J. Keith (Eds.), *New methods for old research* (p. 17). Chicago, IL: Center for Urban Policy, Loyola University of Chicago.

Glenn, C. (1980). Ethical issues in the practice of child psychotherapy. *Professional Psychology, II,* 613–619.

Koffler, D. (1988, February 27). Unanswered questions [Letter to the editor]. *The New York Times,* p. 30.

Laosa, L.M. (1979). Social competence in childhood: Toward a developmental, socioculturally relativistic paradigm. In M.W. Kent & J.E. Rolf (Eds.), *Primary prevention of psychopathology: Vol. III. Social competence in children* (pp. 253–279). Hanover, NH: University Press of New England.

Lincoln, Y.S., & Guba, E.G. (1987, April). *Ethics: The failure of positivist science.* Paper presented at the meeting of the American Educational Research Association, Washington, DC.

Scarr, S. (1988). Race and gender as psychological variables. *American Psychologist, 43,* 56–59.

Sieber, J.E., & Stanley, B. (1988). Ethical and professional dimensions of socially sensitive research. *American Psychologist, 43,* 49–55.

Sigel, I.E. (1978). The development of pictorial comprehension. In B.S. Randhawa & W.E. Coffman (Eds.), *Visual learning, thinking, and communication* (pp. 93–111). New York: Academic Press.

Sigel, I.E. (1983). The ethics of intervention. In I.E. Sigel & L.M. Laosa (Eds.), *Changing families* (pp. 1–21). New York: Plenum.

Sigel, I.E., & Cocking, R.R. Editors' message. *Journal of Applied Developmental Psychology, 1,* i–iii.

Sigel, I.E., & Kelley, T.C. (1988). A cognitive developmental approach to questioning. In J. Dillon (Ed.), *Classroom questioning and discussion: A Multidisciplinary study* (pp. 105–134). Norwood, NJ: Ablex.

Sigel, I.E., & McGillicuddy-DeLisi, A.V. (1984). Parents as teachers of their children: A distancing behavior model. In A.D. Pellegrini & T.D. Yawkey (Eds.), *The development of oral and written language in social contexts* (pp. 71–92). Norwood, NJ: Ablex.

Part III
Ethics and Knowledge Dissemination

10 Ethical Dilemmas in Playing by the Rules: Applied Developmental Research and the Law

Gary B. Melton

"Do you promise to tell the truth, the whole truth, and nothing but the truth, so help you God?"

Through modeling by Perry Mason and, more recently, the partners and associates of McKenzie, Brackman, this question is ingrained in the minds of Americans as a behavioral cue for respect for the legal process. What happens, though, when an expert witness attempts affirmatively to tell the "whole truth," to ensure that the trier of fact is aware of all of the methodological caveats and conflicting findings that might affect the weight placed on a conclusion? The odds are that the answer will be stricken from evidence as unresponsive to the question posed.

This seeming anomaly is illustrative of the ethical issues that arise when psychologists attempt to apply their knowledge to the law. Playing by the rules is itself likely to result in ethical dilemmas for developmental researchers. Such dilemmas arise in large part because the primary purpose of the legal system differs from that of science. As the influential work of John Thibaut, a social psychologist, and Laurens Walker, a law professor, and their colleagues has clarified (see, e.g., Thibaut & Walker, 1978; for a comprehensive review, see Lind & Tyler, 1988), the primary purpose of law is the pursuit of *justice,* but the ultimate goal of science is to illuminate *truth.*

Such purposes are not necessarily compatible. For example, justice is best served by permitting the parties in a dispute to control the production of information. Giving each party the opportunity to put its best case forward—to have a say—promotes the sense of the litigants and the community as a whole that justice is being done. However, such a procedure (exemplified by the Anglo-American tradition of adversary legal process) usually results in the production of evidence that is not representative of the universe of relevant facts. On the other hand, an inquisitorial approach (i.e., an unbiased search for facts by a neutral third party) is well suited to produce a picture that closely approximates reality, but it is also likely to leave the parties and observers unsatisfied. In view of institutional goals, we should not apply an inquisitorial approach to most questions raised in the legal process, but neither should we adopt an adversary procedure for resolution of scientific disputes.

Scientists may protest that a system that blinds itself to the whole truth surely cannot render just decisions. Consider, though, the following hypothetical case.

145

Suppose that the Truthville police place wiretaps on every phone in the village and that they undertake random thorough searches of the homes and personal effects of the Truthvillians. Suppose further that the evidence uncovered in such searches is used to determine the guilt or innocence of all the villagers. Undoubtedly, a more accurate picture would be composed of the true prevalence of crime in Truthville than would appear in another village that guaranteed due process, but would the exercise of state authority in Truthville be just?

To return to the opening vignette, expert witnesses who strive to present the whole truth—in a sense, to *impose* the whole truth on the trier of fact and the parties—may ensure that scientific objectivity is preserved but, in doing so, they imperil the central purpose of the legal system. Whatever the benefits to factfinding per se, intrusion on the parties' ability to present their cases in their best light threatens due process. To be sure, as I shall discuss, misrepresentation of the facts by an expert, whether deliberate or unwitting, is even more disrespectful of legal authority than the expert's attempt to circumvent duly established legal procedures. Nonetheless, developmental psychologists entering the legal arena must be sensitive to the fact that rules established to promote the legitimate goals of the legal system may place them in a position in which they are compelled to abandon some of the norms of science.

RESOLVING CONFLICTS OF PURPOSE

The answer to such a role conflict is, in large part, simply to accept it. In the end, the role conflicts caused by the clash between their duty to promote truth and legal authorities' duty to promote justice strike me as not so serious. First, it should be recognized that lay witnesses also bear a duty of veracity, but they too are not permitted to present evidence outside the strictures of the rules of procedures and evidence. I know of no ethical principle that would justify a place for experts that supersedes the parties' control of their cases. Expert witnesses are not *that* different.

Second, the rules of evidence and psychologists' ethical principles actually are largely compatible. As I will discuss later, expert testimony that violates the ethical duty not to exceed competence is inadmissible under Federal Rule of Evidence 702. When potential expert testimony is so complex that it is inherently misleading when presented in limited time and in a format outside the witness's control, such evidence also is inadmissible (Federal Rule of Evidence 403).[1] I

---

[1] The evidentiary rule barring inherently misleading testimony is compatible with the ethical principle that "[p]sychologists present the science of psychology . . . fairly and accurately, avoiding misrepresentation through sensationalism, exaggeration, or superficiality," in keeping with "the primary obligation to aid the public in developing informed judgments, opinions, and choices" (APA, 1981, Principle 6g).

have previously argued that testimony about post-trauma syndromes may fall into such a category, given evidence that most people have difficulty applying base rates validly (see Melton & Limber, 1989).

Third, truth and justice are penultimate goals subordinate to the still more fundamental value of respect for human dignity, the essence of constitutional guarantees. Psychologists' highest obligation is to "respect the dignity and worth of the individual and strive for the preservation and protection of fundamental human rights" (American Psychological Association [APA], 1981, Preamble). Consistent with that high duty, psychologists agree to "avoid any action that will violate or diminish the legal and civil rights of . . . [persons] who may be affected by their actions" (APA, 1981, Principle 3c). An obvious corollary is that the underlying values of law and psychology are largely consistent.

Applied to the production of evidence, Principle 3c implies a duty of care in the development and presentation of scientific information, so that the factfinder is not misled and so that the parties can determine the rigor and fairness of the procedures used to generate opinion evidence (see, e.g., *United States v. Byers*, 1984, brief of amicus curiae APA and dissenting opinion of J. Bazelon).[2] When the information to be gathered is case-specific, the duty to protect civil rights requires that psychologists not permit themselves to be used as sub rosa law enforcement agents gathering evidence without the subject's knowledge of the purpose of such an investigation (see APA, 1981, Principle 6). Whether purposefully or naively, psychologists may find information ostensibly gathered in confidence used to bolster a criminal or juvenile prosecution, contrary at least to the spirit of the fifth and sixth amendments (see Melton, Petrila, Poythress, & Slobogin, 1987, chap. 3; Slobogin, 1982).

More generally, the duty to promote human dignity requires that psychologists respect the legal rules that have been created to ensure that threats to liberty and property are not taken lightly and that litigants have a say in the disposition of their case. When weighty interests are at stake, it is important to maintain both the appearance and the reality of fairness. Whatever the outcome, psychologists (and others) involved in the investigation or adjudication of a case should behave in such a way that the litigants on both sides will perceive themselves as having been treated fairly (Melton & Limber, 1989). A corollary is that psychologists should avoid intrusions into the province of legal decision makers, a point to which I shall return.

Fourth, psychologists who are knowledgeable about legal rules will find that, when the law presents ethical conflicts, it also often will offer ways out of the conflict. For example, a subpoena that threatens the privacy of research partici-

---

[2] Note the similarity in this regard to the norm of scientific work that requires researchers to make their procedures and data available, under ordinary circumstances, for scrutiny and replication (see Fienberg, Martin, & Straf, 1985; Hedrick, 1988). Such a canon minimizes the probability that social harm will result from reliance on faulty methods or erroneous conclusions (see APA, 1981, Principle 1a; Weithorn, 1987a).

pants may be quashed under rules that limit discovery of embarrassing information, and statutory provisions are available that permit advance protection against subpoena in many instances (see Melton, 1988). Obviously, resolution of conflicts between apparent ethical and legal duties through such creative application of legal rules (see APA, 1981, Principle 3d) can occur only when researchers are knowledgeable about the alternatives and skilled enough in legal analysis that they can construct legal justifications for behavior that is compatible with psychological ethics. Nonetheless, the point is that dilemmas raised by psychological research and practice in the legal system often are tractable through a search for legal solutions to legal dilemmas (see, e.g., Gray & Melton, 1985).

LOSING THE INDIVIDUAL IN THE GROUP

Although an understanding of the traditional conflict of purposes in law and science may diminish the dissonance experienced by expert witnesses uncomfortable with failure fully to "come clean" with the knowledge they possess, the problem does not end there. Questions remain whether scientists should be present in the courtroom at all. Such questions are of two types: (a) inherent philosophical problems in the application of scientific evidence to the adjudication of cases (see generally Monahan & Walker, 1985, 1988), and (b) more familiar issues, most of them probably resolvable through care in opinion formation or through additional research, about the limits of expertise and related questions of competence (see generally McCloskey, Egeth, & McKenna, 1986; Melton & Limber, 1989).

The intrinsic issues in use of social science in legal decision making rest for the most part on the conceptual leap that is required in generalizing from group probability data to individual cases (see Chapter 9). Such issues are most profound in attempting to discern past behavior. For example, when the question is whether a parent abused a child, the probability of a positive answer is, strictly speaking, either 0 or 1. To recognize the actual probabilistic nature of the judgment of a judge or jury is, in effect to negate the presumption of innocence, because the fact that the defendant is on trial indicates a de facto probability of guilt greater than 0 (Tribe, 1971). Moreover, simply knowing some of the characteristics of a defendant will alter the probability assessment, but guilt is supposed to be assessed on the basis only of what the defendant did, not who he is. As a result, courts almost uniformly have excluded offender profile evidence (e.g., abusing parent syndrome) intended to corroborate a criminal or civil charge. Courts are more divided in their approach to profiles of victim characteristics, but the trend is toward exclusion because of their prejudicial effect and often weak scientific foundation.

The least problematic use of profile evidence is in disposition or sentencing. Because the inquiry at that point is future-oriented, it is inherently probabilistic, and use of the most precise probabilities is sensible. However, even in that context, problems remain. Suppose, for example, an arrest before the age of 14 is a predictor in a dispositional table. Suppose, though, the juvenile respondent protests that he was exonerated of the earlier charge. Suppose also that race is a predictor. Do we really want to take race into account in determining whether a juvenile is sent to a training school? Moreover, a juvenile placed in a high-risk category, regardless of the variables used, may argue he or she is different—that he or she has reformed—and that it is unfair to presume that this defendant is among the 40% (hypothetically) for whom the prediction of recidivism will turn out to be a true positive.

In short, a system of individualized justice finds use of probability evidence problematic, whatever the scientific basis for its application. Although this difficulty is certainly a serious problem or morality, it is not so serious a problem of professional ethics. As long as the expert is honest about the limits of knowledge (e.g., the expert does not try to "diagnose" whether abuse occurred), makes clear the leap that is required to move from group data to a determination of facts about an individual, and works diligently to explain problems in interpretation of probability evidence (e.g., the application of base rates), the psychologist is behaving ethically. Nonetheless, the fundamental epistemological and moral problems in use of profile evidence present substantial issues in regard to its admissibility.

KNOWING WHAT YOU DON'T KNOW

Probably the most common and perhaps the most pernicious ethical problem when psychologists sit in the witness box is exceeding the bounds of their competence. Failure to monitor the limits of one's competence to render professional opinions is a clear violation of the Ethical Principles of Psychologists (APA, 1981, Principle 2). When expert witnesses render opinions that go beyond what they know *as psychologists,* they effectively usurp the role of legitimate authority and, in so doing, show disrespect for the community as a whole as well as the individuals directly affected by the litigation. They also violate the duty of fidelity to the profession through accurate representation of the state of knowledge.

Besides violating professional ethics, exceeding competence also should render an expert's opinion inadmissible. Unlike lay (fact) witnesses, experts are permitted to render opinions as well as to describe facts. Ordinarily, the trier of fact (i.e., the judge or the jury) is presumed competent to draw proper inferences from the facts. Therefore, witnesses generally are not permitted to offer opinions (Federal Rule of Evidence 701), because doing so invades the province of duly recognized authority.

Federal Rule of Evidence 702, which has been adopted by most state jurisdictions, not only serves as the standard for admissibility of opinions (as a matter of law), but it also provides a guide for expert witnesses to monitor the limits of their competence (as a matter of ethics). According to Rule 702, an expert's opinion is admissible only "[i]f scientific, technical or other *specialized knowledge* will assist the trier of fact to understand the evidence or to determine a fact in issue" (emphasis added). Accordingly, whenever an expert witness offers an opinion on the stand, he or she is representing that the opinion is based on more than common sense—specifically, that the opinion is derived from a scientific foundation. Therefore, constant self-scrutiny about whether particular opinions could have been developed if the witness were not trained as a psychologist is a useful procedure for determining whether one is beginning to exceed competence.

For example, psychologists in recent years often have been asked to render opinions about whether a child has been abused or even whether a child witness is truthful. Such opinions, which most appellate courts have held to be inadmissible, clearly lack a scientific foundation and should not be offered (Melton & Limber, 1989). Indeed, the examples that I have heard some psychologists give to justify their presenting such opinions actually prove my point. When a psychologist says that a child was sexually abused because the child gave a graphic description of ejaculation, there is no reason to believe that a layperson would not be capable of making the same inference from the facts without the psychologist's opinion. The proper conclusion from the evidence is a matter of common sense. That fact is unaltered by the psychologist's experience with abuse cases or skill as a therapist treating abused children. The question is not whether the psychologist is an expert, but whether the specific opinion is based on an expert judgment.

The duty to stay within the bounds of competence often is violated by psychologists who fail to differentiate scientific and legal/moral judgments. For example, the standard of *best interests of the child* is ubiquitous in children's law. Developmental psychologists reasonably may conclude that they know more than laypersons about the factors affecting children's development. However, when an opinion is rendered in a legal forum about a child's best interests, the psychologist also is implicitly claiming expertise *as a psychologist* in the legal standards about the outcomes that are desirable and their relative weight. In so doing, the psychologist misrepresents the state of scientific knowledge (see APA, 1981, Principle 4g) and exceeds the bounds of competence (see APA, 1981, Principle 2) in a context in which the consequences are profound (see APA, 1981, Principle 1f).

As I have summarized elsewhere, "the best-interests test seems to demand no less than a judicial determination of the desirable traits of a citizen" (Melton et al., 1987, p. 334). Whether a parent who will promote gregariousness is superior to one who will stimulate intellectual growth is a moral decision, not a scientific one. Similarly, whether the law recognizes one outcome as superior to the other is a legal determination, not a scientific one. Analogously, a recommendation about the frequency of visitation to be permitted by a noncustodial parent inherently presumes special moral and legal knowledge about the rights of parents and the traits desired in children. Therefore, psychologists should *never* offer an opinion about the ultimate issue to be determined by the trier of fact (Grisso, 1986; Melton et al., 1987; Weithorn, 1987b; Weithorn & Grisso, 1987).

Even when psychologists do not invade the province of the fact finder, issues remain about the level of scientific foundation necessary to present opinions about social facts. Rule 702 again provides guidance. Opinions, even when derived from specialized knowledge, are admissible only when they "will assist the trier of fact." This standard is incremental. *Some* addition in the fact finder's ability to weigh the evidence is sufficient. Thus, to be admissible, a scientific opinion need not have perfect or even high validity. When opinions are not highly prejudicial (for example, when the aura of the white coat is weak), then even relatively low validity may provide enough foundation for an opinion. On the other hand, in some circumstances, the weight placed on expert opinions is so profound that even a highly valid opinion will not add to the factfinder's ability to weigh the evidence. Similarly, highly complex testimony may mislead more than it assists the factfinder even if the testimony accurately reflects the state of knowledge. To give another scenario, when common (lay) knowledge is great about a particular phenomenon, even highly valid opinions will not aid the factfinder sufficiently to be admissible.

Thus, from an evidentiary perspective, the validity of the opinion that the expert offers is not by itself dispositive of the value of the opinion. Assuming that an opinion has *some* probative value so that its presentation is not a total waste of time, the real question is the validity of the inference that is likely to be drawn by the factfinder. In that regard, the expert's ethical duty is to attempt to frame the opinion in the manner that is most likely to lead to valid comprehension of the significance of the opinion.

This principle has two corollaries that are, to an extent, mutually contradictory. First, a clear presentation that can be easily interpreted by laypersons probably is preferable to testimony that is highly detailed and complex and, in a sense, more accurate.[3] Although a stance of advocacy for one side or the other in litigation is inappropriate for an expert, the expert should be an advocate *for the data*. That principle implies a duty to learn how to present scientific evidence in a way that is comprehensible to the consumer of the information. Second, the expert should be careful to indicate the degree of certainty attached to his or her opinion. Even if it is disquieting for the factfinder (and the expert), illumination

---

[3] The obvious qualifier to this corollary is that when the state of knowledge is so complex that a comprehensible presentation is impossible without seriously misleading the factfinder, the expert's testimony should be inadmissible (Federal Rule of Evidence 403).

of uncertainty about the meaning of behavior promotes justice as much as does an opinion that is closely linked to a psychological "law."

Child custody in divorce is again a good example. There is probably no area of law in which psychologists have been as willing to reach beyond their competence. Perhaps as a result and contrary to the conventional wisdom, clinical testimony is rarely presented in custody disputes, and, when presented, rarely given much weight (Melton, Weithorn, & Slobogin, 1985). The errors are of two sorts. First, as I noted previously, psychologists and other mental health professionals often have invaded the province of the factfinder by presuming to know the meaning of a child's *best interests,* despite evidence that courts and psychologists typically have a different understanding of the term (Lowery, 1981). Second, psychologists often have given the impression of certainty or near-certainty about the likely effects of a custody or visitation alternative. They have done so, despite *"the lack of any methodologically sound empirical evidence allowing psychological predictions as to the effects of various types of custodial placements on children, or whether joint custody, in general, is a better option than single-parent custody"* (Weithorn & Grisso, 1987, p. 161, emphasis in the original).

However, recognition of a high degree of uncertainty about the probable consequences of various dispositions available to the family court does not mean that psychologists have no contribution to make to the resolution of such matters—only that their function may be more to prevent decisions confidently made on the basis of erroneous assumptions than to assist judges to make "correct," confident decisions when they would not otherwise have done so. For example, some parental variables that often are believed intuitively to be highly related to parental ability (e.g., parental mental disorder) actually are, at most, weakly related to child outcomes, when appropriate controls are added for confounding variables (see Melton, 1989; Melton et al., 1987, §12.05). Expert testimony about this body of research may prevent an unwarranted rush to judgment, even if it does not clarify the appropriate result.

Similarly, even "informed speculation" (AKA "educated guesses") may be useful to the factfinder, *if it is presented as such* (Bonnie & Slobogin, 1980; Melton et al., 1987). For example, clinical formulations of the nature of intrafamilial relationships may have little scientific foundation, especially in regard to predictions about their implications for disposition. On the other hand, such opinions are not simply folk wisdom, and they may provide the judge with a way of framing the evidence that otherwise would not have occurred to him or her. Therefore, formulations may assist the trier of fact, if the expert clarifies the degree of uncertainty about their validity. When the level of speculation that underlies a formulation is identified honestly, the judge may decide that the opinion lacks sufficient probative value to be admissible, but the expert will neither have sacrificed professional ethics nor misled the trier of fact.

The general rules of thumb about appropriate expert testimony that I have offered elsewhere are applicable to testimony about developmental issues:

> In summary, although the range of opinions . . . which mental health professionals provide the courts should be narrowed to exclude opinions of a purely moral or legal nature, the door should be left open to professional opinions, including formulations of legally relevant behavior, that might assist (as opposed to overwhelm) the trier of fact. At the same time, mental health professionals should be careful to indicate the level of scientific validity or certainty attached to their opinions. (Melton et al., 1987, p. 17)

THE SUPPRESSION OF DATA

Protection of a Litigant

The nature of the issue. Even when no question exists about the specialized knowledge possessed by an expert, dilemmas still may arise about the limits on openness in presentation of that knowledge. As the vignette that introduced this chapter illustrates, the legal system often neither expects nor even permits full exposition of the findings of research relevant to a particular case. Moreover, when a clinical opinion is involved, the opinion itself and the facts underlying it may be withheld on the basis of constitutional (fifth amendment) or statutory (psychologist-client) privilege.[4] Whether the knowledge possessed by the expert is derived from research or clinical assessment, the evidence gathered by the expert and his or her opinion about it may be sheltered by attorney-client privilege, because the attorney is able to contract for the services of psychological experts to assist in developing theories of the case. Indeed, in criminal cases, failure to provide an indigent defendant with access to an *adversary* expert may violate the sixth amendment right to effective assistance of counsel (*Ake v. Oklahoma*, 1985). In short, regardless of a psychologist's desire to be forthcoming with information relevant to a legal dispute, the party that sought the expert's services may be able to suppress information that is not favorable to its case.

When clinical testimony is involved, this rule of law is likely to produce little dissonance for psychologists, although the application of the rule is hardly un-

---

[4] *Privilege* often is confused with *confidentiality*. Whether or not information is kept confidential from third parties, privilege—the right to exclude information in a legal proceeding—may apply. For example, the contents of a confession obtained according to procedures contrary to the fifth amendment may become widely known (e.g., the contents of the confession may become public in a suppression hearing and disseminated by the press), but it is nonetheless excludable at trial unless the defendant decides to waive privilege.

controversial (compare *People v. Edney,* 1976, and *United States v. Alvarez,* 1975; see generally Melton et al., 1987, chap. 3). Even if experts do not appreciate the fifth and sixth amendment or statutory privilege issues involved, they are likely to be sensitive to confidentiality issues raised more generally in clinical work.

An attempt by a litigant to suppress information may be especially conflict-laden for both the expert and the court when the exercise of privilege may harm an individual who is not a party to the litigation. The most obvious example is the exercise of psychologist-client privilege in child custody disputes (see Melton et al., 1987, §13.04[a]). In jurisdictions that recognize a psychologist-client privilege, that privilege usually is applicable unless the client puts his or her mental state at issue in litigation or expressly waives the privilege. However, the complicating factor in custody disputes is that, under most circumstances, the custodial parent would assert or waive privilege on behalf of a minor child. Obviously, in a custody dispute, the usual presumption that the parent would be acting solely in the child's best interests is untenable, because the parent is an interested party in the dispute. If the child himself or herself is given authority to exercise the privilege, the question will arise of the child's competence to make that decision. Moreover, even if the parent has been the client, the child's right to due process as the subject of the dispute, albeit without standing, may be violated by an assertion of privilege by one or both parents. If family therapy has been the treatment, questions remain whether any of the family members involved in the treatment have expectations of privacy against each other. In short, the clinician may feel torn to protect the interests of various parties and, in any event, the law may be unclear about the legally correct course of action, regardless of the ethics of the situation.

The greatest dissonance for experts, though, is likely to come in the context of suppression of research findings that are unsupportive of the case of the litigant who contracted for the expert's services. In general, openness is the norm of scientific ethics. For example, the duty expressed in the Ethical Principles of Psychologists (APA, 1981) to provide access to one's data is the weakest among the three major ethical codes in social science (Melton, 1988).[5] However, the Ethical Principles do require psychologists, "[i]n publishing reports of their work, . . . never [to] suppress disconfirming data, and . . . [to] acknowledge the existence of alternative hypotheses and explanations of their findings" (Principle 1a).

On the other hand, trial attorneys generally will regard the collection of data for the purpose of litigation to be a work for hire and the researchers themselves to be their agents. Therefore, absent a contract to the contrary, they may expect

---

[5] I am referring to the codes of the American Anthropological Association and the American Sociological Association, as well as the APA.

the researcher to suppress any findings that are not favorable to the party seeking the expert's opinion, at least during the pendency of the litigation and possibly in perpetuity. Only if the party reveals the existence of the research and makes the expert available for subpoena or cross-examination (and the right questions then are asked) will unfavorable findings come to light. Should the expert reveal the findings despite the wishes of the attorney (and arguably in breach of contract)? Pushing the problem back a step, should an expert ever enter into an agreement to conduct or review research when a legal obligation may accrue to quash the findings in some circumstances?

Before I present a hypothetical case to demonstrate the dilemmas that may arise, it may be useful to note that there are other circumstances in which there is a well-established tradition of secret research. The most obvious situation is industrial research. If a psychologist working for a marketing firm discovers a particularly powerful means of persuasion, one can be certain that the information will not enter the public domain, no matter what its significance in the social psychology of attitude and behavior change. Similarly, a discovery of human factors associated with personal computing (a discovery that might have substantial social import—and economic rewards) is unlikely to be shared with the labs of other corporations. More controversially, research related to national security may never be made public, whatever its potential significance for science. With the possible exception of marketing research by toy companies, I am not aware of any situations other than research for litigation in which applied developmental researchers are likely to find themselves with a norm of suppression of data. Nonetheless, the point is that the issue is not unique to the legal context, and the expectation of openness in research is in fact not absolute. In fact, because Principle 1a of the Ethical Principles of Psychologists (APA, 1981) is limited to publication practices, there is no basis for adjudication of ethical complaints related to suppression of negative results, unless there is selective publication.

A hypothetical case. The nature of the dilemmas that consultants in litigation may face can be illustrated by the following hypothetical case. Suppose that an advocacy group for noncustodial fathers decides to develop a test case intended to develop a common-law rule that joint custody is presumptively in the best interest of children in divorce. In the absence of substantial empirical evidence on this question, the attorney for the father then hires a psychologist to conduct research aimed (from the point of view of the litigant) at proving this proposition. The advocacy group pays all expenses related to the research, including the psychologist's fee. Unfortunately, none of the assumptions of the group are supported by the research. Therefore, the attorney directs the psychologist not to reveal that the research has been conducted. Because the research may be adverse to the interests of his clients not only in the test case but in future cases, the psychologist is told never to release the data or even the fact that the research was conducted. What should the psychologist do?

On the one hand, the findings are of substantial social import. If the findings are not released, preventable social harm may result. A psychologist reasonably may conclude that failure to release the results, perhaps even before the litigation is decided, would violate the duty to use scientific knowledge to promote human welfare (APA, 1981, Preamble). Indeed, such a duty may be especially profound in the hypothetical case, because the group most directly affected (i.e., children) is socially and legally dependent. On the other hand, failure to provide litigants with confidential consulting services, including production of scientific evidence, may frustrate the legitimate goals of the legal system. Moreover, as the hypothetical case evolved, a psychologist who failed to protect the confidentiality of the research, including its findings, would be in violation of a duly established contract and arguably in breach of the ethical duty of fidelity—promise-keeping and loyalty to clients (see APA, 1981, Principle 6).

Certainly, reasonable people may disagree about the "correct" solution to the dilemma. In my own view, the preservation of legal system, including the adversary process and the corollary reliance on the parties to determine the evidence to be presented, is so intrinsic to the promotion of justice that I would be inclined to suppress the findings. What is clear, though, is that the resolution of the dilemma at the point raised in the hypothetical case is too late. Researchers should establish clear agreements with attorneys employing them *before* work begins about any limitations that may be imposed on the publication of the findings of the research (APA, 1981, Principle 1b). Psychologists who believe that they would be ethically compelled to publicize the findings in the situation described above should never agree to conduct the research without an agreement in advance that the decision about whether findings merit public release (beyond the possible use in the employer's case) is the psychologist's alone, to be based solely on the scientific and social significance of the findings.

Protection of the Researcher

Sometimes the suppression of data in the legal process is intended to benefit the researcher as much as, or more than, the party who engaged the expert. Indeed, most of the litigation about access to data has focused on researchers' arguments that their own interests and, by extension, the interests of society would be harmed by a requirement to surrender data (see Melton, 1988, and cases cited therein). In such cases, the research typically was not conducted specifically for the purpose of litigation, but the information derived from the research may be relevant to the just resolution of a case.

In arguing, usually successfully, that research data relevant to a question in litigation should be invulnerable to subpoena, researchers commonly have made some combination of the following arguments:

1. A requirement to surrender one's data is time-consuming and sometimes expensive. It is burdensome on the researcher, intrusive on the research

enterprise, and destructive of academic freedom. Therefore, it ultimately is a hindrance to the development of new knowledge.

2. Subpoenae of raw data may deter participation in future research with adverse consequences for both the researcher (who depends on human participants in order to pursue his or her livelihood) and society as a whole (which is less able to generate new knowledge, especially about socially or personally sensitive topics).

3. Akin to usual prohibitions against subpoenae of trade secrets, a requirement to surrender the products of research may result in a deprivation of economic benefit to the researcher without due process of law. Because researchers are dependent on publication of their findings in academic fora for promotion, tenure, merit pay, and so forth, premature release of findings may preclude receipt of such benefits. Furthermore, because such benefits provide the incentives for research, there may be negative social consequences as well as economic losses for the researcher.

4. Forced production of research data may result in erroneous conclusions, because of incomplete data sets, inadequate peer review, or lack of research sophistication in the recipient of the data (Stanley & Stanley, 1988). Besides the possible threats to both justice and social welfare because of mistaken conclusions, there may be an unjust diminution of the researcher's scientific reputation.

Sorting out when the self-interest of the researcher and the public interest are congruent often is not easy in particular cases. Regardless, it is important to emphasize that the law generally has operated on a paradoxical principle that the development of ideas sometimes is facilitated by secrecy, notwithstanding the value on openness that underlies the first amendment and the sixth amendment right to a public trial. Intellectual property law prevents the entrance of individuals' scholarly work into the public domain without their consent, because it is assumed that protection of the economic interests of the individual scholar will create or preserve incentives for production of new knowledge.

Protection of Participants

As the discussion thus far suggests, I am not greatly bothered by the suppression of data in a legal proceeding when the purpose is to promote justice, consistent with the rules of evidence and procedure, or even when it is to protect the research enterprise itself. My greatest concern, though, is about the consequences for research participants that may result from the mandatory disclosure of raw data, pursuant to a subpoena (see Melton, 1988). Such action violates the promises that usually have been made to research participants and sometimes threatens the well-being of participants. Although no jurisdiction has established a statutory researcher-participant privilege, I would argue that the rationale for such a privilege is actually stronger than for a psychologist-client privilege. The same societal interest in preservation of a confidential relationship is present, often there is the same risk of embarrassment or stigma, and there is an equal wrong as a result of a breach of privacy. The costs to the research participant are even more egregious, though, than the costs to the therapy client, because research participants generally have consented to be used for the benefit of others. De facto punishment of such altruism is especially cruel.

To guard against a breach of participant privacy as a result of subpoenae of data, researchers should take action before a subpoena arrives in any study involving sensitive information (e.g., assessments of personality or parental attitudes and behavior; self-reports of illegal behavior). Research may be designed to prevent identifiability of data, or the researcher may obtain a certificate of confidentiality from the relevant institute of the Public Health Service (Boruch & Cecil, 1979, 1983; Gray & Melton, 1985; Melton, 1988; Melton & Gray, 1988).[6]

THE DUTY TO CONDUCT AND DISSEMINATE RESEARCH

Thus far, I have discussed dilemmas that often arise in research in legal contexts. However, those dilemmas should not deter psychologists from developmental research related to law. The duty to promote human welfare (APA, 1981, Preamble and Principle 9) obligates psychologists to consider the issues of most pressing social concern. Surely assumptions that underlie legal policies affecting children and families (or, at the other end of the age spectrum, older adults) fit such a criterion. Moreover, psychologists accept public funds, directly or indirectly, for their training and ongoing work, with an expectation, at least implicitly, of service to humanity through creation and diffusion of scientific knowledge relevant to social welfare. Therefore, the duty of fidelity also pushes toward a psycholegal research agenda.

Simply conducting such research without consideration of design of research to fit pressing policy questions or without attention to diffusion of findings to policy makers does not fulfill the duty. If one is to become a policy researcher, one must do so competently. The implication is that one must be knowledgeable about ways of informing legal decision makers, or at least one must collaborate with scholars who do possess such knowledge and the motivation to follow through on it. Substantial research now exists on the most effective means of diffusing developmental research in particular for use in legal policy (Melton,

---

[6] Researchers interested in obtaining a certificate of confidentiality for research related to mental health should write: Extramural Policy Branch, National Institute of Mental Health, Room 9-95, 5600 Fishers Lane, Rockville, MD 20851.

1987a, 1987c). Although the significance cf such diffusion of knowledge should not be underemphasized, developmental psychologists involved in legally relevant research also must establish reasonable goals for their work.

SUMMARY AND CONCLUSIONS

The ethical foibles that have been common in psychologists' involvement in juvenile and family law have emanated to large extent from unrealistic expectations by the courts or, perhaps even more, by experts themselves. As experts on child development, psychologists often have presumed to be able to define the "right" policy in regard to children and families or disposition in regard to a particular child or family. Indeed, the child mental health and social service professions grew from the juvenile court and, to a large extent, still work in its service (Levine & Levine, 1970; Melton, 1987d, in press), although commonly without critical analysis of its underlying assumptions.

There is a temptation for psychologists (and others) to assume advocates' roles that are derived from ethical and political purposes other than promotion of the interests of children and youth (Melton, 1987b). By the same token, courts often have constructed psychological ruses for policies that obfuscate the actual underlying bases of policy (Melton, 1987e). Psychologists should do the research necessary to test such assumptions, but the goal should be diminution of "psychologizing" in child and family legal policy. The courts often have avoided protection of the rights of children and youth by focusing on their purported incompetence and vulnerability. Careful analysis of what is known and not known about developmental factors related to legal issues and comprehensive research on that which is now known may not result in widespread use of such knowledge by legal decision makers, but it may stimulate a focus on the normative principles that should guide policy. Achievement of such intellectual honesty and concern for personhood of children and youth would be no mean feat.

In the same vein, psychologists who perceive the legal system as undervaluing truth should pay attention to the significance of justice in our society. In so doing, they should be properly respectful of the norms of the legal system, and they should be sure that their clients and the consumers of research in the legal process will feel satisfied that the psychologists' behavior has facilitated the just application of those norms. Achievement of such an end often will require that psychologists not only are committed to obeying legal rules, but that they also understand how to apply those rules in order to fulfill implicit or express promises (e.g., expectations of privacy) to their clients and research participants. Ultimately, such careful attention to the role of psychology in the law is likely to comport with the ethical imperatives embedded in both disciplines.

REFERENCES

Ake v. Oklahoma, 470 U.S. 68 (1985).

American Psychological Association. (1981). Ethical principles of psychologists. *American Psychologist, 36*, 633–638.

Bonnie, R.J., & Slobogin, C. (1980). The role of mental health professionals in the criminal process: The case for informed speculation. *Virginia Law Review, 66*, 427–522.

Boruch, R.F., & Cecil, J. (1979). *Assuring the confidentiality of social research data.* Philadelphia: University of Pennsylvania Press.

Boruch, R.F., & Cecil, J. (Eds.). (1983). *Solutions to ethical and legal problems in social research.* New York: Academic Press.

Fienberg, S.E., Martin, M.E., & Straf, M.L. (Eds.). (1985). *Sharing research data.* Washington, DC: National Academy Press.

Gray, J.N., & Melton, G.B. (1985). The law and ethics of psychosocial research on AIDS. *Nebraska Law Review, 64*, 637–688.

Grisso, T. (1986). *Evaluating competencies: Forensic assessments and instruments.* New York: Plenum.

Hedrick, T.E. (1988). Justifications for the sharing of social science data. *Law and Human Behavior, 12*, 163–171.

Levine, M., & Levine, A. (1970). *A social history of helping services: Court, clinic, school, and community.* New York: Appleton-Century-Croft.

Lind, E.A., & Tyler, T.R. (1988). *The social psychology of procedural justice.* New York: Plenum.

Lowery, C. (1981). Child custody decisions in divorce proceedings: A survey of judges. *Professional Psychology, 12*, 492–498.

McCloskey, M., Egeth, H., & McKenna, J. (Eds.). (1986). The ethics of expert testimony [Special issue]. *Law and Human Behavior, 10*(1/2).

Melton, G.B. (1987a). Bringing psychology to the legal system: Opportunities, obstacles, and efficacy. *American Psychology, 42*, 488–495.

Melton, G.B. (1987b). Children, politics, and morality: The ethics of child advocacy. *Journal of Clinical Child Psychology, 16*, 357–367.

Melton, G.B. (1987c). Guidelines for effective diffusion of child development research into the legal system. In G.B. Melton (Ed.), *Reforming the law: Impact of child development research* (pp. 280–300). New York: Guilford.

Melton, G.B. (1987d). Law and random events: The state of child mental health policy. *International Journal of Law and Psychiatry, 10*, 81–90.

Melton, G.B. (1987e). The clashing of symbols: Prelude to child and family policy. *American Psychologist, 42*, 345–354.

Melton, G.B. (1988). When scientists are adversaries, do participants lose? *Law and Human Behavior, 12*, 191–198.

Melton, G.B. (1989). Untangling the web [Review of *Children at risk: In the web of parental mental illness*]. *Contemporary Psychology, 34*, 266.

Melton, G.B. (in press). Children as objects of social control: Implications for training in children's services. In P.R. Magrab & P. Wohlford (Ed.), *Clinical Training in Psychology: Improving Psychological Services for Children and Adolescents with Severe Mental Disorders.* Washington, DC: American Psychological Association.

Melton, G.B., & Gray, J.N. (1988). Ethical dilemmas in AIDS research: Individual privacy and public health. *American Psychologist, 43*, 60–64.

Melton, G.B., & Limber, S. (1989). Psychologists' involvement in cases of child maltreatment: Limits of role and expertise. *American Psychologist, 44*, 1225–1233.

Melton, G.B., Petrila, J., Poythress, N.G., & Slobogin, C. (1987). *Psychological evaluations for the courts: A handbook for mental health professionals and lawyers.* New York: Guilford.

Melton, G.B., Weithorn, L.A., & Slobogin, C. (1985). *Community mental health centers and the courts: An evaluation of community-based forensic services*. Lincoln: University of Nebraska Press.

Monahan, J., & Walker, L. (1985). *Social science in law*. Mineola, NY: Foundation Press.

Monahan, J., & Walker, L. (1988). Social science research in law: A new paradigm. *American Psychologist, 43*, 465–472.

People v. Edney, 39 N.Y.2d 620, 385 N.Y.S.2d 23, 350 N.E.2d 400 (1976).

Slobogin, C. (1982). *Estelle v. Smith:* The constitutional contours of the forensic evaluation. *Emory Law Journal, 31*, 71–138.

Stanley, B., & Stanley, M. (1988). Data sharing: The primary researcher's perspective. *Law and Human Behavior, 12*, 173–180.

Thibaut, J., & Walker, L. (1978). A theory of procedure. *California Law Review, 66*, 541–566.

Tribe, L.H. (1971). Trial by mathematics: Precision and ritual in the legal process. *Harvard Law Review, 84*, 1329–1393.

United States v. Alvarez, 519 F.2d 1036 (3d Cir. 1975).

United States v. Byers, 740 F.2d 1104 (D.C. Cir. 1984).

Weithorn, L.A. (1987a). Professional responsibility in the dissemination of psychological research in legal contexts. In G.B. Melton (Ed.), *Reforming the law: Impact of child development research* (pp. 253–279). New York: Guilford.

Weithorn, L.A. (1987b). Psychological consultation in divorce custody litigation: Ethical considerations. In L.A. Weithorn (Ed.), *Psychology and child custody determinations: Knowledge, roles, and expertise* (pp. 182–209). Lincoln: University of Nebraska Press.

Weithorn, L.A., & Grisso, T. (1987). Psychological evaluations in divorce custody: Problems, principles, and procedures. In L.A. Weithorn (Ed.), *Psychology and child custody determinations: Knowledge, roles, and expertise* (pp. 157–181). Lincoln: University of Nebraska Press.

11 Ethical Considerations of Psychologists Working in the Media

Robert B. McCall

In his presidential address to the American Psychological Association, George Miller (1969) urged his colleagues to "give psychology away" for the benefit of human welfare and society. Some years later, William Bevan (1982), speaking in the same capacity but confronted with cutbacks in research support, also encouraged psychologists to give the public the benefits of the fruits of their labors, which Bevan observed to be "the most enlightened kind of self-interest" (p. 1316).

By the early 1980s, these admonitions had been put into practice. The American Psychological Association expanded its public information office, created a public information committee within its governance system, purchased the magazine *Psychology Today* from Ziff-Davis, and gave its approval to produce a pilot television magazine program under the joint auspices of *Psychology Today* and the American Psychological Association. While not all these ventures were warmly received or came to fruition, they signaled an increased willingness of psychology as a profession to relate to the media. Further, individual psychologists have been dispensing psychology by appearing as guests on talk shows and, more notably, hosting audience call-in programs on radio and television in which people ask for advice about their personal problems. Such activity has increased so substantially in the last decade that a professional organization, the Association for Media Psychology, was created and has now metamorphosed into an official division of the American Psychological Association.

Not everyone, however, was pleased with these initiatives. Many psychologists were horrified at what they heard other psychologists saying on the airwaves—or what they imagined they might say. Ryan Tweney ("Behavioral Scientists Score Media Psychology . . . ," 1982), an experimental psychologist at Bowling Green State University in Ohio, reportedly argues that audience call-in programs could do more harm than good and would undermine the credibility of psychology, reduce funding for research, and make people less likely to seek help from a psychologist. "There's no peer review, no means of consumers presenting complaints, no follow-up. It's all an unregulated process. . . . It is not at all unreasonable to assume that some media psychologist will make an ass of himself or herself" (p. 2). In response to criticisms of this type, Bruce Marr, a radio professional who started two such talk-radio programs, reportedly said, "I've never seen such petty jealousy and just plain bullshit from some of the APA people" (Rice, 1981, p. 88). And *Newsweek* observed, "never have so many bared so much on the cathode couch—nor generated more static over whether such spectacles serve the public health or merely exploit human pain" (Waters, 1983, p. 116).

This chapter, then, presents a brief modern history of psychologists in the media, especially those who host audience call-in programs, which are the source of most of the ethical concerns. Then the claimed benefits and liabilities of such practices are outlined, followed by a review of the limited research available to document those claims. Finally, major ethical issues are presented, drawing from three sets of ethical guidelines currently drafted.

While these issues have never been studied or discussed with respect to particular subdisciplines of psychology, applied developmentalists should be especially concerned. The main reason is that they are more likely than other professionals to be interviewed by journalists or to appear in the media (for a review, see McCall, 1987). The topics they work with are more in the public interest than those of other disciplines. This will be somewhat more true of those who deliver professional services, but it also pertains to applied scientists. Not surprisingly, then, the issues and literature reviewed below primarily focus on providing psychological services through the media, especially by hosting or participating on broadcast call-in programs in which members of the audience seek personal advice about their problems. But the issues also relate to any professional interviewed by any media, and applied developmentalists and even scientists will be contacted often and asked to respond to personal questions as guests on talk shows.

HISTORY

Talk-radio and television did not start with psychologists. Steve Allen, for example, began television's "Tonight Show" in the 1950s, which consisted of a mixture of entertainment and talk with celebrities. Allen was followed on "Tonight" by Jack Parr and Johnny Carson and by Merv Griffin, Mike Douglas, David Susskind, and Dinah Shore among others on similar productions. These programs were primarily entertainment, but they did suggest, along with the newspaper tabloids and gossip columns, that the private lives of celebrities, at least, were interesting to the public.

But Phil Donahue, who began in 1967 in Dayton, Ohio and was then syndicated out of Chicago in 1974, demonstrated that ordinary people would talk about their problems, and that their private lives and thoughts were also interesting to the public (Shah, 1978; Waters, Maier, & Wilson, 1979).

At the same time, talk radio became popular. These programs began as a means of providing the public with a forum to express their ideas about contemporary social issues. But again, a nonpsychologist, Larry King (Miller, 1979) demonstrated that the intimate details of people's lives, both public figures and private citizens, made fascinating listening.

While the beginning of talk-broadcasting was conducted primarily by radio and television personalities as opposed to psychologists, Joyce Brothers, who first appeared answering questions about prize fighting on the "Sixty-Four Thousand Dollar Question," began to dispense advice in 1958 (Mayer, 1982). But the modern history of psychologists hosting audience call-in programs probably began with Bill Ballence and Toni Grant. In the early 1970s, Ballence, a former disc jockey, began an afternoon show called "The Bill Ballence Feminine Forum" on a Los Angeles talk-radio station (Rice, 1981). The women who called were so willing to bare their hearts and souls on the air and talk about their sex lives and fantasies that this program and a similar one in San Francisco ("California Girl") became known in the trade as "topless radio" (Rice, 1981). Mixed with those who told tales of adultery and unusual sexual practices were some legitimately troubled individuals who seriously needed help. So Ballence brought on a psychologist, Norton Kristy, who was sufficiently successful to provoke the idea of having a female counterpart. Then Toni Grant, a young clinical psychologist, reportedly asked Ballence at a cocktail party for an opportunity to appear as a guest on the program. By the middle 1970s she became a regular (Hackett, 1982; Rice, 1981). The show increased in popularity and was moved to KABC, the top talk-radio station in Los Angeles. Eventually the producers decided that Toni Grant had become the real attraction of the show, and in 1977 "The Toni Grant Show" was launched.

Grant demonstrated that if a psychologist was the host of a program aimed at personal problems, people were even more willing to discuss the intimate details of their lives. They were the same problems that were fictionalized on the soap operas, but these were real (Carter, Howard, Yang, & Gelman, 1979), and talk-radio of this genre became very profitable (Mann, 1980). The movement undoubtedly was facilitated by societal changes, especially the increasing stress in people's lives, the progressive isolation people felt as a result of the mobility of modern society, and the evolving permissiveness of sexual behavior in society and in the media.

Sex, as reported above, was the format for two of the early programs and Don Chamberlain, a radio personality, also hosted a program, "Talk About Sex," in San Francisco in the late 1970s (Hackett, 1982). But discussing real sexual problems on the air gained high national visibility when Ruth Westheimer made guest appearances on Johnny Carson's "Tonight Show" and conducted a radio call-in program in New York on Sunday nights called "Sexually Speaking." Dr. Westheimer studied psychology at the Sorbonne, took a master's degree in sociology at the New School, and received an Ed.D. in Family Studies from Columbia University (Hackett, 1982; Mayer, 1982). Considerable controversy surrounding her and call-in programming in general was ignited by a Wall Street *Journal* article (Mayer, 1982) which documented her popularity as well as the lucrative contracts for books and television programs that were coming her way.

By the early 1980s, nearly every major broadcasting market had at least one psychologist on the air dispensing advice to troubled callers, and many of the problems concerned children and family matters. The professional organizations could no longer ignore the phenomenon. So in January, 1981, the American Psychological Association revised its "Ethical Principles of Psychologists" to permit its members to dispense advice but not to provide individual diagnosis and psychotherapy over the air. On the one hand, the difference between advice and therapy was not specified and the new provision was merely a description of what psychologists who were already in the media claimed to be doing. Besides, giving advice had not been prohibited in the previous version of the "Ethical Principles." On the other hand, the revised statement seemed to sanction psychologists appearing in the media in this manner as long as they utilized "the most current relevant data," exercised "the highest level of professional judgment," and met "the same recognized standards" as apply to psychological services delivered in the context of a professional relationship. Therefore, the new statement did not move the profession forward from an ethical standpoint, but it did acknowledge that delivering some professional services over the airwaves and in other media was a recognized professional activity, and heuristically it stimulated professional debate about the ethical and performance issues.

In March of 1982, the Board of Trustees of the American Psychiatric Association followed suit, issuing a similar statement which read in part: "The American Psychiatric Association encourages the responsible participation of psychiatrists in radio and television programs for the purpose of educating the public about psychiatry, mental illness, and related subjects; and to advise the public on appropriate sources of quality mental health care in the community. . . . It is inappropriate for psychiatrists appearing on radio and/or television to provide any advice which could be considered as therapy to a member of the studio or listening audience. Psychiatrists should not attempt to state a diagnosis or, in any conclusive way, describe the problem that may be troubling the person" ("APA TV and Radio Guidelines," 1982).

At the same time, those mental health professionals, mainly psychologists and psychiatrists but also counselors, social workers, psychiatric nurses, and others, who had the opportunity to appear in the media, began to recognize that they had no training or experience in this activity and sought the help of each other. Jacqueline Bouhoutsos, a past president of the California State Psychological Association and a former member of the Code and Rating Administration of the Motion Picture Association (AMP) of America, began a self-help professional organization in February, 1982, called the Association for Media Psychology ("Media Psychologists Form Association," 1982). These people met twice a year, usually before or after a major convention, and shared their problems, failures, successes, strategies, and concerns. They also created the first set of explicit guidelines and ethical principles for appearing in the media (Broder, 1983).

But many of the most successful (in terms of size of audience) broadcast practitioners were not members of AMP. For example, in 1983 (Barthel, 1983) Toni Grant had 500,000 listeners weekly in Los Angeles alone, Doctor Ruth had 250,000 in New York, Sally Jessy Raphael (a nonpsychologist) broadcast to 115 stations on NBC's Talknet, and Bill Little's show on KMOX in St. Louis could be heard in 44 states. The organization had no real power other than expulsion to enforce its guidelines, and therefore it lacked clout over the field, because the most powerful media psychologists were not members.

But AMP and the phenomenon it represented did have presence. The popularity of the call-in show format plus the substantial salaries and lucrative contracts being offered to a few personalities (Toni Grant was reportedly paid close to $100,000 in 1981 for her show in Los Angeles which grossed nearly $2 million in ad revenues; Rice, 1981), the Ethics Committee of the American Psychological Association decided in 1983 that more specific guidelines and ethical principles were required for psychologists who appeared in the media. Consequently, it appointed a special task force for media psychology which met twice during 1983 to compose such guidelines. These were delivered to the Ethics Committee, which never formally discussed or approved them. Several years later, the Public Information Committee of the American Psychological Association also felt the need to produce guidelines, and members of the old task force began to provoke the Ethics Committee to produce a final set of guidelines for the Association. At this writing, the Ethics Committee is revising the ethical principles and considering the set of three draft guidelines as a basis for statements regarding psychologists in the media.

THE PROS AND CONS OF MEDIA PSYCHOLOGY

The call-in advice program, which often deals with personal problems of children and families, has been the most controversial format, but the issues raised also pertain to other media formats.

One criterion for evaluating these audience call-in advice programs is whether they achieve their goals, which presumably include providing some beneficial mental health service to callers and listeners and contributing positively to the image of psychologists and other mental health professionals as sources of responsible, effective help for people. Considerable debate and precious little data bare on whether the programs accomplish these goals.

Presumed Benefits

Typically, hosts of such programs claim they do not provide psychotherapy to callers (although some television programs depict simulated or actual therapy sessions). But they do argue their programs are "therapeutic" in various ways ("Media Psychology Benefits Many," 1983).

Help those who otherwise would not receive it. One claim is that these programs bring some degree of mental health service to people who otherwise could not or would not contact a mental health professional. "The mental health profession has never solved the problem of making therapy available to everybody who needs it. The radio programs stepped smartly into this gap" (Barthel, 1983, p. 128), *Woman's Day* magazine informed its readers. Toni Grant agrees that she and other hosts or hostesses are giving psychology away for free (Barthel, 1983).

Larry Balter, who hosts a radio call-in program specifically on children and family matters in New York City among other media activities, argues that "a unique advantage to the radio format is that it enables enormous numbers of parents to become aware of options, potential problems and situations, as well as resources about which they otherwise might never had known" (Balter, 1983, p. 38).

Assure that they are not alone. Another claimed benefit is that people see that they are not alone with their problems, that other people have similar difficulties or even worse problems than do they. Balter (1983) argues that "for some parents it is reassuring to know that one is not alone with one's difficulties" (p. 38), and that people can learn from someone else's experience in what Balter calls "vicarious hindsight."

Provide alternatives and hope. Most psychologist hosts attempt to provide a caller with one or more alternative courses of action and to give them some hope and encouragement that their problem can be solved. "On my program," says Sally Jessy Raphael, a nonpsychologist on NBC's nationwide Talknet, "we traffic in hope" (Barthel, 1983, p. 128). Susan Forward, a psychologist on television in Los Angeles, tries to leave callers with some new options, insight into what's happening to them, and ideas on what to do (Mohr, 1983).

Balter agrees (1983). He attempts to help parents understand the child's point of view, to encourage those parents who are on the right track who may be too timid to follow their own instincts, and to offer alternative solutions to what they have already tried. Similarly, Bonnie Ring, formerly on radio in San Francisco, tried to provide callers with greater understanding of themselves and other people, optional courses of action, and reassurance that they can solve their problems ("Media Psychology Benefits Many. . . ," 1983).

Increase referrals. Almost all hosts encourage certain callers to seek professional help, and some make specific referrals to public agencies. Also, many have assistants who help callers, especially those who did not get on the air, find suitable help in the community ("Media Psych Benefits Many. . . ," 1983).

Improve psychology's image. It is widely recognized that seeking professional help carries a stigma for many people, undoubtedly out of ignorance about psychologists and the therapeutic process. Psychologists hosting such programs often argue that they portray a psychologist who is human, caring, reassuring, and not spooky or mysterious. They believe that they help to demystify mental health services and improve the public image of psychologists and other professionals (Barthel, 1983; Mohr, 1983; Waters, 1983). "We make people realize that therapy isn't only for crazy people," claims Toni Grant (Barthel, 1983, p. 133).

Increase awareness. Susan Forward, a specialist on incest, also argues that the programs help make the public aware of problems that otherwise might not be talked about in the public arena (Mohr, 1983).

Liabilities

Opponents of the programs emphasize the potential harm that can be done, which they feel outweighs whatever good is accomplished.

The time is too brief. "I'm very much in favor of the dissemination of psychological information on radio or TV or the general discussion of problems and sources of help," said Willard Gaylin, a psychiatrist and president of the Hastings Center, a research institute devoted to ethical issues in medicine and mental health (Rice, 1981, p. 41). "But these people are giving specific guidance after just a few minutes on the phone. It's hard enough to do that after an hour with a patient in the office."

Similarly, Daniel Goleman (1981), who writes on psychological issues for the New York *Times* and *Psychology Today,* was once auditioned to serve as a host of a television program planned by Goodson-Todman Productions in which people with problems were to compose the studio audience and be interviewed by the host and discussed by the audience. "We never got to sum up the major problems. . . . What could we do if we did? The pace of the show is sure to trivialize even the most pathetic—or sympathetic—varieties of human misery. What of value or insight can be offered in the few minutes between commercials, with no prior encounter and no follow-up meeting?" (Goleman, 1981, p. 39).

In fact, the typical caller gets as little as two and as much as 10 or 12 minutes with an average of about four or five minutes on the air (Balter, 1983). Although the implications of such a brief session are many (see below), distractors of the programs argue that this is simply too little time to be of much help. Worse, the quick judgments required by the host in the absence of complete information might be inappropriate or harmful to the caller and possibly to listeners who believe they have similar problems. "Critics worry that the advice given on TV may be hazardous to a viewer's health" (Kalter, 1983, p. 6).

Creates the wrong public image of psychologists. Critics argue that true therapy cannot be done in a few minutes over the phone, but call-in hosts or hostesses give the public the impression that this is what psychotherapy is like.

For one thing, they give the impression that a problem can be solved in a few minutes—that psychotherapy is a quick fix for problems (Waters, 1983).

Further, real therapists are not always polite, reassuring, gentle, and kind. Kathy Peres, a psychologist who did a television call-in program in Miami and conducted a private practice, reported (personal communication, 1983) that patients who heard her on television were often shocked to find her "much different" in the context of private therapy than she appeared on television, especially when she needed to be confrontational or probing.

Other critics are simply worried that those psychologists appearing in the media as representatives of their disciplines are not very good. Tweney reportedly ("Behavioral Scientists Score Media Psychology . . . ," 1982) worries that some of these on-air psychologists will make mistakes and fools of themselves, which will harm psychology's public image, make it more difficult to obtain research funds, and inhibit those who otherwise might seek professional help. "It's all an unregulated process" (p. 2).

In addition, some argue the discipline should have a say through regulation, credentialing, training, and other means, who is to represent it in such an important way. Others, of course, demur, claiming that broadcasting is free enterprise, that the people professional associations might pick to represent them may not be suitable to the media, and that some of this criticism is simply professional jealousy.

The Research

Many of the claims and criticisms outlined above could be investigated empirically, and some have, although the amount of research available is paltry. In fact, only one serious study of these issues exists. Bouhoutsos, Goodchilds, and Huddy (1986) questioned 368 individuals in two New York and two Los Angeles shopping malls who were divided into listeners of such call-in programs and nonlisteners. In addition, they interviewed 122 callers of one program on WABC in New York (Judith Kuriansky, a psychologist) before, immediately after, and three months after their on-the-air call.

Who listens? Although the shopping-mall sample of potential listeners were better educated than the general population and than is typical of listeners or callers to talk-radio programs, approximately half said they listened to radio and television "programs on which people discussed their personal problems with psychotherapists." Moreover, 64% of those who said they did not listen nevertheless had heard of the programs, and 42% indicated that they did not listen because it wasn't convenient to do so. In fact, only 18% of those shoppers questioned expressed any dislike, disapproval, or discomfort about such programming. The listeners were especially supportive: 86% felt the programs were useful, 82% thought they were unlikely to create problems for people, and 95% said they were definitely worth airing.

Listeners tuned in because they wanted information that would apply to their own lives (36%), to hear about the problems of other people (28%), to learn about psychology (23%), and to be amused or entertained (20%).

Generally the listeners thought the on-the-air therapists were intelligent, interested in the caller, trustworthy, sensitive, and warm, but a few were regarded as abrupt, know-it-all, arrogant, and cold.

Listeners were more confident about their knowledge of psychology than nonlisteners, but their scores were not different from nonlisteners on a 7-item, true/false psychology quiz on the symptoms of psychoses, neuroses, and depression; distinctions between psychologists and psychiatrists; and knowledge of psychotherapy.

Therefore, substantial numbers of people listen to these programs. While they recognize their potential to harm, relatively few think they do. They generally regard the psychologists as intelligent and compassionate, but some are considered abrupt and cold, and they listen primarily to gain information about themselves, other people, and psychology.

Who are the callers? Relative to those who just listened, people who call the psychologist host were less likely to be currently married (24%), more apt to have never married (47%), less well-educated (50% having no more than a high school education), less likely to be currently employed (32%), and more likely to be regular listeners of the programs (46%). Although some people called to offer information, most had a problem, and those problems pertained mainly to social isolation, loneliness, depression, and coping.

Do callers benefit? Immediately after the program, 64% of the callers said they felt better and 57% stated that the call was helpful to them, although 52% would have liked their on-air experience to have lasted longer. Three months later, 66% said they were feeling better about themselves than before they called.

However, callers were asked to rate their well-being on several dimensions before, immediately after, and three months after their appearance. No significant differences in their levels of distress were observed across time.

But, three months after their appearance, callers were asked in open-ended format: "What happened during your call to help or hurt you?" Approximately one-third indicated they had received emotional support or validation, 29% said they received specific advice which helped, 21% increased their understanding of the situation, and 16% felt helped just by talking to someone about their problem. However only 43% provided any answer to this question.

Also, 73% recalled that specific advice had been given them, and 83% of those said they had followed the advice. In contrast, 26% said they had been given a referral, but only 24% of those actually followed through on it.

Finally, callers were asked whether "anything specific" had happened in their lives since being on the program. While 38% said nothing unusual had happened, 16% said they experienced a real improvement in an important relationship and 9% described their work situation as improved.

Of course, these data are difficult to evaluate. Callers to only one program were evaluated, one might expect a certain amount of recovery and good feelings simply because one calls when stress is maximum and it should decline by chance thereafter, patients often politely say they have benefited from a professional encounter even if they have not improved, and no comparison group was studied to determine whether talking with a neighbor or friend might have done just as well.

Callers, however, seemed to be realistic about the potential benefits of their call. "How much advice could I get in a short time?" said one man, and "I wish there were some cure-all answer, but I understand intellectually that there isn't," said another. "It's a quick kind of analysis—it can't be anything but. It gives you some ideas that you haven't thought yet." Another volunteered, "I figure the more I talk and the more ideas I get, the more I can see the light of day."

In addition, most broadcast professionals get letters testifying to their helpfulness, sometimes in serious, perhaps life-threatening, situations. Judith Kuriansky recalls a man who wrote to her saying he had really intended to commit suicide the night he called. "He wrote that just being able to talk to someone about his feelings of not being loved made him change his mind" (Barthel, 1983, p. 133). Sometimes the help comes indirectly. Kuriansky remembers "a woman who was very unhappy because her husband didn't get along with her father. The husband called me the next night; he had heard the program on his car radio and had recognized his wife's voice. He said, 'I always thought she was always nagging, but when I heard her talking to you, I understood for the first time how much I'd hurt her' " (Barthel, 1983, p. 133). Of course, one might assume that those who have been helped are more likely to write the therapist than those who have not been helped; but one also would assume that people who felt harmed would also write.

Therefore, the worst fears of the critics are not validated by these results. Most people felt the experience was positive to neutral, and many more people reported feeling better or having been helped than having been harmed by the experience. The programs are obviously not providing miraculous cures to callers, but people generally feel positive about their experience and somewhat better about their situations and only a few feel they have been harmed.

Are we serving the underserved? A substantial number of the callers rated their well-being with respect to life and coping with problems to be lower than listeners or nonlisteners who did not call. Thus, callers were presumably in greater need of mental health services than the noncalling program audience.

But in another study of 4,900 individuals nationwide who responded to a survey on loneliness, Rubenstein (1981) found 2% had called radio talk shows. They were no more lonely, bored, unhappy, or self-denigrating than the others in the sample who had not called a program. Callers actually had more friends, were more likely to be married, knew their neighbors better, made and received more phone calls, and rated themselves as friendlier, less shy, and more willing to reveal their intimate thoughts and feelings to people they didn't know.

Rubenstein (1981) also informally surveyed 10 callers to Karen Blaker's (a psychiatric nurse) New York call-in radio program. She found that approximately three-quarters of the callers had already discussed their problem with friends or relatives, half had been or still were in psychotherapy, and more than half had called other talk shows about it.

Rubenstein's results are similar to those of early studies of callers to talk-radio programs focusing on current social and political issues rather than personal problems. These surveys showed that people used the programs as a forum to express their ideas (Crittenden, 1971), regarded themselves as socially isolate and lacking in other contacts (Avery, Ellis, & Grover, 1978; Turow, 1974), found the conversation to represent social interaction and companionship, and were accustomed to aggressively seeking out social contacts and companionship (Tramer & Jeffres, 1983). In fact, in the latter study of 181 persons calling four different programs in the summer of 1979 in Cleveland, Ohio, 61% had called before, 41% had called more than four times before, and 19% had called more than 25 times before. Some even estimated they had called more than 100 times. The most frequent callers indicated that they called "seeking companionship."

Therefore, people who call probably do need some help, but the very act of calling reflects a disposition on their part to seek help from mental health professionals, friends, and neighbors, and even other talk shows. Consequently, these are not the most psychological needy people on average, and half have already seen mental health professionals in private contexts. While this may be disappointing to proponents, it should also calm critics. Rubenstein (1981), for example, said, "I am convinced that the mental health of most of the people I spoke with is not in jeopardy from calling a therapist on the air" (p. 90).

But at least a few of the callers are in desperate psychological circumstances and might not seek any other professional help. Rubenstein (1981) describes one religious man who liked "to swing." His wife and his friends would be horrified to know this, and he could not risk seeking professional help. He was even afraid someone might identify him if he called, but admitted "the truth is, I am really looking for help, but I have to do it in a sneaky way" (p. 90). And nearly every host or hostess will tell you they have encountered people who are desperately depressed, suicidal, or unstable, even if they are not the majority of callers.

Do referrals increase? In the Bouhoutsos' et al. (1986) study of callers, only approximately one-fourth of those individuals who had been referred actually said they carried out the referral within three months of the call. But that may be many more people who sought professional help than would have otherwise been the case. Further, referral centers do report informally that the number of calls to them increases when they are mentioned on the air, and some get more clients than they can handle (Barthel, 1983; "Media Psychology Benefits Many. . . ," 1983). Finally, it is known that other types of programs depicting abuse and other psychological problems with a clear message for people to seek help do produce substantial numbers of calls to professional agencies, often by seriously distressed individuals (McCall, 1987).

Conclusion. While the data are skimpy at best, they seem to indicate that neither the grandest claims or the worst criticisms of broadcast call-in programs are likely to be the case. Most of the people who call are not in desperate psychological circumstances, but they do have real problems, ones that may be more appropriate to this format than those of more disturbed individuals. They are accustomed to seeking informal and formal mental health services and frequently call broadcast therapists. Generally they regard their on-air experience positively and feel they have been helped, although it is not clear how substantial the benefit is or whether it would have occurred by talking to a neighbor rather than a professional therapist. Generally, people seem realistic about what they can derive from a brief on-air experience, and few cases of serious harm are reported (but see below). Anecdotally, a few people who call are in serious psychological condition, and some people have been helped substantially.

ETHICAL CONCERNS AND PRINCIPLES

Apart from whether the shows are helpful, some critics have raised serious ethical issues with them, the same issues that have received attention from professional organizations who drafted guidelines for ethical practice in the media. Most are not resolved, and none of the guidelines have been approved by the American Psychological Association at this writing. Both sides of each problem are presented below, and some personal recommendations are offered.

The ethics of professional practice, I am told by Father Val Peter, a former professor of medical ethics at Creighton University and now executive director of Father Flanagan's Boys' Home (personal communication, 1983), can be divided into three broad classes. The first are "canons of *courtesy*"—behavior that is appropriate, polite, and respectful of patients, other therapists, and the profession. The second are "mores"—*customary* professional procedures and reasonable standards of treatment. The third consists of "*right* and *wrong*"—issues of lying, taking advantage of patients, unfairly benefiting from a situation, and doing harm. The ethical issues will be discussed under these categories, which roughly reflect levels of seriousness.

Canons of Courtesy

Generally, concerns and complaints about psychologists in the media often consist of criticisms of style and professional behavior. They are discussed under headings that represent ethical principles contained in at least one of the three guidelines.

When possible, psychologists are urged to provide some information about their degree, training, or special expertise, and not to misrepresent those credentials. The admonition to identify one's credits in the media is understandable, but not always realistic. Generally, the media permit a phrase or at most two to identify the credentials of the guest or host, and this typically involves stating the discipline ("a psychologist"), a title (e.g., professor of psychology, licensed private psychotherapist), and perhaps a special expertise (e.g., a specialist in family violence).

Psychologists, especially those who are not licensed in a state, must be mindful of state laws regarding who may call themselves "a psychologist." A doctorate in psychology is typically not sufficient, except in some states where college professors or government employees are permitted to call themselves psychologists.

Mental health professionals should limit their statements to areas of their special competence. This is not difficult when you are a source for a newspaper interview or even a guest on a broadcast interview program when you can set limits and ground rules beforehand. But if audience call-ins are involved on a broadcast program, and especially if you are the host of a program that specifically deals with the problems of callers, the demands on the breadth of your expertise can be substantial.

Some critics have argued that no one can be sufficiently schooled in all the topics that callers present, even within the child and family area. While some shows specialize in certain topics (e.g., child and family relations, sexual behavior) and some hosts employ assistants who screen out callers who present problems that are off limits, these approaches are often only approximate.

Distinguish between research facts, theory, professional opinion, and speculation. Research (Robinson, 1982) indicates that experts do not label opinion as often as nonexperts and don't refer explicitly to research any more frequently. Experts are vastly more likely to assert facts without substantiation, and they are similar to nonexperts in the frequency of value statements (also typically unlabeled).

While it seems appropriate professional practice to deliberately label these types of assertions, it is often difficult to do so in the media, especially when time is very limited. At least one can label "research," "professional opinion," and "speculation," and psychologists probably should minimize and clearly label political or social advocacy (although situations do exist in which advocacy is appropriate). Of course, misrepresenting the research of other people as one's own; making inaccurate, misleading, or unsubstantiated claims of research findings or therapeutic success, or taking the ideas of others as one's own are serious violations of ethics in any context.

Psychologists must be concerned about the effects of their statements on diverse groups and individuals (e.g., gays, minorities, religious sects, handicapped individuals, the divorced), and must not speak prejudicially or in an unbalanced manner about such groups. The mass media have a mass audience containing members of every possible group and circumstance, so this is a substantial task.

Of course, some groups and circumstances are more likely to have particular problems, commit crimes, spread disease, and possess other negative characteristics, but such information can be presented in a balanced, sensitive, and respectful fashion without extreme generalization and prejudice.

Broadcast psychologists should respect the dignity and worth of callers and avoid being abusive, abrasive, abrupt, cold, arrogant, or demeaning. One general dissatisfaction with psychologists in the media concerns the perception that some are not very pleasant. Some callers have been quickly told that they are "a bad mother" or that they are "stupid" or other epithets. It can become more serious when joking, condemning, or abusive comments are directed to an individual who, unknown to the host at the time, is seriously depressed or suicidal.

Many call-in hosts are worked five or more days a week for two or three hours a day, and are often asked the same questions by different people from one day to the next. After months of programming, it can be difficult to retain one's composure, sensitivity, and support. But other clinical professionals are accustomed to spending eight hours a day in private practice with similar cases week after week and are expected to maintain courtesy and decorum.

Mores

Psychologists hosting shows should be very experienced professionally, trained in the media, and possibly given special credentials. Psychologists experienced at hosting call-in programs recognize the extensive and unique skills required to perform this function well. Not only must one have great breadth of training and experience in interviewing, diagnosing, and treating a great variety of problems, but one needs special *media skills* which are rarely taught in graduate schools. The latter include using brief and clear language understandable to a lay audience, exercising exceptional sensitivity to the words and intonations of a caller's voice, making rapid judgments of the real nature of the caller's problem, offering an extensive repertoire of alternative courses of action that a caller can implement, and developing a sensitivity about what topics and information are interesting to a lay audience.

Because it is a new field, few individuals who become program hosts ever had any training in the media. They learned on the job. Some professionals have quietly stated that perhaps the time has come for a credentialing system specifically for such program hosts that would guarantee stations and listeners certain levels of training and experience in psychology. The stations would have the right to announce such credentialing on the air, and professional associations might monitor hosts and revoke the credential if necessary. No serious efforts in this direction are under way, however.

Psychologists in the media should offer general information about a problem rather than specific advice. Because the amount of information provided to the host by the caller is so limited, psychologists answering call-in questions are often urged to talk generally about the problem raised by the caller rather than direct specific suggestions to the particular caller.

This is well-intentioned, but people do not call for a general lecture on family violence, for example. A wife wants specific suggestions about how to control *her* abusive husband. General information can be provided more easily on interview shows not involving audience call-ins and to reporters doing a story on a particular topic, but the strategy has limits when dealing with audience call-ins.

Psychologists do not provide therapy over the air. The 1981 APA Ethical Principles emphasize, but do not define, the distinction between giving advice and providing therapy. Few broadcast hosts claim that their conversations with callers on the air are therapy. Therapy, some would claim, requires taking an accurate history, assessing nonverbal cues, establishing a professional-client relationship over a substantial period of time, acquiring enough information to make a diagnosis, developing a treatment plan, and establishing criteria for knowing when treatment goals have been met. This is simply not possible under most media circumstances.

Hosts are often encouraged to deliberately inform their audiences that psychotherapy is quite different from what is represented on the program, and anecdotal reports and limited research information suggest that listeners and callers may need such information and reminding. They feel they know more than they do (Bouhoutsos et al., 1986), and they may develop erroneous expectations about therapy by listening to such programs.

Some programs do present actual or simulated therapy on the air. For example, Cable Health Network's "Crisis Counselor" and Daytime's "Living and Loving" use improvisational actors to simulate actual therapy sessions, and Walter Brackelmann conducts on-air counseling sessions with actual subjects on a program called "Couples." Certainly, serious ethical questions arise when actual therapy sessions are broadcast. Although such patients apparently give consent and waive confidentiality, it is questionable whether many of them can be made fully aware of the repercussions of having their session broadcast to an audience that may include some of the individuals they discuss on the air (e.g., an abusing spouse). Further, people get carried away with "being on television." A few minutes into the session they may forget they are being broadcast, and some have been surprised at their own emotions and confessions when they view the program later.

Calls must be carefully and professionally screened. All programs have individuals who screen the calls, but their training and skill varies substantially, and the criteria for who gets on the air sometimes reflects the values of entertainment rather than mental health. Wally Sherwin at KABC ("Toni Grant Show") reportedly said, "We try to get the most entertain—wait, I don't really mean that. I mean the most unusual calls" (Rice, 1981). Generally, screeners look for variety in problems, articulateness of caller, diversity in age (within the 25–50-year-old group that sponsors prefer), and sex. They eliminate obvious psychotics, drunks, ramblers, and obscene individuals. All shows also have a 7-second delay which allows them to kill a call if it becomes offensive.

But many argue that a person's true problem is not always apparent even after an hour of private therapy with a skilled specialist, and it is difficult for screeners and on-air psychologists to discern a serious depressive or suicidal case after only a few minutes of conversation. Also, the criteria are somewhat unfair. Toni Grant admitted, "We really do keep the elderly off the air. They're very hard to listen to. It's sad, but it's a reality of radio programming" (Rice, 1981, p. 88).

A more serious problem may be the individual who does not get on the air. The Los Angeles *Times* reported that a depressed man attempted suicide when his call was put on hold and he thought he would never reach anybody (Barthels, 1983), but such reports are rare. Nevertheless, many hosts employ assistants who talk to all persons who did not get on the air (e.g., Balter, 1983; "Media Psych Benefits Many. . . ," 1983).

There must be follow-up and monitoring. In therapy, when a particular approach does not work, the therapist has the opportunity to contain the damage, repair it, and try another strategy. This is not possible in the case of such programs, even though many hosts encourage their callers to call back if they have another problem or to report how things are going. Some view this limitation as inherent in the enterprise and exceedingly serious in its potential consequences ("Behavioral Scientists Score Media Psychology. . . ," 1982; Rice, 1981). It is sometimes cited as a reason why this activity can *never* be done up to professional standards and in an ethical manner.

A corollary of the fact that no specific credentialing is done for program hosts is that their performance on the air is not monitored. Program hosts, however, are quick to point out that their professional practice is open for all to see and/or hear, and that many more unprofessional and unethical activities occur under the cloak of privacy in traditional therapeutic relationships (Rice, 1981; "Radio Psychology. . . ," 1982).

Right and Wrong

The major serious ethical complaints revolve around the potentially exploitative nature of airing people's problems and the serious harm that may be done to caller and audience by the necessity to make unreasonably quick judgments, diagnoses, and prescriptions for action in the absence of sufficient information.

Such programs must not exploit misery. The primary interest of the media is to deliver an audience to an advertiser; if public health is also served at the same time, so much the better.

Alyce Finell, director of programming for Daytime Cable Channel, put it crisply: "problems have become big business" (Kalter, 1983, p. 5). The media recognize that the appeal of call-in programs is the same as for soap operas (Waters, 1983), but the call-ins are considered "reality programming" (Kalter, 1983). Other critics, especially mental health professionals, have used less sanitized labels: "Its not-so-easy-listening" or "peak-a-boo radio" (Barthel, 1983, p. 128), "it's voyeurism of the ear" (Mayer, 1982, p. 1), and "it's turning neurosis into a spectator sport" (Mayer, 1982, p. 1). Perhaps the most blatant exploitation occurred on the program "So You Think You Got Troubles?!" a nationally syndicated T.V. show that ran for 26 weeks and awarded prize money for the personal problem receiving the best advice as determined by audience vote from a panel consisting of a therapist, minister, and mystic (Kalter, 1983).

The ethical conundrum is that only certain people or problems get on the air, especially the unusual and most intimate, but the short format guarantees that such callers receive little meaningful psychological assistance. In a phrase, the stations, who make an enormous amount of money in advertising revenue, and the therapist benefit more than, and perhaps at the expense of, the callers.

However, some callers are helped. Only a small percentage of callers feel making the call was not worthwhile or that they were ill-treated, they have realistic attitudes about what can be accomplished in a short time, many are in the habit of calling such programs or talking to other people about their problems, and most feel their confidentiality has been maintained (although this is not the case when they appear on television or when they reveal sufficient details that people who know them well can recognize them). Perhaps the exploitation is more in the ear of the listening professional than in the minds of the participants. Yet some people clearly do not fully appreciate the possible liabilities of presenting their problem in public.

A professional must not use his or her patients on the air. The media know that the stories of real people wrestling with real problems is much more interesting to the lay public than a professional describing them second-hand. So broadcasters often request a psychologist to bring people who have experienced a particular problem onto the program to tell their stories to illustrate the problem and perhaps its resolution.

This represents a potential ethical dilemma, because these people have not volunteered to do this, may feel obligated to their therapist, may have extraordinary trust in the therapist and will do something for them that they might not do for someone else, and may not fully understand the possible consequences to them of reliving their problem and of being identified by people who may respond in undesirable ways. These dangers are so great that some professional groups have suggested that psychologists should never ask one of their current or former patients to appear on a program with them.

Other groups have suggested that this should be done only with considerable caution. For example, the psychologist should attempt to make sure that the patient understands the possible benefits and liabilities to their appearance, and the therapist must be prepared to deal at no charge with any undesirable consequences to the patient as a result of this experience. But many psychologists experienced in these matters oppose this liberal stance, because they have seen many people become so excited about being on television that they cannot weigh the potential adverse consequences to them.

A possible compromise is that patients may be used only in non-identifiable formats (anonymously in written articles and with voice and image distorted on radio or television), or in identifiable formats only after careful and open discussion with a second, uninvolved mental health professional who agrees that their participation is without serious risk.

A professional makes no self-referrals in the media. Appearing in the media gives recognition and credibility to a psychologist, and it often leads to increases in the number of people seeking private, paid services from that psychologist. All professional bodies have suggested prohibitions against self-referrals, and some stations require that referrals be made only to public agencies.

Advertising products or services is prohibited. Most professional organizations frown on their members advertising or endorsing for compensation products or services, especially when that professional has not contributed in a substantial way to the creation of the product or the execution of the service. Clear examples of behavior prohibited under this principle include a psychologist advertising a brand of mattress with picture and quotes in newspapers, or a psychologist extolling the psychological benefits of particular cosmetics.

On the other hand, psychologists who write books are clearly permitted to go on talk shows for the purpose of promoting the sale of the book. Also, agencies are frequently contacted by the press when they offer a new service, and psychologists are allowed to advertise their professional services within limits already stated in the "Ethical Principles."

But between these black and white examples lie many shades of gray. If a psychologist consulted with the manufacturer and made at least one suggestion that was implemented in the design of a toy, for example, may their name be used in advertising that toy? Can they make statements regarding the toy's benefits? Can a columnist for a national magazine appear in a 90-second advertisement providing information about a particular problem or topic and concluding that this is what readers can find every month in the magazine? Can this be done only if the information discussed in the TV spot comes directly from that psychologist's column? These examples would be considered at least ethically suspect.

Recently, advertisers have discovered the importance of having their products seen in a nonadvertising context, in the movies, in a dramatic television program, and especially on the news or on talk shows. Many toy companies, for example, ask child psychologists if they will appear as an expert on play or on the effects of television. The psychologist may discuss anything he or she would like, but toys produced by the manufacturer must be used for illustration, the benefits of a particular class of toy must be discussed while examples from the manufacturer's product line are shown to viewers, or the psychologist must assert the developmental importance of play with certain kinds of objects, such as, those of the sponsoring manufacturer. The psychologist is not required to name the manufacturer, the episode appears as an ordinary news or talk interview, the viewer is never informed that the psychologist is sponsored by the manufacturing company, and the psychologist may be compensated from $2,000 to $10,000 plus expenses for a week or two weeks of such appearances.

Generally speaking such activities are considered to be professionally unethical, especially because compensation is being paid to the psychologist to provide a context for advertising a product he or she did not create, and the viewer is not informed of the purpose of the episode. However, presumably it would not be unethical if the psychologist is paid only expenses to appear on a program with no *quid pro quo* regarding content or to appear as an independent psychologist on the same segment with representatives of a toy manufacturer.

But the ethics of professionals limiting advertising may conflict with the law of the land. Laws pertaining to restraint of trade may prevent professional organizations, for example, from prohibiting or limiting their members the right to advertise or endorse products. Such organizations may make "suggestions" but not "guidelines" or "ethical prohibitions" in this regard.

One must not exceed professional responsibility. Perhaps the most serious ethical charge is that the format of call-in programs does not provide the mental health professional with sufficient opportunity to gain adequate information about the nature of the problem and the factors that impinge on it to be able to make professionally responsible suggestions to the caller.

Clinicians know that many clients enter their offices complaining about one problem but actually having another, and it often takes several hour-long sessions to discover all the factors in the persons' background and current circumstances that contribute to the problem and influence the nature of the solution. Yet some broadcast professionals have claimed to be able to diagnose any schizophrenic in two minutes on the telephone, some have told callers they were manic-depressives after two minutes of conversation (Rice, 1981), and some ask shockingly presumptive questions (e.g., "Did your father ever have sex with you?" "You hate your mother, don't you?") after a minute of conversation in an attempt to get quickly at underlying dynamics.

The complaint is that callers are being labeled or diagnosed, deep inferences regarding dynamics are being made, and major life changes are being suggested (e.g. "You should divorce that scoundrel," "You are seriously disturbed and need professional help") on the basis of so little information that they must be inaccurate at very high rates. Such diagnoses and prescriptions could cause irreparable harm, not only to the caller but to listeners who may perceive themselves, accurately or inaccurately, to have the same problem as the caller.

Therefore, most professional associations have suggested that broadcast professionals refrain from making specific diagnoses, using standard diagnostic labels, making deeply interpretive inferences, or prescribing major life-changing courses of action. Instead, broadcast professionals are encouraged to help a caller problem solve, suggest alternative courses of action, or recommend consulting a private professional.

Despite the frequent complaint that unethical practices do occur, the only formal charge of malpractice of which I am aware was a suit that was prepared and then dropped against KABC and Toni Grant for $250,000 claiming that the "verbal abuse, vilification, and psychological assault" a caller experienced caused her severe nervousness, emotional trauma, and loss of ability to breast-feed her infant (Rice, 1981).

OTHER DEALINGS WITH THE MEDIA

Most applied developmental psychologists will not host their own programs, although many will appear on talk shows that have audience call-ins which often present that psychologist with the same ethical dilemmas discussed above. Further, applied child development researchers may be unaccustomed to dealing with specific, personal questions about child rearing which often arise in such contexts, and therefore they may be prone to exceed their competence.

Generally, when appearing on a talk program, with or without audience participation, it is wise to indicate to the program assistants and to the host the kinds of questions you are willing and not willing to deal with. While it is reasonable to indicate that you cannot provide specific diagnosis and treatment suggestions for personal problems, it is helpful to tell the host what you can discuss.

More typically, psychologists will be consulted by newspaper or magazine journalists who want general information about a particular issue or problem or specific information about the professional's research or practice. Suggestions for effective and ethical behavior in such situations have been made in several places (see McCall, 1987). The most important principles suggest you honestly represent your credentials; avoid making self-serving statements; do not deal with questions beyond your sphere of competence; avoid sweeping conclusions or prescriptions for major social or personal change; attempt to label "research," "professional opinion," and "speculation;" acknowledge the work of others when you describe it; and do not accept honoraria beyond expenses for appearances on news, talk, or documentary programs.

Being a source for a newspaper or magazine writer presents special problems, because the writer will select, rephrase, and give emphasis to what you say. You will not have total control over what is published. Many major magazines will check quotes and sometimes facts with you before publishing (McCall, 1987), but most newspaper reporters do not have time and may be insulted if you ask to check what they write. Of course, you are not ethically responsible for what the journalist does to your information, but you must say it right before the reporter can write it right. And if the topic or your views are controversial, be careful not to provide reporters with juicy extreme statements, lest you find them featured in the headline or lead paragraph and your more balanced observations buried later in the article or omitted entirely.

SUMMARY AND CONCLUSIONS

Most ethical issues pertaining to psychologists in the media concern providing personal advice to the audience, especially on radio and TV audience participation programs. Applied developmental issues are frequent topics on these programs and in other media formats.

Research on the benefits and liabilities of personal advice programs is limited. It indicates:

1. The shows are popular, people recognize the potential harm the programs could do but relatively few think they are actually harmful, and listeners find most, but not all, psychologist hosts to be intelligent and compassionate.
2. Callers are more likely to be unmarried, less well-educated, unemployed, and regular listeners of the program who tend to have problems of loneliness, depression, and coping. They often seek help from others for their problems.
3. Callers say they often take the advice they receive on the air, but only a quarter of those referred to professionals actually went. Generally, callers say they are helped by the experience and few claim it was harmful, but the evidence for either outcome is weak.

Three sets of ethical guidelines have been drafted. They purpose:

1. When possible, psychologists should provide some information about their degree, training, or special expertise, and not misrepresent those credentials.
2. Mental health professionals should limit their statements to areas of their special competence.
3. Participants should distinguish between research facts, theory, professional opinion, and speculation.
4. Psychologists must be concerned about the effects of their statements on diverse groups and individuals (e.g., gays, minorities, religious sects, handicapped individuals, the divorced), and they must not speak prejudicially or in an unbalanced manner about such groups.
5. Broadcast psychologists should respect the dignity and worth of callers and avoid being abusive, abrasive, abrupt, cold, arrogant, or demeaning.
6. Psychologists in the media should offer general information about a problem and limit the extent of very personal advice.
7. Psychologists do not provide therapy over the air.
8. Calls must be carefully and professionally screened.
9. There must be follow-up and monitoring.
10. Such programs must not exploit misery.
11. A professional must not use his or her patients on the air.
12. A professional makes no self-referrals in the media.
13. Advertising products or services that the professional did not create or help create is not encouraged.
14. One must not exceed professional responsibility.

Many new inventions or technologies have great potential to contribute to society, but they also may have severe potential to harm (e.g., fire, nuclear energy). Further, it often takes time to perfect a technology and to learn how to use it effectively and responsibly, and some people get hurt during this learning process (e.g., a new airplane design). Also, pioneers, almost by definition, are unusual people and tend not to represent the conservative mainstream of their group, who often oppose their maverick actions.

I believe all of the above themes characterize media psychology during the last 10–15 years. It is an enterprise with great potential to help and risk to harm, we are probably not finished with the development phase of this kind of activity, and some of the first psychologists willing to appear in the media were relatively young, not gray eminences, who enjoyed the opportunity to entertain as well as to help people. Many have dropped out, because their programs were cancelled for one reason or another, the compensation for their media appearances was substantially below what they could make in private practice, they lost their privacy, and they burned out at a demanding and difficult task in which their performance was monitored by thousands everyday.

In my opinion, a few of these individuals are unprofessional, abrupt, abusive, and perhaps unethical. Others, however, do a superb job at a task that demands incredible breadth of knowledge, substantial self-regulation and tact, fast thinking, and judicial selection and translation of complex issues for lay audiences. Moreover, the demands of the media and the profession are often at odds, and some individuals have walked a fine line that serves both groups fairly well.

I believe the question is not whether psychologists or other mental health professionals should communicate through the media, even as call-in guests or hosts. That question implies that if psychologists do not do it, no one will. But nonprofessionals did it initially, are doing it now, and will continue to do it if mental health professionals do not. I have heard programs in which a nonprofessional treated a caller's problem with premature sexual arousal in a light and entertaining way, but in a few minutes a guest psychologist detected depression and suicidal tendencies and dealt with them in a helpful, effective, and professional manner. It was far better to have had the psychologist on the program than to have left this case totally in the hands of a nonprofessional. The proper comparison, then, is whether mental health professionals can do this job better—if not perfectly—than other people, and on balance I think they can.

As with any other task, it can be done well or it can be done poorly. The issues discussed above describe the task and begin to define competent professional performance in this context. We should encourage and reward those professionals who represent our discipline competently by according them the professional status that expertise at this difficult task merits.

REFERENCES

"APA TV and radio guidelines." (1982, March). American Psychiatric Association Board of Trustees.

Avery, R.K., Ellis, D.G., & Glover, T.W. (1978). Patterns of communication on talk radio. *Journal of Broadcasting, 22,* 5–17.

Balter, L. (1983). "Giving away" child psychology over the airwaves. *The Clinical Psychologist, 36,* 37–40.

Barthel, J. (1983, April 26). Hi, you're on the air—What's your problem? *Woman's Day,* pp. 81, 128, 131, 133.

Behavioral scientists score media psychology and its emerging stars. (1982, March 22). *Behavior Today, 13,* 1–2.

Bevan, W. (1982). A sermon of sorts in three plus parts. *American Psychologist, 37,* 1303–1322.

Bouhoutsos, J.C., Goodchilds, J.D., & Huddy, L. (1986). Media psychology: An empirical study of radio call-in psychology programs. *Professional Psychology: Research and Practice, 17,* 408–414.

Broder, M. (1983). *Guidelines for media mental health professionals.* Guidelines Committee, Association for Media Psychology, author.

Carter, B., Howard, L., Yang, J., & Gelman, E. (1979, October 29). Radio's gabfest. *Newsweek,* p. 87.

Crittenden, J. (1971). Democratic functions of the open mike radio forum. *Public Opinion Quarterly, 35,* 200–210.

Ethical principles of psychologists. (1981). *American Psychologist, 36,* 633–638.

Goleman, D. (1981, December). Will the next problem sign in, please! *Psychology Today,* pp. 31–39.

Hackett, G. (1982, May 3). Talking sex with Dr. Ruth. *Newsweek,* p. 78.

Kalter, J. (1983, June 4). No problem is too intimate for your TV therapist. *TV Guide,* pp. 4–6.

Mann, J. (1980, July 7). Talk can be profitable, and radio's proving it. *U.S. News and World Report,* p. 68.

Mayer, J. (1982, February 26). It's 10 p.m.—Do you know where your children are tuned? *Wall Street Journal,* pp. 1, 20.

McCall, R.B. (1987). The media, society, and child development research. In J.D. Osofsky (Ed.), *Handbook of infant development* (pp. 1199–1255). New York: Wiley.

Media psychologists form association. (1982, March 1). *Behavior Today,* p. 4.

Media psychology benefits many consumers and therapists (II). (1983, March 7). *Behavior Today,* pp. 5–6.

Media psychology benefits many consumers and therapists. (1983, February 28). *Behavior Today,* pp. 3–4.

Miller, G.A. (1969). Psychology as a means of promoting human welfare. *American Psychologist, 24,* 1063–1075.

Miller, G.S. (1979, November 13). King of the night: Radio's Larry King gives fans a big lift. *Wall Street Journal, 1,* 37.

Mohr, B. (1983, March 26). Forward with her advice. *San Diego Union,* D1–2.

Rice, B. (1981, December). Call-in therapy: Reach out and shrink someone. *Psychology Today,* pp. 39–43, 87–91.

Robinson, B.E. (1982). Family experts on television talk shows: Facts, values, and half-truths. *Family Relations, 31,* 369–378.

Rubenstein, C. (1981, December). Who calls in? It's not the lonely crowd. *Psychology Today,* pp. 89–90.

Shah, D. (1978, September). Talk, talk, talk. *American Way,* pp. 17–21.

Tramer, H., & Jeffres, L.W. (1983). Talk radio—Forum and companion. *Journal of Broadcasting, 27,* 297–300.

Turow, J. (1974). Talk show radio as interpersonal communication. *Journal of Broadcasting, 18,* 171–179.

Waters, H.F. (1983, November 7). Welcome to therapy theater. *Newsweek,* p. 116.

Waters, H.F., Maier, F., & Wilson, C.H. (1979, October 29). The talk of television. *Newsweek,* pp. 76–82.

12 Ethical Issues in Parent Education

David Elkind

There is no institutionalized apparatus for the dissemination of child development research and theory to parents. As a consequence, a very extensive informal system for conveying this information to parents has developed and flourished. This system includes books, magazines, training programs, and workshops dealing with parenting and childrearing issues. Many of the books, magazine pieces, training programs, and workshops are written or conducted by pediatricians, child psychiatrists, developmental psychologists, and educational psychologists. Others are written and conducted by nonprofessionals.

It is the informality of this information dispersal system which creates the ethical issues. Since there is no professional organization comparable to the APA for parent educators, there are no professional controls over the soundness of the information provided to parents. To be sure, parent educators who are also professionals are bound by the ethics and the ethical constraints of their discipline. But even so, since there is no peer review, there is much greater freedom, in writing or conducting workshops for parents, than there is when writing or conducting workshops for colleagues.

This chapter is primarily concerned with the ethical issues encountered by developmental psychologists who are writing for, lecturing to, or conducting workshops with parents. Many developmentalists, myself included, were drawn into such activities by a genuine concern for the plight of children in our society. Once involved, however, we find ourselves confronted with a number of ethical issues we would never have encountered in the classroom or laboratory. Accordingly, the purpose of the present chapter is threefold: (a) to describe the range of parent education activities that are engaged in by developmental psychologists; (b) to identify and provide examples of the three major types of ethical dilemmas encountered by developmentalists when engaging in these activities; and (c) to suggest some guidelines for dealing with these dilemmas.

PARENT EDUCATION ACTIVITIES

Parenting is not a profession. There are no institutionalized programs for training parents, no scientific journals to disseminate the most current research findings, no requirements for continuing education and so on. And yet there is a great deal of solid information about parenting available in the scientific literature and that data base continues to multiply (e.g., Cath, Gurwitt, & Ross, 1982; Cohen, Cohler, & Weissman, 1984; Jensen & Kingston, 1986). Nonetheless, this material is primarily directed to other professionals. Even the Jensen and Kingston book on *Parenting,* directed at parents, is too technical for all but the most sophisticated layperson.

Accordingly, today as in the past, there is a very real need for people trained in the discipline of child development to translate the research into language and proscriptions that are both understandable and useful for parents. Moving into this field of applied developmental psychology is partly a matter of commitment, partly a matter of chance, and partly a matter of special skills, and, depending upon one's experience, a matter of good fortune or bad luck! In my own case, a vagabond journalistic gene was the culprit and gave me an ear more attuned to the language of parents than to the technical vocabulary of my profession. By whatever circumstances one gets into the parent education business, several different vehicles are available for communicating to parents.

Print and Visual Media

First of all, one can write books for parents. Such books fall within several different classifications. Historically, the oldest and most venerable class of books for parents might be called the parent "handbook." Such "handbooks" present parents with solid information and gentle guidance through the rapids of childrearing. This group would include books like Froebel's *Pedagogics of the Kindergarten* (1904) and Gesell's *The Atlas of Infant Behavior* (1934). Perhaps the most well known and successful book of this genre is Benjamin Spock's *Baby and Child Care* (1976) which continues to be a basic reference for parents. T. Barry Brazelton's books, for example, *Becoming a Family* (1987), as well as recent entrants by Chess and Thomas (1987) and by Bettleheim (1987), also fall within this group.

At the next level are what might be called the "system" books in which the author communicates a particular theory or point of view. Erik Erikson's *Childhood and Society* (1950) and Selma Fraiberg's *The Magic Years* (1959) are typical of this group. These authors present documented child development material from a particular theoretical perspective. Alice Miller's books, for example, *The Drama of the Gifted Child* (1981), as well as my own books, for example, *The Hurried Child* (Elkind, 1981), would also fall marginally within this class. Books within this category are generally professionally sound and are aimed at helping parents as well as other professionals better understand children.

At the next level are what might be called "message" books which are outspokenly "how to." While these books are based on theoretical assumptions, data, and the experience of their authors, their central aim is to provide proscriptions for action rather than information about how children grow and develop.

Hiam Ginott's book, *Between Parent and Child* (1969), falls at the higher end of this genre. At the other end of this spectrum are books which appeal to parent narcissism such as Susan Ludington-Hoe's *How to Have a Smarter Baby* (1985); Eastman and Barr's *Your Child is Smarter than You Think* (1985); and, the Engelmann's *Give Your Child a Superior Mind* (1981).

Another printed source of information for parents is the periodical. Some magazines such as *Parent's Magazine* and *Children* are written exclusively for parents. Others, such as *Redbook, McCalls,* and *Good Housekeeping* run regular columns or articles dealing with child-rearing issues. Many of the articles in these magazines are written by child development professionals who are translating research and theory into popular language and applications for parents. Obviously, many books and articles on child rearing and parenting are written by nonprofessionals but such works will not be considered here inasmuch as we are only concerned with the ethics of child development professionals involved in parent education.

So far I have only listed the range of written materials available to parents. Although videotapes for parents are just beginning to appear on the market, it is likely that these will increase in number and popularity. My guess is that these tapes will follow the pattern of the books, that is, some will be of the "handbook" variety, others will fall within the "system" category, while still others will be distinctively "message"-oriented. Videotapes really hold considerable promise for carrying tried-and-true information about child rearing into the home where parents can view it at their own time and pace. Unfortunately, the power of the technology can also be abused by the unscrupulous message types who play upon paternal anxiety and guilt as well as vanity.

Training Programs

In addition to the print and visual media, there are an increasing number of training programs for parents. As in the case of the print and visual materials, parent training programs can run the range from the professionally responsible to outright exploitative. The guided observation programs, arranged so that parents can learn from observing their own children participating in an early childhood group is an example of a professionally sound training program for parents. In St. Paul, Minnesota, the city provides such programs free of charge along with free child care while the parents are attending the classes. Many similar programs are provided at universities and hospitals for expectant parents, for parents of infants, and for parents with children who have special needs. These programs, aimed at teaching basic parenting skills, are inexpensive and generally most worthwhile.

Other programs for parents have a distinct "message" emphasis. Some of these such as the "P.E.T." training programs and the "Toughlove" meetings can be beneficial to parents who are really struggling and who badly need peer group support. Other message programs are run for profit by nonprofessionals who play on parental anxiety, guilt, and self-interest by claims to create little geniuses. Many of the "message" programs may be run by parents who have been trained by the authors of the program. This practice itself raises ethical issues in connection with the training of those who are to work with parents. Unfortunately, that matter is also outside the province of the present chapter.

ETHICAL DILEMMAS IN PARENT EDUCATION

There are three major, and obviously overlapping, areas of ethical concern among professionals providing education for parents. One of these is primarily professional: "Is the information that I am providing sound, and is the advice that I am offering responsible?" Another is primarily personal: "What are my motives? Does the self-promotion and notoriety that are a part of 'going public' override my commitment to providing the best possible information to parents?" And finally, there is the monetary question: "To what extent is what I am doing determined by the monetary rewards involved?" There are, I am sure, other ethical dilemmas for professionals providing information for parents, but I believe a majority of particular issues can be grouped within these three categories. Again, they are separated only for purposes of exposition and are probably inextricable in fact.

In dealing with ethical dilemmas within any of the categories described above, I have found the book *Getting to Yes* (Fisher & Ury, 1983) a useful guide. Although the book was directed to interindividual conflicts, I have found it helpful in dealing with intraindividual conflicts as well. A central point of the authors' strategy for resolving conflicts is to decide the matter on the basis of some principle rather than on the basis of some motivation, feeling, or desire. Accordingly, when I am confronted with an ethical dilemma, such as those to be described below, I try to find some general principle that will serve to guide my decision. Wherever possible, I look for a principle that would be in keeping with my understanding of the ethical principles of my discipline of developmental psychology.

Professional Dilemmas

A couple of vignettes from my own experience in writing a monthly column for *Parent's Magazine* on older teenagers and a book on preschoolers for parents may help to introduce those ethical dilemmas associated with decisions about the soundness and appropriateness of the material one provides parents.

Weighing the potential risks versus benefits. Recently I did a column on "How Well do you Know your Teenager?" As part of the column I made up a brief test which included some 10 multiple choice items which would permit parents to anticipate their teenager's reactions in a number of different situations from honesty and altruism to family loyalty. Some of the issues were delicate. One question, for example, had a teenager party to a discussion in which his or her parent was criticized and the available choices ranged from active defense to tacit acceptance.

I went back and forth over this issue for weeks. On the one hand, I wanted to raise an important dimension of interpersonal relations between parent and child. On the other hand, by doing so I might bring some parents to believe that their youngster might not defend them when they were attacked. Was I in this way causing unnecessary anxiety and pain for parents in order to make a point? Would the positive benefits for parents outweigh the negatives? For example, to find out how well he or she did, the parent would have to discuss the questions with their teen-ager. Thus, the gains from this parent–child interaction had the potential to be much greater than any negative reactions that might result.

In deciding whether or not to publish the "Do you Know your Teen-ager Test" I tried to find a rule to guide me in this situation. The rule which eventually helped in my decision to publish the test is as follows: To the best of my knowledge and ability to predict, will the presentation do more good than it will do harm? When I examined the issue, discussed it with the editors, and could honestly answer in the affirmative, I decided to publish the piece.

In my recent book, *Miseducation: Preschoolers at Risk* (Elkind, 1987), I discussed the issue of entrance into kindergarten. The research on the so-called "age-effect" is clear-cut. Over the short and long term, on average, the younger children in any given kindergarten class will do more poorly academically than is true for the older children in the class. The research also suggests that neither retention nor transition classes resolve this problem. The best solution is multi-age grouping and flexible curricula at the kindergarten and first-grade levels. In fact, however, since that is not happening, I chose to suggest that parents with children who had summer or fall birthdays keep their children out of school until the following year.

Making this recommendation literally gave me nightmares. The problem is that many parents cannot afford to keep their child home for another year. By economic necessity some parents are forced to put their summer and fall birthday children into kindergarten as soon as, or before, they turn five. Although, on the basis of the research, I believe these parents are putting their children at risk for underachievement, my recommendation is, nonetheless, undemocratic. It can be acted upon only by those parents who can afford to keep their children out of school an extra year or to put their child in a private school. And, yet, I felt I could not deny parents the information or the recommendation.

In deciding to include a recommendation in *Miseducation* that parents of children with summer and fall birthdays hold their children out of school for another year, I drew upon the principle described above: To the best of my knowledge would the recommendation do more good than harm? In general, I have found that parents often read material which reinforces what they already believe. I felt I would be helping those parents who were already leaning in this direction. I also felt strongly that I should give parents who were going to send their children to kindergarten regardless as honest a reading of the situation as I could provide. I saw this as not so much making the choice for them as providing the information with which they could make an informed decision. To salve my conscience, I also urged parents to work with their schools to provide programs that would be appropriate for children at all developmental levels.

Interpreting the literature in a balanced way. Sometimes our professional judgment as to what is sound advice to parents can be co-opted by the social, political, and economic tenor of the times. John Bowlby's (1950) book on *Child Care and the Growth of Love* is a case in point. A central tenet of that book was the concept of "maternal deprivation" according to which the mother's attention to the child is critical during the first three years of life. The idea of maternal deprivation had been making its way into the literature right after World War II, but the reasons are a bit suspect.

During World War II, both in Britain and in the United States, an elaborate day care network was set up that provided round the clock as well as weekend care for women working in defense plants. These programs provided medical care as well as nutritious food programs. After the war, as men began to return from service, many of these day care facilities were closed down. They were "too expensive." In addition, women were losing their jobs to the newly returned service men. The concept of "maternal deprivation" conveniently eased the transition. It was not the expense of the day care programs nor the need of returning service men to find jobs which led to their closure or the movement of women out of the work force. Rather, the dangers of maternal deprivation had to be avoided at all costs.

I am not claiming that Bowlby deliberately introduced these ideas to ease the movement of women out of the work force. Nonetheless, more socially responsive psychiatrists and pediatricians such as D. Winicott (1964/1971) chided Bowlby for perhaps coming out too strongly against all forms of mother–infant separation. Winicott recognized that many women, even after the war, had little choice but to go to work. To tell them to stay home and mind their babies was empty advice that could only add to their guilt and unhappiness. In some cases, it is only in retrospect that we see how we were caught up in social movements (see Chapter 18).

In contemporary writing, Burton White (1975) has had to confront a similar dilemma. He believes, as Bowlby does, that the first three years of life are crucial to the child's life long well-being and advocates mothers staying home and caring for their children during these years. In some ways, his situation parallels mine in recommending that parents with children who have summer or fall birthdays keep their children home. Some parents will not be able to follow that advice and may feel guilty as a result of not doing so. If we really believe the research findings and their practical implications, is it responsible to make recommendations on the basis of these implications even when we know that not all parents will be able to follow that advice?

The issue of providing responsible advice looms large when we speak to broad issues such as the effects of day care on children. Many of us today are reading the research to mean that children in quality child care facilities are in no way harmed thereby. On the other hand, many of us also believe the literature is indicating that very young children can be harmed by low-quality care, which may be more prevalent. In some ways we are co-opted by the times as well. The fact is that more than 50% of women with children under the age of five are in the work force (see Chapter 16). Should we urge them to stay home with their children when we know this is not possible, even when we have reservations about out of home care for infants? Many of us allay our reservations on this issue by urging that one or another parent stay home for at least the first six months. Nonetheless, the pressure to read the research in a way that supports existing social trends is very great and presents a serious ethical dilemma.

Here the principle of more help than harm is often difficult to apply. When the issue is so closely tied to various social dynamics, I think we need to invoke another principle as well. This principle might be phrased as follows: Am I reading the literature in a balanced way and have I taken into account the negative as well as the positive findings? It is very tempting, particularly when we are dealing with a hot social issue, to ignore the data that does not support the hypothesis. Again, I think a general rule should be to review all of the evidence and try to take an objective view. For years, I advocated the retention of children in kindergarten. Over the years parents and teachers had sworn by this practice and I became a believer. I was shocked to find that current research does not support the practice. Rather, it is a conviction that is widely held but not well researched. I had to change my position on retention.

Laboring over ethical decisions. On the other hand, all rules have exceptions. Erik Erikson (1950) once wrote that to be heard in this country you have to take an extreme position and shout it loudly. That is what I have done in my own books written for a popular audience. To get people's attention to problems of hurrying children, misplacing teenagers, and miseducating infants and young children, I had to exaggerate my case. I did so deliberately because I believed the forces working against child rearing were so powerful that the only way to counteract them was to take an extreme position and shout it loudly. In these books I deliberately took an extreme position and minimized the counterargument.

Here we come, perhaps, to a more overriding principle. That is, that we have to be reflective about what we are doing. Knowing that we are making ethical decisions and laboring over them may be as important as the particular decision itself. We may come up with the "wrong" decision. But if that decision is made on the basis of reflection, on a consideration of some basic ethical principles and an honest attempt to apply them, then perhaps that is as much as we can be expected to do.

The foregoing are but a few illustrations of actual dilemmas facing those of us who write for parents. We now need to turn to another set of problems, of equal or greater difficulty, namely the personal ones.

Personal Dilemmas

The personal dilemmas I discuss in this chapter emerge whenever we become the focus of media attention for our views. The issue then becomes that of deciding what our motives really are. "Am I doing this because I really believe in what I am saying or am I doing this because it adds to my fame and noteriety and might also sell more books?" I think we would be less than human if we did not admit to a little ego gratification from being in the public eye. And that egoism is not necessarily bad so long as it is kept in proportion and does not outweigh the commitment to the information being conveyed.

When dealing with personal ethical dilemmas, some different issues come into play. In many ways, the question as to whether or not I am being personally responsible is much more difficult to answer than is the question as to whether or not one is being professionally responsible. We have so many ways of deceiving ourselves, of finding good rather than real reasons for what we are doing, that it is very treacherous territory. A few concrete examples may help to convey this type of dilemma.

Balancing roles. I was asked to appear on the Donahue television show as a counterpoise to Glenn Doman, an entrepreneur who advocates the early intellectual stimulation of infants and children. Dolman (1965) argues that "you can teach a baby anything," particularly if parents buy and use his flashcards. The dilemma was clear. If I don't appear Doman will still be on the show and will get his message across. If I do the show, I in a sense appear as an equal and so legitimize his appearance. I wrestled with the issue and talked it over with friends whom I respect. After considerable soul searching I decided to appear with Doman. It seemed to me that countering his message was the most important consideration.

In this instance I had to deal with another personal as well as professional issue. My appearance on the Donahue show would also mean that my book *The Hurried Child* would be mentioned and hence given more publicity. In addition, I would be appearing on national television, a nice bit of self-promotion. Were these considerations entering into my decision? Yes, to a certain extent they were. On the other hand, I have been doing national television for 20 years, my book had already been out for five years and was doing nicely, one more television appearance was really not going to make that much difference.

Different, but related, ethical issues are presented by figures such as Dr. Ruth Westheimer and Dr. Joyce Brothers. In both cases we have individuals with professional credentials who have become popular media figures. The ethical question here is a complex one. The issue is not whether the individual's professional judgment is compromised by the fact of self-promotion. To some extent the individual reached a position of noteriety via the profession that he or she represents. By becoming a full-time media person, that individual is really no longer a member of the academic profession.

Here, or so it seems to me, is where the ethical conflict emerges. The ethics of broadcasting are not the same as the ethics of psychology (see Chapter 11). If you move from psychology to broadcasting and still maintain your image of being a psychologist, which ethics do you follow? And what if they are in conflict? The real ethical dilemmas of full-time media persons such as "Dr. Ruth" and Joyce Brothers, or professionals invited to speak on radio or television, like myself, would seem to be to resolve the disparity between the roles and ethics of media personalities and professional psychologists. When the ethics guiding these two roles are placed in conflict, if the media decision wins out, than an individual's professional standing is clearly compromised.

Evaluating one's areas of competence. Psychologists in the public eye are often called upon to give opinions on topics which are tangential to their areas of expertise. In the field of parent education clear-cut professional boundaries regarding activities and expertise have yet to be delineated. Thus, evaluating one's ability to be professionally helpful often becomes a personal ethical dilemma. It seems to me that the best way to handle this type of personal ethical dilemma is to get another opinion. Some of us are fortunate enough to have colleagues, mates, or friends whose judgment and integrity we trust. As long as we don't overuse this resource, asking such a person to review the ethical issue is very valuable. Sometimes, when I have been doing a lot of media work over a short time, I tend to lose perspective and have a tendency to become a little grandiose and go beyond my limits. Fortunately, I have a friend who gently suggests that maybe I really do not know enough about that topic to give an expert opinion.

As an example, I was recently called by a publicist at the university who has been a friend over the years. The Baby M case broke and her news director who was giving her a very hard time wanted me to appear on local TV to discuss it. The director didn't know me and asked my publicist friend to make the call. She called and explained that it would be helpful for her relations with the director if I did the show. I am not an expert on adoption, although I did work with a family court for a number of years and did deal with adoption cases, but not of the Baby M variety. Out of compassion for my publicist friend I accepted and appeared on the show. Later I questioned myself about whether that was the right motivation for doing the show. Should we comment on issues which are in some ways tangential to our area of expertise?

When I talked over the Baby M appearance with a friend, it was gently pointed out to me that it really didn't take much persuasion to get me to participate and that my motives were not entirely altruistic. I had gotten a little caught up in the excitement and hype of the case and was not being objective or using my best judgment. Looking back at it, I am a little embarrassed because I know my friend was right. Nonetheless, it is one thing to know something yourself and quite another to get it fully under control. I am working at it.

In my lecture work I sometimes do programs for the students of a school system during the day and a presentation for their parents at night. At one student presentation a 13-year-old girl asked me what to do about her boyfriend who was pressuring her to have sex. I suggested that she tell him "no" and that if that was the only reason he wanted to be friends with her to find someone else. That evening after my lecture to parents, a couple came up to me and introduced themselves as the parents of the girl who had asked the question that afternoon. They were quite angry with me and said, "You didn't even ask her whether or not she loved the boy!"

I explained that if she had wanted to have relations with the boy she wouldn't have asked me the question. The reason she asked, or so it seemed to me, was to get support for not being sexually active. Nonetheless, it raised a serious ethical dilemma for me. Should I answer such questions or refer the young person to her parents? Was I usurping the parental role in giving advice to teen-agers, and did this represent some personal need to be the all-knowing father?

From a purely factual point of view, I could justify my answer. The earlier a girl becomes sexually active the more likely she is to become pregnant and the less likely she is to have successful heterosexual relationships later. Nonetheless, what is my ethical responsibility in this situation? Do I do what I believe to be in the best interest of this girl, or do I recognize that this is a question the girl should put to her parents? Where does my ethical responsibility lie, with the girl or with her parents? And where is my own ego in all of this?

I talked this situation over with some clinician friends. They suggested that I had invited the girl's question by the kind of session I had had with the teenagers. If the groups were structured differently the youngsters might not feel so free to discuss personal issues. Perhaps, in my zeal to talk with teen-agers about the stresses they were experiencing, I was opening up issues that I could not hope to deal with in a short time. Perhaps, it was better not to open them up at all. Although I continue to justify myself to myself, I have stopped running that sort of program for teenagers.

Monetary Issues

Once when I complained to David Rapaport about the meagerness of my NIH postdoctoral stipend he dismissed my complaint with the pronouncement that "Money is corrupting." And he was right of course. At the most fundamental level money means security and beyond that, freedom and power. In our society, as in most societies, it is also a symbol of success or high social standing or both.

Greed is a most likely motive to cause us to compromise our ethical and moral standards. A few of the types of ethical dilemmas centering around money and parent education are described below.

Assessing conflicts of interest. Now that I have attained a certain notoriety, thanks to my popular books, I get many requests to endorse various products from books, to child care products, to toys. Often I am approached to serve as a consultant on a particular project. It not infrequently turns out, however, that the product is already in production and all that is really wanted is an endorsement. The fees involved are often substantial. Do I accept these lucrative arrangements if I genuinely believe the product is worthwhile?

A general rule that helps me in such dilemmas is "Does accepting this money put me in a conflict of interest?" On the basis of this rule I have a policy of not endorsing *any* commercial product. I see myself as an applied developmental psychologist who holds a university professorship. Endorsing products is in conflict with my perception of a university professor. Moreover, it is in conflict with my perception of myself. I do not want parents to buy any given product because I said it was a good product.

But, I am sure someone will say, you write and sell books to parents, where is the difference? The difference is that writing books is something university professors do. It is an accepted way for a professor to earn money over and above his or her salary. Certainly, there is a difference between a textbook and books for parents, but it would be hard to make the case that professors should not write books for the lay public. Moreover, many books for the lay public, including my own, are also used in university courses because of their readability. Accordingly, I see writing books as well within the province of my role as a university professor and endorsing commercial products as in conflict with this role.

One of the most difficult issues in the field of parent education is that of fees for services. In many cases we have to set the fees ourselves and in this way set a price on our value. Clinicians in private practice have general guidelines to go by, but this is less true for those of us who write books, lecture, and do workshops. What should our lecture or consultant fees be? Do we charge what the market will bear or do we follow some more absolute standard?

The issue of fee setting is difficult. But the general principle of accepting money for presenting a lecture or workshop is again in keeping with the role of university professor. To begin with there are university colloquia for which a professor often receives an honorarium. The same is true for invited presentations at conferences. Once one accepts the practice of accepting fees for lectures as part of a university professor's role, the question of how much is no longer an ethical issue.

In many ways this fee issue is comparable to the issue of a university professor's salary. This salary is determined, in many cases, by the professor's merit. The most well known, most productive professors, are also the most well paid. In the same way, a lecture fee will be determined by the lecturer's fame as well as by his or her skill on the platform. For awhile, I felt guilty about charging for lectures. I was cured of that feeling when I found that organizations were selling tickets to the lectures and making money from my presentation. While I have no objection to organizations making money from my presentation, I believe it is only fair to be paid for my work for these organizations.

In short, with respect to monetary issues, I ask whether being paid for what I do is in conflict with my role as university professor. Earning money from writing books and from lecturing is something which university professors do and is an accepted part of their position. Endorsing commercial products is not. Accordingly, while I write books and give lectures, I do not endorse products.

SUMMARY AND CONCLUSION

In this chapter I have briefly sketched some of the activities engaged in by developmental psychologists who are involved in parent education. Although there is no formal mechanism for this type of education, an informal system of books, magazines, and workshops has grown to provide the latest information on child rearing to parents. Books for parents are of the comprehensive handbook, theoretically-oriented system, or hands-on "message" variety. Magazines may be directed entirely to parents or have regular columns on parenting. Workshops can range from those provided in university settings by professionals to those provided in the community by parents trained as workshop leaders.

There are at least three areas of ethical concern encountered by those of us who work in the field of parent education. The first of these is primarily professional and involves issues of what information to convey and how best to convey it. The second area is primarily personal and involves the extent to which the activities we engage in benefit personal ego rather than the parents or audience we are addressing. A last, but by no means least ethical issue, is the monetary one: To what extent are my activities dictated by monetary gain to the exclusion or suppression of my professional responsibilities.

The chapter outlines a few strategies that I have found useful in resolving these ethical dilemmas for myself. First, I try to find some general ethical or professional rule as a guide in making a difficult decision. Second, I try to discuss the issue with others to gain an objective perspective. Third, and perhaps most important, I try to be aware of ethical situations and to be reflective about them and to recognize that I am indeed making an ethical choice. These are personal guidelines, of course, but I hope that they, along with the many personal (and sometimes painful) examples from my own experience will be useful for young people just moving into the important field of parent education.

REFERENCES

Bettelheim, B. (1987). *A good enough parent.* New York: Knopf.

Bowlby, J. (1950). *Child care and the growth of love.* London: Penguin.

Brazelton, T.B. (1987). *Becoming a family.* Reading, MA: Addison-Wesley.

Cath, S.H., Gurwiit, A.R., & Ross, J.M. (Eds.). (1982). *Father and child.* Boston: Little Brown.

Chess, S., & Thomas, A. (1987). *Know your child.* New York: Basic Books.

Cohen, R.S., Cohler, B.J., & Wessman, S.H. (Eds.). (1984). *Parenthood: Psychodynamic perspective.* New York: Guilford.

Doman, G. (1965). *Teach your baby to read.* London: Jonathan Cape.

Eastman, P., & Barr, J.L. (1985). *Your child is smarter than you think.* New York: Morrow.

Elkind, D. (1981). *The hurried child.* Reading, MA.: Addison-Wesley.

Elkind, D. (1987). *Miseducation: Preschoolers at risk.* New York: Knopf.

Engelmann, S., & Engelmann, T. (1981). *Give your child a superior mind.* New York: Cornerstone.

Erikson, E.H. (1950). *Childhood and society.* New York: Norton.

Fisher, R., & Ury, W. (1983). *Getting to yes.* New York: Penguin.

Fraiburg, S.M. (1959). *The magic years.* New York: Charles Scribners & Son.

Froebel, F. (1904). *Pedagogics of the kindergarten.* New York: Appleton.

Gesell, A. (1934). *The atlas of infant behavior.* New Haven, CT: Yale University Press.

Ginott, H. (1969). *Between parent and child.* New York: Avon.

Jensen, L.C., & Kingston, M. (1986). *Parenting.* New York: Holt, Rinehart and Winston.

Ludington-Hoe, S. (1985). *How to have a smarter baby.* New York: Rawson.

Miller, A. (1981). *The drama of the gifted child.* New York: Basic Books.

Spock, B. (1976). *Baby and child care.* New York: Penguin.

White, B. (1975). *The first three years of life.* Englewood Cliffs, NJ: Prentice-Hall.

Winicott, D. W. (1971). *The child, the family and the outside world.* Reading, MA: Addison-Wesley. (Original work published 1964).

Part IV
Ethics and Professional Practice

13 Predictive Parallels Between Clinical and Applied Developmental Psychology*

Warren W. Tryon

Developmental psychology has recently become increasingly concerned with applied problems and contexts (Fisher & Tryon, 1988; Morrison & Keating, 1986; Morrison, Lord, & Keating, 1984; Pion & Lipsy, 1984; Sigel, 1985). These developments can be seen on both the research (Baltes, Reese, & Lipsitt, 1980; Bronfenbrenner, 1977; Kohlberg, 1971; McCall, 1977) and application (Stevenson & Siegel, 1984; Wertlieb, 1983; Zigler, 1980) fronts. Such views of applied developmental psychology consistently combine science and service either through group interventions, consultation, assessment, or direct health care. This interactive combination of research and application constitutes what, in clinical circles, is known as the Boulder Model so named after the 1949 conference on training in clinical psychology held in Boulder, Colorado (cf. Raimy, 1950; Caddy & LaPointe, 1986).

Perhaps the most enduring result of this conference was the view that students of clinical psychology should be trained both as scientists and as professionals. The term "Boulder Model" is used today to refer to training which equally emphasizes scientific and professional practice including prevention as well as treatment. The rationale behind this recommendation was that the psychological science underlying the practice of clinical psychology was insufficiently mature to support exclusive training in professional practice. In contrast, the sciences of chemistry and physiology are sufficiently well developed to warrant training physicians as consumers but not generators of such knowledge, as their entire professional goal is the application of previously discovered knowledge. The argument is that practicing clinical psychologists must also discover new knowledge; that they must generate as well as consume knowledge because their discipline is not yet sufficiently advanced to support a division of labor along researcher/practitioner lines. Clinical (applied) psychologists are in a particularly good situation for conducting meaningful research because they have first-hand contact with the phenomena in need of explanation and consequently are in a good position to formulate and address important research questions.

Clinical psychology has had over 40 years of experience with the Boulder

* I would like to thank David Glenwick, Ph.D. and Celia Fisher, Ph.D. for their helpful comments.

model and sadly enough "the boulder" has cracked into so many pieces that it currently represents a minority position. The major point of the present discussion is that similar pressures will be felt by applied developmental psychology if it continues to promote an interactive combination of research and application. Perhaps applied developmental psychology can benefit from the experience of clinical psychology and make a better go of the Boulder model.

This chapter is divided into three parts. The first section discusses how the initial coordinated Boulder model became unbalanced. Among the relevant pressures were: (a) greater student interest in practice than research; (b) demands for practice but not research thereby impeding research in service delivery settings; and (c) university tenure and promotion emphases on research and publication over service delivery; priorities opposite those of students.

The chapter's second section addresses three aspects of professional development inherent in the application process. Each of these developments consumes human and financial resources and tend to change the focus of the profession and its organizations. The three topics concern: (a) justification for intervention, (b) training developments, and (c) the homogenization of professional training and practice as a consequence of regulation via credentialing.

The third section of this chapter offers some observations and recommendations for how to effectively implement the Boulder model. Much can be learned from the way medicine has structured its better research institutions where application and research have been integrated to the benefit of both. Research funds answer important applied questions, and revenue generated by application supports the infrastructure necessary to conduct meaningful applied research.

BALANCING RESEARCH AND APPLICATION

Student Interests

Undergraduate students are largely interested in the application of psychology to everyday problems rather than in generating new knowledge. This interest extends to the more able students who become graduate students in clinical psychology. The exponential growth of professional schools of clinical psychology (Caddy & LaPointe, 1987) amply testifies to the extreme popularity of programs that emphasize application and provide little, if any, research training.

Interest can be found among graduate students for empirically validating intervention effects. Since these clinicians will typically see individuals, or perhaps families, they would benefit from an understanding of single subject research designs and associated methods of statistical analysis (Barlow & Hersen, 1984; Kazdin, 1982, Tryon, 1982). However, students are typically taught large sample research designs and attendant statistical techniques which they will almost certainly never use professionally unless they are concerned with program evaluation. Individual clinicians simply do not regularly come in contact with large matched experimental and control groups of any kind. The unpleasant experiences typically associated with learning these "research" skills along with the stress of conducting a large N masters thesis and doctoral dissertation usually succeed in extinguishing what little research interest existed during the first year of graduate study, through verbal statements endorsing research remain until submitting their dissertation to the graduate dean.

The rise of applied developmental training in psychology will undoubtedly appeal to and attract many service-minded undergraduate psychology majors. I see no reason why the student interest in applied developmental programs should differ substantially from students entering clinical psychology programs.

My perception of applied developmental psychology is that it also favors the large N research designs found in clinical psychology despite the fact that the developmental perspective theoretically emphasizes change within individuals over time. Greater exploitation of single-subject research designs will broaden the scientific scope of applied developmental psychology in a way that may also be more compatible with student interest. Involvement with large-scale preventive programs calls upon traditional statistical training. Service delivery to individuals requires single-case research designs.

Service Emphasis

Most clinical settings are administrated with an emphasis upon service. Accountability through program evaluation as a whole or by individual clinicians documenting clinical progress are often seen as threatening activities. Current program evaluation often consists of documenting quantity rather than quality of service provided such as the number of clients served during the last fiscal period. It is assumed that "good" services are being provided. If research confirms this perspective, nothing is gained. If research conflicts with this perspective, then much stands to be lost. This reflects the unfortunate administrative commitment to program rather than to problem (see Chapter 3) promoted by various political and financial factors. It would be better if applied developmental psychologists can encourage service delivery centers to make evaluation integral to their service delivery on the basis of finding and refining the most effective treatments possible. This would imbue service providers with the same sense of discovery and inquiry so characteristic of science, which is the spirit of the Boulder model. Applied developmental psychologists will need to persuade potential service delivery centers, or the groups with which they consult, of the desirability to be committed to solving the problem at hand rather than in justifying specific budget lines.

The scarcity of university appointments has set the occasion for many clinical psychology Ph.D. graduates to seek service delivery jobs which, for reasons discussed above, make little if any use of their research training. Hence, from the perspective of the Boulder model, their professional development proceeds in an unbalanced manner.

University Rewards

Professorships are scholarly positions. Accordingly, merit is construed in scholarly terms: publication (journal articles, monographs, and books), presentation of papers at scientific meetings, and obtaining external funding (because these proposals are carefully peer-reviewed by "experts" and few, presumably only the very best, are funded). Provision of clinical services is conspicuously absent from the criteria for promotion, tenure, and merit pay increments. Not surprisingly this places clinical faculty in conflict. Should they curtail their consulting and service delivery activities (especially private practice) and concentrate on professorial duties? Or should they pursue professorial goals until tenure has been obtained and then redirect their efforts to more interesting and financially rewarding service delivery paths?

Choosing either alternative leads to an imbalanced professorship, as viewed from the Boulder model, unless one can find clinical settings in which publishable work can be conducted. More will be said about this matter in the third section of this chapter where we consider how to more effectively implement the Boulder model.

Applied developmental psychologists based in university settings will experience the conflicts described above to the extent that opportunities for applying developmental psychology arise. Will they accept consultant fees and spend time away from the university? Will these experiences translate into publications or other scholarly activities? How much time should be devoted to professional societies and professional issues?

ADDRESSING PARAMOUNT APPLICATION ISSUES

Including application of scientific findings into professional practice sets the occasion for (a) justifying ones interventions, (b) concern over training developments, and (c) involvement with credentialing issues such as licensure and certification.

Justifying Intervention

Clinical psychology began to deliver mental health services in earnest after the Second World War. Because clinical psychology was so new, it lacked a solid research base, thereby justifying the scientist-practitioner model. Every clinical psychologist was to create new knowledge as well as apply existing knowledge.

The major point here is that ethical principles require all applied programs to scientifically validate their interventions prior to, or at least concurrent with, application.

An interesting exception to this perspective was offered by Rodgers (1980). He persuasively argued that the justification for a profession is social need rather than scientific achievement. Physicians became legitimate vendors of health care services long before the dawn of modern medical science because they were perceived to be the most qualified persons to confront disease. Even today, physicians treat terminally ill persons for whom they lack effective interventions, despite the harsh side effects sometimes associated with these treatments. No cure exists for Parkinson's or Alzheimer's disease, which regularly end in death yet, physicians are charged with managing the inevitable deterioration. Competence by training and background legitimatize clinical practice by physicians. People sometimes seek medical attention believing that the physician offers the best available prospect of reestablishing good health even while acknowledging the absence of a cure.

It could be argued that applied psychologists of all persuasions are currently among the most prepared citizens to cope with behavior disorder by virtue of their training and background even if they presently lack adequate scientific basis to justify their current interventions. Two assumptions are implicit in this argument. First is the premise that it is better to do something than nothing, even if it leads to harsh consequences (side effects). Second is the presumption that no other discipline offers a preferable treatment; that is, one that is more efficacious with the same or fewer side effects. Current tensions between organized psychology and psychiatry suggest that any differences in efficacy will be capitalized upon politically and economically.

Developmental psychologists are no doubt equally split over the issue of whether developmental psychology is ready to seriously undertake application of its basic knowledge. The definition of applied developmental psychology is in transition as mentioned in the very beginning of this chapter and in the first chapter of this volume (cf. Fisher & Tryon, 1988). Some may feel that they can only justify a consulting role rather than a direct service delivery role such as developmental testing. Others may disagree. Certainly opinions diverge as to the adequacy of the existing knowledge base to support ethical intervention. We may confidently expect many more articles justifying, or criticizing, applied developmental psychology in the near future.

Training Developments

Caddy and LaPointe (1986) provide a concise but thorough review of training developments in clinical psychology. Koocher (1989, see Chapter 14) gives considerable attention to the ethical concerns surrounding training issues in clinical and applied developmental psychology.

The development of a code of professional ethics was begun at the Boulder Conference thereby recognizing the importance and challenge of moving carefully from the laboratory to the clinic. Emphasis was placed upon establishing a core of minimum standards upon which diverse specialities could be developed. Notice the early concern clinicians had for ethical issues. The present volume reflects a similar concern by promoting ethical awareness among developmental psychologists as they begin to apply their scientific data base to applied issues.

In 1951 Adelphi University initiated a professional training program leading to the Ph.D. degree on the basis that psychology had developed to the point where a practitioner program was warranted. A secondary rational was to increase the supply of professional psychologists to provide mental health services. This was a bold early step designed to emphasize the professional role of the clinical psychologist over that presented by the Boulder model.

The "Boulder" began to crack with two surveys indicating that the modal publications by clinical psychologists was zero (cf. Kelly & Goldberg, 1959; Levy, 1962). It was now clear that clinical psychologists trained as scientists and professionals were not acting like scientists in that they were not publishing papers of either empirical or theoretical import. Moreover, no unpublished research seemed to be going on either. Walsh (1979) indicated that this problem had as much to do with reinforcement contingencies impinging upon professors as with student interests. Academics had little access to clinically important populations and therefore tended to research topics that students saw as sterile. Consequently, students were neither interested in pursuing such efforts postdoctorally nor did their positions in applied settings reward this kind of behavior. Academic credit derived primarily from publishing rather than from service delivery, which further undermined the Boulder Model within the very academic motherland that was charged with its nurturance. Walsh (1979) indicated that we were training neither good researchers nor competent clinicians. These conclusions strengthened the earlier request by Rodgers (1980) to separate professional (clinical) psychology from academic (scientific) psychology.

At this point, professional psychology began to re-evaluate its basic model indicating that the road to professional development is not always a smooth, linear, and gradual process. The next several paragraphs reflect differing perspectives regarding the proper training of clinical psychologists. Initially, the Boulder model governed almost all training programs. Greater professional emphasis would come mainly through the establishment of new programs that could rapidly generate graduates who would subsequently come to dominate the membership of the American Psychological Association and its governing bodies.

The Committee on Scientific and Professional Aims of Psychology, more popularly known as the Clark Committee (Caddy & LaPointe, 1986), met in 1963 to discuss ways of strengthening professional training in clinical psychology. They suggested separate training for clinical psychologists based upon an apprenticeship model leading to a degree other than the Ph.D.. The Psy.D. (Doctor of Psychology) degree is the current descendant of this recommendation.

The Conference on the Professional Preparation of Clinical Psychologists, also known as the Chicago Conference of 1965 (Caddy & LaPointe, 1986), considered alternative models such as psychologist–psychotherapist and research-clinician but, because of their much narrower scope, rejected them in favor of the scientist-professional model. It was concluded that such narrow models did not do justice to psychologists or the settings in which they were employed. It was also recommended that clinical psychology programs increase the number of practicing clinicians appointed to their faculties and that professional activities be rewarded the same as scientific activities.

Homogenization

Application of research findings brings one into contact with the public either directly through service delivery or indirectly through consultation. Either way, one is in a position to influence the lives of other people either through action or inaction, by useful information and by mistakes. The public has a right to be protected, and psychologists are ethically bound to respect this right. Consequently, quality control issues emerge in the form of credential requirements and associated training implications.

The American Psychological Association is organized around divisions in response to the divergent interests of psychologists and their varying professional identities. Hence, we have separate divisions of clinical, developmental, and community psychology despite many communalities. As academic disciplines, no objection exists to their separate identity. But the final common pathway of application appears to set the occasion for professional homogenization.

The number and size of ethics manuals published by the American Psychological Association has steadily increased over the years. The standards necessary to obtain State licensure have been raised in recent years. Certification bodies such as the National Register of Health Service Providers in Psychology and the American Board of Psychology have increased their scope in recent times. These events rightfully reflect the ever greater role clinical psychologists have played in applying psychological knowledge to social-emotional-behavioral problems.

Another factor favoring the homogenization of training was establishment of The Council for the National Register of Health Service Providers in Psychology (Zimet & Wellner, 1977) in 1974 to certify psychologists as appropriate for third party (insurance) payments by virtue of their clinical training. Standards were established and a register kept to certify psychologists as eligible for third party payments. Because of the economic consequences of being excluded from insurance payments, these criteria constitute a de facto training standard.

Fisher and Koocher (1987) discuss the homogenization of training for all applied psychologists (e.g., developmental, cognitive, etc.) brought about by accreditation. Protecting the consumer requires that minimal standards be set. These standards usually translate into core courses and training experiences. Divergent specialities often have difficulty deciding upon how much and what kind of common training to require given the limited time students are in graduate training.

The history of training programs and professional development within psychology has clearly shown evidence of homogenization over the years. Clinical and counseling psychology, for example, began as quite disparate programs but have now essentially merged into a single professional preparation, despite being administered through different academic departments.

Today training of Applied Developmental Psychologists is just emerging with care being taken to insure that training be based upon sound developmental principles (Scholnick, Fisher, Brown, & Sigel, 1988). It is suggested that the developmental perspective brought by applied developmental psychologists makes a contribution distinctively different from that of clinical psychologists in general and clinical child psychologists in particular. If developmental principles are as important as they are alleged to be, then why should they not be incorporated into the practice of child clinical psychology? Do these principles really require a separate Ph.D. program for their implementation? Is there a basis for separate specialization? It is understandable that developmental programs would wish to retain administrative control over their programs in order to better manage the evolution of applied developmental psychology. However, state licensing boards and other officials will need to be educated regarding why applied developmental psychology should be considered as a separate discipline (see Chapter 14).

Homogenization of training and service is a prominent theme within medicine. Medical training requires a common M.D. program prior to specialization. Note that this common training is concerned with practice rather than research, which is considered one of the possible specializations one can go into after receiving their M.D. degree. Some programs offer an M.D.-Ph.D. combination to reflect this training sequence. Notice that the emphasis is upon first training the student to become a general practitioner who then may either begin clinical practice or continue training in a specialty, which could be research. Most likely, the student with an interest in research would pursue specialty training in an area such as psychiatry or neurology prior to research training. The primary alternative for the research-oriented student is to seek a Ph.D. in the aspect of Biology or Chemistry of their choice. This action generally separates them from the health care delivery system.

The fact that service delivery is funded by the health care industry suggests that the medical model will be closely followed as tried and true. Matarazzo (1987) recently extended this view further by arguing that "there is only one psychology, no specialities, but many applications."

EFFECTIVELY IMPLEMENTING THE BOULDER MODEL

The following comments are primarily directed at a direct service delivery conception of applied developmental psychology. I have omitted discussion of consulting applications because, to my knowledge, they have not consistently integrated research and practice.

Despite the early problems psychologists had with the medical model (Ullman & Krasner, 1969), medicine has effectively implemented the scientist-practitioner model at some institutions. I am speaking of departments where clinical services are provided according to structured protocols, thereby collecting information capable of supporting publishable conclusions. Faculty and students have opportunity to gain firsthand experience with the disorders (disease entities) that they specialize in rather than analogue populations selected from essentially normal undergraduates. Implementation of the structured protocols provide students with valuable clinical experience in testing (evaluating) and treating the type of people with whom they will work after graduation. Students also have opportunities to observe faculty administer tests. Results of treatments are directly generalizable to other clinical samples, unlike results obtained from analogue studies, whose subjects often differ in severity, age, socioeconomic class, and so on from clinic populations.

Useful health services are provided to the community during the research and training process. Third party reimbursements fund some of the expenses associated with the research and training process. The resulting clinical infrastructure provides at least two benefits. First, it allows one to admirably complete the "Resources and Environment" section of Federal grant applications. One can show that an adequate subject population, both in kind and numbers, is available. Second, it becomes feasible to provide faculty with office space for private practice to augment their institutional salaries. This benefits the institution in two major ways. First, it raises total compensation to a point where the very best clinical investigators can be recruited and retained. Second, it reduces incentives to spend time off campus and away from students while engaged in the same health service delivery.

Conducting applied (clinical) research within a health care delivery system enriches both the research and health care. Each provides funding and resources from which the other benefits. Research dollars provide the latest treatment by specialists, often at reduced private cost to patients. Third party payments for service delivery helps provide the infrastructure within which truly important research can be accomplished.

The scientist-professional model as implemented above contains all of the elements necessary to make applied science work well. Perhaps applied developmental psychology may try to create this type of setting, through consortium arrangement, if the university does not have a health service delivery system or is unwilling or unable to provide a psychological clinic. Contracts with outside agencies for service provision by students and faculty could also be developed. Such funds would support faculty on their consulting days and throughout the summer months when teaching positions are particularly scarce and students have extra time for professional development. Students could even be charged a summer tuition for the privilege of assisting in the services delivered by faculty.

This would implement the apprenticeship model called for by the Clark committee.

Perhaps the greatest lesson to be learned from clinical psychology is the difficulty of successfully implementing the highly desirable Boulder or Scientist-Professional Model. Peterson (1969), Albee (1970), Albee and Loeffler (1971), and Meehl (1971) questioned the ethics of providing students with scientific training they would not use at the expense of clinical training upon which quality service depended. Quality control of professional competence is important to maintain.

ADVANTAGES TO CAPITALIZE UPON

Applied developmental psychology has three advantages that may help it implement the Boulder Model better than clinical psychology. First, applied developmental psychology has a stronger scientific tradition and literature base to build upon than did clinical psychology at a comparable point in its professional development. Second, whereas the professional role crystalized early in clinical psychology under pressures to provide immediate clinical service, applied developmental psychology is still deciding on what are appropriate professional roles for its practitioners. Third, applied developmental psychology is beginning at a time when the concept of prevention and early intervention are much more accepted than they were when clinical psychology began.

SUMMARY AND CONCLUSIONS

The scientist-practitioner model, idealized as the Boulder model of clinical psychology, is characteristic of current trends in applied developmental psychology but was difficult to implement in clinical psychology for several reasons that are discussed in this chapter. It is difficult to balance research and application for three reasons. First, students are rather more interested in application than in research. This is partly due, in my view, to the emphasis upon research designs and statistical techniques that they will have little, if any, opportunity to use professionally and therefore are functionally irrelevant to them. Second, most service delivery institutions are more committed to administering and defending budget lines than in applying science in its most effective form. Applied developmental psychologists will benefit by persuading service delivery institutions to be problem-rather than program-oriented. The third factor stems from the fact that universities are constructed to reward scholarly activities only. The scarcity of service delivery institutions which are supportive of research creates an undesirable forced choice situation that would not serve applied developmental psychology well.

Choosing to apply scientific findings in the public domain, either directly through service delivery or indirectly through consultation, necessarily engages three professional issues. The first concerns the justification for application. This can come either from the published literature or from the argument that specialized training makes applied developmental psychologists best suited for the practical role they have chosen to play. The second concern is with training developments, to insure that students are properly prepared to carry out their professional responsibilities. Third, the necessity to protect the public interest fosters similarity in training among applied fields of psychology. Matarazzo (1987) has argued in favor of this view by indicating that "there is only one psychology, no specialities, but many applications."

Finally, we considered medical examples where the Boulder model was effectively implemented to the benefit of both research and practice. These institutions embody a commitment to scientific issues as well as to service delivery.

REFERENCES

Albee, G.W. (1970). The short, unhappy life of clinical psychology. *Psychology Today, 4*, 42–74.

Albee, G.W., & Loeffler, E. (1971). Role conflicts in psychology and their implications for a revaluation of training models. *Canadian Psychologist, 4*, 465–481.

Baltes, P.B., Reese, H.W., & Lipsitt, P.L. (1980). Life-span developmental psychology. *Annual Review of Psychology, 31*, 65–110.

Barlow, D.H., & Hersen, M. (1984). *Single-case experimental designs: Strategies for studying behavior change* (2nd ed.). New York: Pergamon Press.

Bronfenbrenner, U. (1977). Toward an experimental ecology of human development. *American Psychologist, 32*, 513–531.

Caddy, G.R., & LaPointe, L.L. (1986). The training of professional psychologists: Historical developments and present trends. In G.S. Tryon (Ed.), *The professional practice of psychology* (pp. 3–49). Norwood, NJ: Ablex.

Fisher, C.B., & Koocher, G.P. (1987). *To be or not to be: The accreation dilemma for APA and emerging specialities.* Unpublished manuscript.

Fisher, C.B., & Tryon, W.W. (1988). Ethical issues in the research and practice of applied developmental psychology. *Journal of Applied Developmental Psychology, 9*, 27–39.

Kazdin, A.E. (1982). *Single-case research designs: Methods for clinical and applied settings.* New York: Oxford University Press.

Kelly, E.L., & Goldberg, L.R. (1959). Correlates of later performance and specialization in psychology: A follow-up study of the trainees assessed in the VA selection research project. *Psychological Monographs, 73* (12, Whole No. 482), 1–32.

Kohlberg, L. (1971). From is to ought: How to commit the naturalistic fallacy and get away with it in the study of moral development. In T. Mischel (Ed.), *Cognitive development and epistemology* (pp. 151–235). New York: Academic Press.

Koocher, G.P. (1990). Practicing applied developmental psychology: Playing the game to win. In C.B. Fisher & W.W. Tryon (Eds.), *Ethics in applied developmental psychology.* Norwood, NJ: Ablex.

Levy, L.H. (1962). The skew in clinical psychology. *American Psychologist, 17*, 244–249.

Matarazzo, J.D. (1987). There is only one psychology, no specialities, but many applications. *American Psychologist, 42*, 893–903.

McCall, R.B. (1977). Challenges to a science of developmental psychology. *Child Development, 48,* 333–344.

Meehl, P.E. (1971). A scientific, scholarly, nonresearch doctorate for clinical practitioners: Arguments pro and con. In R.R. Holt (Ed.), *New horizons for psychotherapy: Autonomy as a profession.* New York: International Universities Press.

Morrison, F.J., & Keating, D.P. (1986). *Applied developmental psychology* (Vol. 2). Orlando, FL: Academic Press, Inc.

Morrison, F.J., Lord, C., & Keating, D.P. (1984). *Applied developmental psychology* (Vol. 1). Orlando, FL: Academic Press.

Pion, G.M., & Lipsy, M.W. (1984). Psychology and society: The challenge of change. *American Psychologist, 39,* 739–754.

Rodgers, D.A. (1980). The status of psychology in hospitals: Technicians or professionals. *The Clinical Psychologist, 33,* 5–7.

Scholnick, E.K., Fisher, C.B., Brown, A., & Sigel, I. (1988, Spring). Report on Applied Developmental Psychology. *American Psychological Association Division 7 Newsletter,* pp. 6–10.

Sigel, I.E. (1985). *Advances in applied developmental psychology* (Vol. 1). Norwood, NJ: Ablex.

Stevenson, H.W., & Siegel, A.S. (1984). *Child development research and social policy* (Vol. 1). Chicago, IL: The University of Chicago Press.

Tryon, W.S. (1982). A simplified time-series analysis for evaluating treatment interventions. *Journal of Applied Behavior Analysis, 15,* 423–429.

Ullman, L.P., & Krasner, L. (1969). *A psychological approach to abnormal behavior.* Englewood Cliffs, NJ: Prentice-Hall.

Walsh, J. (1979). Professional psychologists seek to change roles and rules in the field. *Science, 203,* 338–340.

Wertlieb, D. (1983). Some foundations and directions for applied developmental psychology. *Journal of Applied Developmental Psychology, 4,* 349–358.

Zigler, E. (1980). Welcoming a new journal. *Journal of Applied Developmental Psychology, 1,* 1–6.

Zimet, C.N., & Wellner, A. (1977). The council for the National Register of Health Service Providers in Psychology. *International Encyclopedia of Neurology, Psychiatry, Psychoanalysis, and Psychology, 5,* 329–332.

14 Practicing Applied Developmental Psychology: Playing the Game You Can't Win*

Gerald P. Koocher

WHAT IS APPLIED DEVELOPMENTAL PSYCHOLOGY ANYWAY?

While there are many training programs in psychology designed to teach application of developmental principles and research to serve human needs different labels are often used. Some might be called programs in clinical-child psychology, pediatric psychology, or school psychology. In this chapter, however, applied developmental psychology will be used to describe other programs which evolved out of academic developmental psychology as opposed to the more traditional human service programs in psychology (i.e., clinical, counseling, and school psychology). A survey conducted under the auspices of the American Psychological Association's Division of Developmental Psychology in 1986 (Shantz, 1987) analyzed survey data from 35 such programs. The result is an interesting and instructive picture of this evolving speciality.

Although developmental psychologists have long engaged in teaching, research, and consultation with significant beneficial applications, the formation of programs to train applied developmental psychologists is a relatively recent event. Wertlieb (1983) cites three factors that account for these developments: (a) increasing dissatisfaction with traditional training models, (b) increasing social pressures for within and outside the field for contributions to social problem-solving and public policy formation, and (c) a changing employment market where fewer academicians and more practitioners are demanded. The survey noted above found programs using many different descriptive titles including: Child and Family; Developmental Disabilities; Human Development; and Child, Family, Community; a well as applied developmental psychology. The survey revealed that nearly half of such doctoral programs began in 1980 or later with 74% evolving after 1970. When asked whether the program prepares students for state licensing or certification 43% replied in the negative and 54% in the affirmative (some programs were uncertain). Of the 54% which indicated that their

---

* An earlier version of this chapter was presented at the 95th Annual Convention of the American Psychological Association, New York, NY, August 31, 1987.

program prepares students for licensing, nearly all indicated that they considered such preparation optional.

Forty-eight percent of the programs were housed in departments of psychology, while the rest were in such departments or colleges as education, human development, child and family development, human ecology, social ecology, individual and family studies, child study, and family resources and consumer sciences. Only a third of these programs offered or required courses on intervention programs and techniques or program evaluation methods. More than half offered no courses in developmental disabilities, and just over half offered any courses in family systems or family functioning. The use of practica and field placements were equally uneven and the mission statements of the programs were often rather vague in describing the professional roles to which their graduates might aspire.

There have been specific attempts to define the field of applied developmental psychology (see, for example: Fisher & Tryon, 1988; Scholwick, Fisher, Brown, & Sigel, 1988; Zigler & Finn, 1984; as well as the symposium of papers on the definition of and training in applied developmental psychology published in volume 4 (1983) of the *Journal of Applied Developmental Psychology*.) Such efforts, however, have generally been ignored by departments or programs which have recast themselves as engaged in applied developmental training with little, if any, attention to the meaning of such a change. Most of the efforts to define the field seem to agree that a wide spectrum of activities in both knowledge generation and knowledge application are appropriate. Such activities might include research designed to address social concerns, design and evaluation of primary prevention programs, family education, and family or individual-oriented direct interventions. The chief problem is that few newly recast programs give much consideration to where their students will fit along this continuum of activities.

Applied developmental psychology programs often do not have a very clear vision of the specific activities in which their students ought to engage during or after their academic training. As a result, program faculty often fail to consider whether the students who graduate from their programs will need to qualify for licensing. This lack of vision and thoughtful planning leaves graduates of such programs vulnerable to many difficulties as they seek employment and often relegates them to a kind of netherworld of job opportunities.

TRENDS IN PROFESSIONAL REGULATION

As these programs in applied developmental psychology have been quietly evolving in the background, psychological practitioners regularly contend with each other over policies of who should deliver what type of services to whom. Professional association boards and committees as well as statutory licensing bodies have been active in this arena for at least three decades. Ironically, the academic and research psychologists most centrally involved in the evolution of applied developmental psychology programs have remained aloof from such activities. The net result is that they and the graduates of their programs are increasingly being excluded from practice opportunities, not so much because of regulatory malevolence as because of their own lack of attention to and participation in the process.

Some developmental psychologists reading this chapter may ask themselves, "Why should I care about accreditation or licensing if I am not delivering clinical services?" The most simple answer is that society, in the form of regulatory aspects of government, is increasingly forcing consumer protection and other accountability mechanisms on professionals who interact with the public. This includes consulting and public education. More complex answers involve consideration of the training and employment needs of their students, as detailed below.

One important trend in professional regulation has been the requirement of a doctoral degree in psychology. Those of use who serve on state licensing or certification boards are continually troubled by the broad range of individuals with quite diverse training (not necessarily related to psychological practice) who claim to be and seek licensure as psychologists. People with degrees in pastoral care, rehabilitation, special education, social and human relations, home and family life, general studies, health and physical education have all sought licensing and recognition as health service providers in psychology (Keith-Spiegel & Koocher, 1985). At the same time, the survey cited earlier revealed less than half of the programs in applied developmental psychology are housed in psychology departments. The American Psychological Association's *General Guidelines for providers of Psychological Services* (APA, 1987), and *Model Act for State Licensure of Psychologists* (APA, 1987) both specify that the doctoral degree of the practitioner be in psychology. This stands in contrast to days gone by when degrees in "closely related fields" were tolerated. Indeed, the *Model Act* specifies that all degrees should preferably be from APA-accredited programs for candidates to be licensed after 1995. At this time there seems little prospect that the APA accreditation program will be expanded to include applied developmental psychology.

Another major trend has involved specification of curriculum elements as a prerequisite for professional practice. At the very least these would include coursework in psychological assessment and interventions, yet the survey (Shantz, 1987) suggests that two-thirds of applied developmental psychology programs do not offer or require such course work. Aside from the difficulty graduates of such programs will have in becoming licensed, one wonders what faculty members have in mind when they purport to train applied psychologists without assessment or intervention skills (see Chapter 7 for a discussion of essential curriculum requirements for training in developmental intervention). How are they to recognize pathology, adequately measure developmental progression, or assess behavioral change?

Restricted access to internship and practica which includes supervision by licensed psychologists is also an increasingly important trend. Although the APA Council of Representatives has voted that it is "not necessarily inappropriate" for approved internship facilities to offer training to well-qualified applicants from programs in developmental psychology (Abeles, 1984, p. 647), access to students from applied developmental psychology programs remains limited. Internship and practicum sites expect students to have at least a core of coursework in assessment and intervention, which is often not provided by their academic programs. Thus students in applied developmental psychology programs are often not well prepared to compete for access to such experiential programs. This will cause additional barriers for those who wish to be licensed, because every jurisdiction requires a substantial amount of supervised experience by licensed psychologists and a prerequisite to be seated for the licensing examination. In addition, faculty members teaching in applied developmental psychology programs are often not licensed themselves. Some such faculty have simply never bothered to seek licensure or have found it irrelevant to their work. Other faculty do not themselves have adequate credentials for state licensing. As a result, many programs staffed by such faculty do not have the capacity to provide their students with requisite in-house supervision for licensing purposes.

A classic example of the problem exists at the Graduate School of Education at a local university. A small doctoral program exists within the school in "Counseling and Consulting Psychology." A certain mix of institutional arrogance and ambivalence has enabled that program to avoid seeking American Psychological Association accreditation to date. Faculty members have been known to observe, "We don't need to seek accreditation or be like everyone else, students will continue to enroll here anyway." Others note that clinical programs are expensive to operate, relative to research/academic programs since they require small class sizes for clinical course of practicum instruction. A dean is unlikely to approve development of such programs during times of fiscal restraint. Still others argue that students would not want to take the extra coursework or time to complete a degree program which would be required, were the program to move toward APA accreditation standards. Nonetheless, the current program is clearly a psychology program and it's graduates have routinely been granted admission to candidacy for licensure by the Massachusetts Board of Registration in Psychology.

Elsewhere in the same School of Education students are granted degrees in "Human Development." Although the faculty of both programs overlaps to some degree and includes many fine psychologists, these degrees are not necessarily equivalent to degrees in psychology. On the surface (i.e., in its catalogues) the school makes no claim to be training professional psychologists, yet many students quite clearly intend to practice applied developmental psychology in public schools, other educational settings, or private practice following graduation. When applying for licensure such students must routinely shoulder the burden of proving that their doctorates are psychological in content and nature.

New legislation and regulations have been passed which will shut the door to licensure in Massachusetts on graduates without degrees in *psychology,* and eventually require that all licensed psychologists have a common core curriculum. All graduate programs in the state whose students routinely apply for licensure were notified and two public hearings were held. Who came to discuss the issues on behalf of the School of Education? The only representative was an unofficial one, a first-year graduate student who was legitimately concerned as to whether she would be able to practice upon completion of her degree. Unfortunately, such disinterest in professional regulation on the part of developmental psychologists is not atypical nor limited to Massachusetts. Students from such programs are the ultimate victims of their faculty's indifference.

Such attitudes on the part of faculty in developmental programs leaves all decisions regarding the boundaries of applied developmental psychology activities to statutory licensing boards. Developmental psychology faculty members seldom seek appointment to or serve on such panels. As a result, graduates of their programs will increasingly be forced to seek legitimacy and employment through "clinical" standards for which they will generally be ill-prepared.

WHAT ARE THE CENTRAL ISSUES?

The reader should not confuse the practice of "professional psychology" with only those services offered through mental health settings or private practice offices. Any psychologist who is offering services to the public may be considered a professional psychologist. From the perspective of applied developmental psychology activities family education, developmental assessment, and the design or implementation of primary prevention programs are all examples of professional services. In addition, the distinction between "experimental" and "control" groups in developmental research can also tread a very fine line as a professional psychological practice activity (see Chapters 3 and 4).

There are essentially four types of professional psychologists who comprise the bulk of the problem. First, are those psychologists trained as human service providers (e.g., clinical or counseling psychology graduates) who want to serve children or families, but have no specific child-oriented training. Second, there are psychologists with degrees in developmental psychology, child development, or human development who have applied training and want to serve children or who wish to develop applied skills, but do not have traditional assessment or intervention training. Third, there are those psychologists in the previously mentioned groups who begin evaluating or treating children or families without specialized training. Finally, there are practitioners trained solely in theories of child or adult psychopathology, who cannot assess children or adults with respect to normal human development.

Psychologists in this latter category are clearly in violation of the *Ethical Principles of Psychologists,* (APA, 1981) especially *Principle 2* (competence) and *Principle 6* (welfare of the consumer). Unfortunately, they are not likely to get caught unless or until they make serious mistakes. That is to say, the public is unlikely to recognize their incompetence from the outset and enforcement bodies such as ethics committees or licensing boards are not likely to catch them until a serious problem leads to a complaint. Even when they are caught, enforcement is hardly certain (Hogan, 1979; Koocher, 1979).

It is possible to complete an APA-approved doctoral program in clinical or counseling psychology, for example, without ever seeing a child client or taking a course in developmental psychology. Many psychologists practicing family therapy have never studied developmental psychology or child psychopathology. Too often psychologists who have completed their doctorates and licensure requirements seem to have the attitude that they can read a book or take a workshop on a new technique or treatment modality and then begin immediately to use it in their practices. Because of their relative lack of insight with respect to their own competencies and weaknesses, such colleagues are unlikely to step forward and identify themselves.

There are also "adult-trained" clinical or counseling psychologists who would like to acquire developmentally focused child training. There are significant financial disincentives for such individuals to revert to training status in order to acquire the experience they should have. Although it is worth noting that they exist in significant numbers, they are not the prime focus of this chapter. The best means to influence ethical conduct by such adult-trained practitioners is by improving the teaching of professional ethics in graduate programs, so that such values are inculcated in students at their most formative stages. This should in turn be followed by vigorous efforts within the professional community to sensitize more senior practitioners to issues related to placing appropriate limits on one's practice.

The developmental psychologist who wants to learn "clinical," "counseling," or other applied skills is often immediately regarded with suspicion by practitioner colleagues. Graduates of applied developmental psychology programs are often cast as "trying to sneak in the back door" (Orgel, 1983) or as intending to be designated a clinician by nontraditional means. Even the term "retread" implies a backward or regressive movement, "a going back," rather than a more appropriate view of one's professional career as a continuing evolution or lifelong process of career competence development. The prevalent retread views tend to be predicated on an assumption that there is a single route to competence in professional practice. In any case, psychologists who wish to develop such new skills must also identify and then locate appropriate and relevant training while facing economic burdens similar to those of the so-called "adult" practitioner. The developmentalists are, however, at some specific disadvantage by virtue of the traditional views of applied training which tend to cast them as "back door" clinicians.

RETRAINING OR COMPETENCE BUILDING?

American psychology has officially addressed the problem of the developmental psychologist who wishes to retrain as practitioner, while ignoring the "adult" practitioner. A specific mechanism in the form of retraining or so-called "retread" programs has emerged with detailed policy recommendations (American Psychological Association, 1976, 1977). Psychologists who wish to switch from being a developmental psychologist to a clinical, counseling, or school psychologist are told what to do:

> "Go back to school. Go to a program specially designed to retrain psychologists and fulfill all of the formal requirements of the degree you seek, which were not a part of your initial doctorate in psychology." Candidates are told to expect that they will be given due credit for previously satisfied coursework requirements and are cautioned that a mere internship or practicum experience does not constitute adequate retraining. (American Psychological Association, 1976, p. 6)

Although the APA Council hoped to encourage universities and professional schools to offer such programs the response has been underwhelming. One informal assessment (Koocher, 1984) suggests that the total number of such openings in such programs in the United States is less than 200 per year, and most of the programs require two to three years of full-time study. Tuition is substantial in such programs, since the nature of the teaching components and necessary practica generally require low student-to-faculty ratios.

The current system obviously makes it quite difficult for a psychologist in midcareer to change specialities. As suggested above, the senior psychologist who trained at a time (years ago) when current requirements had yet to be formulated is likely to be closed out entirely. There are many such colleagues, who prefer to remain anonymous, who are boxed into an interesting paradox. They regularly teach students in clinical or counseling courses at advanced levels, but under current credential restrictions are not permitted to practice what they are teaching others to practice. While this presumed incompetence to practice is a technical presumption of questionable validity, it is nonetheless built into many credentialing systems in psychology.

The American Psychological Association treats graduates of applied developmental psychology programs exactly the same as those from traditional programs in developmental psychology. Based on the survey data collected by the Division of Developmental Psychology, that appears to be a wise practice, since the training offered through such programs varies so widely.

WHO NEEDS THE RETRAINING?

Current policy as articulated in the American Psychological Association's standards and model statute, cited above, is directed toward clinical, counseling, and school psychology. These policies imply that retraining in a formal program is the only true road to practitioner competence. I refer to this assumption as the "single route theory." It clearly exists as a professional ideal in defiance of empirical reality. There are many competent clinicians who acquired their skills in other ways, including virtually all of those who trained in the 1940s and 1950s, when clinical psychology was in its infancy and toddlerhood. It has been argued that current credentials in psychology hold little predictive validity for competent professional practice (Gross, 1978; Hogan, 1979; Koocher, 1979), and the Standards for Providers of Psychological Services make no pretense of assuring competence.

While professional standards may provide some low-level protection against outright quackery, there is little or no evidence of their validity as guides to practitioner competence. The notion that a single prescribed type of program is the sole route to develop professional skill for highly specific service applications flies in the face of common sense. The important question is not how to turn developmental psychologists into child clinicians or school psychologists, but rather how to provide the nonclinician with the skills necessary to perform some valuable professional services competently and recognize such competence with appropriate credentials to admit such individuals to the practice of psychology. There is no easy way to provide the necessary training; it is expensive and time consuming for both the trainers and the trainees. In order to reach valid answers to such questions developmental psychologists and their practitioner colleagues must begin a genuine dialogue on appropriate training for all those who provide direct services to children, youth, and families.

This will require that the faculty of applied developmental psychology degree programs declare themselves as such, and make certain that the degrees they offer are listed as degrees in *psychology*. Curricula must be revised to conform with existing professional and statutory requirements. Faculty members must familiarize themselves with the standards for professional practice and become full participants in continuing discussions around the validity and evolution of such standards. They must participate in the regulatory process, rather than remain aloof from it. Students must be provided with clear and specific statements regarding the limitations they will face in professional practice, both before entering an academic program and continually throughout the program. So long as applied developmental psychology programs exist without such changes the faculty are little more than unethical and inconsiderate coaches inviting students to become players in a game they cannot possibly win.

THE FUTURE

The dark tone used above is meant to underscore the need to take current trends in professional regulation seriously while opportunity for self-direction remains available. We can make changes now that will provide graduates of applied developmental programs with career opportunities along one or more avenues yet to be decided upon. To remain inactive in this respect leaves students in an untenable situation and that is unethical.

SUMMARY AND CONCLUSIONS

As employment possibilities in academia and research funding opportunities in developmental psychology have become more difficult to find, both graduate students and fully trained psychologists with degrees in developmental psychology are increasingly seeking to broaden their employment opportunities. Applied developmental psychology is a natural outgrowth of this trend. Simultaneously, psychologists trained as human service providers by more traditional routes (e.g., clinical, counseling, and school psychologists) have sought to restrict access to public practice by persons without traditionally defined professional credentials. Professional associations and state regulatory bodies have generally supported such restrictions in the name of consumer protection. As a result, it will become increasingly difficult for applied developmental psychologists to practice (as opposed to teach and conduct research), even if they are well-trained and competent to perform tasks more often associated with human service or health service providers. Educational institutions and some faculty compound the problem by ignoring or remaining aloof from the regulatory process both within the profession and within governmental entities. Much can be done to alleviate this problem once it is recognized. To continue to sidestep these important matters is unethical given the consequences for current students.

REFERENCES

Abeles, N. (1984). Proceedings of the American Psychological Association, Incorporated, for the year 1983. *American Psychologist, 39*, 604–638.

American Psychological Association. (1976, January 23–25). Policy on Psychologists Wishing to Change Their Specialty. *Minutes of the Council of Representatives.*

American Psychological Association. (1977). *Standards for Providers of Psychological Services.* Washington, DC: Author.

American Psychological Association (1981). Ethical principles of psychologists. *American Psychologist, 36*, 633–638.

American Psychological Association. (1987). General guidelines for providers of psychological services. *American Psychologist, 42*, 712–723.

American Psychological Association. (1987). Model act for state licensure of psychologists. *American Psychologist, 42*, 696–703.

Fisher, C.B., & Tryon, W.W. (1988). Ethical issues in the research and practice of applied developmental psychology. *Journal of Applied Developmental Psychology, 9*, 27–39.

Gross, S.J. (1978). The myth of professional licensing. *American Psychologist, 33*, 1009–1016.

Hogan, D.B. (1979). *The Regulation of Psychotherapists: Volume 1. A study in the Philosophy and Practice of Professional Regulation.* Cambridge, MA.: Ballinger.

Keith-Spiegel, P.C., & Koocher, G.P. (1985). *Ethics in psychology: Professional standards and cases.* New York: Random House.

Koocher, G.P. (1979). Credentialing in psychology: Close encounters with competence? *American Psychologist, 34*, 696–702.

Koocher, G.P. (1984, Summer). Competence in serving children: Credentials, protectionism and public policy. *APA Division of Developmental Psychology Newsletter,* pp. 35–42.

Orgel, S.A. (1983). Role of the internship in respecialization. *The Clinical Psychologist, 36*, 71–72.

Scholnick, E.K., Fisher, C.B., Brown, A., & Sigel, I. (1988, Spring). Report on applied developmental psychology. *APA Division of Developmental Psychology Newsletter,* pp. 6–10.

Shantz, C. (1987, Spring). Report on applied developmental psychology programs. *APA Division of Developmental Psychology Newsletter,* pp. 1–13.

Wertlieb, D. (1983). Some foundations and directions for applied developmental psychology. *Journal of Applied Developmental Psychology, 4*, 349–358.

Zigler, E., & Finn, M. (1984). Applied developmental psychology. In M.H. Bornstein & M.E. Lamb (Eds.), *Developmental psychology: An advanced textbook* (pp. 451–492). Hillsdale, NJ: Lawrence Erlbaum Associates, Inc.

Part V
Ethics, Cultural Diversity, and Social Bias

Part V
Ethics, Cultural Diversity, and Social Bias

15 Population Generalizability, Cultural Sensitivity, and Ethical Dilemmas*

Luis M. Laosa

Applied psychologists who provide services in nations composed of multiple and widely varied cultural groups, such as the United States, face certain ethical dilemmas that would not arise in more homogeneous societies. These ethical dilemmas, the focus of this chapter, revolve around the concept of population validity.[1]

Population validity refers to the generalizability of research findings across different populations. In this regard it is important to keep in mind that a research finding is an interpretation of data obtained from a sample representing a particular population (Messick, 1975). A measure of a psychological construct may or may not have the same or even similar psychometric properties or patterns of relationship with other variables in different populations (Laosa, 1981b). Thus, an inference may be valid for one population and not for another; an inference is valid for a particular population to the extent that it leads to correct judgments about members of that population (Breland, 1979).

Operationally, the concept has been variously labeled *population validity, population generalizability, ecological validity, differential validity, population transportability,* and *population transferability.* Granted that generalizability is an aspect of validity, the term *validity* conveys additional meanings in the measurement literature; for this reason and because the issue is clearly one of generalizability, Messick (1980, 1987) recommends use of the term *population generalizability* in preference to the others. The latter term is used generally in this chapter.

Emphasis on generalizability was stimulated in the behavioral and measurement sciences by Campbell and Stanley's (1966) discussion of what they called *external validity.* Their point was one of methodological rigor: In conducting an experiment, the researcher hopes that the results are broadly representative of different time periods, settings, and groups of people. Attention should be given,

* Work on parts of this chapter was made possible by a grant from the William T. Grant Foundation, which the author gratefully acknowledges. The author presented portions of this chapter in a symposium at the 95th Annual Convention of the American Psychological Association.

[1] Although the point of reference in this chapter is applied developmental psychology, the issues also apply to other psychological specialties and other fields as well, including, of course, education, psychiatry, and social service, and they apply to both professional practice and policy making.

therefore, to uncontrolled variables that may pose threats to the representativeness, or generalizability, of the findings.

Fundamentally, population generalizability is a special case of the broader concern in science for replicability—the canon that one investigator's results should be again obtainable independently by another investigator or by the same investigator using a different sample from the same presumed population. Population generalizability is also a special case of construct validity, as noted above, because evidence of generalizability always contributes either to firming up or undercutting construct interpretation (American Educational Research Association, American Psychological Association, & National Council on Measurement in Education, 1985; Messick, 1987).

Statistically, the concept is embodied in moderator variables and person-by-treatment interactions.[2] Findings involving moderator or interaction effects, or their absence, are important in current practice, policy, theory, and metatheory because often such statistical effects are viewed as the most representative models of reality (Cronbach, 1987; Laosa, 1982a, in press).[3] Rooted in a different methodological approach, ethnographic studies (e.g., Cole & Griffin, 1987) yield rich descriptive data that also contribute to our understanding of how populations and contexts interact.

Regardless of discipline or methodology, however, *once we accept as plausible a hypothetical model of reality in which interactions may occur between population-specific characteristics and particular stimuli, then the generalizability of treatment effects can never be taken for granted. Neither can it ever be assumed, therefore, in the absence of proper evidence, that the outcome of a particular service, intervention, or policy will be the same in different populations.* Before turning to the ethical issues involved, let us examine recent research evidence bearing on the tenability of the model.

RESEARCH EVIDENCE

To illustrate the issues just raised, consider recent examples from the research literature. Specifically, let us look at selected studies based respectively on four

---

[2] The term *treatment* is used in the very general sense that it conveys in experimental or quasiexperimental research and not necessarily in its medical sense.

[3] Basically, studies of these topics compare regression slopes. With criterion C, predictor X, and groups of people defined on some basis, the C on X regression can be evaluated in each group. The hypothesized effect may be represented also by analyzing all cases together in a regression equation with three predictors—the original predictor, the grouping variable, and a product term, which represents the interaction. Various tests of significance for such models have been proposed, and they differ in statistical power (Cronbach, 1987). Another approach to representing mathematically the concept of population generalizability is through structural equation procedures, such as those advanced by Jöreskog (see Hayduk, 1987). Degree of generalizability is determined by simultaneously testing the fit of a hypothetical model to two or more groups.

different types of research methodology, each addressing a different facet of the problem.

Research on Classroom Processes

The research literature concerning the effects of classroom processes on students' development is not only of interest to applied developmental psychologists, but recently it also has attracted the close attention of policy makers. Roused by the educational excellence movement, policy makers are turning to this literature in their search for ways to improve the U.S. educational system in relation to those of ascending nations (see, e.g., U.S. Department of Education, 1986).

Research during the past 15 years on the linkages between teachers' behaviors in the classroom and their students' development of academic skills in the elementary grades has produced a small knowledge base concerning the dynamics of classroom processes and how such processes may affect children's learning and development. In their recent review of this literature, Brophy and Good (1986) concluded that even the most widely replicated findings on the relationships between classroom processes and students' educational development must be qualified by references to statistical interactions. Usually, these interactions involve minor elaborations of main trends, but occasionally interactions are more powerful than main effects. Such interactions, some of which appear repeatedly and thus constitute well-established findings, suggest that the effects on children of particular instructional environments vary as a function of the child's characteristics. Some of these characteristics stem from the child's sociocultural background.

A recent study by Wong Fillmore and her colleagues (Wong Fillmore, Ammon, McLaughlin, & Ammon, 1985) illustrates the nature of such interactions. It is one of several studies commissioned by the then-National Institute of Education to determine, through research, how best to meet the educational needs of children in the United States with limited English-language proficiency. Specifically, the study was designed to discover what aspects of classroom structure, teaching practices, and patterns of language use in the classroom had the strongest impact on the child's English-language development over the course of the school year. The analyses examined the oral English-language development of elementary school children from two different ethnic groups—Chinese and Hispanic.

A main effect in the data showed that children with initially low proficiency in English made large gains in oral language development if they were placed in classrooms in which they had numerous opportunities to interact with native English-speaking peers; such peer interactions appeared to be less influential once the children were further along in their learning of English. Further analyses revealed, however, that these results were true to a much greater extent for Hispanic than for Chinese children. Chinese children whose initial knowledge of English was limited and who were in classes in which there were many opportunities to interact with native English-speaking classmates did not show the kind of improvement in English-language skills found among the Hispanic children in such situations. Chinese children developed better in classrooms where teachers closely supervised the learning activities and kept students on task. Wong Fillmore et al. concluded that "the Chinese children seemed much more directly dependent on their interactions with the teacher than was the case for the Hispanic children" (p. 331). It is as if the Chinese children viewed the adult authority figure as the source of knowledge, whereas the Hispanic children profited from the chance to interact with peers who were good language models. Thus it seems that different kinds of instructional approaches work best with different cultural groups. Had the researchers included only a single ethnic group in their study, or had they aggregated the groups in their analyses, the important statistical interaction—and thus the helpful finding bearing on population generalizability—would have been masked.

Consistent with our concern with generalizability, it should be recalled that broad sociodemographic classifications such as *Hispanic* or *Asian* may each contain various ethnocultural groups (Laosa, 1988) and thus mask significant population diversity. Those familiar with the Hispanic population, for example, know that it is composed of several different ethnic groups, including Mexican Americans (Chicanos), Cuban Americans, Puerto Ricans, and other Spanish-speaking national-origin groups. Although these groups share many characteristics in common, there are also important cultural, historical, and sociodemographic differences, and these may limit the generalizability of research findings. It is therefore disappointing that a detailed ethnic breakdown of the study sample was not reported. This omission does not detract, however, from the study's value in illustrating the concept of population-by-treatment interaction, since cultural differences between Hispanics and Chinese are doubtless much greater on the average than those between detailed ethnic groups within these two broad populations.

Experimental Laboratory Research

Further evidence bearing on the question of population-by-treatment interactions comes from a recent experiment by Tuck (1985) comparing Black and White children's performance under varied task conditions. The study was designed to test the general proposition that an ethnic group's culturally rooted behavior patterns and traditions foster the development of particular response styles in its members, and that such Black-White differences as we observe nationally in scholastic attainment levels (see, e.g., Laosa, 1985) can be explained partly on the basis of differences in the response styles characteristic of the two groups.

Tuck's hypotheses stem from a conceptual framework suggested by Boykin (1983). This conception holds that while the beliefs and values of many Black Americans are shaped primarily by the dominant society, some of their beliefs, values, and behaviors are rooted in a traditional African ethos cultivated among Black Americans. Cultural styles inherent in this ethos are seen as clashing with those of the dominant Euro-American system (see also Shade, 1982). Analogous conceptions have been advanced for other ethnic groups (e.g., Cárdenas & Cárdenas, 1977; Heath, 1983; Laosa, 1977b, 1982b; Philips, 1974).

Tuck's study centered on one of the Black cultural styles discussed by Boykin: *psychological verve,* defined as "the tendency to attend to several concerns at once and to shift focus among them rather than focus on a single concern or a series of concerns in a sequential fashion; the inclination towards the energetic, the intense, the stimulating and the lively" (Tuck, 1985, p. 20; see also Boykin, 1983). Tuck hypothesized that Black-White differences in performance are a function of task format. She predicted that Blacks, because of their presumed higher psychological verve, would perform better in tasks with a varied format. To test this hypothesis, Tuck evaluated Black and White children's performance in cognitive-perceptual tasks under varied- and nonvaried-format conditions. The tasks were of four types—color matching, schema reproduction, listening, and scanning. Each child was administered 10 exemplars of each task type. Half of the 40 exemplars were presented in a nonvaried format, and the other half in a varied format, as follows. In the nonvaried format condition 5 exemplars of one task type were presented first and were then followed by 5 exemplars of a second type, and so on. In the varied format condition the remaining 20 exemplars were presented in a random sequential order without regard for type. Each child participated in both conditions, in a counterbalanced-order design. Performance level was the number of exemplars performed correctly.

All the children were of low socioeconomic status because, as Tuck reasoned, low-income Blacks, more than those in the middle class, have experienced isolation from mainstream Euro-American society and thus are more likely to maintain "Afrocentric orientations and cultural styles" (p. 44); also, such children are at particularly high risk for school failure. The sample consisted of 120 Black and White fourth- and sixth-graders.

Of particular interest to us here are the results of an analysis of variance in which Tuck used ethnic group, grade, sex, and format condition as independent factors and performance level as the dependent variable. The ethnic group, grade, and condition main effects were significant, favoring Whites, the higher grade, and the varied format condition. Also significant, however, was the interaction between ethnic group and condition. This interaction revealed that under the nonvaried format condition, Whites outperformed Blacks, whereas under the varied format condition, the two ethnic groups performed at the same level. Confirming Tuck's hypothesis, the results suggest that a varied format facilitates the performance of Blacks, so that in tasks presented in this type of format, Blacks and Whites perform at the same level. The broader significance of Tuck's finding lies in the support it provides for the view that under conditions consistent with their cultural styles, Blacks demonstrate performance levels equal to Whites; and that the lower academic performance of Blacks stems from an incompatibility between Black cultural styles and those styles inherent in the Euro-American schooling system.

The implications of Tuck's finding for the design of instructional methods and curricula are clear. Less obvious perhaps are the implications for assessment. Standardized achievement tests, as Tuck points out, are usually presented under a relatively nonvaried format condition. It therefore seems reasonable to hypothesize, on the basis of Tuck's finding, that under a more varied format condition test scores might reflect with greater accuracy the true ability of higher-verve children.

Research on Families' Ideologies

Complementing the studies demonstrating culture-by-treatment interaction effects, such as those just described, are findings from research focusing on the naturally occurring characteristics of diverse cultural groups. The latter type of research provides additional evidence bearing on population generalizability.

One such study, conducted in Israel by Frankel and Roer-Bornstein (1982), compared the modernization of infant-rearing ideologies of two ethnic communities—Yemenite and Kurdish Jews—by interviewing the grandmother and granddaughter generations. Both communities immigrated to Israel about 30 years ago. In Israel, the families selected for study lived in ethnically homogeneous semicommunal farming villages, which were similar in socioeconomic level and located in a single political district. It was thus possible to compare the changes in two very different cultural traditions that had experienced very similar modern influences.

The results of Frankel and Roer-Bornstein's study showed that tradition interacted with modern influences in promoting a differential receptivity to such influences. This finding demonstrates that different traditional ideologies may differentially facilitate the assimilation of modern values. The study suggests that parental behaviors reflecting a "modern" psychological image of the child do not seem equally reasonable or comprehensible to different ethnic groups. In the communities studied by Frankel and Roer-Bornstein, many of those child-rearing practices stressed by contemporary developmental psychology (e.g., certain forms of mother-child interaction, approaches to infant cognitive stimulation) appeared more acceptable to Yemenite than to Kurdish mothers. Women of the Yemenite granddaughter generation appeared to have a tradition "that meshes with the behavioral demands of many constructs of modern intervention" (p. 38). In discussing the implications of their findings for policies aimed at "making nontraditional perspectives or ideologies accessible to traditional communities" (p. 37), Frankel and Roer-Bornstein concluded that the design of intervention programs should not necessarily be uniform across different ethnic cultures—

that a population's "cultural readiness" to assimilate an extraneous ideology would have to be accommodated by corresponding variations in the design of interventions.

Observational Research on Mother-Child Interactions

Further evidence relevant to population generalizability comes from studies based on direct observations of behaviors within the family, including some of my own research on mother-child interactions. In a series of analyses (Laosa, 1980a, 1981a, 1982b), I compared the teaching strategies of mothers in two distinct U.S. ethnic groups: Chicano (Mexican-American) and non-Hispanic White (Euro-American). These two broad populations are known to differ markedly from one another in average academic achievement and schooling attainment level, a longstanding and serious problem facing the U.S. educational system (Brown, Rosen, Hill, & Olivas, 1980; Laosa, 1985). A principal aim of this study was to contribute empirical data explaining the nationally observed ethnic-group difference in school performance. In particular, a research objective was to ascertain whether differences exist in the strategies that Chicano and non-Hispanic White mothers use in teaching their own children. In the context of the continuity-discontinuity view of school performance, each sociocultural population is seen as having evolved its own—relatively unique—ways of teaching and learning. To the extent that the teaching or learning processes characteristic of a particular population differ from those of the school classroom, children from that population will experience *discontinuity* between the home and school environments. From this conceptual perspective, the wider or more abrupt the discontinuity, the greater will be the child's difficulty with school functioning.

Chicano and non-Hispanic White mothers were observed in their respective homes teaching cognitive-perceptual tasks to their own 5-year-old children (Laosa, 1980a, 1981a, 1982b). The families in the samples were selected to represent as closely as possible these two U.S. populations with regard to the distributions of parental schooling level and socioeconomic status. Using the Maternal Teaching Observation Technique (Laosa, 1980b), trained observers recorded the frequency of occurrence of specific categories of teaching behavior.

The data revealed significant ethnic-group differences for several teaching behavior categories. Some teaching strategies occurred much more frequently in one ethnic group than in the other, while the reverse was true of other teaching strategies. The direction of the differences was in accord with the hypothesis: Compared to the Chicano mothers the non-Hispanic White mothers taught in a style resembling more closely the academic teaching mode one would expect to find in a school classroom. Further, the ethnic-group differences in maternal teaching strategies became nonsignificant when statistically controlled for the mothers' schooling levels (Laosa, 1980a). These findings are harmonious with a continuity-discontinuity explanation of school performance (see Laosa, 1982b).

Two related mechanisms may account for the hypothesized influence of maternal teaching strategies on children's school performance—both may operate concurrently. One mechanism bears on the child's learning strategies; the other involves more broadly communicative traditions or relational styles. Consider that, at least hypothetically, a mother's habitual choice of teaching strategies will influence her child's development of *learning strategies*—the child's characteristic approaches to learning; that is, the student's preferred or most proficient way of approaching a learning or problem-solving task (Laosa, 1977a, 1982b). As such, the child who experiences greater home-school continuity in teaching strategies is likely to have a decided advantage over children with less continuity—that child may well have learned to master in the home the form and dynamics of teaching and learning processes that have adaptive value in the classroom (Laosa, 1977b, 1979, 1982b).

More broadly, one may speak of differences in *communicative traditions*. Mastery of the phonological, syntactic, and semantic rules of a language is not sufficient to guarantee appropriate use of language. In order to operate acceptably to others in society, children and adults must know what forms of verbal and nonverbal behavior are appropriate in which social context. In this view, people in face-to-face interaction become environments for each other—environments that change from moment to moment. With each change, "the role relationships among participants are redistributed to produce differing configurations of concerted action" (Erickson & Schultz, 1977, p. 6). Sociolinguists studying such configurations have found them to be marked by ways of speaking, listening, getting the floor, holding it, and leading and following. Postural and proxemic patterns, too, are instances of culturally conventional signals that show how messages are to be interpreted. Considering that schools are places where students and teachers come together without sharing the same body of implicit assumptions, one wonders about students who are labeled as "inattentive," "unmotivated," "uncooperative," "immature," and perhaps even "academically slow." Do ethnic minority children who "misbehave" repeatedly in school do so mainly out of disrespect for teachers, lack of motivation, low intelligence? Are they often simply confused by the classroom as a social milieu? Are there features of the cognitive and social environment—as that environment is enacted interactionally—that are difficult for children to make sense of when they come from a communicative tradition that differs from that of the teacher (Erikson & Schultz, 1977; Florio, 1976)? A growing body of research (for a recent review see Farr, 1986) suggests that the communicative systems with which people unconsciously operate may conflict with and thus interfere with all teaching and learning processes in the classroom. Put in terms of population generalizability, the teaching strategies that "work" when applied to students from a particular family background may not do as well for other learners.

RESEARCH, APPLICATION, AND ETHICS

As the empirical and theoretical work reviewed in the preceding sections show, important issues are presently being illuminated concerning the intricate linkages among sociocultural, developmental, and intervention variables. Inquiry into these challenging questions is still in its infancy, however, and the area is fertile for further advances.

In the realm of basic psychological research, population generalizability remains a *scientific* concern. In applied psychology, by contrast, population generalizability emerges as an *ethical* issue. It is an ethical issue because in the absence of evidence regarding population generalizability, we cannot predict the outcome of a research application to a population different from the one that yielded the research finding, as indeed the studies reviewed above suggest. The outcome of the application might differ from the intended one—it might be ineffective and harmless or possibly harmful in a different population. Thus, an ethical question centers on whether—or under what circumstances—it is within the bounds of professional ethics to devise, recommend, or implement a service or intervention when the scientific basis lending validity to the practical application arises from research on a sociocultural population different from the one of the intended service recipients.

What is the applied psychologist to do in the absence of research evidence on the adequacy or effectiveness that a standard mainstream service may have for members of the client's sociocultural group? Further, what is one to do when such evidence exists, but it suggests that the service of choice for the mainstream might be inappropriate or ineffective if applied to the nonmainstream population? How can one meet the latter population's need for professional services? Ethically, what should one do in each of these situations? Various solutions, discussed below, have been proposed.

POPULATION SENSITIVITY

The concept of population sensitivity embodies several approaches that have been proposed toward the solution of the aforementioned issues. *Population sensitivity* refers to an orientation that seeks to make policies, services, or institutions harmonious with the basic values and characteristics of diverse populations.

Emphasis on population sensitivity was stimulated by two historical trends that converged in the 1960s. Together these developments focused public attention on the need for population-sensitive policies and services (Rogler, Malgady, Costantino, & Blumenthal, 1987). First was the civil rights movement, which sought to make the institutional structure of U.S. society more responsive to the needs of Blacks and other minority groups and to increase their participation in a pluralistic democracy. Second were the policies and programs of the War on

Poverty, which aimed at reducing social, educational, and economic inequalities and at improving the circumstances of the poor and of the disadvantaged minorities (Laosa, 1984). Services thus began to be extended to formerly ignored groups. These attempts brought in relief deficiencies in the traditional service approaches, as it became increasingly apparent that there were unexpected difficulties in applying such services to these groups. Based largely on the needs and characteristics of the mainstream Euro-American (i.e., White) middle class, the newly extended services often proved to be of questionable effectiveness when applied to persons of other sociocultural backgrounds. Pleas for population-sensitive services ensued (Laosa, 1983; Rogler et al., 1987). More recently, the rapid growth of ethnocultural diversity in our society has brought a renewed sense of urgency to the concept of population sensitivity.

The operational counterpart of population sensitivity is the concept of *matching services to populations*. No consensus exists regarding the proper approach for such matching on the basis of social or cultural variables. There are those, on the one hand, who argue that the services for the mainstream can be effectively extended to special populations via techniques designed to facilitate cross-group application. A contrasting view advocates the development of alternative services designed especially to match a particular population's characteristics and problems. Still others take various positions between these two views (cf., Au & Jordan, 1981; Heitler, 1976; Rogler et al., 1987; Szapocznik, Scopetta, & King, 1978). The issue is further complicated by the fact that individuals may shift their respective positions as a function of focal population and type of policy, service, or institution.

In conceptualizing population-sensitive endeavors, it is helpful to use Rogler and associates' (1987) lucid classification of mental health services for Hispanics and think of four different levels of sensitivity, each of which is reflected in a particular type of approach. On the first level of population sensitivity are approaches that aim at increasing a special population's access to a mainstream service or institution. On the next level are approaches that intend to identify those individuals from the special population who are sufficiently acculturated into the mainstream population to be appropriately and effectively served as members of the mainstream. On the third level are approaches that seek to adapt a mainstream service or institution to fit the characteristics of the special population. Finally, on the fourth level are those approaches that aspire to design a policy, service, or institution specifically tailored to fit a particular population and meet its special needs. Let us illustrate with examples each level of population sensitivity.

Increasing Access

A good example of the first level of population sensitivity comes from the field of mental health. On the basis of both research and clinical practice, mental health practitioners have been aware for some time that persons from the lower so-cioeconomic strata face various problems of access to conventional psycho-therapeutic methods. After reviewing the literature on the problems encountered in providing traditional psychotherapy to this special population, Heitler (1976) concluded that these clients "are the most likely . . . to bring to therapy an array of values, life styles, and expectations of therapy which clash sharply with the working orientation of traditional psychotherapists. . . . There is now a substan-tial body of theory and research evidence to suggest that some mutuality of patient-therapist role expectations . . . is crucial" (p. 340). Some mental health professionals have attempted to bring about this mutuality by socializing the client into the role expectations held for them by the therapist through preparato-ry interviews or role induction procedures.

Ethnolinguistic minorities constitute another set of populations encountering serious barriers to conventional mental health services. For these populations, too, a variety of attempts have been made in recent years to develop more accessible treatment programs. Many treatment innovators have focused their primary efforts on hiring bilingual and bicultural staff (Rogler et al., 1987), thus overcoming the most obvious communication barrier that exists between these clients and staff. One of these efforts has been described by Acosta and Cristo (1981). Assuming that Hispanics' needs for mental health services would likely continue to exceed the availability of Spanish-speaking therapists, Acosta and Cristo developed a bilingual interpreter program in a psychiatric clinic located in a large Mexican-American community in Los Angeles. Interpreters were re-cruited from the same neighborhoods as the clients and trained in language-translation skills, basic concepts of psychotherapy, and the terminology used in clinical settings. Another role created for the interpreters was that of cultural consultants, explaining to English-speaking therapists the meanings conveyed by patients during therapy. Acknowledging the awkwardness and risks inherent in introducing a third party into a psychotherapeutic relationship, Acosta and Cristo (1981) reported that the percentage of Spanish-speaking clients admitted to the clinic more than doubled, evidence of the success of this population-sensitive program in increasing accessibility of services.

A final example of an effort aimed at increasing a special population's access to mainstream resources is the computer education program of the Center for the Development of Non-formal Education in Austin, Texas. This innovative inter-vention was designed by Vargas-Adams and associates to provide bilingual com-puter education for children and families in a low-income Mexican-American community (Cole & Griffin, 1987). Situated in a barrio-based "Computer House," it makes available to the children and their parents a series of teaching and learning resources, including Atari 800 and 400 computers, thus helping members of this special population become better acquainted with technological resources that otherwise would remain largely out of their reach (see Martinez & Mead, 1988).

All such forms of increasing accessibility represent the first level of population sensitivity.

Selecting Services to Fit the Population

Once access is gained, yet another level of concern calls for population sensitivity. The concern now is with the fundamental characteristics of the service or institution, specifically its appropriateness for the service recipient. As Rogler and colleagues (1987) aptly put it, without this level of concern a population could be in the incongruous situation of having greater access to inappropriate services or institutions. Because the goal of population sensitivity is services and institutions that accord with the needs of the individual, on this level the distinctions between group and individual differences may become blurred (cf. Snow, 1986). Indeed, on the second level of population sensitivity the goal is to identify those persons who, because of their similarity to the mainstream population on some relevant individual-difference dimension, could appropriately benefit from a standard service.

From the field of mental health comes the sensible proposal that the choice of services should be based on an objective assessment of the degree of acculturation manifested by the individual client. In preparing for a decision regarding the treatment of choice, the psychologist conducts an assessment of the client's level of acculturation to the mainstream. This dimension reflects how much the ethnic minority individual's personality has incorporated the values, beliefs, and modes of behavior characteristic of the mainstream culture (Berry, Trimble, & Olmedo, 1986). If the client's score on the acculturation scale is sufficiently high to seem to warrant it, the client is then treated in the same manner as the members of the mainstream (Rogler et al., 1987). In the field of bilingual education the analogous concern is with assessing the language-minority student's English proficiency level in order to make entry/exit decisions regarding eligibility for participation in a special program for such students or assignment to a regular English-language classroom.

In sum, on the second level of population sensitivity, the approach involves distinguishing between those individuals who can be treated as members of the mainstream and those who require special treatment reflecting their relevant population-specific characteristics. It is the latter group that brings out the need for the next level of population sensitivity (Rogler et al., 1987).

Modifying Services to Fit the Population

If services can be *selected* to fit the characteristics of the individual, so too can services and institutions be *adapted* to fit the characteristics of the individual. As such, on the third level of population sensitivity the aim is to identify elements of the nonmainstream population's culture and use them to complement or modify a mainstream service or institution. The intention is to accomplish this incorporation without abandoning or compromising the fundamental functions and character of the service or institution (Rogler et al., 1987). Two notable efforts to adapt mainstream services to the modal cultural characteristics of special populations are those originating at the Spanish Family Guidance Clinic in Miami, Florida, and at the Kamehameha Early Education Program in Honolulu, Hawaii.

Spanish Family Guidance Clinic. The Spanish Family Guidance Clinic is situated in a large Cuban-American community. As with other refugee or émigré populations, special problems in this community include those resulting from the impact of the stresses of acculturation on psychosocial functioning and mental health. The approach employed by Szapocznik and his associates at the Spanish Family Guidance Clinic has been to examine the "characteristics and unique needs of its [Cuban-American] client population, and to establish treatment methods that respect and preserve the cultural characteristics of the . . . clients. . . . by adapting the treatment to the client" (Szapocznik, Scopetta, & King, 1978, p. 113). Through their initial clinical observations and systematic research comparing Cuban and Anglo Americans, Szapocznik and his co-workers identified several relevant dimensions on which these two cultural groups seem to differ (Szapocznik, Kurtines, & Hanna, 1979; Szapocznik, Scopetta, Aranalde, & Kurtines, 1978). One dimension appears to be a generally stronger tendency among Cubans for lineality in family relationships. It was also observed that behavior disorders (such as drug abuse and antisocial comportment) in young Cuban-American clients tended to be accompanied by a breakdown of the lineal relational pattern in the family. This breakdown appears to reflect intergenerational differences in acculturation, as the youngsters seemed to be acculturating at a faster rate than their parents. Interestingly, clinical experience suggested that in these cases, the "desired therapeutic outcomes are reached most expeditiously by restoring the lineal-hierarchical relational structure to the family" (Szapocznik, Scopetta, & King, 1978, p. 116). Hence, by incorporating elements of Cuban culture in the therapeutic relationship, the Spanish Family Guidance Clinic's treatment method seeks to restore the family's lineal milieu and reaffirm the parents' authority. Once this is accomplished, the family is then taught the skills necessary to "negotiate" the youngster's differentiation from the family. Szapocznik and colleagues propose that this "culturally sanctioned framework" (p. 117) is a necessary condition for the process of individuation of the Cuban-American youngster to take place.

The cultural dimension is further capitalized upon by incorporating it in the client-therapist relationship. To this end, the culturally prescribed relational style may receive the support of the therapist in various components of the treatment, such as in the manner the therapist relates to the client by recognizing the client's perception of the therapist's role as functioning within a hierarchical relationship. In sum, on the basis of their clinical observations and systematic research, the staff of the Spanish Family Guidance Clinic have elaborated a model of the psychology of the Cuban family and, using this model, have adapted a U.S. mainstream form of family therapy for use as a treatment of choice for Cuban-American clients.

Kamehameha Early Education Program. A particularly well-researched attempt at adapting institutional services to fit the cultural characteristics of a special population is the Kamehameha Early Education Program. The Kamehameha program's primary goal is to discover instructional methods that are effective in teaching Hawaiian children of Polynesian background to read English. As a group, descendants of the Polynesian inhabitants of the Hawaiian Islands, especially those of low socioeconomic status, fare poorly in school, a major problem being with the children's development of reading skills—schools with large Hawaiian populations typically score within the first or second stanine on standardized tests of reading achievement (Au & Jordan, 1981).

Operating an experimental school (kindergarten through third grade), the Kamehameha staff have developed, after years of sustained research and experimentation, a program that is quite successful in developing Hawaiian children's reading skills (Au & Jordan, 1981). The program attempts to take account of the cultural background and abilities developed by the children in the home and to design an instructional arrangement that is both culturally congruent with home and community practices and manageable in the public schools. A central assumption of their research and development has been that the sources of Hawaiian children's school failure are discrepancies between the styles of learning in the home and those in the school, and that an understanding of these cultural differences may offer insights into ways of creating school environments in which these children can succeed (Au & Jordan, 1981; Cazden, 1981).

The origins of the present Kamehameha program are traceable to the 1960s, when studies conducted by social scientists in Hawaiian-ancestry communities began to yield descriptions of the culture and styles of interaction characteristic of this population. This research stimulated questions and hypotheses about discrepancies in styles of learning affecting the development of children from this ethnolinguistic group—about differences between the ways Hawaiian children learn at home or among their peers and the ways in which they are expected to learn in school. It is hypothesized that such differences may prevent or interfere with learning to read because the children find themselves in classroom instructional situations that are incongruent with the learning strategies already familiar to them; if school learning contexts and classroom teaching strategies could be changed so as to make them more similar to those the children are accustomed to, learning might improve. Building on the findings from these studies, the Kamehameha program was created as a research and development project aimed at finding ways of improving the school performance of educationally at risk Hawaiian children (Au & Jordan, 1981; Cazden, 1981; Jordan, Au, & Joesting, 1983).

The effectiveness of the Kamehameha program is attributed largely to its use of a special type of reading lesson, one that resembles *talk-story,* a unique speech activity that occurs naturally and frequently in Hawaiian culture. The activity is characterized by overlapping speech and cooperative production of narrative by several speakers (Au & Jordan, 1981). In the reading lesson the teacher therefore allows the children to discuss text ideas using rules for speaking and turn-taking similar to those in talk-story. Au and Jordan emphasize that the reading lesson is not isomorphic with these cultural forms. It does, however, exhibit several similarities to them, and "in responding to these similarities, the children are able to apply their abilities to the task of learning to read to a greater degree than they can in conventional reading lessons" (p. 151).

Significantly, efforts to apply the Kamehameha program to another cultural population have not been successful. To test the generalizability hypothesis, in recent years the Kamehameha team has also operated a research-and-development site on the Navajo reservation of northern Arizona, selected because of the sharp contrasts of the two cultures. With Navajo children, key features of the program have not functioned well. The reason appears to be differences in the *participation structures* (i.e., communicative traditions)—modes of organization by which everyday interaction is conducted; the rules governing speaking, attending, and turn-taking among interactional partners—characteristic of the Navajo and Hawaiian cultures. Accordingly, Navajo and Hawaiian versions of the program have emerged with clear differences (Jordan, Tharp, & Vogt, 1985—cited in Tharp, n.d.).

The projects just described that are taking place at the Spanish Family Guidance Clinic and the Kamehameha Early Education Program represent outstanding examples of the third level of population sensitivity—namely, efforts aimed at adapting a mainstream service, institution, or policy in order to accommodate the sociocultural characteristics of a special population, thereby syntonically enhancing its appropriateness and effectiveness for members of that population.

Developing Services to Fit the Population

Whereas the level of population sensitivity just described stresses *adapting* mainstream services, the fourth and highest level reflects approaches that aim at *creating* services specifically to meet the special needs of the focal population and to do so in a manner consistent with that population's values, traditions, and other cultural characteristics. *Cuento* or folktale therapy, a recent creation by Costantino, Malgady, and Rogler (1986), illustrates this level of population sensitivity.

Cuento therapy is a psychotherapeutic technique for psychologically distressed Puerto Rican children. It was designed for second-generation mainland children who may find themselves in conflict as a result of competing demands from their two different cultures. Based on the principles of social learning theory, the technique takes as its medium the folktales of Puerto Rican culture. The objective of telling folktales to the children in this context is to transmit cultural values, foster pride in the Puerto Rican cultural heritage, and reinforce adaptive behavior. Because the folktales convey a message or a moral to be emulated, folktale characters are presented with therapeutic intent as models of adaptive emotional and behavioral functioning within the Puerto Rican and U.S. mainstream cultures. By presenting culturally familiar characters of the same ethnicity as the children, the folktales are intended to model functionally adaptive behaviors. To conduct the therapy, a bilingual and bicultural therapist reads the folktales in both English and Spanish to the children and then leads a group discussion of the meaning or moral of the story, emphasizing the "good" and "bad" behaviors of the characters. In the next step of the intervention, the group participants role-play the various characters in the story. This activity is videotaped, and subsequently the children view themselves on tape and discuss the role-playing activities with the therapist in relation to their own personal problems. The therapist then proposes new scenarios for role playing, and the children act out solutions to problems presented in the scenarios while the therapist verbally reinforces adaptive behaviors and corrects maladaptive ones. Recent evaluation research by Costantino et al. (1986) suggests that for Puerto Rican children, this technique is more effective than conventional group therapy. Cuento therapy, then, illustrates the fourth and highest level of population sensitivity—a service that is structured in the client's rather than in the professional's sociocultural background.

WEIGHING THE RISKS AND BENEFITS

Few would argue against recognizing and being sensitive to the client's population-derived individuality. On the other hand, population-sensitive practices are not necessarily free of risk.

An unintended outcome of a population-sensitive service or policy may be differential expectations. In order to adapt services, classifications of individuals often must be made. But in some contexts, particularly in institutional settings, classification can have undesirable consequences. When an organization is required to "process" a large number of people, for example, classification can become functional for bureaucratic purposes rather than serve its original intent (Doyle, 1985).

Another potential risk involved in the provision of population-sensitive services may be differential quality. Consider, for example, attempts to adapt instructional services in schools. Differentiation of instruction may engender fundamental differences in curriculum. These differences may occur both in the amount that is covered and the fundamental character of the material covered. Given the contingencies of time and resources in schools, population-sensitive instruction may restrict the special population to a narrow band of the curriculum (Doyle, 1985).

Yet another possible, undesigned consequence of a population-sensitive approach may be an undue constriction of focus. That is to say, the public's or the professionals' attention may become confined to part of the special population's range of needs and characteristics—to the exclusion of other, perhaps equally relevant, variables for that population. On this point, we are reminded of Good and Stipeck's (1983) discussion of the pros and cons of adaptive instruction, in which they expressed fear that an undue emphasis on a single dimension (e.g., learning style) can lead to neglecting other important factors in learning.

It is ironic that dilemmas of stereotyping or of misjudging the complexity of problems can emerge from population-sensitive services, which themselves arose in response to negative stereotypes and simplistic assumptions. Those who favor population-sensitive approaches argue, however, that there are ways of designing such services so as to avoid or minimize risks (e.g., Trueba, 1988; Weisner, Gallimore, & Jordan, 1988). Certainly, perils attend whenever analyses that hold at the group level are applied indiscriminately to the individuals in the group. This is, of course, as true for the mainstream as for nonmainstream populations, and it is just as serious a generalizability problem as that of generalizing across populations.

Given that population-sensitive practices are not necessarily free of risk to the individuals being served, evaluations of the applied psychologist's professional conduct should incorporate the following questions: (a) In deciding upon the service to be rendered, were the expected benefits properly weighed against the potential risks? (b) Was the service-receiver made properly aware of any known potential risks or side effects? (c) Was the service-receiver included as a participant in the decision-making process leading to the practical application? (d) Was there a mechanism adopted for continuously monitoring the service or policy for unanticipated undesirable consequences?

As the discussion thus far indicates, in moving from scientific research to applied practice the central question shifts from "How can the service, institution, or policy be made more accessible or adaptable to the special population?" (or "How can the individual's needs be met in a population-sensitive manner?") to "When is a population-sensitive approach necessary, and what are its consequences?" Both sets of questions are important for the development of knowledge about population-sensitive approaches, but the latter set further uncovers a particularly heavy ethical burden for the applied professional.

SEPARATION AND EQUALITY

Related to the issue of potential risk is an additional set of difficult ethical problems, which depend more broadly on societal questions of separation and equality. If alternative services are developed for special populations, then these populations will be separated, at least to some degree, from the mainstream. Can uniform standards of quality be formulated between the mainstream services and the population-sensitive services? If such standards of quality are formulated, are they, or can they be, uniformly enforced?

Aside from whether the particular population-sensitive approach involves separation and thus some degree of segregation *during* the course of the service, will a further social distancing (in the society at large) between the nonmainstream and mainstream populations be among the effects of the population-sensitive service or policy? Is such distance a valued or desirable state of affairs (other things being equal)? If there were disagreement on this question, who would decide whether to make the population-sensitive service an available option?

One of the underlying currents in these tensions and indeed in the very concept of population sensitivity is the age-old philosophic problem of the relation between the universal and the particular. This is an intellectual issue, certainly, but one that ultimately finds expression in the political arena. It is helpful to keep in mind the three basic units of a social entity: the society—that is, the structure and functions of its human compositions; the group, namely a coherent subgroup with identifying characteristics by objective criteria and speaking with a common voice on some issues; and the individual. It is the "jostling of interests of the three units [that] forms the stuff of politics" (Holmes, 1988, p. 238). People differ as to the priority they accord to the three units, and this difference varies with the decision to be made. As an extant or proposed policy or practice may be, and in any case, is believed by some to be supportive and by others prejudicial to the larger society or some of its groups, societal conflict is at hand. Much of this conflict results from "competing claims for sensitivity to alleged common characteristics of the larger society, to the desires of coherent groups, and to the asserted 'rights' of individuals" (Holmes, 1988, p. 238).

Embedded as each individual is in his or her own particular sociocultural context, applied psychologists cannot escape these conflicts (Fisher & Tryon, 1988; Laosa, 1983; Messick 1980, 1986; Sigel, 1983). A heavy ethical burden thereby falls on the applied psychologist.

These ethical dilemmas are reflected in the apparent ambivalence toward ethnic and racial diversity evident in U.S. public policies. In effect, the government's role in ethnicity has oscillated between "color consciousness" and "color blindness." We have seen the nation's dominant orientation shift from a color-conscious approach to policy, as reflected in the laws enacted in southern states in the 1830s prohibiting literacy instruction of Blacks (Bremner, 1970) and the practice in the southwest until more recently prohibiting Mexican-American children from using their native language in schools under penalty of punishment (Laosa, 1984), to the color-blind orientation evident in the Civil Rights Act of 1964. The nation then shifted again to a color-conscious philosophy as expressed in affirmative action policies in employment and the requirements for bilingual education in public elementary and secondary schools (Glazer, 1982; Laosa, 1984; Takaki, 1982), and back again to the present color-blind course reflected in the retreat of the federal government from involvement in civil rights issues and also evident in the English-language-only movement. The color-bind society, which places a premium on individual effort, right, responsibility, and reward, seems inextricably entwined with the color-conscious society, which sets the individual in the context of the group for the purpose of maximizing equity in the "allotment of societal shares" (Van Horne, 1982, p. ix). Those who favor group entitlement (e.g., Takaki, 1982) argue that such entitlement serves to increase the chances of the individuals composing the group to win for themselves the shares they might otherwise have been unable to appropriate, given a range of disadvantages—race, language, poor education, unfamiliarity with certain institutional social norms—"in open brute competition of individuals qua individuals" (Van Horne, 1982, p. ix). Others ask whether a color-conscious public policy runs a terribly high risk of inequity and injustice to the individual qua individual insofar as group entitlement supersedes individual rights (e.g., Glazer, 1982, 1983). Implicit in the latter question is the presumption that the risk of inequity and injustice of a color-conscious public policy is greater than that of a color-blind public policy (Van Horne, 1982). Often, both sides of the debate seem to ascribe moral superiority to their respective positions. It is difficult to ignore, however, that color-conscious public policies created many of the present social inequalities that color-blind public policies allow to persist. There is a compelling irony in this history. Van Horne (1982, p. x) has put it well: "Color-conscious public policies gave rise to the demands for color-blind ones, which in turn have given rise to a new demand for color-conscious ones."

SUMMARY AND CONCLUSIONS

Applied psychologists in nations comprising diverse sociocultural groups, such as the United States, face special ethical dilemmas. These ethical issues revolve around the concept of *population generalizability,* which refers to the applicability of research findings across different populations. Important empirical and theoretical advances relevant to this concept are being made in various disciplines. The emerging evidence increasingly supports a general model of reality in which interactions may occur between population-specific characteristics and particular stimuli. Accepting this model we can never take for granted, in the absence of proper generalizability evidence, that the impact or outcome of a particular service, institution, or policy will be the same for different populations.

In the realm of basic research, population generalizability remains a *scientific* concern, whereas in applied psychology it becomes an *ethical* issue. It is an ethical issue because we cannot predict the effects of a particular service, intervention, or policy on populations different from the samples that yielded the research findings. The outcome of the application might differ from the intended one. An ethical question, therefore, is whether—or under what circumstances—it is within the bounds of professional ethics to prescribe or recommend a service or intervention for members of a population on which no relevant research evidence is available.

Population sensitivity refers to an orientation that seeks to make services, institutions, or policies harmonious with the basic values, needs, and characteristics of diverse populations. Population-sensitive efforts may occur on four levels (Rogler et al., 1987): On the first level are attempts to increase a nonmainstream population's access to a mainstream service or institution—usually by adding a complementary feature to the standard service or institution. On the next level of population sensitivity are approaches that intend to identify those individuals from a nonmainstream population who are sufficiently acculturated to be served as members of the mainstream. The third level reflects efforts to adapt a mainstream service to a nonmainstream population. On the fourth and highest level are services especially designed for a particular population.

Although few people would argue against recognizing and being sensitive to the client's population-derived individuality, population-sensitive services are not necessarily free of risk. Possible unintended consequences include different expectations according to group membership and different quality of service. On the other hand, advocates of population-sensitive approaches contend that there are ways of designing such services so as to avoid or minimize these risks.

Because potential risks may be involved in population-sensitive services, the following questions should be incorporated in evaluating the applied psychologist's professional conduct: (a) In deciding upon the service, were the expected benefits carefully weighed against the potential risks? (b) Was the service-receiver properly informed of any known potential risks or side effects? (c) Was the service-receiver included as an active participant in the decision-making process leading to the practical application? (d) Was a mechanism adopted for continuously monitoring for unintended consequences?

Related to issues of risk are ethical dilemmas that pertain more broadly to societal questions of separation and equality. Will participation in a population-sensitive service entail separation from the mainstream group? Can uniform standards of quality be formulated between the population-sensitive services and the mainstream services? If such standards are formulated, are they, or can they be, uniformly enforced? Aside from whether population-sensitive services may involve separation and therefore some segregation *during* the service, additional questions arise: Will a population-sensitive approach to services lead to a further distancing in the society at large between nonmainstream populations and the mainstream? Is such distancing desirable (all else equal)? Who decides whether to make population-sensitive services an available option?

These ethical dilemmas are reflected in the apparent ambivalence toward ethnic and racial diversity evident in U.S. public policies. The government's dominant orientation has shifted back and forth between a "color-conscious" and a "color-blind" role. Much of the conflict arises from competing claims between sensitivity to alleged common characteristics of the larger society, to the needs and desires of coherent groups, and to the asserted "rights" of individuals (Holmes, 1988). Embedded in his or her own particular sociocultural background, the applied psychologist cannot escape these conflicts. This introduces a sensitive ethical task into the latter's professional role.

The dearth of research evidence pertaining to population generalizability adds considerably to the ethical burden of the applied psychologist. Given the emerging evidence on the perils involved in generalizing research findings across populations, what is the applied psychologist to do in the absence of scientific information pertaining specifically to the client's sociocultural background? Is it preferable in such circumstances to abstain from intervention in order to avoid potential or unknown risks? Should one treat the client in the same manner as one would someone from a population about which there are relevant data—and hope that the outcome will be the same in both populations? How can one meet the client's needs for professional services? How can the level of decision making in such cases be improved? Ethically, what should one do in each of these situations?

With the growing sociocultural diversity in this society, the knotty ethical concerns raised in this chapter are bound to arise with increasing frequency. A framework for dealing with these pressing issues is therefore needed. This nascent framework, presently sketched only in broad outline, should be one in which these ethical dilemmas are dealt with in the context of an ongoing interplay between research and application. Specifically, the framework should include three basic elements: (a) a scrutiny of the empirical evidence that justifies a particular application to members of a specific population; but, in the absence of this evidential basis, (b) an examination of plausible rational justifications; and (c) the design of experimental applications intended to test the hypothesis of population generalizability through evaluation research.

REFERENCES

Acosta, F.X., & Cristo, M.H. (1981). Development of a bilingual interpreter program: An alternative model for Spanish-speaking services. *Professional Psychology, 12,* 474–482.

American Educational Research Association, American Psychological Association, & National Council on Measurement in Education. (1985). *Standards for educational and psychological testing.* Washington, DC: American Psychological Association.

Au, K.H., & Jordan, C. (1981). Teaching reading to Hawaiian children: Finding a culturally appropriate solution. In H.T. Trueba, G.P. Guthrie, & K.H. Au (Eds.), *Culture and the bilingual classroom: Studies in classroom ethnography* (pp. 139–152). Rowley, MA: Newbury House.

Berry, J.W., Trimble, J.E., & Olmedo, E.L. (1986). Assessment of acculturation. In W.J. Lonner &

J.W. Berry (Eds.), *Field methods in cross-cultural research* (pp. 291–349). Beverly Hills, CA: Sage.

Boykin, A.W. (1983). The academic performance of Afro-American children. In J.T. Spence (Ed.), *Achievement and achievement motives: Psychological and sociological approaches* (pp. 321–371). San Francisco: W.H. Freeman.

Breland, H.M. (1979). *Population validity and college entrance measures.* New York: College Entrance Examination Board.

Bremner, R.H. (Ed.). (1970). *Children and youth in America: A documentary history. Vol. 1: 1600–1865.* Cambridge, MA: Harvard University Press.

Brophy, J., & Good, T.L. (1986). Teacher behavior and student achievement. In M.C. Wittrock (Ed.), *Handbook of research on teaching* (pp. 328–375). New York: Macmillan.

Brown, G.H., Rosen, N.L., Hill, S.T., & Olivas, M.A. (1980). *The condition of education for Hispanic Americans.* Washington, DC: U.S. Government Printing Office.

Campbell, D.T., & Stanley, J.C. (1966). *Experimental and quasi-experimental designs for research.* Chicago, IL: Rand McNally.

Cárdenas, J.A., & Cárdenas, B. (1977). *The theory of incompatibilities: A conceptual framework for responding to the educational needs of Mexican American children.* San Antonio, TX: Intercultural Development Research Association.

Cazden, C.B. (Ed.). (1981). *Designing reading instruction for cultural minorities: The case of the Kamehameha Early Education Program.* Cambridge, MA: Graduate School of Education, Harvard University.

Cole, M., & Griffin, P. (1987). *Contextual factors in education: Improving science and mathematics education for minorities and women.* Madison, WI: Wisconsin Center for Education Research, University of Wisconsin.

Costantino, G., Malgady, R.G., & Rogler, L.H. (1986). Cuento therapy: A culturally sensitive modality for Puerto Rican children. *Journal of Consulting and Clinical Psychology, 54,* 639–645.

Cronbach, L.J. (1987). Statistical tests for moderator variables: Flaws in analyses recently proposed. *Psychological Bulletin, 102,* 414–417.

Doyle, W. (1985). The knowledge base for adaptive instruction: A perspective from classroom research. In M.C. Wang & H.J. Walberg (Eds.), *Adapting instruction to individual differences* (pp. 91–102). Berkeley, CA: McCutchan.

Erickson, F., & Schultz, J. (1977). When is a context? Some issues and methods in the analysis of social competence. *The Quarterly Newsletter of the Institute for Comparative Human Development, 1*(2), 5–10.

Farr, M. (1986). Language, culture, and writing: Sociolinguistic foundations of research on writing. In E.Z. Rothkopf (Ed.), *Review of research in education* (Vol. 13, pp. 195–223). Washington, DC: American Educational Research Association.

Fisher, C.B., & Tryon, W.W. (1988). Ethical issues in the research and practice of applied developmental psychology. *Journal of Applied Developmental Psychology, 9,* 27–39.

Florio, S. (1976). *Issues in the analysis of the structure and quality of classroom interaction.* Unpublished qualifying paper, Graduate School of Education, Harvard University.

Frankel, D.G., & Roer-Bornstein, D. (1982). Traditional and modern contributions to changing infant-rearing ideologies of two ethnic communities. *Monographs of the Society for Research in Child Development, 47*(4, Serial No. 196).

Glazer, N. (1982). Government and the American ethnic pattern. In W.A. Van Horne (Ed.), *Ethnicity and public policy: Vol. 1* (pp. 24–41). Milwaukee, WI: American Ethnic Studies Coordinating Committee/Urban Corridor Consortium, University of Wisconsin System.

Glazer, N. (1983). *Ethnic dilemmas: 1964–1982.* Cambridge, MA: Harvard University Press.

Good, T.L., & Stipek, D.J. (1983). Individual differences in the classroom: A psychological perspective. In G.D. Fenstermacher & J.I. Goodlad (Eds.), *Individual differences and the common curriculum* (pp. 9–43). Eighty-second yearbook of the National Society for the Study of Education. Part I. Chicago, IL: University of Chicago Press.

Hayduk, L.A. (1987). *Structural equation modeling with LISREL: Essentials and advances.* Baltimore, MD: Johns Hopkins University Press.

Heath, S.B. (1983). *Ways with words: Language, life, and work in communities and classrooms.* Cambridge: Cambridge University Press.

Heitler, J.B. (1976). Preparatory techniques in initiating expressive psychotherapy with lower-class, unsophisticated patients. *Psychological Bulletin, 83,* 339–352.

Holmes, M. (1988). The fortress monastery: The future of the common core. In I. Westbury & A.C. Purves (Eds.), *Cultural literacy and the idea of general education* (pp. 231–258). Eighty-seventh yearbook of the National Society for the Study of Education. Part II. Chicago, IL: University of Chicago Press.

Jordan, C., Au, K.H., & Joesting, A.K. (1983). Patterns of classroom interaction with Pacific Islands children: The importance of cultural differences. In M. Chu-Chang & V. Rodriguez (Eds.), *Asian- and Pacific-American perspectives in bilingual education* (pp. 216–242). New York: Teachers College Press.

Laosa, L.M. (1977a). Cognitive styles and learning strategies research: Some of the areas in which psychology can contribute to personalized instruction in multicultural education. *Journal of Teacher Education, 28*(3), 26–30.

Laosa, L.M. (1977b). Socialization, education, and continuity: The importance of the sociocultural context. *Young Children, 32*(5), 21–27.

Laosa, L.M. (1979). Social competence in childhood: Toward a developmental, socioculturally relativistic paradigm. In M.W. Kent & J.E. Rolf (Eds.), *Primary prevention of psychopathology: Vol. 3. Social competence in children* (pp. 253–279). Hanover, NH: University Press of New England.

Laosa, L.M. (1980a). Maternal teaching strategies in Chicano and Anglo-American families: The influence of culture and education on maternal behavior. *Child Development, 51,* 759–765.

Laosa, L.M. (1980b). Measures for the study of maternal teaching strategies. *Applied Psychological Measurement, 4,* 355–366.

Laosa, L.M. (1981a). Maternal behavior: Sociocultural diversity in modes of family interaction. In R.W. Henderson (Ed.), *Parent-child interaction: Theory, research, and prospects* (pp. 125–167). New York: Academic.

Laosa, L.M. (1981b). *Statistical explorations of the structural organization of maternal teaching behaviors in Chicano and non-Hispanic White families.* Invited paper presented at the Conference on the Influences of Home Environments on School Achievement, Wisconsin Research and Development Center for Individualized Schooling, School of Education, University of Wisconsin, Madison.

Laosa, L.M. (1982a). Families as facilitators of children's intellectual development at 3 years of age: A causal analysis. In L.M. Laosa & I.E. Sigel (Eds.), *Families as learning environments for children* (pp. 1–45). New York: Plenum.

Laosa, L.M. (1982b). School, occupation, culture, and family: The impact of parental schooling on the parent-child relationship. *Journal of Educational Psychology, 74,* 791–827.

Laosa, L.M. (1983). Parent education, cultural pluralism, and public policy: The uncertain connection. In R. Haskins & D. Adams (Eds.), *Parent education and public policy* (pp. 331–345). Norwood, NJ: Ablex.

Laosa, L.M. (1984). Social policies toward children of diverse ethnic, racial, and language groups in the United States. In H.W. Stevenson & A.E. Siegel (Eds.), *Child development research and social policy* (Vol. 1, pp. 1–109). Chicago: University of Chicago Press.

Laosa, L.M. (1985). *Ethnic, racial, and language group differences in the experiences of adolescents in the United States.* Invited paper presented at the Workshop on Adolescence and

Adolescent Development, convened by the Committee on Child Development Research and Public Policy of the National Academy of Sciences, Woods Hole, MA.

Laosa, L.M. (1988). Ethnicity and single parenting in the United States. In E.M. Hetherington & J.D. Arasteh (Eds.), *Impact of divorce, single parenting, and stepparenting on children* (pp. 23–49). Hillsdale, NJ: Erlbaum.

Laosa, L.M. (in press). Psychosocial stress, coping, and development of Hispanic immigrant children. In F.C. Serafica, A.I. Schwebel, R.K. Russel, P.D. Isaac, & L. Myers (Eds.), *Mental health of ethnic minorities*. New York: Praeger.

Martinez, M.E., & Mead, N.A. (1988). *Computer competence: The first national assessment.* (Report No. 17-CC-01). Princeton, NJ: Educational Testing Service.

Messick, S.J. (1975). The standard problem: Meaning and values in measurement and evaluation. *American Psychologist, 30,* 955–966.

Messick, S.J. (1980). Test validity and the ethics of assessment. *American Psychologist, 35,* 1012–1027.

Messick, S.J. (1986). *The once and future issues of validity: Assessing the meaning and consequences of measurement.* (Report No. RR-86-30). Princeton, NJ: Educational Testing Service.

Messick, S.J. (1987). *Validity.* (Report No. RR-87-40). Princeton, NJ: Educational Testing Service.

Philips, S.U. (1974). *The invisible culture: Communication in classroom and community on the Warm Springs Reservation.* Unpublished doctoral dissertation, University of Pennsylvania.

Rogler, L.H., Malgady, R.G., Costantino, G., & Blumenthal, R. (1987). What do culturally sensitive mental health services mean? The case of Hispanics. *American Psychologist, 42,* 565–570.

Shade, B.J. (1982). Afro-American cognitive style: A variable in school success? *Review of Educational Research, 52,* 219–244.

Sigel, I.E. (1983). The ethics of intervention. In I.E. Sigel & L.M. Laosa (Eds.), *Changing families* (pp. 1–21). New York: Plenum.

Snow, R.E. (1986). Individual differences and the design of educational programs. *American Psychologist, 41,* 1029–1039.

Szapocznik, J., Kurtines, W., & Hanna, N. (1979). Comparison of Cuban and Anglo-American cultural values in a clinical population. *Journal of Consulting and Clinical Psychology, 47,* 623–624.

Szapocznik, J., Scopetta, M.A., Aranalde, M.A., & Kurtines, W. (1978). Cuban value structure: Treatment implications. *Journal of Consulting and Clinical Psychology, 46,* 961–970.

Szapocznik, J., Scopetta, M.A., & King, O.E. (1978). Theory and practice in matching treatment to the special characteristics and problems of Cuban immigrants. *Journal of Community Psychology, 6,* 112–122.

Takaki, R. (1982). Reflections on racial patterns in America: An historical perspective. In W.A. Van Horne (Ed.), *Ethnicity and public policy: Vol. 1* (pp. 1–23). Milwaukee, WI: American Ethnic Studies Coordinating Committee/Urban Corridor Consortium, University of Wisconsin System.

Tharp, R.G. (n.d.) *Psychocultural variables and constants: Effects on teaching and learning in schools.* Unpublished paper. Honolulu: University of Hawaii.

Trueba, H.T. (1988). Culturally based explanations of minority students' academic achievement. *Anthropology and Education Quarterly, 19,* 270–287.

Tuck, K.D. (1985). *Verve effects: The relationship of task performance to stimulus preference and variability in low-income Black and White children.* Unpublished doctoral dissertation, Howard University.

U.S. Department of Education. (1986). *What works: Research about teaching and learning.* Washington, DC: U.S. Department of Education.

Van Horne, W.A. (1982). Preface. In W.A. Van Horne (Ed.), *Ethnicity and public policy: Vol. 1* (pp. v–xvii). Milwaukee, WI: American Ethnic Studies Coordinating Committee/Urban Corridor Consortium, University of Wisconsin System.

Weisner, T.S., Gallimore, R., & Jordan, C. (1988). Unpackaging cultural effects on classroom learning: Native Hawaiian peer assistance and child-generated activity. *Anthropology and Education Quarterly, 19,* 327–353.

Wong Fillmore, L., Ammon, P., McLaughlin, B., & Ammon, M.S. (1985). *Learning English through bilingual instruction: Final report submitted to the National Institute of Education.* Berkeley and Santa Cruz: University of California.

. . . .

16 Bias and Social Responsibility in the Study of Maternal Employment*

Lois Wladis Hoffman

Research on the effects of maternal employment on the family and the child has yielded some important insights into the socialization process. We know, for example, that children as young as 5 with employed mothers have a less traditional view of the roles of men and women than do those whose mothers are full-time homemakers (Hartley, 1960; Miller, 1975). Furthermore, although parental attitudes also affect this relationship (Baruch, 1972; Galambos, Peterson, & Lenerz, 1988; Hoffman, 1963b), it holds even when attitudes are controlled, suggesting that the process involved is partly a cognitive one in which children draw conclusions about the nature of the world—and gender—from their own observations of parental roles. Either the fact of the mother's employment itself, or resulting changes in the family structure and division of labor, affect the child's concept of the competence of women. Recent findings suggesting that parent attitudes and behavior toward preschool daughters may be more favorable in the employed-mother family, while they are more favorable toward sons in the full-time homemaker family, have led to new hypotheses about the child's role as elicitor of parental responses under different conditions of stress (Bronfenbrenner & Crouter, 1982; Hoffman 1986). Insights have also recently been gained from this research into the role of the father in the child's cognitive development (Gottfried, Gottfried, & Bathurst, 1988); into patterns of parent-child interaction and child behavior studied longitudinally over the early years (Easterbrooks & Goldberg, 1989); into the role of prenatal maternal attitudes in subsequent maternal behavior (Hock, DeMeis, & McBride, 1988); and into the timing of various kinds of separation experiences during the early years and its significance for early child development (Jacobson & Wille, 1984; Thompson, Lamb, & Estes 1982; Weinraub, Jaeger, & Hoffman, 1988).

For many social scientists, however, and for policy makers, professionals concerned with the public service, media people, and much of the lay public, the value of this work lies in its practical application. Although there is now greater comfort with the fact that the vast majority of mothers of school-aged children

* This chapter was written during a stay at the Bellagio Study and Conference Center. I want to express my appreciation to the Rockefeller Foundation and the staff at the Center for providing this opportunity for uninterrupted work.

are currently employed (71% in two-parent families; 74% in single-parent families), there is considerable public concern about recent shifts in employment patterns among mothers of infants and preschoolers. In 1987, 52% of all mothers with infants one year of age and younger were in the labor force; five years earlier the rate was 43%, and ten years before it was only 33% (U.S. Bureau of Labor Statistics, 1987). Because of concern about the consequences of these new employment patterns, maternal employment has reemerged as a salient social issue, and questions of ethics, social responsibility, and potential bias in the interpretation of results are inescapable. In this chapter, we will consider the bias of the scientist and how it affects the scientific process, and issues of ethics and social responsibility involved in the communication of the research to the public.

BIAS IN THE SCIENTIFIC PROCESS

Scientists have biases. These can come from commitments to a particular theory or methodology, to a concern that the results will be publishable, or to an investment in the social implications of the work. The bias itself may be an unconscious one and it may affect the work in a way that the researcher does not realize. The process of peer evaluation and integration with other results serves to correct errors in research that come from both inept work and unconscious bias. But the reviewer also may have biases which affect the evaluation. When these biases coincide, the reviewer can be blinded in the same way as the researcher. However, in an area of investigation, such as the study of maternal employment, where researchers do not hold the same bias, the peer review process can facilitate scientific progress. Nothing sharpens a reviewer's acumen like disagreement with the theoretical or applied implications of the work under review. Three points at which the scientist's bias affects the maternal employment research will be discussed: (a) in the persistence with which the researcher pursues differences between employed and nonemployed mother groups; (b) in the conclusions drawn from the research; and (c) in the peer review process.

Persistence in Pursuing Differences

To say that the scientist has a bias does not necessarily imply his or her work is defective. While it may sometimes obscure judgment, it may also lead to a more diligent analysis of the data. In the study of maternal employment, it has more often had the latter effect.

Since the early 1960s, the point has repeatedly been made that maternal employment is not so potent a variable that a simple comparison between children with employed mothers and those with nonemployed mothers could be expected to yield significant differences, once extraneous variables such as social class, single parent status, family size, and gender of the child were controlled

(Hoffman, 1963a; Siegel & Haas, 1963; Stolz, 1960). To reveal differences, comparisons had to be made within subgroups based on these variables because the relationships were different for boys than for girls and for different social status groups. In addition, effects varied depending on the attitudes of the parents, the number of hours of employment, and the ages of the children. If one really wanted to show differences associated with maternal employment, then as now, one had to make special efforts to reveal them. This was the approach used by investigators who simply wanted to understand the issue, or who were motivated to show differences—in either direction. However, there were several studies, particularly during the 1970s, when the goal seemed to be to prove the null hypothesis of no difference (Hoffman, 1984b). This was not peculiar to studies of maternal employment; individual studies and comprehensive reviews of gender differences (Maccoby & Jacklyn, 1974) also took this approach during the period. Nevertheless, it is true that if the researcher was satisfied with the demonstration of no difference between the children of employed and non-employed mothers, he or she could simply stop at that point in the analysis.

To understand the role of the mother's employment status, however, or to make the research useful for social action, one had to push on. It is the research which did persist in the effort to reveal differences that has been most important in uncovering the empirical relationships that help us understand how the mother's employment status does affect the child's development. Yet much of this work, like the studies that reported no difference, was motivated by a kind of bias. Often the researcher pursued the analysis in order to demonstrate a particular effect. Since the effect was not observed for the whole sample, it might be observed for some specified subgroups. A review of some of the findings in the maternal employment literature will be provided here both to demonstrate the patterns that were revealed by subgroup analysis and also to provide a summary of substantive results as a basis for the subsequent discussion.

Research results. The more specified analyses enables one to see the possible advantages of maternal employment for daughters. School-aged daughters of employed mothers, across the social classes, viewed females as less restricted in their roles and competencies, exhibited more independence and occupational commitment, and more often saw their mothers as someone they admired (Hoffman, 1979). The data for sons, on the other hand, indicated a more mixed picture. In blue-collar families, sons and daughters both have often been shown to have higher scores on measures of cognitive and socio-emotional adjustment though in at least one analysis (Milne, Myers, Rosenthal, & Ginsberg, 1986) they were found to have lower scores on cognitive measures, and the sons have sometimes shown less closeness with their fathers. In the middle class, sons as well as daughters with employed mothers have often been found to have higher scores on adjustment measures, but in some of the older studies the sons sometimes showed lower scores on grade-school achievement and I.Q. tests (Hoffman, 1979). Several studies have found higher scores on various cognitive indices for employed mothers' children in economically disadvantaged groups (Cherry & Eaton, 1977; Milne, Myers, Rosenthal, & Ginsberg, 1986).

The recent research with infants and young children has as yet revealed few differences in the characteristics of the children with employed and nonemployed mothers, even in longitudinal research (Hoffman, 1989; Gottfried & Gottfried, 1988). While there is some suggestion in the data that the young child with an employed mother is less compliant and more peer-oriented, this seems to depend in part on the nature of the nonmaternal care (Clarke-Stewart, 1988, 1989). Data suggest that the number of hours the mother is employed is important, with a curvilinear relationship emerging—suggesting positive effects at least on the mother-child interaction from part-time employment and negative effects when the mother's employment exceeds 40 hours a week (Owen & Cox, 1988).

A considerable number of investigations have looked at differences in the security of attachment between infants whose mothers have been employed full-time during the first year of their lives and those whose mothers have been employed part-time or not at all. Although most of these studies found no significant differences, the accumulation of results across studies has been interpreted by some as indicating a greater risk of insecure attachment on the part of infants with full-time employed mothers. Serious questions have been raised about the attachment studies, however, including concern with the validity of the attachment measure and the problem of self-selection (Belsky, 1988; Clarke-Stewart, 1988, 1989; Hoffman, 1989).

As with the research on older children, the gender of the child seems to make a difference. Several studies suggest that parents' attitudes and interaction are more positive in employed-mother families when they have daughters, and more positive in nonemployed-mother families when they have sons (Bronfenbrenner, Alvarez, & Henderson, 1984; Bronfenbrenner & Crouter, 1982; Hoffman, 1984c).

The findings reported here, though not necessarily strong, are honest findings. They were revealed because the researchers examined special aspects of the maternal employment situation. This is a valuable contribution. Nevertheless, it was often the researcher's expectations about maternal employment that led to the particular analyses. Revealing the positive effects for school-aged daughters was at least consistent with the Women's Movement of the 1970s. It required a concept that the status of the mother in the family was likely to be affected by her economic role and was important for the daughter's development. To consider the diminished traditionalism of the daughter a positive outcome required a belief that sex-role traditionalism was limiting to female development. Furthermore, to find effects on social development that could be deemed healthy required relinquishing some of the earlier measures of female adjustment which included within them the concept that dependency was an important part of femininity (Bem, 1975). Much of the motivation for this line of research was an interest in finding the precursors for high achievement in women.

The analysis that revealed a possible relationship between maternal employment and the security of attachment is also an example of motivated perseverance. In a review published in 1984, the reviewer accurately reported that no study to date had found significantly more mother–infant insecure attachment in full-time employed mother families (Hoffman, 1984a). Two studies since then have found this relationship (Barglow, Vaughn, & Molitor, 1987; Belsky & Rovine, 1988). However, to strengthen the case for an insecure attachment across studies and in individual investigations, three different devices have subsequently been used:

1. Father-infant attachment was also measured and infants were classified as having at least one insecure attachment. With this measure, a significant relationship emerged (Owen & Cox, 1988).
2. Part-time employment, which had been eliminated from most of the studies (Chase-Lansdale & Owen, 1987), was included with the non-employed group (Belsky, 1988).
3. Data were accumulated from different studies and combined yielding a significant difference between the mothers who were employed full-time during the first year of the child's life and those who were either employed part-time or not at all (Belsky, 1988).

Again, to say that these analyses reflected the researchers' bent is not to invalidate the results. We are simply here pointing out that a researcher's viewpoint can affect the nature and extent of the analyses conducted.

Conclusions Drawn

It is probably in the drawing of conclusions from the empirical analysis that research bias most often enters. As an obvious example, one can say "In eight independent comparisons there were no significant differences" or "Although there were no significant differences, in seven of the eight independent comparisons the direction of the differences was the same and in no case did the direction go the other way." Each statement may be accurate but the implications drawn from them are quite different. Similarly, some researchers will note when the number of significant relationships revealed by their analyses is less than chance and thus not to be trusted, while others will pluck out the few significant results from an extensive battery of statistical tests and present them as valid results.

Researchers also differ in the extent to which they indicate the weaknesses of their data. For example, most studies of maternal employment cannot distinguish effects of employment from selective factors—that is, the mothers who chose to enter the labor market may be different from those who did not and thus the supposed effects of employment status may be a result of preexisting differences between the two groups of mothers. There is wide variation in the degree to which researchers raise this caution in interpreting the data.

Bias can also occur in drawing conclusions if the researcher chooses to focus on certain aspects and neglect others. For example, several studies have found that when maternal employment exceeds 40 hours, a strain is introduced into the mother–child relationship that is not apparent at less than 40 hours. Some researchers, in their conclusions, will emphasize the strain (Owen & Cox, 1988) while others will emphasize its absence (Gottfried, Gottfried, & Bathurst, 1988). Both patterns are present in the data and reported; it is only the emphasis that is different.

A more blatant example of this is in the report of Belsky and Rovine (1988). These researchers found that infant boys who received nonmaternal care for 35 or more hours per week were more likely to show an insecure attachment to their fathers, and also that infant girls experiencing full-time maternal care (less than 11 hours of nonmaternal care) were more likely to show insecure attachment to their fathers. That is, when mothers were employed full-time, father–infant attachment was less likely to be secure for sons than when mothers were not employed full-time; when mothers were full-time homemakers, father–infant attachment was less likely to be secure for daughters than when mothers were employed. The finding for boys, in this study, is a major part of the subsequent analysis and conclusions.[1] The data for girls, however, are dismissed: "No further discussion of this unanticipated but nevertheless intriguing result will appear in this report" (p. 14). The authors explain this decision by saying that the finding for girls has not been reported in any previous work. It might be noted that the finding for boys was obtained only once before and in that study it was only a transitional result noted at 12 months but not at 18 (Owen, Easterbrooks, Chase-Lansdale, & Goldberg, 1984). Nevertheless, the thrust of the conclusion was toward the dangers of maternal employment for attachment security and the counterevidence for daughters was not picked up in that article nor in subsequent ones.

Peer Review

The imperfections in the research process are often ironed out in peer review. Peer review comes in at two major points: when the article reporting the research is submitted for publication and when the results are discussed in published research reviews. Even though the reviewer may have his or her own bias, the outside evaluation is likely to be valuable for detecting flaws or alternative interpretations.

---

[1] The combined measure showing "at least one insecure attachment" is examined for boys but not girls.

Evaluation for publication decisions. Most professional journals require at least two reviews and each review must indicate the reasons behind the evaluation and include suggestions for improvement. Thus, it seems unlikely that an acceptable article would be blocked from publication because of reviewer bias. In most cases, the original submission is modified in response to reviewer criticisms and this usually results in a better manuscript. The more critical review, by this route, often results in the most improved resubmission. Thus, the process often works best when the author and the reviewer have conflicting biases.

For example, in one of the first articles on maternal employment and mother–infant interaction, a study of premature infants, a reviewer noticed that the employed mothers were more likely to be unmarried and also that their infants were lower in birthweight. The submission was not rejected but it was suggested that the author carry out additional analyses to see if the observation that the quality of mother–infant interaction during the second year was lower when the mother was employed would be sustained with these variables controlled. Although the number of cases in the study was too small to control both variables simultaneously, the author was able to show that the main effect persisted when each control was separately introduced. The strength of the results were thus enhanced by the review process. There are many similar examples where reviewers' comments have resulted in additional analyses, alternative interpretations of results, or the introduction of cautions about the limitations of the data. Furthermore, as suggested above, the quality of the report may be improved even in cases where the reviewer is motivated by lack of enthusiasm for the results. It is quite possible that the observation that additional controls were needed in the above example might have been missed if the reviewer were satisfied with the original results, but the criticism was a valid one nonetheless, and the data were strengthened by the suggestion.

A recent example, however, shows how bias can actually be introduced in the review process. Chase-Lansdale and Owen (1987) recently published an investigation comparing the security of parent–infant attachment in families where the mother had returned to full-time employment within six months of the child's birth and families where the mother was home full-time. There were no significant differences in mother–infant attachment for either sons or daughters. When this article was submitted for publication, an anonymous reviewer noted that some of the subjects had been recruited prenatally and were part of a previously studied sample while others were recruited for this particular study. The reviewer proposed that subjects whose research involvement preceded the birth of the child would be less self-selected for the quality of the mother–child relationship than those recruited postnatally when the relationship was apparent. In itself, this is an interesting idea. However, in this case the reviewer apparently saw this problem as an explanation for why the authors had failed to find that employed mothers had less secure attachments, because they were required to compare the security of attachment between prenatally and postnatally recruited subjects *only for the employed-mother group* (personal communication). They were not asked to perform the same test on the nonemployed group, though the same prenatal-versus-postnatal argument could be made there; and they were not asked to compare the employed and nonemployed groups separately for the prenatally and postnatally recruited subjects, though that is obviously more germane.

The requested analysis did show more insecure attachment in the prenatally recruited group of employed mothers than in the postnatally recruited group of employed mothers, and this was reported in the published article. The additional analysis required by the reviewer does not, in fact, change the original results. While it is interesting to consider that subjects recruited before the child's birth may be less self-selected for security of attachment, there is no evidence that this is related to employment status nor that it affects the results of this study. Nevertheless, the inclusion of this particular analysis in the final publication has led to a misinterpretation in subsequent review articles which have reported it as a post-hoc analysis that invalidates the major findings (Belsky, 1988).

Published reviews. Peer review for publication decisions may not always operate as effectively as one might wish, but it is a valuable system for maintaining quality and minimizing bias even when it relies on the existence of conflicting biases. An additional route by which balance is obtained is through review articles. Since the late 1950s, articles have appeared which have attempted to integrate, interpret, and criticize the research on maternal employment (e.g., Belsky, 1988; Bronfenbrenner & Crouter, 1982; Etaugh, 1974; Heyns, 1982; Hoffman, 1963a, 1974, 1979, 1980; Maccoby, 1958; Siegel & Haas, 1963; Stolz, 1960; Zaslow, unpublished manuscript).

Integrative reviews have a number of advantages over individual research reports. The reviewer can discern common trends across studies and pull out results that were too weak in the individual research to warrant attention. By this process, the reviewer, like the original researcher, can point out patterns selectively. The finding, for example, noted by Hoffman (1979), that daughters of employed mothers show more independence was supported not so much by any individual study, but by a recurring pattern across studies. In this context, the excellent early study by Siegel and her colleagues (1959) reported data suggesting that the preschool daughters, but not the sons, of employed mothers seemed more independent in behavioral observations. In the article reporting the study, the emphasis was on the absence of differences between employed and nonemployed mothers' children, but in the review, the pattern of daughters' independence revealed in the tables was picked up.

There are many other examples. Thus, several reviewers have noted that maternal employment seems to have different significance for sons than for daughters, and this observation is often based on noting similarities across studies even when the original researcher did not include the result in his/her conclusions (Bronfenbrenner & Crouter, 1982; Hoffman, 1974, 1979, 1984a; Zaslow, unpublished manuscript). As noted earlier, reviewers have recently combined the data from studies of maternal employment and mother–infant attachment among mothers who are employed full-time during the child's first year (Belsky, 1988; Clarke-Stewart, 1989), though very few of the individual studies found a significant relationship.

In addition, the integrative review is also a vehicle for criticism. Divergent findings and methodological weaknesses are noted. And in these reviews, as in the evaluations for publication decision, one can often discern a tendency to be less critical when results conform to ones expectations and astute to detect flaws when they disagree. As an example, several reviews have recently questioned the validity of the Ainsworth Strange Situation measure (Ainsworth, Blehar, Waters, & Wall, 1978) as an indication of security of attachment when the infant has experienced routine nonmaternal care (Clark-Stewart, 1988, 1989; Hoffman, 1989). This criticism takes note of the fact that the measure was established and validated on a population of children for whom the experimental situation created a state of moderate stress. The situation consists of the following events: The child and mother enter an unfamiliar room, a pleasant but unknown woman enters, there are two brief separations when the mother leaves the room. The situation was designed to create moderate stress and thus to activate attachment behavior, and previous work has identified certain behavior patterns as indicating the quality of the child's attachment to the mother. One pattern of insecure attachment, called "anxious avoidant," often appears to be an independent coping style, but in a situation of stress has been shown to be a defensive reaction (Sroufe & Waters, 1977). Recently, however, it has been pointed out that the degree of stress experienced by the child will be affected by the strangeness of the situation. For the child whose mother is employed full-time, the situation may seem similar to accustomed routines. The independent behavior of the child may thus not reflect anxious-avoidant attachment but simply a lack of stress. This position has been bolstered by evidence indicating that the measure did not predict subsequent behavior for the children of employed mothers as it did for nonemployed (Vaughn, Deane, & Waters, 1985).

This criticism provides a valuable insight and it has been extended to explain some unexpected cross-cultural findings which used the Ainsworth measure: The attachment scores of Japanese children suggest they may be overly stressed in the situation while Israeli children in kibbutzim may be, like the American children of employed mothers, insufficiently stressed (Clarke-Stewart, 1988; Sagi & Lewkowicz, 1987; Takehashi, 1986). What is noteworthy here, however, is that this criticism has emerged just when the first evidence has been reported suggesting that infants with full-time employed mothers may be insecurely attached, and particularly may show the anxious-avoidant pattern (Barglow, Vaughn, & Molitor, 1987; Belsky & Rovine, 1988). As indicated before, this does not invalidate the criticism, but it does suggest a motivation for its emergence.

Another important methodological issue that has been raised in recent years pertains to cohort effects. Because of the recent increases in the employment of mothers of infants and preschool children, a considerable amount of the research has focused on the effects of the mother's employment during the child's early years. Because it is difficult to measure enduring qualities in young children, researchers now often rely on retrospective data, or they take advantage of existing longitudinal data sets. A major problem with this procedure, however, is that the mothers who were employed during the children's preschool years in such studies were extremely unusual. They are likely to have been highly professional and career-oriented, unmarried, or in poverty circumstances. So few mothers of young children were employed in the 1950s and 1960s that the pattern occurred only under unusual circumstances and it is difficult to disentangle the effects of employment status from other special aspects of the situation. Furthermore, any implications of these studies for present times when such employment has become modal are unknown. These problems have been discussed in several recent reviews (Hoffman, 1984a; 1986).

A particular controversy connected with this issue arose in the research of Milne, Myers, Rosenthal, and Ginsberg (1986). This analysis used data obtained in 1976 through 1981. Their findings, extensively reported in the mass media (Mann, 1983), were that high school students whose mothers had been employed, and particularly those in white, intact families, obtained lower scores on reading and mathematics achievement tests.[2] However, a reanalysis of this same data set by Heyns and Castambis (1986) revealed that the source of the negative effects was carried by the "small number of mothers who worked full-time *prior to 1970*" (p. 140, italics mine).

The importance of review by one's peers was highlighted in this case. The Milne data were released to the press before they were even submitted for publication. Headlined first in the *Washington Post,* articles across the country soon featured the discovery that the children of working mothers performed inadequately in school. The prepublication reports by the researchers (Ginsberg, Milne, Myers, & Rosenthal, 1984; Milne, Myers, Ellman, & Ginsberg, 1983) were more qualified than the newspaper accounts, but did, nonetheless, include results and analyses that the authors revised before the data were eventually published three years later. Furthermore, when it was published, it was presented along with a prepared critique, comment, and rejoinder (Heyns & Castambis, 1986). The analysis was flawed, and the reanalysis by Heyns and Castambis which indicated this and pointed out the cohort problem was undertaken largely because of the first author's previously indicated interest in the methodological issues (Heyns, 1982). Nevertheless, the drama and attention were no doubt heightened by the social significance of the topic. The incident also reveals a problem to be considered more fully in the next section of this paper: While the

---

[2] The original reports made broader assertions but these results emerged as the strongest claims in the published version.

scientific publication was modified and monitored, there was no retraction in the public press.

COMMUNICATION TO THE PUBLIC

A serious dilemma exists for the social scientist whose work focuses on a social issue because there is a need for scientific information on which to base action, but the actual data are limited and easily misinterpreted. On the one hand, he or she recognizes that the work is socially significant and that in addition to its scientific merit, there are implications for social policy and individual decisions. The practitioner and the policy maker have a need for knowledge in the areas in which they must act. They need to know what research has uncovered in order to make the best possible decision. On the other hand, most of us realize that any given study may be flawed and is at least limited by the few variables that can be accommodated within the design, by special characteristics of the sample, and by other factors that prevent a fully adequate portrayal of the phenomenon under investigation. Even groups of studies are limited because the results are probabilistic and restricted by the measures used and most research designs. If there were total consensus in the results of studies of maternal employment, we would still not know if suggested effects of maternal employment were not simply a function of selective factors—which mothers chose to work and which to stay home—or if the absence of suggested effects reflected our failure to examine the right variables or to discover sleeper effects through longitudinal designs. Furthermore, highly significant differences between groups still mean that the presumed effects did not occur in many cases, often even in the majority of cases.

Individual Decision

For all of these reasons, those who know the data best are often the ones most reluctant to give advice. As a concrete example, consider the currently common question: Will there be a negative effect on the child's emotional development if the mother returns to work full-time before the child's first birthday? It is clear from what has already been discussed in this chapter that we do not know the answer, but it is also likely that it is unanswerable. If there were a perfectly measured, unquestionably established relationship between the mother's employment status during the first year and the security of the child's attachment, what would we know? Hock, DeMeis, and McBride (1988) have demonstrated that the attitudes of mothers in the maternity hospital predict to both subsequent attachment behavior and employment decision. Mothers who are not concerned about attachment and separation are more likely to seek early employment. Thus, we cannot know whether any relationship between employment status and attachment security is causal, or whether it merely indicates that the group who return to employment soon after the birth includes more women who are likely to have insecurely attached infants—not because of their employment but because of their attitudes and behavior. There is no way to escape the problem of self-selection.

In addition, even if the research could establish cause-effect relationships, its value for individual decisions would be limited. Any effect of the mother's employment status would be mediated through many other variables—the particular mother, the particular child, the family situation, the nature of the nonmaternal care, how that care compares to the care the mother would otherwise be providing, ad infinitum. General prescriptions, such as the admonition that mothers should not work if the child is under three (White, 1980), cannot be research-based. There are data, in fact, that indicate that mothers of infants who are home full-time but conflicted about this choice are less sensitive and responsive to their infants than employed mothers, whatever their preference (Dienstag, 1986). While some mothers do very well with the full-time care of an infant, others may be more effective in this role when they are also employed.

What the ethical researcher should not do in communicating research findings to the public is to report the data with more certainty than they warrant, to strip the data of their necessary qualifications, or to draw action implications beyond what is known—and then to claim these conclusions are empirically based. In the area of maternal employment, there is much of value that can be communicated to the public, but honesty and scientific integrity need to be maintained. If data are discussed, their frailties must also be described. It is a feasible task. Sandra Scarr, in a taped radio interview broadcast on "All Things Considered," included an explanation of the validity issues surrounding the Ainsworth Strange Situation measure along with her discussion of the research findings. It was brief and clear. Hoffman, on the *Today Show*, explained why data showing that extra environmental input led to sizable I.Q. gains in an environmentally deprived sample of babies, could not be generalized to a middle-class situation. In mass media communication, as in college teaching, a major goal should be to increase understanding of the nature, and limitations, of scientific findings. Since there are many who assert questionable conclusions in the name of science, it is very important to increase the public's knowledge of how to interpret research results.

There is actually a great deal that the research has revealed that can be helpful to individuals. The data have shown potential advantages and pitfalls of each employment status—the full-time homemaker, part-time employment, full-time employment, and more than full-time employment (Hoffman, 1979, 1989). They have sensitized us to the many other aspects of family life that interact with the mother's employment status and affect the outcomes for children. The findings, however, are complex, often tentative, and always affected by the social context in which they were obtained. Their value for individuals depends on communicating these complexities, whether the communication is a direct one from the scientist or through someone in the media. If it is not true, it is not useful.

Social Policy

Perhaps the clearest implication for social policy stems not from the psychologist's research but directly from the census tables. In 1987, close to 57% of the mothers in the United States with children under six years of age were in the labor force (U.S. Bureau of Labor Statistics, 1987). The data from previous years clearly indicate an upward trend and both extrapolation from these figures and analysis of the social changes that have led to this new pattern (Hoffman, 1984c) indicate that, though the pace may slacken, this trend will continue. There is a need for preschool care. A considerable amount of research has examined the various kinds of preschool care and considered the different dimensions to determine effects on children (Clarke-Stewart, 1988, 1989; Clarke-Stewart & Fein, 1983; Phillips, 1987). While the results of this work are not definitive, there are findings that could be useful in setting up preschool care programs and evaluation criteria for government or individual use.

On the other hand, the implications for social policy that can be drawn from the research on the effects of maternal employment on children are not as clear. As with drawing conclusions for individual use, the research rarely yields cause-effect statements, and thus the policy implications are limited. An interesting example can be seen in the following: Studies that have examined maternal employment and the characteristics of children from economically disadvantaged populations have typically found that the children with employed mothers score higher on various indices of cognitive performance and social adjustment (Heyns, 1982; Hoffman, 1980; Milne et al., 1986). If this relationship is a causal one, if the mother's employment is a cause of these positive outcomes, then one might conclude that receivers of federal funds such as Aid to Families with Dependent Children (AFDC) should be encouraged to seek employment rather than supported to stay home. However, it is also possible that the relationship exists because in circumstances of poverty, the mothers who have fewer children, more adults in the family, better education, less personal distress, and more organized lives are the ones who are employed and the advantages their children show are a function of these qualities and not employment per se. That is, the empirical relationship may reflect selective factors, not causality, and if this is the basis for the relationship, forcing the nonemployed mothers into the labor force might exacerbate an already very difficult situation.

Moreover, even if causality were established, the social policy implication would depend on the reason for the effects. In economically disadvantaged families, maternal employment makes a considerable difference in the per capita income and offers a financial advantage over AFDC. Per capita income is itself related to children's cognitive performance (Cherry & Eaton, 1977), and thus a very different social policy implication might be to increase the AFDC payments in order to bring these children up to the others' level. In this example, the existing data are inadequate to yield policy implications, but they do indicate future research projects that could more accurately inform policy. Research specifically geared toward policy may often be necessary to bridge field research with policy decision.

There are only a few areas where policy implications can clearly be drawn from existing data. One possible example is the recurring finding that part-time employment often offers advantages over either nonemployment or full-time employment. The pattern has been found in several studies over the years, but most recently in research with preschool children that examined the quality of mother–infant interaction or the mother's attitude toward the child and enthusiasm for mothering (Bronfenbrenner, Alvarez, & Henderson, 1984; Hoffman, 1984c; Schwartz, 1983). There are also data that suggest that when family circumstances make either full-time mothering or full-time employment stressful for the mother, such as when there is a handicapped child, part-time employment may be particularly advantageous (Hoffman, 1986). Yet part-time jobs are difficult to find and often lacking in employee benefits. Extending benefits to part-time employment, facilitating job-sharing, and redefining work units to fit part-time packages would fill an important need.

Reporting the Data

There have been some scholarly attempts to cope with the dilemma of recognizing the importance of making social science data available to the public, while also exercising concerns that the data not be distorted in the process. The volumes that make up the *Reviews of Child Development Research* (Hoffman & Hoffman, 1964) and books such as *Child Development Research and Social Policy* (Stevenson & Siegel, 1984) are examples. These publications consist of chapters in which social scientists review the research organized around social issues, reporting the results with their qualifications but without jargon. These chapters are reviewed by other scholars and often by experts with more applied experience. Thus, the data are made available to practitioners, journalists, and policy makers without the miscommunication and oversimplification that sometimes occurs. An outstanding example of this in the area of maternal employment is the two volume set, *Families that Work* and *Working Families,* edited by Kamerman and Hayes (1982, 1983). In addition, some of the individual reviews are useful in this way (Hoffman, 1984a; Clarke-Stewart, 1989).

Probably the route by which most individuals learn about the impact of maternal employment on children, however, is through newspapers and magazines. Newspapers in particular, perhaps because of deadline requirements or the competition for bylines, often report results from unpublished single studies, fail to check the veracity of their article with the researchers, and are attracted to the sensational (see Chapter 9). It is, of course, more sensational to report effects than to say that most studies found no differences and the researcher who is most likely to make unqualified claims is the most likely to be quoted in the mass media. The attention given the research by Milne and her colleagues, already discussed, is one example. Recently an article, also from the *Washington Post*, was syndicated throughout the country with glaring headlines such as "The Lifelong Harm of Leaving Infants in Strangers' Care" (Rosenfeld, 1986). In Minneapolis, the *Star and Tribune*, published a response by Shirley Moore (1986), but in most cities the emotionally charged article appeared unchallenged.

Researchers can exert some control over how their work is used by the media. Often when asked for a phone comment by a writer, I find they are willing instead to accept a published review by mail. The writer's understanding of the nature of the research and the complexities of the issue is more likely to be enhanced by that route, and the quality of the article being prepared as well as future ones may be improved. Some newspapers, like the *New York Times*, and many magazines, are willing to check what they have written with the researcher before it is published. One can often request this as a condition of cooperation. Social responsibility requires some surveillance over at least the reporting of ones own work. And it is particularly evident when there is a willingness to write a rebuttal to what seems to be an inaccurate or misleading report of ones area of specialty (Chess, 1987; Heyns & Catsambis, 1986; Moore, 1986; Philips, McCartney, Scarr, & Howes, 1987).

Television has also shown interest in the effects of maternal employment, and researchers sometimes have an opportunity for direct contact with a wide audience. Depending on the nature of the program, however, television can be a strange media for the researcher (as can radio; see Chapter 11). For example, the television format can place researchers, who are often unfamiliar with giving their messages in short, concise statements, at a considerable disadvantage. Asked a question, the researcher may begin by expressing caveats or a relatively esoteric point and miss the opportunity to state his/her position. Or, when invited in pairs to represent different viewpoints on maternal employment, some researchers become angry and state their positions in stronger terms than they really believe. Offering viewers various possible interpretations of the maternal employment research is a good idea. Some training in this skill can be helpful as this is a valuable vehicle for communicating research results with the awareness that legitimate investigators can draw different conclusions.

SUMMARY AND CONCLUSIONS

In this chapter, two issues have been considered that arise in studying the effects of the mother's employment status on the child: bias in the scientific process and communication to the public. When one studies a social issue like maternal employment, one must deal with potential bias—in the conducting of research, in its interpretation, and in the evaluations of others work. Some of this bias is an inescapable part of all science; some is because there are implications about which it is difficult to maintain neutrality. Bias, however, does not necessarily mean the research is faulted. It can be a spur to new analyses and stimulate insights. Because the bias of the researchers in this area is not the same, there are checks and balances. Through peer review and dialogue, the system is self-correcting and research is advanced.

But the checks and balances of peer review are not effective in the communication of research to the public. Public communications are often not peer-reviewed and results are reported without the necessary qualifications. While there is a social responsibility to make findings available for social policy and individual decision, there is also a responsibility to communicate the results accurately, and to educate the public about what the data can and cannot say. The tentative nature of our findings, their susceptibility to different interpretations, and the complications of translating them into individual or policy actions must be communicated to achieve an ethical science.

REFERENCES

Ainsworth, M., Blehar, M., Waters, E., & Wall, S. (1978). *Patterns of attachment.* Hillsdale, NJ: Lawrence Erlbaum Associates, Inc.

Barglow, P., Vaughn, B., & Molitor, N. (1987). Effects of maternal absence due to employment on the quality of infant-mother attachment in a low-risk sample. *Child Development, 58*(4), 945–954.

Baruch, G.K. (1972). Maternal influences upon college women's attitudes toward women and work. *Developmental Psychology, 6,* 32–37.

Belsky, J. (1988). The "effects" of infant day care reconsidered. *Early Childhood Research Quarterly, 3,* 235–272.

Belsky, J., & Rovine, M.J. (1988). Nonmaternal care in the first year of life and the security of infant-parent attachment. *Child Development, 59,* 157–167.

Bem, S.I. (1975). Sex-role adaptability: One consequence of psychological androgyny. *Journal of Personality and Social Psychology, 31,* 634–643.

Bronfenbrenner, U., Alvarez, W.F., & Henderson, C.R., Jr. (1984). Working and watching: Maternal employment status and parents' perceptions of their three-year-old children. *Child Development, 55,* 1362–1378.

Bronfenbrenner, U., & Crouter, A. (1982). Work and family through time and space. In S.B. Kamerman & C.D. Hayes (Eds.), *Families that work: Children in a changing world* (pp. 39–83). Washington, DC: National Academy Press.

Chase-Lansdale, P.L., & Owen, M.T. (1987). Maternal employment in a family context: Effects on infant-mother and infant-father attachments. *Child Development, 58,* 1505–1512.

Cherry, R.R., & Eaton, E.L. (1977). Physical and cognitive development in children of low-income mothers working in the child's early years. *Child Development, 48,* 158–166.

Chess, S. (1987, February). Comments: "Infant day care: A cause for concern." *Zero to Three,* pp. 24–25.

Clarke-Stewart, K.A. (1988). The 'effects' of infant day care reconsidered: Risks for parents, children and researchers. *Early Childhood Research Quarterly, 3,* 293–318.

Clarke-Stewart, K.A. (1989). Infant day care: Maligned or malignant? *American Psychologist, 44,* 266–273.

Clarke-Stewart, K.A., & Fein, G.G. (1983). Early childhood programs. In P.H. Mussen (Ed.), *Handbook of child psychology, Volume 2. Infancy and developmental psychobiology* (pp. 917–1000). New York: Wiley.

Dienstag, E.L. (1986, August). *The transition to parenthood in working and non-working pariparous mothers*. A paper presented at the 94th Annual Convention of the American Psychological Association, Washington, DC.

Easterbrook, M.A., & Goldberg, W.A. (1989). Security of toddler-parent attachment: Relation to children's socio-personality functioning during kindergarten. In M. Greenberg, D. Cicchetti, & M. Cummings (Eds.), *Attachment in preschool years: Theory, Research, and Intervention*. Chicago: University of Chicago Press.

Etaugh, C. (1974). Effects of maternal employment on children: A review of recent research. *Merrill-Palmer Quarterly, 19–20*, 71–98.

Galambos, N.L., Petersen, A.C., & Lenerz, K. (1988). Maternal employment and sex-typing in early adolescence: Contemporaneous and longitudinal relations. In A.E. Gottfried & A.W. Gottfried (Eds.), *Maternal employment and children's development: Longitudinal research* (pp. 59–84). New York: Plenum.

Ginsberg, A., Milne, A.M., Myers, D.E., & Rosenthal, A.S. (1984). *Single parents, working mothers and the educational achievement of school children* (Contracts No. 300-80-0778 and No. 300-83-0211). Washington, DC: U.S. Department of Education.

Gottfried, A.E., & Gottfried, A.W. (Eds.). (1988). *Maternal employment and children's development: Longitudinal research*. New York: Plenum.

Gottfried, A.E., Gottfried, A.W., & Bathurst, K. (1988). Maternal employment, family environment and children's development: Infancy through the school years. In A.E. Gottfried & A.W. Gottfried (Eds.), *Maternal employment and children's development: Longitudinal research* (pp. 11–58). New York: Plenum.

Hartley, R.E. (1960). Children's concepts of male and female roles. *Merrill-Palmer Quarterly, 6*, 83–91.

Heyns, B. (1982). The influence of parents' work on children's school achievement. In S.B. Kamerman & C.D. Hayes (Eds.), *Families that work: Children in a changing world* (pp. 229–267). Washington, DC: Academy Press.

Heyns, B. & Catsambis, S. (1986). Mother's employment and children's achievement: A critique. *Sociology of Education, 59*(3), 140–151.

Hock, E., DeMeis, D., & McBride, S. (1988). Maternal separation anxiety: Its role in the balance of employment and motherhood in mothers of infants. In A.E. Gottfried & A.W. Gottfried (Eds.), *Maternal employment and children's development: Longitudinal research*. New York: Plenum.

Hoffman, L.W. (1963a). Effects on children: Summary and discussion. In F.I. Nye & L.W. Hoffman (Eds.), *The employed mother in America* (pp. 190–214). Chicago: Rand McNally.

Hoffman, L.W. (1963b). Parental power relations and the division of household tasks. In F.I. Nye & L.W. Hoffman (Eds.), *The employed mother in America* (pp. 215–230). Chicago: Rand McNally.

Hoffman, L.W. (1974). Effects of maternal employment on the child: A review of the research. *Developmental Psychology, 10*, 204–228.

Hoffman, L.W. (1979). Maternal employment: 1979. *American Psychologist, 34*, 859–865.

Hoffman, L.W. (1980). The effects of maternal employment on the academic attitudes and performance of school-age children. *School Psychology Review, 9*, 319–336.

Hoffman, L.W. (1984a). Maternal employment and the young child. In M. Perlmutter (Ed.), *Parent–child interaction and parent–child relations in child development. The Minnesota Symposia on Child Psychology* (Vol. 17, pp. 101–128). Hillsdale, NJ: Lawrence Erlbaum Associates, Inc.

Hoffman, L.W. (1984b). The study of employed mothers over half a century. In M. Lewin (Ed.), *In the shadow of the past: Psychology portrays the sexes* (pp. 295–319). New York: Columbia University Press.

Hoffman, L.W. (1984c). Work, family and the socialization of the child. In R.D. Parke (Ed.), *The family: Review of child development research* (Vol. 7, pp. 223–282). Chicago: University of Chicago Press.

Hoffman, L.W. (1986). Work, family and the child. In M.S. Pallak & R.O. Perloff (Eds.), *Psychology and work: Productivity, change, and employment* (pp. 173–220). Master Lecture Series, American Psychological Association, Washington, DC.

Hoffman, L.W. (1989). Effects of maternal employment in the two- parent family: A review of recent research. *American Psychologist, 44*(2), 283–292.

Hoffman, M.L., & Hoffman, L.W. (Eds.). (1964). *Review of child development research* (Vol. 1). New York: Russell Sage.

Jacobson, J.L., & Wille, D.E. (1984). Influence of attachment and separation experience on separation distress at 18 months. *Developmental Psychology, 20*(3), 477–484.

Kamerman, S.B., & Hayes, C.D. (Eds.). (1982). *Families that work: Children in a changing world.* Washington, DC: National Academy Press.

Kamerman, S.B., & Hayes, C.D. (Eds.). (1983). *Working families.* Washington, DC: National Academy Press.

Maccoby, E.E. (1958). Children and working mothers. *Children, 5*, 83–89.

Maccoby, E.E., & Jacklyn, C. (1974). *Psychology of Sex Differences.* Stanford, CA: Stanford University Press.

Mann, J. (1983, June). Working. *Washington Post*, p. 11A.

Miller, S.M. (1975). Effects of maternal employment on sex role perception, interests and self-esteem in kindergarten girls. *Developmental Psychology, 11*, 405–406.

Milne, A.M., Myers, D.E., Elman, F.M., & Ginsberg, A. (1983, June). *Single parents, working mothers and the educational achievement of elementary school age children.* Unpublished paper.

Milne, A., Myers, D., Rosenthal, A., & Ginsberg, A. (1986). Single parents, working mothers, and the educational achievement of school children. *Sociology of Education, 59*(3), 125–139.

Moore, S. (1986, December). Day-care debate should focus on variable quality of the facilities. *Minneapolis Star and Tribune*, p. 2A.

Owen, M.T., & Cox, M.J. (1988). Maternal employment and the transition to parenthood. In A.E. Gottfried & A.W. Gottfried (Eds.), *Maternal employment and children's development: Longitudinal research.* New York: Plenum.

Owen, M.T., Easterbrooks, M.A., Chase-Lansdale, L., & Goldberg, W.A. (1984). The relation between maternal employment status and the stability of attachments to mother and father. *Child Development, 55*, 1894–1901.

Phillips, D.A. (Ed.). (1987). *Quality in child care: What does research tell us? Research Monographs of the National Association for the Education of Young Children, Vol. 1.* Washington, DC: National Association for the Education of Young Children.

Phillips, D.A., McKartney, K., Scarr, S., & Howes, C. (1987, February). Selective review of infant day care research: A cause for concern! *Zero to Three*, pp. 18–21.

Rosenfeld, M. (1986, November). The lifelong harm of leaving infants in strangers' care. *Minneapolis Star and Tribune*, pp. 10–11.

Sagi, A., & Lewkowicz, K.S. (1987). A cross-cultural evaluation of attachment research. In L.W. Hoffman, C. Tavecchio, & M.H. van IJzendoorn (Eds.), *Attachment in social networks.* Amsterdam: North-Holland.

Schwartz, P. (1983). Length of day care attendance and attachment behavior in 18-month-old infants. *Child Development, 54*, 1073–1078.

Siegel, A.E., & Haas, M.B. (1963). The working mother: A review of research. *Child Development, 34*, 513–542.

Siegel, A.E., Stolz, L.M., Hitchcock, E.A., & Adamson, J.M. (1959). Dependence and independence in the children of working mothers. *Child Development, 30,* 533–546.

Sroufe, L.A., & Waters, E. (1977). Heart rate as a convergent measure in clinical and developmental research. *Merrill-Palmer Quarterly, 23*(1), 5–25.

Stevenson, H., & Siegel, A. (Eds.). (1984), *Child development research and social policy.* Chicago: Chicago University Press.

Stolz, L.M. (1960). Effects of maternal employment on children: evidence from research. *Child Development, 31,* 749–783.

Takahashi, K. (1986). Examining the strange-situation procedure with Japanese mothers and 12-month-old infant. *Developmental Psychology, 22,* 256–270.

U.S. Bureau of Labor Statistics. (1987, August). Press release. *USDL,* pp. 87–345.

Vaughn, B.E., Deane, K.E., & Waters, E. (1985). The impact of out-of-home care on child-mother attachment quality: Another look at some enduring questions. In I. Bretherton & E. Waters (Eds.), Growing points of attachment theory and research. *Monographs of the Society for Research in Child Development, 55* (1–2, Serial No. 209).

Weinraub, M., Jaeger, E., & Hoffman, L.W. (1988). Predicting infant outcomes in families of employed and non-employed mothers. *Early Childhood Research Quarterly, 3,* 361–378.

White, B.L. (1980). *A parent's guide to the first three years.* Engelwood Cliffs, NJ: Prentice-Hall.

Zaslow, M.J. *Sex differences in children's response to maternal employment.* Unpublished manuscript. Prepared for the Committee on Child Development Research and Public Policy, National Research Council, Washington, DC.

17 The Ethics of Research and Intervention with Ethnic Minority Parents and their Children

Harriette Pipes McAdoo

The field of applied developmental psychology is emerging within traditional graduate programs in developmental psychology spawning a broad spectrum of activities and training programs (Fisher & Tryon, 1988). One issue that must be examined in great detail as the field develops is the ethical treatment of ethnically diverse minority families and their children. As parameters are laid out, it is essential that families from ethnic minority groups, particularly those of color, are handled within the normal context of the field. Content on these ethnic groups and culturally sensitive materials must be incorporated initially as the field is being developed, rather than tacked on as a political afterthought. To successfully integrate cultural sensitivity into the science and practice of applied developmental psychology requires an understanding of (a) problems associated with the generation of knowledge about families and children of ethnically and culturally diverse groups; (b) ethnic minority family patterns; and (c) the special problems facing ethnic minority children and adolescents. This chapter addresses these three areas.

THE GENERATION OF KNOWLEDGE ABOUT ETHNIC MINORITY FAMILIES

Ours is a culture with a multinational, multiethnic, and multiracial population that is growing towards a majority of persons in 2,000 AD. It is unfortunate that cultural differences are so often given second-class status. Persons who come from ethnically diverse groups are too often treated simply as minorities, a diminishment of groups of peoples and families. Their acceptance by researchers and practitioners, is, unfortunately, based upon how close they approximate the norm of middle-class white families and children. They are often depicted within the literature as negations or deviations from normal families. Cultural components are often ignored in the intervention process.

To promote this "minority" approach is to deny the infusion of elements from an individual's culture or country of origin that may contribute to effective coping strategies (Barrera, 1988; Balgopal, 1988; Bowman, 1988). These strategies are helpful within present day society, as individuals move into more mainstream culture. Only by appreciating existing patterns and the sources of their origin can developmentalists work with ethnic minority individuals in a culturally sensitive manner.

Presentation of Ethnic Families in the Literature

Forty years ago Black families appeared in the works of Herskovits (1930) and Franklin Frazier (1932, 1939, 1957). Frazier began the first series of empirical studies on African-Americans opening the way for many to follow. Over a decade later, the study of ethnic families was invigorated with the works of Billingsley (1968) as the first of many authors who discussed the Black family within the context of social systems. Billingsley's work and the writings of Willie (1970) and Staples (1971) presented the Black family not simply as a stereotype, but as a viable, adaptive entity with functional systems. Scanzoni (1971) continued the empirical study of diverse Black families. These writings were partially in response to the negative stereotypes presented in the social science and public policy literature (Moynihan, 1965). Indeed, Hill (1971) startled the field when he listed the strengths of Black families. Works that followed presented a base of knowledge about families of African descent including the socialization of Black children (McAdoo, 1974), enthnographic work on Black women (Ladner, 1972; Stack, 1975) and key components of Black families (McAdoo, 1988a).

Simultaneously new knowledge on Native American and Chicano families were being presented by Alvirez, Bean, and Williams (1981), de la Garza, Kruszewski, and Arcimega (1971) and Stanton (1972). The book *Ethnic families in America: Patterns and Variations,* edited by Mindel and Haberstein (1976, 1981), made a real contribution to the field. In this book Price wrote about North American Indian families and Huang covered Chinese-American families.

The growth of publishing on ethnic families increased near the end of the 1970s. Kagen and Ender (1975) and Laosa (1978, 1980) compared Chicano and Anglo-American families in their maternal teaching styles. Durrett, O'Brien, and Pennebacker (1975) discussed child-rearing in Black, White, and Mexican-American families. Virgil (1980) traced ethnic families beginning with Indians and moved on to Chicanos. The most comprehensive presentation of all American ethnic groups was presented in 1980 in the *Harvard Encyclopedia of Ethnic Groups,* although the emphasis was on ethnic groups and not on families and children per se.

While the literature was beginning to be written and collected on ethnic families, it was surprising that most of these works were usually in books. Few of these articles were in professional journals. Those who were working in the field of family ethnicity knew of these writings, but the wider audience of developmental psychologists, family practitioners, and other mental health professionals did not read the books.

Methodological Problems in the Study of Ethnic Families

The most frequent methodological problem in the study of ethnic minority families and children is that of sample selection. Too often middle-class white family members are compared with lower-class Chicano, Native American, or African American families. When this is done, it is impossible to factor out the real contributions of race or class. When class and race are confounded, professionals who intervene in the lives of ethnic children and families work with faulty and ineffective information.

Marie Peters (1985) has identified six additional methodological problems common to research on ethnic minority families: (a) Many studies do not specify the race or culture of the sample, thus ignoring culture-specific influences; (b) Ethnic families tend to be viewed in a monolithic manner. Few studies use both middle and working class families; (c) When more than one race is studied, only comparative statistics, rather than ethnomethodological or descriptive analyses are employed; (d) Only problem families are investigated (poor mothers, delinquent boys, pregnant girls, nonsupportive fathers), rather than the majority of ordinary families in which few problems are present; (e) When ethnic families are studied, the research design is often changed. When white families are the target the researcher may be interested in process or how various influences affect the subjects; when the family is a member of an ethnic group the central concern may be intervention; (f) The presence of an outside "expert" of another race or culture often presents an unmeasured influence.

Applied developmental psychologists interested in parent and child relations will find many of these patterns of methodological weakness in studies of minority families. The reader should keep in mind the tentative nature of conclusions drawn from minority family research as we move to the next section on ethnic minority family patterns.

ETHNIC MINORITY FAMILY PATTERNS

Minority families, particularly those who are in need of supportive services, often share a commonality of cultural patterns that appears to cross ethnic groups. McAdoo (1978) described these patterns as follows:

> There are involvements and frequent interactions with close kin.
> Extended family patterns are important and often include friends who become fictive kin.
> Poverty is widespread because of isolation from economic and social supports of the broader community.
> Conflict occurs between the family and the wider society when the child ventures into the society and faces conflicting values.

>Subcultural members are viewed by the wider society in a stereotypical manner that does not allow deviations.
>
>There is a lack of respect for their cultural uniqueness.

While there may be differences between ethnic families on other variables, these patterns are common for most members of different ethnic groups, particularly those of color. On the other hand, the communal and cooperative values that have been attributed to ethnic groups are not always found. Although extended family social support systems are common in minority families, not all minority families have a warm support system upon which they may call.

While poorer families are more involved in the patterns described above, it is a mistake to assume that with educational and occupational mobility there will be a lessening of involvement in cultural patterns. Patterns of interacting within families are not easily given up. For example, parents who have become upwardly mobile have been found to continue to maintain cultural patterns of intimate social support, but in different contexts and with gifts that flow outward more than inward within the family (McAdoo, 1988b).

Diversity of Child-Rearing Patterns

There have been few comprehensive studies of child-rearing styles that cut across both social class and ethnic group. Our knowledge about child rearing within ethnic families is limited to data from studies, with small and limited samples, or anecdotal descriptions of families. One must, therefore, be careful in the interpretations that are made and the programs that are implemented for these parents and children.

Ethnic minority parents in two-parent homes and mothers in single-parent homes have been successful in raising normal healthy children in a variety of environments. The key ethnic child-rearing fact is that there are diverse child-rearing styles that may differ slightly from the mainstream family. For example, empirical results have failed to support the stereotype that permissive child rearing is a common pattern in Mexican-American, Black, or Native American families (Mindel & Haberstein, 1981). Rather, the behaviors of ethnic minority parents have been found to vary with the educational level of the mother; with those who are higher status using the authoritative patterns associated with competitive and individualistic middle-class White American values (Baumrind, 1971; Radin, 1982).

The above indicates how one must be careful in stereotyping. Successful intervention with members of ethnic minority groups requires knowledge of the families from which they come. The responses and accommodations that families make to cultural forces will also vary as a function of the degree of adversity and isolation from mainstream American life. For example, an applied developmental psychologist, a family life educator, or family therapist who believes that second-generation Chicano or Asian families are similar to those who are recent immigrants will approach them in the wrong manner.

ETHNIC MINORITY CHILDREN AND ADOLESCENTS

Ethnic Minority Children

Ethnic minority children live the effect of being members of a minority group in a culture that does not value their uniqueness. Their cultural, socioeconomic, and educational environments are unique and reflect the group's status within society. While most minority children are made to feel different, not all children are in a devalued status.

An example of the unique environments of ethnics can be shown in the many Asian-American groups. As members of a stereotyped minority, Asians are viewed in a monolithic manner that is positive, but still hurtful for them. They are felt to be achievers and to excel in math and science. This may be fine for the majority of these children, except for those Asian children who do not fare well in either subject. Those who may be artistic or who may simply not be bright are made to feel even more rejected. They often receive unusual pressure from their parents and community.

Ethnic Minority Families

On the other hand, negative images are held about black, Native American, and some Hispanic children. The further a child deviates from society's image of the idealized white child the more he or she is devalued. In applied developmental work, it is imperative that commonly held community values are not replicated, but are examined and that interventions are both sensitive to values and protective for the child. We must value the uniqueness of children, whatever their cultural or racial group membership may be, and provide them with the support and tools necessary for growth and development.

Self-esteem and racial identity within minority children. The treatment of ethnic children will have an impact on their racial attitudes and self-esteem. Racial socialization refers to how parents prepare their children for adulthood in their ethnic group. All parents of ethnic minority children must introduce their children to the world and prepare them for the roles they will be allowed to play.

These roles are determined by the history of that ethnic group within our country and by the life chances their parents perceive for them. Parents and significant others may misinterpret these roles and prevent their children from taking advantage of opportunities. Or, parents may misread the cues and prepare children for roles not available to them. In order to aid the development of ethnic minority children, professionals must work within the child's social and family environment.

The route to socialization will have an impact on feelings of self-worth. All children, regardless of their racial group, desire to be a member of the dominant group as preschool children. Their identification with their own ethnic group firms as they grow up and develop a sense of their place in the environment. Ethnic children who learn it is all right to be a member of an ethnic group and identify with their social category will feel positive about their group membership. They can develop feelings of self-worth and value through an understanding that the prejudices they encounter come from problems within the dominant group rather than from within themselves. Without a cultural link there is the danger of having an adult who is neither comfortable nor accepted within his or her social group or the larger society. Such dislocated individuals are too often found in ethnic minority groups of lower status. Those who want to read further in this area should refer to the works of Cross (1987), H. McAdoo (1988), M. McAdoo (1985), Peters (1988), and Phinney and Rotherarm (1987).

Ethnic Minority Adolescents

Important life decisions are made during adolescence. During this period of uncertainty families may experience stress and conflict. This is particularly true for the ethnic minority family in which the adolescent is striving to assume his or her place in a world that is less than accepting. Three problems for those who work with ethnic minority adolescents are: (a) lowered educational achievement; (b) the prospect of underemployment and unemployment; and (c) the possibility of adolescent pregnancy. The issues are separate yet interrelated. Young ethnic men and women receive neither proper education nor skill training to allow them entrance into the changing labor market. While black youth have received the most notoriety on these counts, the risks are also rampant for Hispanic, Native American, recent Cuban, Chinese, and other Asian immigrant youth. Intervention is needed within each group and the procedures must differ with their respective cultures.

Young men without good jobs cannot assume the role of head of the household or loving parent. They will therefore father children with no hopes of raising them in a "traditional" family. Young girls will become pregnant with the knowledge that the father of their children will not assume responsible roles in their future. Their children will have limited contact with their natural fathers and the fathers' role may be assumed by other men in their lives (Furstenberg & Gunn, 1987). Matters will be even more complicated as a high proportion of ethnic minority young men will be institutionalized (Edleman, 1987; Gibbs, 1988). There are many odds against young minority men. An almost fatalistic view of their future predominates their lives.

We are rapidly entering a period in which new jobs for minority youth will be available only at the service level, with low pay and limited futures. We must work within the school system and in the community to prepare students to be self-sufficient. They will need to stay in school and to be realistic in their occupational planning.

Adolescent mothers and single parent families. Marriage is often viewed as a means of economic survival, but many minority mothers, especially Hispanic and Black mothers tend to remain single. The academic and social performance of children of former adolescent mothers is related to variables such as maternal age and the amount of time the young mother spent with her child. A comprehensive review of school-age parenting and a view of the history of the problems of early child-bearing is presented by Hayes (1987).

When designing research or interventions, applied developmental psychologists must clarify distinctions between female-headed families and those families started with adolescent mothers. Female heads of families are more often previously divorced adult women, not teenage mothers. Even in black families, whose level of single parenting is 50%, the majority of female heads of households were previously married. This distinction is often confused in the social science literature and is important when one works with these families.

Adolescent sexual behavior. It is important that the conflicting premarital attitudes and values that are held by an economically diverse group of high school students is known. The applied developmentalist will need to know more about what this age group thinks and feels to design programs that are effective in preventing pregnancy.

According to Danziger (1986), young girls pass through four "decision points" along the path toward adolescent pregnancy: (a) the decision to be sexually active; (b) the choice of whether contraception will be used; (c) how to handle the pregnancy; and (d) how to support the child. Intervention at these four stages may be effective. They are periods where the culturally sensitive intervener can work with the adolescent, her parent(s), and the community to provide accurate information and effective programs. I believe clinics within the schools or the immediate area should provide comprehensive mental and physical care. This view is still controversial (see Chapter 2) and will necessitate the combined efforts of parents and professionals. Together, they must work on programs to make services available to young people and to provide choices consistent with religious and moral beliefs.

The following vignette illustrates the importance of a culturally sensitive approach to adolescent sexual behavior. Juan and Maria are attractive 16-year-old Puerto-Rican high school students who are both from large extended families and are active in their local parish. Juan has lost interest in school, has limited training, and is working part-time at a fast food establishment. He is full of his perceived male role, loves dancing, and appears older than he is. Maria is a good student and could go on to college. She tends to be shy and follows others in her social life. Maria also is feeling the pressure from her friends about having a boy friend and making him happy. Her parents are beginning to hint that she should decide on her future. Maria and Juan become sexually involved. They indicate that they do not feel that there is a chance that they will get pregnant. They do not use contraceptives, because of religious prohibition and because Juan does not like to use devices. It can be predicted that a pregnancy will occur if they continue, for over 30% of the girls in Maria's school do get pregnant.

What cultural factors must be considered in designing an intervention for adolescents like Maria and Juan? First, one should be aware of the peer and subtle family pressures being placed on Maria, as well as the strong influence of the church. How will these effect Maria's fortitude to remain chaste in an area in which girls are making other decisions? Effective intervention can best be implemented by psychologists who are aware of the cultural restrictions of Juan and Maria's environment and who have been involved in the community for a length of time. For example, will Juan be able to receive counseling and specialized training to better his job prospects? Is it more appropriate to expect that Juan and Maria will have a baby and prepare the family and the couple for the future? Finally, a culturally sensitive professional, recognizing that intervention will be most successful when conducted in collaboration with members of the minority adolescent's social milieu, will provide parents and teachers in the community with information (in nontechnical language) which will help them assist their children with these important life decisions. A good presentation of a cultural sensitive approach to Black families has been recently completed by Boyd-Franklin (1988).

SUMMARY AND CONCLUSIONS

An understanding of ethnic minority families in contemporary society requires an appreciation of the social forces exerted upon them (McAdoo & Terborg-Penn, 1985). The ethical treatment of ethnically diverse minority families also requires that the applied developmental psychologist recognize his or her unconscious prejudicial attitudes. It is impossible to grow up in a society such as ours and not have some vestiges of prejudice. This is true both for mainstream psychologists as well as those who are members of ethnic minorities.

Applied developmental psychologists not of color must assess their own personal perceptions of ethnic groups and the stereotypes they hold. This may be a painful process. Yet, only by coming to grips with the perceptions that are held about other groups can one examine them for accuracy and attempt to change or modify those that are faulty.

Positive stereotypes can be as painful as negative ones. Ethnic minority members often face the imposition of stereotyped expectations that preclude their performance as individuals. By attempting to deal with ethnic minorities as a monolith, interventionists are denying the members of different groups their individuality. An applied developmental approach to research and intervention must, therefore, incorporate respect for diversity of all individuals.

Applied developmental psychologists who are members of ethnic groups of color have to work within a dual consciousness as they approach their families. Members of ethnically diverse minorities often experience life within this dual consciousness. They are prepared to become members of the great American mainstream and at the same time they are socialized to become members of their own racial, ethnic, or religious group. DuBois (1903) first presented this dilemma in reference to African-Americans but it holds true for all ethnic minority groups. He described the constant problem of seeing oneself and one's group through the eyes of others. Developmental psychologists of color must present their families in order that nonethnic persons may understand them better. At the same time they will have to avoid becoming emotional and identified with these families.

The field of applied developmental psychology has started to approach individuals in need of services that are sensitive to the cultural dimensions of their lives. Psychologists, family life educators, teachers, therapists, and policy analysts will benefit from an objective, realistic approach to ethnic minority families. As we begin to approach the 21st century, it is imperative that we accept and respect more readily the strengths that are present in culturally diverse families.

REFERENCES

Alvirez, D., Bean, F., & Williams, D. (1981). The Mexican American Family. In C.R. Mindel & R. Haberstein (Ed.), *Ethic families in American: Patterns and variations.* New York: Elsevier.

Balgopal, P. (1988). *Social networks and Asian Indian families.* In C. Jacobs & D. Bowles (Eds.), *Ethnicity and race, critical concepts in social work* (pp. 18–33). Silver Springs, MD: National Association of Social Workers, Inc.

Barrera, M. (1988). Models of social support and life stress, beyond the buffering hypothesis. In L. Cohen (Ed.), *Life events and psychological functioning, theoretical and methodolical issues* (pp. 211–236). Newbury Park, CA: Sage Publications.

Baumrind, D. (1971). Harmonious parents and their preschool children. *Developmental Psychology, 4,* 99–102.

Billingsley, A. (1968). *Black families in white America.* Englewood, NJ: Prentice-Hall.

Boyd-Franklin, N. (1988). *Black families in therapy, A multisystems approach.* New York: Guilford.

Bowman, P. (1988). *Postindustrial displacement and family role strains: Challenges to the black family.* In P. Voydanoff & L. Majka (Eds.), *Families and economic distress, coping strategies and social policy* (pp. 75–97). Newbury Park, CA: Sage Publishers.

Cross, W. (1987). A two-factor theory of black identity: Implications for the study of identity development in minority children. In J. Phinney & M.J. Rotheram (Ed.), *Children's ethnic socialization, pluralism and development* (pp. 117–133). Newbury Park, CA.: Sage Publications.

Danziger, S., Haneman, R., & Plotnick, R. (1986). Antipoverty policy: Effects on the poor and the nonpoor. *Fighting Poverty: What Works & What Doesn't* (pp. 50–77). Cambridge, MA: Harvard University Press.

de la Garza, R., Kruszewski, Z., & Arcimega, T. (Eds.). (1971). *Chicano and Native American, the territorial minorities.* Englewood Cliffs, NJ: Prentice-Hall.

DuBois, W.E.B. (1967). *The souls of black folk.* New York: Fawcett Publications. (Original work published 1903).

Edelman, M. (1987). *Families in peril: An agenda for social change.* Cambridge, MA: Harvard University Press.

Fisher, C.B., & Tryon, W.W. (1988). Ethical issues in the research and practice of applied developmental psychology. *Journal of Applied Developmental Psychology, 9,* 27–39.

Frazier, F. (1932). *The Negro family in Chicago.* Chicago: University of Chicago.

Frazier, F. (1939). *The Negro family in the United States.* Chicago: University of Chicago.

Frazier, F. (1957). *Black bourgeoisie: The rise of a new middle class in the United States.* New York: Free Press.

Furstenberg, F., & Brooks-Gunn, J. (1987). *Adolescent mothers later in life.* Cambridge: Cambridge University Press.

Gibbs, J. (Ed.). (1988). *Young, black, and male in America.* (Dover, MA: Auburn House.

Hayes, C. (Ed.). (1987). *Risking the future, adolescent sexuality, pregnancy, and childbearing.* Washington, DC: National Research Press.

Herskovitz, M. (1930). *The myth of the Negro past.* New York: Harper and Row.

Hill, R. (1971). *Strengths of black families.* Washington, DC: National Urban League.

Huang, L. (1981). The Chinese American family. In C. Mindel & R. Haberstein (Eds.), *Ethic families in American: Patterns and variations* (pp. 115–141). New York: Elsevier.

Kagan, S., & Ender, P. (1975). Maternal response to success and failure of Anglo-American, Mexican-American, and Mexican Children. *Child Development, 46,* 452–458.

Ladner, J. (1972). *Tomorrow's tomorrow: The Black woman.* Garden City, NY: Anchor.

Laosa, L. (1978). Maternal teaching strategies in Chicano families of varied educational and socioeconomic levels. *Child Development, 49,* 1129–1135.

Laosa, L. (1980). Maternal teaching strategies in Chicano and Anglo-American families: The influence of culture and education on maternal behavior. *Child Development, 51,* 759–765.

McAdoo, H. (1974). The socialization of Black children: Priorities for research. In L. Gary (Ed.), *Social research and the black community: Selected issues and priorities.* Washington, DC: Howard University, Institute for Urban Affairs and Research.

McAdoo, H. (1978). Minority families. In J. Stevens (Ed.), *Mother/child, Father/child: Relationships* (pp. 177–195). Washington, DC: National Association for Education of Young Child.

McAdoo, H. (1988a). *Black families* (2nd ed.). Newbury Park, CA: Sage Publications.

McAdoo, H. (1988b). Transgenerational patterns of upwardly mobility in African-American families. In H. McAdoo (Ed.), *Black families.* Newbury Park, CA: Sage Publications.

McAdoo, H., & Terborg-Penn, R. (1985). Historical trends and perspectives of Afro-American families. *Trends in History, 3*(3/4), 97–111.

McAdoo, J. (1985). Modification of racial attitudes and preferences in young Black children. In H. McAdoo & J. McAdoo (Ed.), *Black children, social, educational, and parental environments* (pp. 243–256). Beverly Hills, CA.: Sage Publications.

Mindel, C. & Haberstein, R. (Eds.). (1981). *Ethnic families in American: patterns and variations* (2nd ed.). New York: Elsevier.

Moynihan, D. (1965). *The Negro family-The case for national action.* Washington, DC: Office of Policy Planning and Research, U.S. Department of Labor.

Peters, M. (1985). Racial socialization of young black children. In H. McAdoo & J. McAdoo (Eds.), *Black children, social, educational, and parental environments.* Beverly Hills, CA: Sage Publications.

Peters, M. (1988). Parenting in black families with young children, A historical perspective. In H. McAdoo (Ed.), *Black families* (2nd ed.). Newbury Park, CA: Sage Publications.

Phinney, J., & Rotheram, M.J. (Ed.). (1987). *Children's ethnic socialization, pluralism and development*. Newbury Park, CA: Sage Publications.

Price, J. (1981). North American Indian Families. In C. Mindel & R. Haberstein (Eds.), *Ethic families in American: Patterns and variations* (pp. 245–268). New York: Elsevier.

Radin, N. (1982). Role sharing fathers and preschoolers. In M. Lamb (Ed.), *Nontraditional families: Parenting and child development* (pp. 173–204). Hillsdale, NJ: Erlbaum.

Scanzoni, J. (1971). *The Black family in modern society*. Boston: Allyn and Bacon.

Stack, D. (1975). *All our kin*. New York: Harper and Row.

Staples, R. (1986). *The Black family, essay and studies* (3rd Ed.). Belmont, CA: Wadsworth. (Original work published 1971).

Stanton, R. (1972). A comparison of Mexican and Mexican-American families. *The Family Coordinator, 21*, 325–330.

Willie, C. (1970). *The family life of Black people*. Columbus, OH: Charles Merrill.

Virgil, J. (1980). *From Indians to Chicanos: A sociocultural history*. New York: C.V. Mosby.

18 Cultural Forces Leading To Scientific Developmental Psychology*

James Youniss

In 1905, G. Stanley Hall, the founder of developmental psychology (Sears, 1975; Siegel & White, 1982), told members of the Young Men's Christian Association that "full knowledge of [Jesus's] mind would be the only complete normal psychology. His pedagogy is normative . . . Scripture is the world's great text-book in psychology. . ." (Hall, 1905a, p. 486). In the same year, Hall published one of his own speeches, given at the University of Virginia, in the *Pedagogical Seminary*, of which he was the editor. He expressed the following view: "No two races in history, taken as a whole, differ so much in their traits, both physical and psychic, as the Caucasian and the African. The color of the skin and the crookedness of the hair are only the outward signs of many far deeper differences . . . cranial capacity, vita sexualis, . . . temperament, disposition, character, . . . [and] emotional traits (Hall, 1905b, p. 358).

The purpose of these introductory examples is not to paint Hall as a religious zealot or racial bigot, which he probably was not (Muschinske, 1977), but to illustrate common nineteenth century biases which Hall appears to have brought to the field of child studies. The present chapter looks at the period 1870–1930, when the discipline of developmental psychology was taking shape in the United States. It begins with the era of "child saving" (Platt, 1969) when reformers focused on children in the effort to break cycles of crime and poverty. Two reformers are presented as examples of the general outlook that "saving" fundamentally entailed religious conversion which was believed essential for good citizenship. The focus of reform was on immigrant children whose parents were thought incapable of exerting proper socialization and moral training. This incapacity was attributed to racial traits, religious backwardness, and moral weakness.

When G. Stanley Hall took up the study of children, he inherited these cultural views. Although he was an empirical scientist who was open to data, he viewed results through the child-saving perspective. He stressed racial dif-

* Bruce Ross and Robert Sears read earlier drafts of this chapter and offered comments and criticisms. I appreciate their frankness and willingness to share insights on the history of our discipline in a spirit of helpfulness. I appreciate also the thoughtful suggestions of the editors of this volume.

ferences, put emphasis on the role of Christian training, and supported institutions, such as the YMCA, Boy Scouts, and the Sunday School movement, which made up for lack of parental guidance. For Hall, basic psychological processes and extant religious doctrine were assumed to be obviously compatible. For example, the cultural phenomenon of being religiously born again (Kett, 1977), was seen by Hall as evidence for a psychologically fundamental truth about adolescence. It appears that Hall did not see a need to guard against the intrusion of cultural beliefs into psychological studies, but he brought them into his psychology and made them compatible and conforming.

Hall presented a problem for his successors who wanted to build an "objective" psychology that was scientific in the modern sense, circa 1920–30. These psychologists were operating in a changed cultural context when racial and religious identifications were receding in the face of intellectual pluralism and secularism. It is interesting to note that when the Society for Research in Development was forming in the late 1920s, its advocates consciously sought to disassociate themselves from Hall's reform mentality with its inherent religious, racial, and political presumptions. In retrospect, it is not surprising that these advocates of the new discipline adopted the stance that they wanted knowledge which was free from external influences and value predispositions. However, like the child savers and Hall before them, these developmental psychologists were no less reacting to cultural forces, albeit different ones. They sought a psychology which would not arrange individuals from various ethnic backgrounds in preconceived hierarchies. This "inclusive" psychology probably reflected the fact that millions of immigrants from foreign cultures had rather quickly adapted to the United States and their children became productive citizens whose diverse talents helped to sustain American culture rather than destroy it. For these psychologists, the aim was to study childhood, meant as a universal category, as opposed to documenting differences among "Irish," "Italian," "Jewish," and "Slavic" children.

What is the usefulness of this excursion into history for a volume dedicated to contemporary ethical issues? I suggest that this chapter might contribute to the growing realization that developmental psychology can be enriched from a deeper understanding of its relations with our society and culture. It is no longer credible to argue that our methods allow us to see childhood naturally and freshly, as if it were an "object" with independent existence (Kessen, 1979). Childhood is an important item in the culture and owes its definition, in part, to the culture. When we come to study children, we do so with predispositions that are supported by laws, customs, religious beliefs, economic factors, and political ideology which necessarily shape our conclusions (Boli-Bennett & Meyer, 1978; Riegel, 1972). Insofar as psychologists recommend courses of action toward children and interventions in the lives of families, we are responsible to seek self-understanding in our views. It is now broadly understood that recommendations are not dictated by data but follow as well from interests which we bring to our studies (Steiner, 1976). An ethically mature developmental psychology would not deny its debt to social and cultural forces but seek to know them better for itself and the persons it serves (Wertsch & Youniss, 1987; Youniss, 1983).

THE NINETEENTH-CENTURY REFORMERS

In 1875, William Letchworth was commissioned by the New York Senate to survey all residential care facilities for children in the state. He personally visited each and submitted a report which described numbers and kinds of children, financial status and sources of support, and, often, daily regimen for children as well as the philosophy of those in charge of the homes. In presenting his report, Letchworth focused on the good that these homes were doing for the state, especially because they were providing a Christian upbringing to children who might otherwise not be exposed to the advantages of American Protestant family life. Letchworth was aware of the prevalent theory that by socializing children into the proper Christian value system, reformers could stem poverty and break the cycle of crime which was perpetuated through families. He justified the focus of reform on children by quoting from a report submitted to the State of Pennsylvania: "To busy ourselves alone with mature and developed crime, and to ignore the breeding mass of embryonic vice beneath, from which it is steadily supplied, is an attempt to dam the river at its mouth when it has grown into an irresistible torrent . . ." (p. 26).

Letchworth was typical for his day in centering attention on children as the hope for the nation's future. In reading his report, one can see the reasons residential care was needed. Periodic outbreaks of cholera and the Civil War had caused many households to be without a male head. In addition, many immigrant children had parents who were living but who were unable to provide adequate care because of lack of employment and degraded living circumstances. Letchworth believed that these children should not be made to fend for themselves on the streets. That would only lead to furthering lives of poverty and crime. He believed that they should be exposed to a religious and moral upbringing which would result in the formation of good citizens: "The building of all true character must rest on a religious basis. Unless the child learns its obligations to the Deity to begin with, and is taught the importance of living an upright life, it can hardly be expected to become a good citizen. Enlargement upon a point so universally conceded would seem to be superfluous" (p. 20).

One can readily see why Letchworth also believed that it was proper for children to be taken from their parents if these parents failed to provide proper moral guidance. He asserted that when parents had become "demoralized" it was the state's duty to take their children from them: "It rescues from criminality, builds up character, and breaks off the line of hereditary pauperism, and is a remedy applied to the very fountain-source of the evils which undermine society" (p. 96). Letchworth was no oddity but one of a number of leading citizens who viewed the mass of urban immigrants as a threat to the American way of life. They saw the crowded neighborhoods as breeding grounds for poverty and crime, which would ultimately lead to society's downfall. Philanthropic associations, such as the Home for Little Wanderers, viewed these parents as "ignorant, intemperate, and vicious", and felt justified in having them surrender legal rights of their children. "When their parents or guardians can be persuaded to give the Mission legal control of [the children], they are taken under our immediate care. . . ." But when parents did not grant the right, children were taken anyway: "We gather into day and Sunday-schools all the children we can reach, whose parents will not surrender them to the Mission or consent to their being sent away" (Quoted by Letchworth, 1875, p. 254).

This same logic can be found in Charles Loring Brace who became the head of the Children's Aid Society (CAS), which was founded in New York in 1853, in large part, to provide shelter for the thousands of homeless and vagrant youth of New York. In 1880, Brace, a Protestant minister and then director of the CAS, published a third edition of a book in which he described his work with the poor in New York city. It was called *The Dangerous Classes of New York and Twenty Years Work among Them*. He emphasized the incapacity of many immigrant parents to rear their children properly as Christians and Americans. He, as Letchworth, saw it necessary to capture these children in order to deter future crime and poverty. To achieve these ends, the CAS established several homes for children around the city. These homes provided bed and board to an estimated 12,000 children per year. For example, in the first 18 years of its existence, the Society's Home for Newsboys on 18th St. lodged 91,326 boys who paid 6 cents for a bed and bath and 4 cents for a hot meal. Other homes were scattered across the city and supplied services for girls as for boys (p. 315, 329, 337, 338).

Brace, like the Little Wanderers Association, viewed these homes as catchments for the ultimate purpose of religious and moral conversion. The tactic was to invite youngsters in off the street, to give them decent food and warm bed, and then to capture their souls for Christianity. In speaking of the homes for newsboys, Brace said the following: "The first thing . . . was to treat the lads as independent little dealers . . . to offer them more for their money [by way of lodging and meals] than they could get anywhere else. Moral, educational, and religious influences were to come afterward. Serving them through their interests, we had permanent hold of them. . ." (pp. 100–01).

Brace defined the "dangerous classes" as "mainly American-born, but the children of Irish and German immigrants" (p. 27). Brace saw these masses as a threat to American democracy, citing the "terrible Communist outbreak in Paris" and seeing the same "explosive elements" operating in New York (p. 29). For Brace, the CAS "must employ the powers of education, and above all, the boundless force of religion to elevate the race above the tyranny . . ." of its destructive habits, such as alcoholism. "The subject of applying Religion as a lever to raise up the class of neglected children whom we have been describing, is a difficult one, but vital to the Science of reform. The objects of those engaged in laboring for this class are to raise them above temptation, to make them of more value to themselves, and to Society, and, if possible, to elevate them to the highest range of life, where the whole character is governed by Religion" (p. 418).

As did the Home for the Little Wanderers, Brace believed that children ought to be separated from negligent parents. The "permanent hold" Brace wanted, extended to creating new identities for youths who were sent from the city to be resettled out west. The CAS established a system whereby boys, found in the city, were sent to live with farm families in Indiana, Michigan, and the like. Brace hoped to "make an honest, hard-working Western pioneer" out of the "rough thieving New York vagrant" (p. 114). This program was extensive and one wonders why so little has been made of it in the study of the history of child psychology. Jackson (1986) estimates that the CAS relocated 129,000 youths from New York to the American frontier over a 50-year period.

Letchworth and Brace are described here as representatives of the child-saving era which preceded Hall and established a viewpoint on the importance of childhood for the young nation. An earlier generation of reformers had expended effort on proselytizing adult immigrants, but their general failure encouraged a turn to children whom they saw as more likely candidates for conversion (Lane, 1932). While "child saving" connoted attempts to stem delinquency and poverty, it also denoted the securing of children's religious salvation. For Brace's generation, good citizenship and religiousness were nearly synonymous. But not all religions were equal. Brace was a direct critic of Catholicism which was the religion of many recent immigrants. He viewed it as inimical to citizenship in democratic America. He believed that the Catholic church in the United States had "lost its inspiration" (p. 156). "A great obstacle in our own particular experience was . . . the superstitious opposition of the poor. This was undoubtedly cultivated by priests, who seem seldom gifted with the broad spirit of humanity of their brethren in Europe" (p. 244). Brace, of course, advocated public education in opposition to Church-sponsored schools. "The system of Free [public] schools is the life-blood of the nation. If it be corrupted with priestcraft, or destroyed by our dissensions, our vitality as a republican people is gone" (p. 426). And "under no circumstances should the Protestants of the nation allow the Free schools to be broken up. They are the foundation of the republic, the bulwark of Protestantism and civilization" (p. 426).

In review, Letchworth and Brace are offered as two examples of late-nineteenth-century reformers who illustrate the ideology which motivated the child-saving movement. It seems reasonable to suggest that when Hall began his work with children, clear categories had already been established for thinking about their "nature" and about the political value of their socialization. The term children was embedded in concerns that were religious, racial, and political in character. Hall and others could not have been expected to approach the study of children freshly, as if they were visitors from another planet. Children had been made the objects of concern for those who feared social disorganization and those who cared about the nation's future. The legacy of these reformers was a hierarchical scheme with American democracy, Protestant values, and the Anglo race at the top. Foreigners, non-Protestants, and immigrants from scattered places posed a question about America's survival. The tactic many reformers shared was to save America through its children. They chose to drive a wedge between the young and their parents and, thereby, hoped to create a new genera- tion that would accept American-Protestant values in responsible citizenship. Here is the thought captured in an anonymous voice cited by Letchworth: "There is a point in each young life, where, if withdrawn from moral pitfalls into the sunlight of Christian nurture, the child may be thus saved for this life and the next" (p. 184).

These children, whose parents came from Catholic countries and did not speak English, needed to be exposed to Protestant values which were central to American democracy and the nation's social order. Because Protestantism was nearly synonymous with the nation's political identity, the child savers can be seen as trying also to preserve the young nation from disorder which the press of immigrants let loose (Wiebe, 1967). Protestant Christianity and patriotism were two sides of one coin that gave reformers their purpose for action and concern for children. Foster care, apprenticeship, and wanting to stem poverty and crime should not be minimized. Nevertheless, to skip over the interlocked goals of religious conversion and political formation is to overlook a crucial point of child welfare in the late nineteenth century (Wertsch & Youniss, 1987).

G. STANLEY HALL

In the present chapter, G. Stanley Hall is depicted as a transitional figure who brought nineteenth century thinking about children into the twentieth century birth of the modern discipline of developmental psychology. As the founder of the discipline, Hall is properly credited with making empirical studies of children the grounds for theory about development (Siegel & White, 1982). In this regard, he can be seen as the pioneer, founder of the empirical science of child develop- ment. There is, however, another side to Hall. He was a product of the nineteenth century in ways that John Watson, for example, was not. This side of Hall looked on children not as abstract representatives of natural processes but as particular cases of their social and religious roots. Before proceeding, I want to repeat that this is not an attempt to portray Hall as a religious bigot or a racist. Muschinske (1977) proposes that Hall was not vicious, but was in step with his times when racial and religious categories were central identifications. Hall believed for example, that blacks and Indians had not evolved as far as whites; but, in this, he was not alone in wanting to provide "a 'scientific' rationale for the popular prejudices of his day" (p. 334). Hence, his words may be read as stemming, not from spite, but from the spirit of the culture. In brief, it would be inappropriate to use contemporary criteria for judging Hall; the attempt here is rather to seek an understanding of how he reflected his times and the extant culture (see Ross, 1972).

A sample of his religious presuppositions is found in Hall's classic book: *Adolescence* (1904). Throughout the 81-page chapter XIV, "The Adolescent Psychology of Conversion," Hall paraphrases Christian theology as if it could be taken for granted and was integral to psychological knowledge. One of the goals of his chapter was to show that during adolescence, religious conversion, also called "rebirth" or "being born again," was *natural* in the sense of inherency. In making his case, Hall recalls that religious revivals were a traditional part of the regimen on college campuses in the United States. He noted that at Yale's revival in 1802, one-third of the students were converted while over the next 40 years, 15 more revivals were held on Yale's campus. He adds: "Princeton was no less favored." And: "Durfee makes the early history of Williams College to consist chiefly of efforts to secure the conversion of students" (p. 287). With an eye to the present, Hall continues: "The traditions of revivalism long lingered, and are yet strong in some of the older American colleges" (p. 287).

It is evident that the importance of religious conversion was not a product of Hall's imagination but was shared in academic circles at large. At the same time, Hall gave this event a strong psychological meaning. Conversion denoted that a young man would attest to the religious heritage of his father by making a public statement in which he accepted Christianity. By tradition, the time for this attestation was near the end of adolescence (Kett, 1977). Hall did not create the concept of adolescence anew, but he took a social-cultural convention from its eighteenth and nineteenth century American religious and cultural context and inserted it, almost whole, into scientific psychology. Notice how he endowed the concept with strong terms implying developmental necessity: "In its most funda- mental sense, conversion is a natural, normal, universal, and necessary process at the stage when life pivots over an autocentric to an heterocentric basis" (p. 301).

There can be little doubt that Hall believed religion to be a central charac- teristic of psychological existence. By implication, one can also see that Hall believed Christianity to hold priority in this regard. The revivals of which he writes belonged to the "eclectic Protestantism" (Smith, 1957) which was prac- ticed at the nation's major colleges where the sons of the elite spent their "pivot- al" years. It was part of the American heritage, marked as the first and second "awakenings," which were designed to strengthen the nation's waning religious spirit. An equally strong case is found in a 1905 address Hall gave to the Young Men's Christian Association. He noted: "I love and honor this association be- cause it marked practically the first recognition in Christiandom of the true meaning and value of youth. . . Your work begins at the pubertal epoch when religion is rather sudden and, more than at any other time of life, needed against the flood of temptations that now beset the young man, and when true piety can be purest and deepest" (p. 479). Hall clearly believed that religion and psychology were naturally conjoined. It is fitting that he concluded this speech with the motto: "Jesus for young men and young men for Jesus" (p. 486).

Just as central to Hall's thinking was the category of race, which, during the era of immigration, entailed a comparison between the white "native" American Protestants and the Catholic or Jewish newcomers. Samelson (1978) has carefully noted that Hall's contemporaries in the field of psychology had made race a focus of their studies. Several experiments were conducted to compare traits among Nordic, Alpine, Mediterranean, and other "races." This search continued at least until the 1930s when the ethnic composition of the profession of psychology changed so as to make race typing self-defeating. Insofar as Hall openly expressed racial views which would not have been tolerated a generation later, he can be seen as a definite representative of the nineteenth century. Some excerpts from a (1905b) article by Hall in his own *Pedagogical Seminary* illustrate the point.

"Special studies show that the negro child up to about twelve is quite as bright as the white child; but when this [sexual] instinct develops it is earlier, more sudden, and far more likely permanently to retard mental and moral growth than in the white who shoots ahead. . . . W. H. Thomas, himself a negro, . . . says, 'The chief and overpowering element in his [the negro's] make-up is an imperious sexual impulse, which, aroused at the slightest incentive, sweeps aside all restraint.' This he deems the chief cause of the arrest of the higher development of this tropical race" (p. 362).

Hall believed that reconstruction in the South had erroneously pushed the blacks beyond their evolutionary capability (see also Muschinske, 1977, p. 333). He therefore, praised reactions against having granted blacks the right to vote. "These [reactionary] methods were a slow development of a reaction by intelligent citizens against a saturnalia of political corruption that arose under negro rule. . . . If anyone doubts the evil of wholesale negro suffrage he should glance at the literature" (p. 365).

At the end of this article, Hall spoke about future actions. The negro should "make his own social life . . . and recognize that his race has gifts that others lack—such as an intense and large emotional life, an exquisite sensitiveness to nature, gifts in the field of music and oratory, a peculiar depth of religious life (connected in part with the sense of dependence, which is its psychic root), a strong belief in invisible powers . . ." (p. 367). A confirming sense of how Hall fit into the tenor of his time and was not eccentric can be judged from the fact that Hall chose to reprint this article from a public lecture that he had delivered at the University of Virginia in July, 1905.

Lastly on this point, it is worth noting that Hall was not an aberrant thinker among the reformers of his day. For comparison, consider the following. In

1896, three authors were commissioned to provide a description of life in New York City. One, Mrs. Helen Campbell, "city missionary and philanthropist," reported her findings in 23 chapters of the book, *Darkness and Daylight, or, Lights and Shadows of New York Life*. She described life in New York's 32,000 tenement houses and the relation between physical conditions and "moral habits." She focused on racial traits that were accepted as truisms of the day. Here is an excerpt from her description of the character of the New York poor on whose living conditions she reported: "They are a class apart, the poor Irish forming by far the larger proportion. They retain all the most brutal characteristics of the Irish peasant at home, but without the redeeming light-heartedness, the tender impulses, the strong affections of that most perplexing people. Sullen, malicious, conscienceless, with no capacity for enjoyment save in drink and the lowest forms of debauchery, they are filling our prisons and reformatories, marching in an ever-increasing army through the quiet country, and making a reign of terror wherever their footsteps are heard. With a little added intelligence they become Socialists, doing their heartiest to ruin the institutions by which they live" (pp. 109–110).

Hall's contributions to the early formation of developmental psychology as a science are documented carefully by Siegel and White (1982). The present description is meant to show another side to Hall's thinking. He seems to have been very much a part of his times when scholars thought of persons as members of racial groups with known traits that were based in biological evolution. Further, Hall took a strong stand on religiousness as basic to psychological structure. All who have written about Hall call him a complex person with a fierce intellectual curiosity and desire to organize facts into general principles (Ross, 1972). It is important not to judge his ideas from a present-day perspective. He seems to follow a line of thinking that was already evident in reformers, such as Letchworth and Brace. Hall, of course, sought to move beyond them as he consciously collected empirical evidence that would inform his theory of development. Nevertheless, his orientation to science was countered with presumptions about religion and race that resulted in a partitioning of children into types which were products of his evolutionary theory. Whites were at the top, while others were ordered below in lesser ranks. Hall is a major actor for our discipline with his feet planted in two centuries. He perpetuated the 19th century concern for the integrity of the United States as it met the challenges of immigration and pluralism. At the same time, he had a twentieth century outlook on a science of childhood that was open to empirical evidence which would, eventually, come to challenge the ideas held by its predecessors.

CONTEMPORARY DEVELOPMENTAL PSYCHOLOGY AND SRCD

Sears (1975), Rheingold (1986), and Smuts (1986) have recently offered fresh evidence about the formal origins of the Society for Research in Child Development (SRCD). Robert Woodworth, a respected experimental psychologist at Columbia University, was in 1924 made chairman of the Committee on Child Welfare and Child Development for the National Research Council. Through this office he sponsored the formation of SRCD, whose inaugural meeting occurred in June of 1933 at the fourth convention of the Committee. The formation of the Committee was sparked by the low test scores of World War One military recruits and the aim was to seek a remedy via intervention into children's early experience (Smuts, 1986). According to Smuts, care was taken to present the Committee's purpose in terms of "research." A strategy was adopted to restrict "its function to research and [assure] that its scientific status was not tainted by association with child welfare or parent training activities" (Smuts, 1986, p. 112).

Another sponsor of the fledgling field was the Laura Spelman Rockefeller Fund which supported the establishment of child study institutes at several universities. A major figure responsible for funding was Lawrence Frank (see Cravens, 1985; Sears, 1975). He echoed Woodworth in his advice to the discipline to keep itself away from practical application while maintaining a research posture. He told the Committee to portray itself "as rigidly a scientific enterprise as possible and minimize references to child welfare implications and obligations" (quoted in Smuts, 1986, p. 112). Bird Baldwin, director of the Iowa Child Welfare Station, and a member of the Committee said at the 1925 meeting: "We are concerned with a scientific analysis of the fundamental scientific problems underlying childhood rather than with formulating remedial measures or outlining methods of training" (quoted in Smuts, 1986, p. 112).

One can hardly miss the sharp division between Hall and those who followed him in the field only a generation later. In 1909, Hall sponsored a meeting of the Child Conference for Research and Welfare at Clark University. He envisioned that this Conference would "establish relations between scientific study and practical work for children" (p. IX). Hall believed that the "time had come at least to consider a society of societies that might pool knowledge, organize endeavor, and thus increase efficiency" (p. IX). He noted that this was the 'century of the child' and saw that a "science of the child" could be put to work to enhance "philanthropic and pedagogic" work in the United States. The contrast is obvious; Hall wanted to unite science with reform, while his successors wanted to separate them and focus solely on science. How might we account for this shift in outlook over such a brief period? Hall and Brace before him, looked to children as the means to reform society, to create a nation of like-minded people. They operated in a time when leadership in the United States took its Protestant origins and millennial destiny for granted. Immigrants from diverse cultures and religions constituted a threat to this vision. For Brace, the antidote was conversion to the eclectic Protestantism with which America's elite identified. For Hall, religious categories were merged with psychological terms; yet the same themes were present although in muted forms.

World War One may have been the watershed which sharply brought nineteenth-century thinking into perspective, made it appear anachronistic, and prompted a modern outlook. Americans of German heritage showed loyalty to the United States during the war. Likewise, the institutional Catholic Church strongly supported the nations's war effort and as a consequence, it was difficult to perpetuate the image that Catholic immigrant groups were antithetical to America's interests (Dolan, 1985). Catholics had moved into positions of political power; mayors in Boston and New York were Catholic Irishmen and one Catholic Irish mayor of New York openly challenged the professional adequacy of Catholic-sponsored charities. While ethnic groups might remain oppositional to each other, it became outmoded for the governing class and intellectuals to maintain racial and religious stereotypes. A new secularism was in place and American academics gave their allegiance to the rationality of science rather than to old formulas which were based in religious authority (Cravens, 1985). Previously, Catholicism connoted papal authority, which induced a veil of ignorance and a threat of divided loyalty for Catholic immigrants. Now, religion of all sorts was beginning to be seen as an authoritarian force which might stand in the way of rationally obtained knowledge.

Racial categories, also, began to be viewed with scientific caution (Woodworth, 1910). Samelson (1978) has tracked the meaning of race in psychology during this period. In the first two decades of this century, studies of race were associated with the search for racial types, character traits, and differences in intelligence. By the 1930s, however, focus was shifted to investigations of *prejudice,* or why persons in one group or class perceived persons in other groups or classes stereotypically rather than objectively. Samelson proposes that the shift corresponded with the upward mobility of immigrants into the science of psychology. The previous subjects of study became the investigators. Consequently, it became more feasible to search for general laws of behavior, in which everyone participated, rather than look for causes of Irish degeneracy, German obdurateness, Jewish brashness, or other derisive racial emblems.

Cravens (1985) has noted moreover that the genetic base for racial characteristics also began to fall from favor at this time. The nineteenth century reformers had held that there was a genetic basis for crime, degeneracy, and limitations in intelligence. But studies at the Iowa Child Welfare Station countered belief in the genetic limitation of IQ and opened the way for a new environmentalism. This allowed psychologists to study early determinants of intelligence and to base achievement in experience, or circumstance, rather than in unalterable genes. Perhaps this was the last straw which was needed to break with the nineteenth century conception of religious and racial child types. Henceforth, psychologists could think in terms of children *in general* who behaved according to processes that were natural and universal. Whether a child became successful in school or became a criminal was not due to religious or racial inheritance but depended on the conditions in which that child was reared. More broadly, the behavior of children no longer had to be judged against one ideal, namely the norm of white middle-class Protestants. To modern scholars of that day, pluralism was valued rather than condemned. No more did the narrow definitions of Hall et al. seem presumptively correct. In fact they seemed wrong and anachronistic. Already, when Thorndike read Hall's 1905 book on adolescence, he acerbicly judged it to be "full of errors, masturbation, and Jesus" (cited in Siegel & White, 1982, p. 270). Surely by the 1930s, the views that Hall had taken for granted were no longer credible to mainstream scholars.

John B. Watson was no less forthright than Thorndike. He saw the new psychology of his day to be the replacement for the very ideas Hall held dear. For example, Watson (1925) believed that philosophy was disappearing to become merged into the history of science. Likewise, religion was being "replaced among the educated by experimental ethics" (p. 18). Watson, of course, also denied the usefulness of genetic explanations of criminal character: "There is no such thing as an inheritance of *capacity, talent, temperament, mental constitution,* and *characteristics* . . . a certain type of structure, plus early training— *slanting*— accounts for adult performance" (p. 74). Watson saw psychology as the path to a new order that sharply divided the nineteenth from the twentieth century thinker. He spoke of a "new universe" (p. 248), whereas Hall was content with adding psychological concepts to the old order. A final point of contrast is now cited. Recall Hall's praise of the YMCA in 1905. Here is Watson's (1928) assessment in his book: *Psychological Care of Infant and Child.* "Girls should not have as companions only girls [nor boys only boys]. The majority of parents somehow feel safe if their boys run with boys and their girls with girls. Nothing is further from the truth and the parents who resign their girls only to girl companions, girl scouting organizations, the YWCA; and their boys to boys' camps, Boy Scouts and to the YMCA . . . are pursuing an unwise and dangerous course of conduct" (pp. 178–179).

SUMMARY AND CONCLUSIONS

The foregoing sketches comprise an attempt to show the close association between concepts of childhood and structural features of our society. It seems clear that child savers such as Letchworth and Brace made the child a repository of hope for the nation's future. The child was counted on for reviving a sagging fervor for religion and for strengthening the threatened bond between politics and Protestant values. To think about children's development, then, entailed a set of interests that had their roots in late-nineteenth-century America's issue-laden conditions. It appears that G. Stanley Hall picked up the same themes when he addressed children and youth. Political, religious, and racial themes are quite evident in his psychology. He was pro-American and against the rise of socialism. He held that whites had achieved the highest evolutionary niche, and he equated the "true" psychology with Christian doctrine. Hence, Hall had little difficulty in relating knowledge to practice within an overt ideological frame. One did not just study children to learn about childhood. Rather, knowledge was to be used for their good as well as the nation's welfare. Moreover, if one wanted to know what to study, the places to look were the traditions of Christianity and American Protestantism.

During the 1920s and 1930s, many developmental psychologists consciously sought to sever ties with this ideological past. Indeed, they adopted a credo of science which asserted that their methods yielded knowledge which was free of ideology. With the advantage of hindsight, one can now see that this position was, itself, driven by social and ideological forces. The attempt to escape ideology may be understood as an effort to adapt to a secular and pluralistic America in which religious and racial divisions were no longer appropriate. Diverse immigrant groups, which appeared eccentric and alien when they initially arrived, factually proved to be acceptable as they worked their way into the nation's fabric as workers and good citizens. In the face of this demonstration, psychologists stopped emphasizing racial traits and their putative biological basis and began to deal with childhood in a universal sense. They accepted the argument that childhood was a time for shaping the future adult, but unlike the child savers, they did not stress interrupting parent-child transmission. Rather, they sought to understand the processes by which experiences determined personal characteristics.

It seems evident that the early developmental psychologists were dealing with more than the study of children. Their predecessors had concerns about poverty, about crime, about immigrant families, and about the Protestant basis of the nation. When they began to study children, they had similar concerns plus additional desires to get beyond the ideological morass in which Hall et al. seemed to be trapped. The new scientific methodology of the day appeared to be the antidote they needed to escape old biases which reinforced racial stereotypes and religious sectarianism. The new methodology promised to remove the investigator, in the subjective sense, from the knowledge process so that the result would be the collection of facts eventually synthesized in rational theory.

We should now be able to see why this choice was attractive at the time but also realize why it is necessary to revise that viewpoint today. There is no reason to suspect that we, at present, are any less products of our day than our forbearers were of their times. The only difference might be that we are better able to inspect them retrospectively than we are able to look clearly at ourselves. We also have the advantage of the historical record which should help us be cautious of claims regarding objective knowledge, now or in the past.

This leads to the obvious question of how we might begin to gain the reflective insight that would help us understand the ideological forces which are operating in our discipline today. I would like to suggest one approach and a theory to support it. The basic idea behind contextual analysis is that knowledge is a social construction rather than a discovery of preexisting objects. The discipline of developmental psychology would benefit from studies that made clearer how phenomena and problems come to be defined as they are in our field. In sociological studies, the area of the social construction of social problems is fairly advanced (Schneider, 1985). The goal of this endeavor is to provide an "account for the emergence and maintenance of claim-making and responding activities" (Kitsuse & Spector, 1973, p. 445). A pertinent example for developmentalists is found in Pfohl's (1977) account of how social forces led to deviant labeling for child abuse and how this led to criminal legislation in the 1960s. The point is that already known behavior is given new definition and public awareness changes attitudes toward it. Soon, the behavior takes on a life of its own as it becomes a phenomenon within the culture which distinguishes good from bad persons and calls for remedies that require the intervention of experts.

Another example is found in analysis offered by Steiner (1976) regarding federal legislation on child welfare and family policy. Several well-known developmental researchers appeared as expert witnesses before congressional committees and presented results of research to support one or another kind of action, such as Head Start and School Lunch programs. Steiner identifies their part in the process of problem construction but considers it alongside the parts played by other equally or more powerful actors. The latter included: lobbying groups for children's rights, such as the Children's Defense Fund; lobbying associations which represented employment interests, such as the School Food Service Association; monetary interests, such as the American Dairy association; and professional groups, such as the National Education Association. Accounts such as this imply that views of what children are, the needs they have, or how needs should be redressed are complex products of the multiple interests which are brought to bear on issues. It seems unreasonable to suggest that developmental psychology, which is enmeshed in the process, could somehow participate in the construction yet stay removed so as not to be influenced by it.

Lastly, it is suggested that we institute opportunities for exchanges of ideas within the discipline as well as between it and other interest groups. Insofar as the aim is to gain reflective clarity on forces affecting our discipline, we can gain from activities in which several actors are brought together to discuss their respective views and interests face-to-face. Lack of such activity has no doubt encouraged developmental psychologists to perceive the "sidedness" in others outside their field while they have been able to maintain the self-perception that they themselves are disinterested observers of children. A case in point is found in recent discussions of daycare that are focused selectively on security of attachment when it is evident that the matter involves parents as well as children, work as well as care, wages as well as roles, and costs as well as ideals. The fact is that the broader discussion is occurring outside our discipline. By remaining narrowly focused, psychologists may exclude themselves as rightful participants. More open communication between psychologists and others should lead to identification of interests in all parties and ultimately enrich understanding of children in our culture and society (Youniss, 1983). That understanding is, of course, prerequisite for any attempt to argue for a universal concept of childhood or to propose ways to enhance children's development today as in the past.

REFERENCES

Brace, C.L. (1880). *The dangerous classes of New York and twenty years work among them.* New York: Wynkoop & Hallenbeck.
Boli-Bennett, J., & Meyer, J. (1978). The ideology of childhood and the state. *American Sociological Review, 43,* 797–812.
Campbell, H. (1896). *Darkness and daylight; or light and shadows of New York life.* Hartford, CT: Hartford Publishing Co.
Cravens, H. (1985). The wandering IQ: American culture and mental testing. *Human Development, 28,* 113–130.
Dolan, J. (1985). *The American Catholic experience: A history from colonial times to the present.* Garden City, NY: Doubleday.
Hall, G.S. (1904). *Adolescence* (Vol. II). New York: D. Appleton.
Hall, G.S. (1905a). The efficiency of the religious work of the Young Men's Christian Association. *Pedagogical Seminary, 12,* 478–489.
Hall, G.S. (1905b). The negro in Africa and America. *Pedagogical Seminary, 12,* 350–368.
Hall, G.S. (1909). *Proceedings of the child conference for research and welfare.* New York: G.E. Stechert.
Jackson, D.D. (1986). It took trains to put street kids on the right track out of the slums. *Smithsonian, 17,* 94–103.
Kessen, W. (1979). The American child and other cultural inventions. *American Psychologist, 34,* 815–820.
Kett, J.F. (1977). *Rites of passage.* New York: Basic Books.
Kitsuse, J.I., & Spector, M. (1973). Toward a sociology of social problems. *Social Problems, 20,* 407–419.
Lane, F.E. (1932). *American charities and the child of the immigrant.* New York: Paulist Press.
Letchworth, W.P. (1974). *Homes of homeless children.* New York: Arno Press. (Original work published 1974)
Muschinske, D. (1977). The nonwhite as child: G. Stanley Hall on the education of nonwhite peoples. *Journal of the History of the Behavioral Sciences, 13,* 328–336.
Pfohl, S.J. (1977). The "discovery" of child abuse. *Social Problems, 24,* 310–323.
Platt, A. (1969). *The child savers.* Chicago: University of Chicago Press.
Rheingold, H.L. (1986). The first twenty-five years of the Society for Research in Child Development. In A.B. Smuts & J.W. Hagen (Eds.), *History and research in child development* (Vol. 50). Monographs of the Society for Research in Child Development.
Riegel, K.F. (1972). The influence of economic and political ideologies on the development of developmental psychology. *Psychological Bulletin, 78,* 129–141.
Ross, D. (1972). *The psychologist as prophet.* Chicago: University of Chicago Press.
Samelson, F. (1978). From 'race psychology' to 'studies of prejudice': Some observations on the thematic reversal in social psychology. *Journal of History in the Behavioral Sciences, 14,* 265–278.
Schneider, J.W. (1985). Social problems theory: The constructivist view. *Annual Review of Sociology, 11,* 209–29.

Sears, R.R. (1975). Your ancients revisited. In M. Hetherington (Ed.), *Review of child development research*. Chicago: University of Chicago Press.

Siegel, A.W., & White, S.H. (1982). The child study movement. In H.W. Reese (Ed.), *Advances in child development and behavior* (pp. 233–285). New York: Academic Press.

Smith, T.L. (1957). *Revivalism and social reform: American Protestantism on the eve of the Civil War*. Baltimore: Johns Hopkins University Press.

Smuts, A.B. (1986). The National Research Council Committee on Child Development and the founding of the Society for Research in Child Development, 1925–1933. In A.B. Smuts & J.W. Hagen (Eds.), *History and research in child development* (Vol 50). Monographs of the Society for Research in Child Development.

Steiner, G.Y. (1976). *The children's cause*. Washington, DC: Brookings Institution.

Watson, J.B. (1925). *Behaviorism*. New York: Norton.

Watson, J.B. (1928). *Psychological care of infant and child*. New York: Norton.

Wertsch, J.V., & Youniss, J. (1987). Contextualizing the investigator: The case of developmental psychology. *Human Development, 30*, 18–31.

Weibe, R.H. (1967). *The search for order, 1877–1920*. New York: Hill and Wang.

Woodworth, R.S. (1910). Racial differences in mental traits. *Science, 31*, 171–186.

Youniss, J. (1983). Beyond ideology to the universals of development. In D. Kuhn & J.A. Meacham (Eds.), *On the development of developmental psychology*. Basel: Karger.

Part VI
Commentary

19 Developmental Psychology in the Real World: A Perspective on Its Ethical Issues

M. Brewster Smith

The rich and varied contributions to this ground-breaking volume provide the reader with a thought-provoking experience, as Drs. Fisher and Tryon have skillfully planned. I think everyone reading it who is concerned with the ethics of psychological research and practice, or who is involved in applied developmental psychology, will emerge with at least several important new ideas, and with perspectives beyond those attainable within our own separate niches. Readers will not have found a codification of answers to ethical dilemmas. Rather, they will have been exposed to the ethical thinking of a stellar selection of experienced psychologists, representing a remarkably broad spectrum of applied developmental interests and activities.

My induction to the issues of this book dates from two decades ago when I joined Stuart Cook's committee that developed the American Psychological Association's guidelines on the ethics of research involving human participants (Ad Hoc Committee, 1973). In the years since, I have been involved recurrently with ethical issues raised by psychological research, including participation in the necessarily bureaucratized process in which research ethics has been formalized in government regulations and in the institutional review committees these regulations brought into being. I have also had to think about how these issues impinge on child development research (Smith, 1967). So I find the down-to-earth concreteness of the ethical concerns treated in most of the chapters refreshing and satisfying. The book gets back to the spirit of the Cook Committee which collected critical incidents of ethical problems in the actual conduct of research. This approach followed the example of the earlier committee chaired by Nicholas Hobbs that formulated APA's initial general code of ethics (American Psychological Association, 1953). The reader is plunged into real, consequential issues in context, confronted with genuine human puzzles and with the attempts of wise and humane psychologists to deal with them—people who don't necessarily agree with each other.

In their introductory chapter, the editors give an able survey of the book's contents, putting its contributions in coherent order. It would be pointless for me to produce an idiosyncratic duplication of their effort. Rather, I shall comment selectively on what I have found in this volume, hoping, of course, to give further impetus to ideas that strike me as especially valuable.

To begin with, a word is in order about the wide range of activities included in "applied developmental psychology," the ethical aspects of which are our present concern. These activities range from applied academic research of the sort that frequents our developmental journals through "interventions" in various institutional and interpersonal settings and their evaluation, and from policy research of various sorts to instruction and communication offered to special audiences or to the general public through the mass media. Is this a coherent, emerging field, covering a terrain that overlaps at its boundaries with academic developmental psychology, community psychology, educational and school psychology, counseling and child clinical psychology, and journalism? For the purposes of this volume, it hardly matters, because there is so much to gain from putting side by side the issues of ethics and social responsibility that arise across the full spectrum of developmental psychology's involvement with human welfare. (The absence of issues distinctive of the gerontological context needs explicit recognition, however: a reasonable limitation but one not signaled by the title.) All the same, it is clear that the participants in the book have different conceptions of the potential field in mind as they write from their own special sectors of it. Thus, Koocher's concern with the ethics of training doctoral students in applied developmental psychology without preparing them for state licensing (or without seeing to it that licensing laws make a place for them) obviously bears upon one conception of the applied developmentalist as involved in service delivery, but not necessarily upon many of the roles in research and communication that are also considered in this volume. Whether a licensed specialty of applied developmental psychology should be promoted is an issue raised but not pursued here.

Sieber sets the tone of the book with her distinction between the "little ethical problems" in research that federal guidelines and institutional review committees are mostly concerned with, and the "big" ethical problem that is generally ignored, that of doing useless, perhaps harmful, research. I want to extend her contrast a bit to compare scrupulosity about the issues of risk, informed consent, and confidentiality with which federal regulations and APA research principles are concerned, important as they are, with the broader issue of whether the research in question—or other activity in the broad spectrum of applied developmental psychology—really contributes to usable knowledge, or to helping children, parents, teachers, and mental health professionals in other ways in their common interest in promoting optimal human development.

Most of the chapters focus on the big ethical problems in this extended sense. But as Sieber realizes and Baumrind and Fisher & Rosendahl in particular spell out, the "little" problems turn out to be big ones too. The principles set forth by APA and SRCD do cover a good deal of the ground under consideration. All the same, the procedures that are federally mandated for ethical review concern research, not the full gamut of applied developmental psychology, and they were drawn with the problems of biomedical research mainly in view—a realm in which the potential harms as well as benefits are more immediately visible and dramatic than in most psychological and social research. The authors of these chapters are concerned for the most part with decisions that cut across traditional distinctions between ethics, pragmatics, and politics. That is the consequence of taking seriously and responsibly the increased involvement of developmental psychology in the "real world."

In the narrower area of research ethics, I have observed (Smith, 1976) that our APA principles derive from two mainly independent and not always compatible sources in philosophical tradition—utilitarian concern with harm vs. benefit, and deontological concern with respect for individual autonomy—informed consent. These foci remain central here, but the present broader context highlights for me two additional underlying themes (which, to be sure, have obvious links to the foregoing clusters): *competence* and *justice*.

Competence figures prominently in the general APA ethical principles, and arises as an ethical concern across the entire range of applied developmental psychology as treated in this volume. Incompetent research is unethical, so considerations of validity, reliability, and population generalizability get proper attention, especially in the chapters by Sieber, Scarr, and Laosa. A related issue challenges the adequacy, the competence of even the best research to prescribe policy. Given serious reservations about the probative value of empirical findings, with which we have to come to terms in this post-positivist era, I was delighted with Baumrind's formula: Wouldn't it always be better, when we communicate our research conclusions in settings in which their implications might be acted upon, to use the language of discovery—"we have good grounds for believing . . ."—rather than the language of proof—"we have demonstrated . . ."? That would help to keep policy decisions in the realm of politics where of course they belong (though we could hope for better politics than we have been producing lately.) Our research as well as our more speculative theorizing can be valuable in suggesting frames and means-end relationships for the development of policy even when we cannot in good conscience prescribe it. We are in a better position ethically, pragmatically, and politically when we are scrupulous about the limitations of our contributions. Several authors, especially Hoffman and Sigel, touch on the importance and the difficulty of ethical performance in this respect, given the temptations, even the normative demands, of journalism and other segments of the "consuming" public. Still other issues of competence are raised in media psychology, discussed by McCall and Elkind, in expert testimony by Melton, and in the more clinical interventions that especially concern Koocher and Tryon.

The substantial concern with *justice* throughout the volume reflects a shift in our socio-cultural and political priorities since psychologists began to be systematically concerned with their professional ethics—an example of how our activities are embedded in history and culture, still another theme to be examined shortly in its own right. We are coming to realize that the United States is a multiethnic, multiracial, dual-gender society in which the old metaphor of the melting pot assimilating newcomers to the WASP tradition of the Founding *Fathers* can no longer work for us. Especially as we look at our nation's children, we see gross disparities in opportunity and in the grounds for sustaining hopefulness, disparities linked with poverty, race, and ethnicity, and gender too. If we are genuinely concerned with the big ethical problem—how to be most helpful to the development of children, where help is most needed, we must inevitably give high priority to concerns of justice toward the groups that have historically been treated unjustly. These concerns permeate the volume but are focal in the chapters by Laosa and McAdoo.

There are genuine ethical dilemmas here. In recent years, spokespersons for disadvantaged minorities have castigated research that displayed the damage done to members of ethnic minorities as "blaming the victim" (Ryan, 1971). The problem is real: showing the disabilities resulting from injustice *can* be used to justify continued injustice in allocating resources and opportunities, since the scars on the damaged undercut their ability to compete equally. But it can also be used to call for recompense and remedy. Touchy issues of ethnic self-esteem are involved in ways that sometimes replace "blame the victim" with "kill the messenger." Sandra Scarr (1988) has discussed elsewhere some of the ethical issues of doing research in this treacherous area, in which she has shown great courage and competence. I come down on the side of truth and integrity as likely in the long run to favor justice, but we also need to sponsor justice for its own sake.

Also in regard to justice, Melton's chapter on applied developmental research and the law provided what struck me as my most novel insight from the book, explaining more clearly than I have seen elsewhere the good sense that is responsible for the bad fit between the Anglo-American legal system and psychological and social science. I was well aware of their substantial incompatibility, which makes the relations between law and psychology difficult and sometimes embarrassing. I had previously thought that the core issue was the conflict between the voluntarism of law (free will, choice, which may be impaired by circumstance and disease) and the determinism of scientific psychology, and on that issue I was ready to side with legal tradition. Melton persuades me that the root incompatibility is deeper. Science seeks truth, and law seeks justice. In the good case, these value-directives converge, but since neither truth nor justice can ever be determined absolutely, the historically developed strategies to promote the approximate attainment of each (science and law) diverge. I have not encountered before such a persuasive defense of our adversarial legal system. And I take very seriously Melton's forthright and firm prescriptions and proscriptions for the behavior of psychological expert witnesses, given the key role of child psychologists in custody hearings.

The older issues of harm-benefit and respect-autonomy also get appropriate attention in this volume. Psychologists need to be reminded of a central tenet of the Hippocratic tradition noted by Baumrind: nonmaleficence should take priority over beneficence. Above all, we should do no harm. But that intuitively convincing prescription seems to conflict with Sieber's observation that applied psychologists are irrationally risk-aversive, that we avoid possibly important contributions because of our fear of being shown up, if not our fear of harmful effects. We need to be sensitized to this dilemma.

Given the special vulnerability of the very young (and also the very old, though their situation is only briefly discussed), the context in which issues of harm-benefit and autonomy must be considered are different for this volume than for psychology in general. Harm-benefit takes priority for the young and vulnerable, though Baumrind and Fisher & Rosendahl keep before us the importance of assent/consent on the part of child participants as well as their legal representatives.

I am pleased not to see any signs in this book of the perniciously mistaken view that it is possible to balance harms and benefits in a quasiquantitative way in making the ethical decisions most frequently required of research psychologists. Such balancing does make sense when decisions for the medical treatment of an individual case are at issue: does the proposed treatment have a sufficient probability of helping the patient to balance the known and unknown risks to the patient? It is equally pertinent to educational and other nonmedical interventions that might harm or benefit their recipients. But the balancing makes no quantitative sense at all when gains from research to science, or to other people in the same problem category, are compared with risks to a target individual. Investigators, therapists, and interveners have to make such choices without the possibility of help or justification from any quasiformula. The inherent ambiguities of harm-benefit analysis properly throw the emphasis toward informed consent as the dominant criterion.

Throughout this book, another consensual theme informs the discussion of ethical issues. Pervading the discussions is agreement that social science and developmental psychology are embedded in their historical, sociocultural context whether their practitioners know it or not, and they had better know it. This relatively new insight is developed most explicitly by Danish, by Lerner and Tubman, and by Youniss, but it permeates the book. Though he is not explicitly recognized in the volume, John Dewey should be acknowledged as the patron saint of this *transactional* view of human social reality, in which stimuli and responses constitute one another, people evoke their own environments which go on to shape them in turn, children and parents and teachers are embedded in interknitted spiraling feedback loops, and researchers and their subjects-participants are consequentially involved with one another as well as embedded in their variant of historical culture (Dewey, 1896; Dewey & Bentley, 1949). Our scientific agenda in developmental psychology and our ethical concerns are both emergent in a particular sociohistorical context. Especially when, as applied psychologists, we think of ourselves as promoting human betterment, it be-hooves us to remember that our ideas of "betterment" are historically and cultur-ally specific. As we look back on the earlier history of developmental psychol-ogy with Youniss and find it benighted (though I agree with his wish that we be kindly in our judgments), we should temper our own tendencies toward abso-lutism in our present value judgments.

We should temper them, but we should not lose self-confidence in nihilistic relativism. All of us are creatures of the history and culture of our own cohorts in American society, but through social science including the empirical tradition of developmental psychology and through open democratic debate informed by philosophy and commonsense, we are capable of criticizing our own society, including what we do with our children and adolescents, and even capable of looking a step or so ahead. We are better off in this respect than our predecessors. That degree of independence of perspective gives plenty of room for useful research and professional expertise in applied developmental psychology. Con-textualism need not entail blind relativism. Yes, recognition that our scientific assumptions as well as the unexamined assumptions of common sense are social constructions may shake our old, historically unwarranted certitude. But this recognition should not undermine the basis for careful, critical, empirical inquiry aimed at *advancing* our understanding of human development in society, and for professional involvement to use that knowledge for human betterment. Of course, our understanding of what we regard as human betterment will keep on changing: no matter. Each cohort, each generation, each individual has its own differentiated agenda, and the interplay among these is one of the challenges and delights of our human condition in a mainly democratic society.

We are provided in this book with sustenance to maintain our morale against the relativistic side effects of contextualism as it has commonly been interpreted. I am particularly encouraged by Hoffman's close analysis of how implicit value agendas in research on the effects of maternal employment on children have helped rather than harmed the emergence of truth in research. She tells us how researchers with strong value commitments do not let favored hypotheses die, but keep on looking for at least interaction effects, with generally good consequences for truth and probably for human welfare. Her down-to-earth account helps to correct the common assumption that the distortion imposed by scientists' own values necessarily corrupts or impedes attainment of scientific understanding. I especially welcome her testimony because I see it as supporting my continued faith in *progress* in science (with technology, it is to me the only domain in which that tattered concept still makes sense), a strong defense of the scientific ideal that is being challenged rather inappropriately by humanists and postmodernist philosophers.

The importance of context, which in developmental psychology requires ref-erence to the major influence of Urie Bronfenbrenner's (1977) ecological approach, also is critical in other major contributions to this book. Lewis's challenging discussion of program evaluation should be taken very seriously. I agree that when even very competent summative evaluations are conducted to assess interventions that essentially involve single procedures, the results are foreordained to be negative. That is because the vicious or benign developmental spirals with which interventions intersect involve many components that interact within a system context. It is naive to expect a single-factor intervention to make much difference in a quasiexperimental test, especially in the short run. So in the rare cases in which serious summative evaluation is actually undertaken, it may well be in the service of political purposes informed by understanding in advance that negative results are probable. There are morals here both for the pragmatics of intervention and the politics and ethics of evaluation. (I wish, all the same, that Lewis had not used the unnecessary example of nuclear deterrence to argue for defensible policy stands on the basis of face validity in the absence of empirical evidence. It is a bad example. Not only is there no empirical evidence in support of the theory—granted that the major powers have not yet got into nuclear war with each other—but by now there are also other reasonable grounds for thinking it outmoded, mistaken, and dangerous.)

The contextual approach also informs Sieber's impressive discussion of adolescent involvement with alcohol. As psychologists, we are as easily misled as the public by the labels that we and our colleagues invent, which freeze issues into formats that defy solution. Sieber's treatment of adolescent alcohol problems in their social context joins with Hoffman's discussion of the effects of maternal employment and Scarr's account of her long-term research in Bermuda to give us invaluable food for thought. Here we encounter the big and little ethical issues in context, and while we need the guidance of general principles, principles are not enough.

Principles, of course, arise from different philosophical and religious premises, and people who start from different premises cannot make much sense to each other. Certainly they cannot convince each other; one can hope that they can accommodate to each other politically and politely, though the recent politics of birth control and abortion dims these hopes (Smith, 1987). Each of us has probably worked out his or her own tacit ad hoc version of ethical principles derived from our several involvements with the history of our culture and of our science within it, now challenged by our worldwide involvement and the hoped for emergence of worldwide social science. This book should help all of us to think through our more difficult decisions as they affect research and practice concerning human development, and to become more explicit in our ethical decisions. We all are properly guided by federal rules and maybe also by APA or SRCD guidelines. But these do not help us as much as we want with the serious ethical problems, problems that we may not even be fully aware of before facing issues such as those discussed in this book. When all is said and done, each of us is challenged to be socially responsible in our research and practice—and given our predictable bias to be self-serving, we are also well advised to consult our colleagues on the harder decisions.

Remember what some of the authors have said, distilling wisdom from hard-earned experience:

> Scientific integrity is the crux of what I mean by doing well . . . We cannot control, though we can influence, the use that is made of the knowledge we produce. We *can* control our own conduct, fulfilling our fiduciary obligations fruitfully and behave with utmost integrity, aspiring to do no harm, in our efforts to do good well. (Baumrind)

> Achievement of such intellectual honesty and concern for personhood of children and youth would be no mean feat. (Melton)

> Perhaps most important, I try to be aware of ethical situations and to be reflective about them and to recognize that I am indeed making an ethical choice. (Elkind)

> Perhaps, the best summary statement is that research investigators in any field, but particularly in applied psychology, must have consummate *integrity* and *truthfulness* to themselves. From these flow ethical behavior to others. (Scarr)

These are variations on the same theme. Ethical practice depends on information and sensitization (to which this book contributes much), and on reflectiveness and integrity, which are a challenge to us all.

REFERENCES

Ad Hoc Committee on Ethical Standards in Psychological Research. (1973). *Ethical principles in the conduct of research with human participants.* Washington, DC: American Psychological Association.

American Psychological Association. (1953). *Ethical standards of psychologists.* Washington, DC: American Psychological Association.

Bronfenbrenner, U. (1977). Toward an experimental ecology of human development. *American Psychologist, 32,* 512–531.

Dewey, J. (1896). The reflex arc concept in psychology. *Psychological Review, 3,* 357–370.

Dewey, J. & Bentley, A.F. (1949). *Knowing and the known.* Boston, MA: Beacon.

Ryan, W. (1971). *Blaming the victim.* New York: Pantheon.

Scarr, S. (1988). Race and gender as psychological variables: social and ethical issues. *American Psychologist, 43,* 56–59.

Smith, M.B. (1967). Conflicting values affecting behavioral research with children. *Children, 14,* 53–58.

Smith, M.B. (1976). Some perspectives on ethical/political issues in social science research. *Personality and Social Psychology Bulletin, 2,* 445–453.

Smith, M.B. (1987). Value dilemmas and public health: A psychologist's perspective. *International Quarterly of Community Health Education, 7,*(2) 79–90.

Author Index

Philips, S.U., 231, *250*
Phinney, J., 278, *283*
Piaget, J., 52, *59*
Pion, G.M., 93, *111*, 203, *214*
Pion, G.W., 43, *59*
Platt, A., 285, *299*
Plotnick, R., *281*
Poythress, N.G., 147, 150, 151, 152, 153, 154, *161*
Pratto, D., 97, *111*
Price, J., *283*
Price, R., 102, 103, 109, *111*

R
Rachal, J.V., 72, *78*
Radin, N., 276, *283*
Ragozin, A.S., 48, *58*
Rappaport, J., 93, 96, *111*
Reese, H.W., 95, *110*, 118, *129*, 202, *213*
Reid, J., 51, *59*
Rheingold, H.L., 293, *299*
Ricciuti, A., 32, 34, *41*
Ricciuti, H., 83, *91*
Rice, B., 165, 167, 169, 177, 178, 181, 182, *185*
Riegel, K.F., 114, 118, 125, *130*, 286, *299*
Robinson, B.E., 175, *185*
Robinson, N.M., 48, *58*
Rochat, R.W., 62, *77*
Rodgers, D.A., 207, 208, *214*
Rodman, H., 97, *111*
Roer-Bornstein, D., 232, *248*
Rogler, L.H., 235, 236, 237, 239, 241, 142, 146, *248, 250*
Rosen, N.L., 233, *248*
Rosenfeld, M., 267, *270*
Rosenthal, A.S., 255, 256, 262, *269, 270*
Ross, D., 291, 293, *299*
Ross, J.M., 188, *199*
Ross. L., 52, *58*
Rotherman, M.J., 278, *283*
Rovine, M.J., 39, *41*, 257, 258, 261, *268*
Royce, J., 126, *130*
Rubenstein, C., 172, 173, *185*
Ryan, W., 96, *111*, 306, *310*
Ryaff, C.D., 121, *130*

S
Sagi, A., 261, *270*
Salks, M.J., 49, *58*
Samelson, F., 292, 295, *299*
Sarawon, S.B., 44, *59*, 69, *78*, 123, 127, *130*

Scanzoni, J., 274, *283*
Scarr, S., 29, 31, 32, 33, 34, 39, 40, *41*, 44, *59*, 120, *130*, 136, *142*, 267, *270*, 306, *310*
Schaeffer, S., 88, *91*
Schiff, M., 38, *41*
Schneider, H.G., 48, *58*
Schneider, J.W., 298, *299*
Schneirla, T.C., 116, 118, 119, 128, *130, 131*
Scholnick, E.K., 2, 3, *13*, 210, *214*, 216, *224*
Schuckit, M.A., 62, *78*
Schultz, J., 234, *248*
Schwartz, P., 266, *270*
Scopetta, M.A., 236, 239, *250*
Scott, C., 23, *28*
Scriven, M., 101, *111*
Sears, R.R., 1, *13*, 285, 293, 294, *300*
Serianni, E., 63, *77*
Shade, B.J., 231, *250*
Shah, D., 164, *185*
Shanab, M.E., 19, *28*
Shantz, C., 215, 217, *224*
Shaw, G.B., 83, *91*
Sieber, J.E., 8, 10, *13*, 52, *59*, 136, *142*
Siegal, H.A., 62, *77*
Siegel, A.E., 25, *28*, 255, 260, 264, *270*, 271, 285, 290, 293, 296, *300*
Siegel, A.S., 203, *214*
Siegel, A.W., 1, *13*
Sigel, I.E., 2, 3, *13*, 49, *59*, 134, 136, 137, 138, 141, *142*, 203, 210, *214*, 216, *224, 244, 250*
Sigman, M., 122, *131*
Skimnner, E.A., 118, 122, *130*
Slobogin, C., 147, 150, 151, 152, 153, 154, 160, *161*
Smart, R.G., 75, *78*
Smith, E.A., 25, *28*
Smith, J.C., 62, *77*
Smith, M.B., 57, *59*, 303, 305, 309, *310*
Smith, S.S., 102, 103, 109, *111*
Smith, T.L., 291, *300*
Smuts, A.B., 293, 294, *300*
Smyer, M.A., 46, *58*, 93, 95, *110*
Snipper, A., 126, *130*
Snortum, J.R., 73, *77*
Snow, R.E., 238, *250*
Snyder, M., 120, *131*
Sorell, G.T., 118, 122, *130*
Sotsky, S.M., 55, *58*
Spector, M., 298, *299*
Spock, B., 188, *199*

Subject Index

Speculation, 175
The Star and Tribune, 267
Statutory privilege, 153–54, 157–58
Step-by-step assessment, 101
Stepping stone hypothesis, 23–24
Stereotyping, 243, 292, 295
Students Against Drunk Driving (SADD), 76
Studies, balanced interpretation, 192–93
Subgroup analysis, 255–57
Subject recruitment, 38, 259–60
Subpoenae, and research data, 156–58
Substance abuse programs, 75–76, 103–108
Success criteria, 85–86
Suicidal symptoms, 11, 51

T

Talk About Sex (Chamberlain), 165
Talk-broadcasting, 164–65, 172–73
Talk-story, 241
Target population, 96–97
Task format, 230–32
Technology, 70, 97–99
Television, and researchers, 267
Temporal theory, 88–89, 122–25
Tenement houses, and "moral habits", 293
Tertiary prevention, 95
Testimony, 151–52, 175
Theories, 69, 88–89, 95, 107
Theories of development, and societal
        functioning, 95
Theory, and practice, 69
Thorndike, Ashley H., 296
Today Show, 264
Token funding, 22–23
The Toni Grant Show, 165, 177
Tonight Show (Carson), 165
Toughlove training program, 189
Traditional ideologies, 232–33
Training, 108–09, 189–90, 207–210, 220–21

Transactional view of social reality, 307
Translation, 9–10, 61
Treatment programs, 31, 54–55, 102–103
Truth and justice, conflict of, 145–46

U

Ubiquitous changes, 124–25
Unintended consequences, 95
Universal help, concept of, 84–85
University of Virginia, 285
Unpopular research results, 39–40
Useful research, design of, 61–67

V

Validity, 63–64
Value assimilation, 232–33
Value-free knowledge, 20
Values, 10–12, 24–26, 37–38, 63, 70–71,
        95–97
Victim blaming, 96
Victim characteristics, 148
Volunteer participation, 54

W

War on Poverty, 235–36
Washington Post, 267
Watson, John B., 290, 296
Westheimer, Ruth, 165–67, 194
Williams College, 291
Within-person change, 4–6
Woodworth, Robert, 294

Y

Yale University, 291
Young Men's Christian Association, 285–86,
        291, 296

Z

Zimbardo study, 21